UNDERSTANDING
SPIRITUAL
GIFTS

Also by Robert L. Thomas

Evangelical Hermeneutics

The Jesus Crisis (gen. ed., with F. David Farnell)

The Master's Perspective on Biblical Prophecy
(gen. ed., with Richard Mayhue)

The Master's Perspective on Contemporary Issues (gen. ed.)

The Master's Perspective on Difficult Passages (gen. ed.)

The Master's Perspective on Pastoral Ministry
(gen. ed., with Richard Mayhue)

Three Views on the Origins of the Synoptic Gospels
(gen. ed.)

UNDERSTANDING SPIRITUAL GIFTS

A Verse-by-Verse Study of 1 Corinthians 12–14

ROBERT L. THOMAS
REVISED EDITION

kregel
PUBLICATIONS

Grand Rapids, MI 49501

Understanding Spiritual Gifts: A Verse-by-Verse Study of 1 Corinthians 12–14

Copyright © 1978, 1999 by Robert L. Thomas
Second Edition

Published by Kregel Publications, a division of Kregel, Inc., P.O. Box 2607, Grand Rapids, MI 49501.

Unless otherwise indicated, Scripture quotations are from the *New American Standard Bible*, © the Lockman Foundation 1960, 1962, 1963, 1968, 1971, 1972, 1973, 1975, 1977.

Library of Congress Cataloging-in-Publication Data
Thomas, Robert L.
    Understanding spiritual gifts: a verse-by-verse study of 1 Corinthians 12–14 / Robert L. Thomas —Rev. ed.
        p.   cm.
    Includes bibliographical references and indexes.
    1. Bible. N.T. Corinthians, 1st, XII–XIV—Commentaries. 2. Gifts, spiritual—Biblical teaching. I. Title.
BS2675.3.T47   1999   227'.2077—dc21   98-41465
                                                         CIP
ISBN 0-8254-3829-2

Printed in the United States of America

2 3 4 5 6 / 08 07 06 05 04

To my wife, Joan,
my partner of forty-five years

CONTENTS

CONTENTS

PREFACE TO THE SECOND EDITION

This second edition of *Understanding Spiritual Gifts* is an updating and expansion of the original edition that appeared in 1978.

The body of Christ grows most rapidly as its spiritual gifts function properly. In recent times many Christians have come to recognize this, and a keen interest in spiritual gifts is now widespread, an interest that will surely mean increased effectiveness for the church as time goes on. No passage of Scripture is of greater importance in understanding spiritual gifts than 1 Corinthians 12–14, as the introductory formula "Now concerning spiritual gifts" in 12:1 explicitly says.

Citations from these three chapters have been numerous in discussions of spiritual gifts, but detailed studies endeavoring to present a cohesive analysis of the entire passage have not been so frequent. The goal of this book is to take a step toward filling this void. All biblical quotations throughout this exposition either are from the *New American Standard Bible* or are those of the author. The study, however, ultimately stems from the Greek text of the passage.

The introductory chapter presents a preview of the entire passage, including a detailed outline showing the overall literary framework. Chapters one through six constitute a more in-depth examination. Explanatory notes that are cross-referenced with the main discussion appear at the end of the book. The explanatory notes, an attempt to clarify and justify certain conclusions incorporated into the study, will be most beneficial to those with facility in New Testament Greek. Documentation within them refers to an author's last name, the date of his work, and the pagination. By referring to the Bibliography of Works Cited at the end of the volume, one can locate complete publication data for these sources.

Six appendixes at the rear of the volume offer more detailed discussions of specific areas of interest. Since the release of the first edition of this work, interest in the gift of prophecy has grown widely, so the first four appendixes focus especially on further elaboration on that gift. Appendix A contributes more information to the discussion regarding revelatory and confirmatory gifts. Appendixes B, C, and D offer further insights into recent discussions about the gift of prophecy, with Appendix B evaluating a recently popularized perspective on the gift, Appendix C drawing upon Revelation 22:18 for further understanding of prophecy, and Appendix D relating the gift to the formation of the New Testament canon. Appendix E lists the eighteen spiritual gifts referred to in the New Testament, and Appendix F has practical suggestions for discovering and implementing the eight gifts that remain in operation at present.

It is not the purpose of this work to delve into matters of an introductory nature. For the sake of this discussion, the authenticity and integrity of 1 Corinthians are presupposed. Paul wrote the epistle to Corinth near the close of his three-year ministry in Ephesus, in the spring of 55 (Acts 19:1–20; 20:31). This was some five or six years after his founding of the church at Corinth (cf. Acts 18:1–18).

The author wishes to express his gratitude to Mike Canham, Kurt Gebhards, and Tim Gombis for their assistance in compiling the indexes.

ROBERT L. THOMAS

PREVIEW OF I CORINTHIANS 12-14

Paul received several perplexing questions from the Corinthian Christians about matters that puzzled them. Among these were questions about spiritual gifts—how they could and should be used to benefit the Christian assembly in Corinth.

I. Uniqueness of Spiritual Gifts (12:1-3)

The opening paragraph of his answer specifies uniqueness common to all spiritual gifts. The Corinthian Christians had known what it was to be moved by forces outside themselves, demonic forces. Very clear distinctions existed between these forces and powers operative in the gifts. To think that satanic emissaries are incapable of producing counterfeits for any proper function of the Holy Spirit is a mistake. Great precautions are necessary to keep from confusing these misrepresentations with genuine divine operations. Real gifts of the Spirit have an unmistakable earmark: a willing acknowledgment of Jesus as Lord with conviction of mind and devotion of soul. Such a cry of adoration can come from no lesser source. An endowment of this nature is uniquely from God.

II. Unified Source of Spiritual Gifts: The Triune God (12:4-11)

A general criterion of spiritual gifts having been divulged, the writer proceeds with some specifics. The source of these abilities is one, not many. All come from one God who is three in personality: the Father, the Son, and the Holy Spirit. Though various in form and whether referred to as "gifts" (v. 4), "ministries" (v. 5), or "effects" (v. 6), they are all alike in purpose: "for the common good" (v. 7). A partial list of gifts in verses 8-10 illustrates charismatic variety. Hand in hand with said variety, however, is the common origin of all the phenomena: the Holy Spirit is the distributor of every bestowment in accordance with

His own will (v. 11). Each Christian has received a gift (or gifts) to be used for the good of the rest.

III. Unified Nature of Spiritual Gifts: A Spiritual Body (12:12–31a)
    A. Declaration of Unity (12:12–13)

        Coupled with the oneness of common origin is the spiritual product of one common organism, "the body of Christ." Interestingly, this body is always the figure used when the apostle discusses spiritual gifts (Rom. 12:4–5; Eph. 4:4, 12, 16). In declaring emphatically the unity of Christ's body, verses 12–13 launch a discussion of the body extending through the remainder of chapter 12. It is like a physical body in this respect. Though composed of many and varying members, the body is still one, every member having been inducted into the body through "baptism by the Holy Spirit." No matter how assorted the backgrounds, all have been made a unit in this spiritual organism, the life principle of which is Christ Himself.

    B. Interrelation Because of Unity (12:14–26)
        1. Need for lesser members (12:14–20)

           Variety of charismatic manifestations matches variety of members in the physical body. Such diversification involves, first of all, the danger of underestimating the importance of certain gifts, just as a foot might feel inferior to a hand and conclude its part in the body is unnecessary, so one with a lesser gift might demean himself. This is erroneous. Every member is an integral part of the body and is therefore necessary.

        2. Neediness of greater members (12:21–24a)

           A second and opposite danger is that of overestimating a member's importance. One with superior gifts may view himself as self-sufficient and consequently not dependent on those with lesser abilities. Lest he do this and look with disdain on abilities inferior to his, Paul warns that no gift is so great as to be functional apart from the rest. The eye *does* need the hand if the body is to perform normally. Just as the most talented athlete cannot single-handedly carry his team to victory, neither can a highly gifted individual solo successfully in the work of God.

        3. Provision for mutual concern (12:24b–26)

           As members of this body, Christians must exhibit the same mutual concern as found among members of the human body, particularly so in implementing spiritual gifts. Continued awareness of mutual need one for the other is of highest priority. The teacher needs the evangelist, or he will have no one to teach.

The evangelist needs a Christian with the gift of helps, or his ministry dies from lack of support. So it goes throughout the body. The body stands together or it falls. Separated, the members are spiritual invalids, but together they grow and mature "to the measure of the stature which belongs to the fulness of Christ" (Eph. 4:13).

C. Utilization for Unified Output (12:27–31a)

Sequential arrangement of gifts at this point indicates that some are more strategic in producing growth than others. This gradation in productivity does not erase the mutual concern just advocated, but encourages a local assembly to cultivate those gifts that result in more benefit for all. For maximum output, the body would do well to emphasize those functions near the top of the list, such as apostles and prophets. Clearly, no single gift is the possession of every Christian, so all could not lay claim to apostleship. Yet at whatever time the local group had access to an apostle, they could do nothing better for themselves than to seek his services rather than preferring gifts lower in the list. By emphasizing gifts most conducive to edification, a local body accelerates spiritual progress.

IV. Unquestioned Superiority of Spiritual Fruit: Love (12:31b–13:13)

A. Preeminence of Love (12:31b–13:3)

Mention of the "greater" (or "greatest") gift in verse 12:31a needs qualification, because spiritual gifts are not the ultimate. A "more excellent way" than spiritual gifts—even the greatest of them—is the way of love. Love surpasses the gifts in importance, but does not exclude them. It is a distinct entity, and damage results when gifts become an end in themselves at the expense of love. Without love, gifts are useless. Specifically alluded to are tongues (13:1), prophecy, wisdom, knowledge, faith (13:2), and helps (13:3). That love should be the preeminent quality comes as no surprise from a God who is love and who left one new commandment: "Love one another, even as I have loved you" (John 13:34).

B. Perfections of Love (13:4–7)

A partial list of love's independent excellencies follows the portrayal of love's indispensability. Fifteen characteristics of love appear, fifteen that are most appropriate to affairs in Corinth. The chief quality needed then, as it is now, was such selfless concern as is described in this paragraph.

C. Permanence of Love (13:8–13)

1. Permanence stated (13:8a)

Even these fifteen superlatives do not exhaust the properties of love. Its permanence is well worth separate mention. Its unending duration is unique, even among other important Christian qualities.

2. Permanence contrasted with temporary gifts (13:8b–12)

    a. Passing of gifts (13:8b). An emphasis on love's permanence relates it first to three important spiritual functions: prophecy, tongues, and knowledge. These three gifts—one for inspired speech (prophecy), another for evidential demonstration (tongues), and another for supernatural enlightenment (knowledge)—ranked high in the esteem of either Paul or his readers or both. Yet none of the three could compare with love's lasting value.

    b. Partial nature of gifts (v. 9). The ninth verse explains the temporality of these gifts. They were at best incomplete functions of a body still in its infancy.

    c. Replacing of gifts (vv. 10–12). Paul conceived of a time when this body would progress from childhood to maturity, when these and other gifts pertaining to earlier stages of the church's corporate life would no longer be operative. That maturity would come either with the church's growth into possession of its own completed Scriptures (v. 11), or else with the return of Christ to receive the church into His personal presence (v. 12). Which of these would happen first the writer did not know. From a twentieth-century perspective, it is obvious that the completed New Testament canon has already become a reality. But the body of Christ still awaits its ultimate maturity at the return of Christ.

3. Permanence clarified (13:13)

    Two more Christian virtues enrich the contrast between love and gifts. These two, faith and hope, along with love, abide throughout the present age and in this respect have a guaranteed longevity beyond that of prophecy, tongues, and knowledge. That famous triad of virtues characterizes a well-balanced Christian life. But even among these three, one virtue stands above the others. When the other two reach their culmination at the return of Christ, love alone will remain. Or in other words: "The greatest of these is love."

V. Unified Purpose of Spiritual Gifts: Edification (14:1–36)

  A. Edification Through Prophecy: Unconditional (14:1–5)

    Following his parenthetical but supremely important discussion of love's indispensability, Paul returns to the point he left at 12:31a.

Love is the only suitable atmosphere in which to cultivate spiritual gifts, and it even dictated which gifts were preferable. At this point a comparison begins between two gifts to show which is desirable in light of loving consideration for others. One of the two was valued quite highly by the writer—the gift of prophecy (12:28)—and the other by the Corinthians—the gift of tongues (14:23). In a comparison of the two, prophecy was clearly the most beneficial because it always and unconditionally resulted in edification for the church. Love required the church's edification to take precedence over the building up of a single member when that member was the speaker, since love "does not seek its own" (13:5).

B. Edification Through Tongues: Conditional (14:6–19)

    1. The profitless use: without interpretation (14:6–12)

In contrast to unconditional edification through prophecy, tongues could not edify without the fulfillment of one condition: interpretation had to follow. Three examples prove the uselessness of unaccompanied tongues: the personal example of Paul, inanimate musical instruments, and a personal encounter with someone of a different linguistic background. In light of tongues' insufficiency when alone, zeal for spiritual gifts must follow channels that will produce maximum benefit for the church.

    2. The profitable use: with interpretation (14:13–19)

The profitable use of tongues in Christian gatherings was the other side of the issue. If church growth was to come, it had to be through the gift of interpretation. Only by this means could those other than the speaker receive necessary instruction. Paul had this unwavering objective in his own service to other Christians. He required his readers to weigh their own spoken ministries according to the same value system.

C. Proper Places for Tongues and Prophecy (14:20–25)

After a discussion of the impropriety of uninterpreted tongues, clarification of the proper surroundings and purpose of this gift is next in order. A mature Christian outlook recognized tongues to be designed for unbelievers rather than believers. Conversely, prophecy had its function among believers, not unbelievers. Even an unbelieving visitor in Christian worship, with no experience in tongues, could verify this fact. He could certify the propriety of prophecy, but not tongues, for a believing audience. Tongues provided a sign such as was needed where non-Christians listened, but such an evidential mark was superfluous among Christians.

D. Proper Procedures with Tongues and Prophecy (14:26–33a)

    1. General: edification, not confusion (14:26)

Just as proper places existed for tongues and prophecy, proper procedures for the two also needed to govern. A general criterion applicable to any speaking gift, not just these two, is that it contribute toward church edification. If spiritual growth of the total body does not result, it is improper procedure. On the other hand, if everyone receives upbuilding, the highest objective of a gift is attained.

2. Tongues regulated (14:27–28)

Though the primary function of tongues was among unbelievers, they possibly could have a positive effect among believers. Interpretation legitimized tongues for Christian worship. Without an interpreter, the tongues speaker was to remain silent.

3. Prophecy regulated (14:29–33a)

As with tongues, certain regulations with prophecy bound the readers as well. Speaking in sequence was a primary principle because of the nature of God Himself. He is a God of order, not of confusion or uproar. People assembled in His name should take care to maintain peaceful circumstances to facilitate maximum instruction and growth.

E. Women in Worship (14:33b–36)

For a second time in the epistle, women in worship receive special attention (cf. 11:2–16). Paul intends males to play the leading part, so whenever women assume leadership, as apparently they were doing, he offers a word of sharp correction. He advocates equality of the two sexes, but with equal dogmatism speaks of needed submission of one toward the other, whether at home or in church.

VI. Unified Perspective of Spiritual Gifts: Orderly Conduct (14:37–40)

A. Divine Authority (14:37–38)

Before closing the section, Paul wants his readers to understand two matters very clearly. The first is his own absolute authority from the Lord to write what he has written. These issues are not open to debate or compromise. They are directives from a divine source.

B. Decent Application (14:39–40)

The other aspect to be understood clearly is the orderly exercise and arrangement of gifts in the assembly, including an order of priorities for gifts and a general procedure characterized by its beauty and resemblance to a well-ordered military unit. Harmony should always prevail, since this is the only way compatible with love and self-effacing conduct toward other people.

Chapter One

UNIQUENESS OF SPIRITUAL GIFTS

12:1–3

1 Now concerning spiritual gifts, brethren, I do not want you to be unaware.

2 You know that when you were pagans, you were led astray to the dumb idols, however you were led.

3 Therefore I make known to you, that no one speaking by the Spirit of God says, "Jesus is accursed"; and no one can say, "Jesus is Lord," except by the Holy Spirit.

"Spiritual" means different things to different people. To the majority, it probably carries the connotation of something sacred or ecclesiastical in contrast to what is merely secular. To most it describes a plane of living higher than that usually experienced on a day-to-day basis, since it points to what is religious by nature.

In general, the same is true of the Christians who lived many years ago in the city of Corinth. Those early Christians saw something desirable in the spiritual side of life. Otherwise, Paul would not have devoted extensive sections of his first epistle to them to correcting some of their misunderstandings about spiritual things (cf. 1 Cor. 2:10–3:4; 12–14). This study will devote its attention to a later section of the epistle, the twelfth through the fourteenth chapters. This portion treats a specific subject, that of *spirituals* (the Greek expression of 12:1 when rendered literally) in the realm of gifts or endowments by the Holy Spirit. Chapters 2–3 discuss "spirituals" more generally by describing broader spiritual qualifications of Christians.

12:1—The topic: spiritual gifts. That Paul in 12:1 has come to a new subject in the epistle is obvious from his "Now concerning spiritual gifts." Previously, at 11:2, he had begun instructions about conduct in public meetings of the Corinthian church. Now, in chapters 12–14, he deals with how to employ spiritual gifts in those same public assemblies of the church. The Corinthians saw a need in this area, as well as in other areas, and had sent a letter to Paul via three of their members: Stephanas, Fortunatus, and Achaicus (1 Cor. 16:17). "Now concerning" or an equivalent expression in 7:1, 25; 8:1; 11:2; and 16:1 identifies answers to questions found in the letter. This is the formula utilized at the outset of chapter 12.[1]

The Corinthian request was probably similar to this: "As you know, Paul, we have many richly gifted people in our church (cf. 1 Cor. 1:5–7), and they all desire to participate in every service. This is particularly true of those possessing the spiritual gift of tongues. Because of this, great confusion reigns whenever we get together. What advice can you give to resolve this problem?"

In response, the writer of this epistle under the inspiration of the Holy Spirit launches an extended treatment of the subject of spiritual gifts. It is as though Paul were saying, "Your questions have no quick answer. A proper solution entails having a broad understanding of the whole area of spiritual gifts, so that you can see clearly the answer to your particular problem."

In inaugurating his detailed excursus in 12:1–3, Paul does not make it immediately evident whether he has in mind spiritual persons or spiritual gifts. But his subject becomes obvious in the verses immediately following (12:4–11): he intends to speak of the latter.[2] He has used the same word earlier in the epistle to depict spiritual persons (2:15; 3:1), but the richly gifted Corinthians were not spiritual persons because of the carnality that reigned among them (1 Cor. 3:1–4). In chapter 12 and following, Paul obviously deals with their gifts and not their spiritual sensitivity, a quality they lacked. They possessed and exercised spiritual gifts but were not at the moment in intimate fellowship with the Spirit.

"Spiritual gifts" (literally "spirituals," *pneumatikōn*) is one of five ways Paul has of designating this kind of activity, the other four being found in 12:4 ("gifts"), 5 ("ministries"), 6 ("effects"), and 7 ("manifestation"). The present expression, also found in 14:1, emphasizes the part of the Holy Spirit in the functioning of gifts. The person of the Holy Spirit receives even greater emphasis in a form of Greek expression found in 14:12 where "spiritual gifts" is more accurately "spirits," or "Holy Spirit manifestations." Any ministry or operation finding its source in the third Person of the Godhead is bound to be supernatural in nature. Such functioning goes beyond anything that merely human powers can produce and, of course, exceeds the potential of a non-Christian, since the Holy Spirit does not indwell him or her.

Delving into this section of Scripture will greatly enhance a Christian's understanding of this area of service. This is not the only New Testament discussion of gifts, since Romans 12:3–8, Ephesians 4:7–16, and 1 Peter 4:10–11 have relevance here too. But 1 Corinthians 12–14 has by far the most extended instruction. It was due to his desire to bring Christians into fuller awareness of this subject that Paul penned the words to Corinth in the first place ("I do not want you to be unaware," 12:1; cf. Rom. 1:13, 11:25; 1 Cor. 10:1; 2 Cor. 1:8; 1 Thess. 4:13). Paul's habit was to specify removal of ignorance when he wanted to emphasize an important subject about which his readers were misinformed. Yet he always broached his discussion with a touch of tenderness by his use of the familiar "brethren," an emblem of closeness and endearment within the family of God. The strong words that follow often contain elements of rebuke, but the author always tempered his word of rebuke with a feeling of love.

12:2—The temptation: confusion of spiritual gifts. What was the need for such detailed instruction about spiritual gifts? To be sure, the Corinthians had asked for advice, but Paul went far beyond what they had asked, indicating the great importance he attached to the subject. He must have had deeper reasons.

Verse 2 states specifically why such great urgency attached itself to this matter: Christians tended to equate unusual pneumatic conditions accompanying gifts with similar conditions and experiences they had before becoming Christians. That raised an alarming possibility, since nothing could be more unworthy than to attribute such heathen activities to the Holy Spirit.

The second verse, though brief, describes vividly the condition of an unsaved person. He is a "pagan" (or a "Gentile") and not a Christian, or member of "the church of God" (1 Cor. 10:32). Specifically, the Corinthian readers were also non-Jews, and as such, completely gullible to the idolatry that so characterized the world of that time (as it does the world at the turn of the twenty-first century). It is even clearer in 1 Corinthians 10:19–21 that the idol worshipped was not merely an inanimate object, but one that exercised a positive control over its victims by means of "demons" who were so intricately bound up in the idol. These fallen angels have power to exercise unrestrained control over a person in his non-Christian condition, and some aspects of this control had apparently carried over into the Christian state of some of Paul's Corinthian acquaintances. This was so much the case that they had on occasion confused demonic leading in their lives with that of the Holy Spirit.

That was a deplorable state of affairs, and Paul's utter alarm upon discovering this to be true among his own converts is completely understandable. The capricious will of these satanic emissaries governs the direction in which the unsaved person travels. He is as helpless as a prisoner, being led farther and farther away from the right path. Though he may feel all the while that he acts of his own free will, he is actually the victim of this "dumb" or "speechless" idol (cf. Ps. 115:5; Hab. 2:18) and the personal forces of evil associated with it.

As depressing as it is, one can still conceive of such a thing with a non-Christian. But of deeper concern is that these Christians had mistaken this demonic leading for the leading of the Holy Spirit. Parallels between the two were sufficient to confuse the readers. So here Paul states once and for all that the leading of such ungodly agencies is to be distinguished from being led in paths of righteousness by the Holy Spirit (cf. Rom. 8:14; Gal. 5:18).

12:3—The test: distinguishing of spiritual gifts. In light of ignorance about the subject (v. 1) and consequent confusion and failure to distinguish the Holy Spirit's activity from heathen and demonic leadings (v. 2), Paul now presents a test by which to distinguish the two leadings. The presence of counterfeit spiritual gifts need be tolerated no longer. A suitable test applied to an utterance makes its source immediately obvious, whether it is the Spirit of God or not.

To clarify this crucial matter, a twofold criterion exists for making a distinction between heathen and Christian phenomena.

1. The first aspect of the test is negative: "No one speaking by the Spirit of God says, 'Jesus is accursed'" (12:3). A slightly different rendering more accurately represents "accursed" as "anathema." Though reconstructing a historical circumstance in which the Corinthian assembly heard and approved such words as this is difficult, apparently this very thing did occur.[3] Otherwise, Paul would not have offered this word of correction. It is indeed perplexing that this went on among early Christians, and a careful examination of all the factors involved is obligatory to comprehend the ecclesiastical climate to which Paul addressed these words. Then and only then can one know how to apply the test. The following questions need answers: (a) What person would make such a statement? To whom does the test apply? (b) Where was the statement made? In what surroundings does the test apply? (c) What was the condition of the person at the time of his statement? Is emotionalism a part of the explanation? (d) What is the nature of the declaration about Jesus? How serious is a pronouncement of "anathema"? (e) Why would such a statement be tolerated and even approved by some who heard it? Does the test in any way relate to wrong doctrine? It is only by answering these questions thoroughly that the real implication of such a criterion will be clear.

Question (a). As startling as it is, the person making such a statement must have been a professing Christian. If this was not so, no need would exist to propose a test to determine the source of the statement. An unbeliever could not have spoken such a statement through the Holy Spirit's enabling. Whatever else the Corinthian Christians lacked in discernment, they surely understood that the Spirit of God had not taken up His residence in a person without conversion. Furthermore, the person in question probably was a Gentile, the reference to Gentiles in verse 2, as well as the numerical majority of Gentiles in this church, arguing for this.

Question (b). The declaration, "Jesus is anathema," must have been made in Christian surroundings. A trial setting, whether Jewish or Gentile, is out of keeping with 1 Corinthians 11:2–14:40. These are matters that transpired in conjunction with Christian worship, and the setting of a Christian assembly is the only reasonable explanation. For such a pronouncement to come in Christian surroundings brings even more consternation.

Question (c). A state of ecstasy and outward excitement in the individual speaking should be understood in conjunction with the declaration. This is the only sense in which a parallel with the frenzied inspiration of verse 2 can be drawn. When a person was beside himself with excitement, some accepted this as evidence of the Spirit's presence and activity, recalling the accusation of drunkenness against the earliest Christians on the Day of Pentecost (Acts 2:13, 15). Indeed, it is the disposition of some to accept the truthfulness of any statement if it is made with enough enthusiasm. Paul cautions against this natural inclination, however. A person allowing himself to come under control of forces outside himself has no guarantee of divine inspiration, for there are inspirations that proceed from other sources as well (cf. 12:2). Therefore, a state of uncontrolled emotionalism not from God lay behind the cursing of Jesus.

Question (d). The word "anathema" signals the presence of a Jewish influence upon the speaker. It is a translation of the Hebrew term designating what was devoted to God in order to bring about its destruction. In other words, it was a Jewish term for excommunication. Deuteronomy 21:23 may offer a limited explanation of how such an utterance originated: "He who is hanged [upon the tree] is accursed of God." Since there was in Corinth an element of judaistic teaching arising among the followers of Peter (1 Cor. 1:12) and evidenced by the Hebrew claims of false apostles (2 Cor. 11:22), it is not difficult to see how a Gentile speaker could have had his thinking colored to the point where he could make such a declaration about the historical Jesus. This form of curse, then, amounts to as strong a word of condemnation as one could bring against another.

Question (e). An explanation of why such a statement was tolerated with approval in a Christian meeting is still lacking. It is probably to be supplied in the answer to this fifth question, which notes an incipient heresy about the person of Christ among the Corinthian Christians. It is not suggested that a fully developed system of Gnosticism (a heretical sect founded in the second century and characterized by its belief in salvation by knowledge) was present in Corinth, but that small beginning of heresy that eventually grew into this cult had already begun to appear in Corinth. For example, the presence of some within the church who did not have an unswerving loyalty to Jesus as Lord is implied in 16:22: "If any one does not love the Lord, let him be accursed." In addition to this, just a few months later, another epistle notes the presence of those in Corinth who preached another Jesus (2 Cor. 11:3-4). What was the particular belief of such heretics? They made a distinction between the historical person Jesus and the Christ who was only spirit. They taught that the spirit of Christ descended upon the man Jesus at His baptism, but departed from Him prior to His crucifixion, with the result that the man Jesus died just as any other criminal. Therefore, no spiritual benefits issued from His death.

The presence of other doctrinal aberrations among the Corinthians, such as their misunderstanding of Christ's resurrection (1 Cor. 15), lends credence to finding heresy as the ultimate explanation of the words "Jesus is anathema." This heresy that denied a real union between the historical Jesus and the Christ received a more direct refutation before the close of the first century in 1 John 2:22 and 4:1-3. Since this was a heresy that received as much or more attention than any other from orthodox Christianity during the first century, it is quite probable that it lies at the bottom of why the Corinthian assembly tolerated such a statement and some of its members even granted approval to it.

The negative aspect of testing utterances, therefore, ultimately has to do with doctrinal conformity. To be sure, the test involved other elements, but Paul would have his readers know that no spiritual gift would result in a statement that was contrary to the truth. The test of doctrinal orthodoxy must constantly apply to spiritual gifts: to be accepted as valid, the spoken manifestation must agree with what has come to be written down in God's Word.

2. The second aspect of testing spiritual gifts is positive: "No one can say, 'Jesus is Lord,' except by the Holy Spirit" (12:3). This step involves full confession of the Lordship of Jesus along with full allegiance to Him. Any time one makes this acknowledgment with conviction, it is a cry of adoration and an act of homage on his part. Of course, a skeptic may mouth the words in mockery with the result that it proves nothing at all. It is not such empty words that constitute the test. It is rather the ability to utter these words out of deepest conviction that demonstrates the genuineness of a spiritual gift behind the utterance.

Yet the positive side of Paul's test must go even deeper than measuring sincere devotion. In light of the doctrinal conformity insisted upon in the negative side, it is highly probable that something doctrinal is likewise at stake in this positive word. Closer scrutiny verifies that suspicion. The Greek word *Kurios*, translated into English by "Lord," is the regular New Testament means for translating the Old Testament name of God (referred to often as the *tetragrammaton*). That name, represented in the Old Testament by "the LORD" or "Jehovah," was the name that God appropriated to Himself in Exodus 3:14. Hence, the Spirit-prompted confession that distinguishes the true spiritual gift from the counterfeit includes an acknowledgment that Jesus is God as well as man (cf. 1 John 4:1–3).

If it appears to be stretching the context to attach that Old Testament significance to *Kurios*, one should remember that "anathema," with which the name stands in antithesis, conveys a very strong Jewish, Old Testament tone.

In view of all this, we are justified to conclude that the test of verse 3, along with various side issues, is primarily theological in nature and insists upon an accurate view of the person of Jesus Christ. It is only as one maintains the correct view of Him as the God-man that he can confidently identify the activity of the Holy Spirit and spiritual gifts through members of the body of Christ.

First Corinthians 12:1–3, therefore, impressively emphasizes the uniqueness of spiritual gifts. Nothing is comparable to them in any other realm. Consistency in conveying a proper picture of Jesus, not only as the Son of Man, but also as the Son of God characterizes the true gift. Any representation that falls short of this ideal marks itself as an imitation and, if spiritual health is to prevail, ministry within the body of Christ must do without that imitation.

Chapter Two

UNIFIED SOURCE OF SPIRITUAL GIFTS: THE TRIUNE GOD

12:4–11

4 Now there are varieties of gifts, but the same Spirit.

5 And there are varieties of ministries, and the same Lord.

6 And there are varieties of effects, but the same God who works all things in all persons.

7 But to each one is given the manifestation of the Spirit for the common good.

8 For to one is given the word of wisdom through the Spirit, and to another the word of knowledge according to the same Spirit;

9 to another faith by the same Spirit, and to another gifts of healing by the one Spirit,

10 and to another the effecting of miracles, and to another prophecy, and to another the distinguishing of spirits, to another various kinds of tongues, and to another the interpretation of tongues.

11 But one and the same Spirit works all these things, distributing to each one individually just as He wills.

The fact that by one simple test spiritual gifts are distinguishable from counterfeit spiritual activities does not mean that all spiritual gifts are the same. Diversity is the feature that emerges immediately in 1 Corinthians 12:4. Assuredly, spiritual gifts are unique and are to be distinguished carefully in the broader field of spiritual manifestations (12:1-3). Yet this uniqueness does not entail fitting every one of them into the same mold.

Side by side with this variety, verses 4-11 emphasize the one source from which all proceed. Each gift exhibits itself in a different manner and with a value distinct to itself, but no matter what the manner or value of manifestation, each one is traceable to the Father, Son, and Holy Spirit.

12:4—Gifts of grace from the one Holy Spirit. The fourth verse moves quickly into this new phase of the subject. Instead of continuing a treatment of how to distinguish good spiritual activities from bad, the discussion now focuses more specifically on good spiritual activities alone and how distinctions exist among them. "Varieties"[1] emphasizes by its threefold repetition that no Christian is a carbon copy of another when it comes to spiritual gifts. This initial mention of differences implicitly forecasts the list of gifts found in verses 8-10, where gifts not only differ from one another but also fall into distinct categories. As is recorded elsewhere, they are gifts that differ "according to the grace given to us" (Rom. 12:6).

"Varieties" are first of all characterized as "gifts" (*charismatōn*, 12:4). The Greek expression more fully describes them as "gifts of grace." They are unearned, being prompted purely by God's unmerited favor toward individuals in the body of Christ. The thought aligns with 12:11, where the sovereign will of God alone determines how the gifts are distributed.

After noticing the "varieties of grace gifts," Paul quickly qualifies that variety by noting the unity that lies behind all the gifts. No matter how many and large the differences, the same Spirit of God is the origin. A list of specific gifts is about to appear (12:8-10), each one having its own characteristics, but one and the same Person produces them all, none other than He who dwells within every believer in Christ (cf. 1 Cor. 6:19).

Implicit in this unity of source is a remedy to a Corinthian problem. The very gifts that Paul goes on to list in verses 8-10 are those that, utilized by carnal men, have caused division among Christians. Because of these gifts' spectacular character, individual members of Christ's body enjoyed particular prominence, a prominence that was in turn used to create a party spirit. Paul wanted his readers to know that this schismatic abuse was not of the Spirit. This third Person of the Trinity does not fight against Himself. That these gifts might be used to create division is completely contrary to His intent.

12:5—Services from the one Lord Jesus Christ. Another designation complements "varieties" in verse 5. It is "ministries" or "services" (*diakoniōn*). This designation looks at spiritual gifts as creating benefits for others. The ultimate in Christ's bestowal of gifts is the service they enable one to render. This thread of emphasis runs throughout chapters 12–14 and is well summed up by the nature of love that "is kind [or useful]" (13:4) and "does not seek its own" (13:5).

"The same Lord" (12:5) provides additional evidence favoring the case for unity. The second Person of the Trinity joins the third (12:4) as the source of services performed through spiritual gifts. If this is not sufficiently clear here, a further word written a few years later in Ephesians 4:11 reveals Jesus Christ's part in bestowing such gifts. It is under His authority and for His purposes that they operate, and none escapes His surveillance. Of course, He is not at variance with Himself. How then could anyone justify the use of gifts as a springboard for promoting schism among Christians?

12:6—Results from the one Father. The sixth verse adds another word about varieties, this time in connection with the good effects wrought by spiritual gifts. "Varieties of effects" is the third expression in as many verses depicting spiritual gifts. The "operations" or "effects" (*energēmatōn*, 12:6), focus upon the miraculous things wrought wherever spiritual gifts are operative. Such "energizings" are clearly supernatural. Divine power is at work, a power demonstrating its presence in such things as removal of mountains through the gift of faith (1 Cor. 13:2).

Along with implying this additional aspect of spiritual gifts, Paul reinforces his argument for unity a third time. This he does by reference to God the Father, a singular person in contrast to the "varieties of effects." One and the same God stands behind all the effects, and surely He is not in conflict with Himself. Beginning with the third Person of the Trinity, the text has now included all three Persons and reached a climax with its mention of the first Person. Other passages that group the Father, Son, and Holy Spirit in the same context are Matthew 3:16–17 (the baptism of Christ); 2 Corinthians 13:14 (the threefold benediction); and Ephesians 4:4–6 (another list of unifying factors in Christ's body). The Father has given Jesus Christ as Lord of the church and has sent the Holy Spirit to function in the body of Christ as described in this chapter. The Spirit is the immediate agent of the verse 6 effects (a related word rendered "works" in v. 11) because He is the one whom the Father has chosen to be His representative in dispensing the gifts, carrying out the services, and reaping the beneficial results ("all things") in all people involved with Christ's body ("in all persons").

12:7—Many manifestations for one purpose. In spite of the variety expressed in verses 4–6, however, each gift does not involve a separate intent. A new word to characterize spiritual gifts occurs in verse 7: a gift is a "manifestation" or "exhibition" (*phanerōsis*). The word signals another aspect of spiritual gifts, the element of display. The activity is by nature outgoing, with the result that it touches other lives. It must be seen, heard, or in some manner experienced by at least one person other than the gifted one. The Giver never intended any spiritual gift for private purposes, and to the extent that anyone uses a gift that way, he or she abuses that given ability. Unless this principle governs, the body of Christ cannot realize "the common good" (12:7) or "edification" (14:12).

Returning again to the matter of source, the text repeats that the manifestation is "of the Spirit."[2] The Holy Spirit's part in these phenomena has already been the subject in verses 3–4 above. In essence, He exhibits His bestowal in the operation of various gifts. His part as dispenser is reiterated again in verse 11 below: "distributing to each one individually just as He wills."

Two significant features characterize this Spirit-produced exhibition.

1. It is "to each one." The wording in verse 7 lays heaviest emphasis on this. It is as though the Holy Spirit through Paul would proclaim loudly that gifts of the Spirit are not reserved for a few outstanding people. Every single Christian, whoever he is and no matter when he lives, possesses a spiritual endowment. The discussion constantly returns to this common characteristic. For example, in verses 8–10 the words "to one . . . to another . . ." and so on, take their cue from this universal characteristic. The same strain continues in the words "to each one individually" (v. 11). Nor does this chapter exhaust Paul's attention to this universality. In the companion section of Romans, it is "as God has allotted to each a measure of faith" (12:3). In Ephesians also, some time later, Paul comes back to this theme: "But to each one of us grace was given according to the measure of Christ's gift" (Eph. 4:7). If there is one well-established teaching in this field, it is that every Christian has at least one gift.

2. Secondary emphasis in verse 7 falls on "for the common good" or "for profit." Here in summary is the purpose of Spirit-produced manifestations. Each one has a spiritual ability for the purpose of benefiting the rest of the body of Christ. It is important to observe in 1 Corinthians 12–14 that the profit or edification is not for the benefit of the individual possessing the gift. That is not the goal. In fact, to use a gift for one's own gratification is selfishness, neglecting the guidelines of love. As such, it is a sin against the Giver of the gift, as well as against those for whose benefit the gift should have been used. The consideration constantly before Paul's mind was, "What shall I profit you?" (1 Cor. 14:6), not "How can I profit myself?" Let it be known once and for all: God never intended any spiritual gift for private benefit. Every gifted person is primarily responsible to serve the rest of Christ's body with whatever abilities he has from God.

12:8—Sample gifts: two gifts for the mind. To confirm his word about spiritual manifestations, Paul now embarks upon a list of typical gifts (12:8–10)—ways in which the Spirit manifests His bestowal through different individuals. The gifts mentioned here were those that lent themselves to schisms because their supernatural nature was most conspicuous. The divisive Corinthians appear to have craved these because of their obsession with the personal attention they attracted. The nine gifts in this list fall into three categories marked by alternating Greek words for "another." Six times in the list the "another" stands for "another of the same kind," but two times "another" means "another of a different kind."[3] These latter two occurrences mark beginnings of the second and third divisions of the list and occur in conjunction with "faith" (v. 9) and "kinds of tongues" (v. 10).

In part one of the list, the result is two gifts, wisdom and knowledge, which entail insights granted to the mind. These are "revelatory" gifts in that they included matter granted in one way or another by direct revelation. People became channels used by God to convey His mind to the church. The next part of the list consists of five gifts grouped in accordance with their confirmatory character. Without leaving the intellect in abeyance, the gifts of faith, healing, miracles, prophecy, and discernment more peculiarly involved the human will. Volitionally, certain ones had abilities to perform feats that would confirm divinely granted revelations in the eyes of men. Thus, the second category of gifts supported the first. Though revealing divine power, in the main, these were void of informational content.

The third part of the list, tongues and interpretation, was also confirmatory (cf. 1 Cor. 14:22), but differs from the second in that intellect was largely in abeyance when anyone used tongues (cf. 1 Cor. 14:2). The listing places interpretation here because of its connection with tongues as a solution to the unintelligibility of tongues.

Taking up the first category, verse 8 depicts two gifts—or manifestations—that pertain more particularly to the mind: an utterance prompted by wisdom and an utterance prompted by knowledge.

"The word of wisdom." The widespread occurrence of "wisdom" in the Word of God is obvious to any Bible reader. The gift so labeled, however, has a more restricted sense because it refers to a specific spiritual function of which only a certain group in the body of Christ has been capable. That specialized sense is understandable in light of 1 Corinthians 2:6–13.[4] In this earlier section of the epistle, Paul describes himself in connection with other apostolic and missionary teachers, such as Apollos and Cephas (cf. 1 Cor. 1:12; 3:4–6). As divine mouthpieces, they spoke "God's wisdom in a mystery, the hidden wisdom" (1 Cor. 2:7). By mentioning wisdom in connection with "mystery" and what is "hidden," this passage points clearly to divine revelation received by these early Christian leaders, which they in turn

transformed into words for communicating to others of their generation. It is the process of receiving and communicating this special revelation that is discussed in the paragraph through 2:13.

It is, therefore, in connection with the word of wisdom that Paul in 1 Corinthians 13:2 refers to the gift of prophecy and the understanding of all mysteries. At strategic times throughout Bible history, God has spoken directly to His servants, that they in turn might communicate His message to people at large. The period following Pentecost was one such strategic era. Special need arose for an understanding of hitherto unrevealed truths in order for the church to grow into an instrument for encircling the globe with the message of Christ. The spiritual gift of wisdom to certain first-generation Christians was the means God adopted.

Much information thus revealed became permanently recorded in the pages of the New Testament. Nevertheless, it is probable that much that God chose to reveal had only a temporary usefulness for the local circumstances of first-century Christians. This information did not become a part of God's written revelation.

Noteworthy among those who received this gift was the apostle Paul himself. Peter referred to Paul's particular endowment when he wrote, "Just as also our beloved brother Paul, according to the *wisdom* given him, wrote to you" (2 Peter 3:15, italics added). Among the mysteries so abundantly revealed to Paul were the final destiny of Israel (Rom. 11:25) and joint participation in the same body by Jews and Gentiles on an equal basis (Eph. 3:1–7).

It is worth repeating that this gift is not the same as the wisdom available to all Christians. The demands of life are such that no Christian can stand merely on his own wisdom. He needs divine enlightenment to face various circumstances of life, and this too is "wisdom" (cf. James 1:5). Wisdom in this more general sense is available to all Christians, but is not the same as *"the word of wisdom."*

"The word of knowledge." The other gift of the intellect belongs to the same group as the word of wisdom. In other words, the word of knowledge is in the same revelatory category as the former gift of verse 8. Yet a distinction exists between them. While the word of wisdom brought direct revelation, the word of knowledge was the ability to grasp that objective revelatory data and by inspiration apply it in various connections.

The relation of knowledge to prophecy (and hence to wisdom also) is demonstrated in 1 Corinthians 13:2, where the follow-up statement regarding prophecy includes the understanding of not only "all mysteries" but also "all knowledge." This also means, of course, an overlapping of knowledge and apostleship which, along with its other features, provided for authoritative communication of the message of Christ.

The revelatory nature of knowledge surfaces again in Colossians 2:2–3, where it occurs in connection with "God's mystery," "hidden," and "wisdom." Second Peter 3:1–2 illustrates how it functioned in a revelatory manner. Peter, the divinely inspired writer, took teachings given earlier by "the holy prophets" and "your apostles" and applied these earlier, direct revelations to new circumstances of the late sixties in connection with "mockers" (2 Peter 3:3). That was a new situation that demanded special insights. Jude did a similar thing later in his epistle (Jude 17–18). Once again, it is obvious that all inspired applications of divine revelation did not find their places in the permanent record of the New Testament. The pages of Holy Scripture do, however, record those applications of the gift that were of lasting value to the church of all generations.

Another precautionary word is in order. Distinct from "the word of knowledge," a more general knowledge is the common resource of all believers in Christ. It is in reference to this more general category of knowledge that the Scripture commands Christians to grow continually throughout their lives (cf. 2 Peter 3:18).

The Holy Spirit makes a point of noting His own place with each of the gifts of verse 8. The word of wisdom is "through" or "by" the Spirit. This means that He is the intermediary, or medium of communication, through whom God revealed mysteries to His apostles and prophets. The word of knowledge is "according to" the same Spirit. This means that knowledge gained by those possessing this special ability was in perfect accord with the will of the Holy Spirit. The gift introduced no deviation from the straight line of divine truth expressed in the "word of wisdom," on which the "word of knowledge" was dependent.

12:9—Sample gifts: two gifts for the will. Verse 9 introduces a new category of gifted persons, a category that includes the next five gifts in the list. A different Greek word for "another" in connection with "faith" signals the transition. The gift of faith is "another of a different kind," whereas the rest, with the exception of the fourth occurrence of "another" in verse 10, are "another of the same kind." This variation in wording points to an accompanying shift in the character of the gifts to follow.

The first gift in this category, the gift of faith, provides the unifying factor in this new group. Whatever involves faith automatically entails the decision-making faculty of the human make-up, for no one has ever exercised faith unless he had a will to do so. It is therefore the aspect of human will that looms largest in this portion of the gift list.

The gift of "faith." In addition to furnishing the unifying aspect for the present series of gifts, "faith" is distinct as a separate gift in itself. One should not confuse the gift of faith with the more general faith that is common to all

Christians. The more general sense of faith is not limited to a certain group within the body of Christ, since it is by such a volitional exercise that every believer initially enters the body of Christ.

The gift of faith, on the other hand, had to do with a more intensive manifestation of trust, a specialized function of which only certain Christians were capable. This unusual ability enabled a person to believe God in the face of enormous obstacles. The obstacles came in wide variety to the first-century church. With such a gift, however, the child of God could trust Him to the extent that God intervened and produced a means for overcoming that obstacle. The gift of faith apparently fulfilled the same confirmatory function as did other gifts in its category.

Paul alludes to this special capability once again in 1 Corinthians 13:2: "And if I have all faith, so as to remove mountains, but do not have love, I am nothing." The idea of removing mountains, of course, goes back to the teachings of the Lord Jesus (Matt. 17:20), where He promised His immediate followers this special ability after He had demonstrated the removal of an obstacle by casting a demon from a child.

The kinship between the gifts of faith and prophecy, which comes later in this same group of five, is conspicuous in Paul's statement of Acts 27:25: "For I believe God, that it will turn out exactly as I have been told." In making his prophecy regarding the safety of the ship's crew, Paul did so under the full persuasion that God would perform the miraculous thing he had predicted, which very thing God did (Acts 27:44). His special gift of faith enabled him to make such a dogmatic prediction.

That certain individuals had this special capability, however, does not excuse other Christians from failure to live by faith. This quality of life is a general Christian responsibility, as well as a special capability possessed by only some in Christ's body. It is the general responsibility that is referred to when the Scripture records, "We walk by faith" (2 Cor. 5:7), or when it speaks of "faith working through love" (Gal. 5:6). Hence, no Christian can afford to turn his back on trust in God as a basic rule of life.

"Gifts of healings." The book of Acts is replete with instances when a second kind of faith-oriented gift was in action, "gifts of healings." (Both words are plural in the Greek, pointing to a variety of such gifts designed for different kinds of sicknesses.) A crippled man was healed in Acts 3:6–8. Many of the sick were healed in Acts 5:15–16. Paralyzed and lame people were healed in Acts 8:7. A blind man received his sight and a paralyzed man the use of his limbs in Acts 9:17–18, 33–35. Diseased people were healed in Acts 19:12, as was one afflicted with fever and dysentery in Acts 28:8.

As reflected in all these situations, the gifts of healings did not result from human medical practice but had to do with cures wrought by special spiritual power. As is true with other spiritual gifts, this was an ability bestowed upon some in the church, but not all. When in possession of this ability, a person became the specific divine channel for producing a miraculous cure for a physical problem. This is not to say that the same individual could cure every illness he confronted, for healing was not always what God wanted (cf. 2 Cor. 12:8–9). But he did become the vehicle of God in set circumstances for accomplishing such a spectacular work.

In grasping the purpose of this gift, it is important that one understand the circumstances in which God was pleased to manifest it. The example of Acts 3:6–8 is an illustration. On this occasion, Peter exercised the gift in restoring a crippled man to normal health, and through this miraculous deed gained a hearing for the dramatic sermon delivered on this very occasion (Acts 3:12–26). Without the bodily restoration, Peter would have had no audience. With the miraculous cure, he had a stamp of divine approval on what he had to say to the Jewish audience on that significant day. The healing obviously served to verify Peter's words in the minds of his listeners.

"Gifts of healing," then, were part of the "miracles and wonders and signs" that God granted through Jesus (Acts 2:22) and His disciples following Pentecost (Acts 2:43; 4:30; 5:12; 6:8; 8:13; 14:3; 15:12). They all served to confirm the gospel message in a day when no verified, written New Testament existed.

An important emphasis in connection with this gift, as well as with those that have preceded it, is that divine healing through the gift of healing is not the only divine healing spoken of in the Bible. In fact, the gift as an authenticating mark upon a certain individual and his message in the first century A.D. is different from God's commitment to heal the sick then and now in answer to prayer (cf. James 5:15). It is the privilege, even the responsibility, of every Christian to pray for physical healing, even though no individual in this day and time possesses the gift of healing. The day of divine healing has not passed, though the day of divine healers has. Healing goes on, but miraculous confirmation of specific individuals as vehicles of divine revelation does not because of the completion of New Testament revelation.

The recurring emphasis in the paragraph (vv. 4–11) upon the unified source of all the gifts is worthy of another mention. Faith is "by the same Spirit" (v. 9). To be sure, variety characterizes different members of any body, but the Holy Spirit Himself is the agent for producing whatever variety there is. The Greek preposition translated "by" both times in verse 9 varies from the word for "by" in verse 8. In verse 9, "by" carries the connotation "in the power of" the one Spirit. The end result is essentially the same, however. The same Person lies behind the operation each time, and the net result because of this unified source must be unity among Christians.

12:10—Sample gifts: three more gifts for the will and two gifts for the tongue.

"*Effecting of miracles.*" A third gift in the category of faith and healings is "effectings [the word is plural in the Greek, standing for individual cases where miracles were performed] of miracles." While miracles were broader than healings, which covered only one type of miracle, they were not as general as faith; miracles were only one way in which the gift of faith manifested itself. A sample miracle that was not a healing, strictly speaking, was bringing a person back to life (cf. Acts 9:40).

Another instance of this gift's operation occurs in the blinding of Elymas (Acts 13:8–11). The net result of this judgment against an adversary was to bring special attention to what Paul had to say following the miraculous feat (Acts 13:12). The confirmatory effect of the gift of miracles is thus like the effect of other gifts in this second category: these are a means for validating God's spokesmen and their messages. Such a need existed only so long as the church was without its own authenticated written revelation, a condition that prevailed through the first century A.D. Once all had been written that God wanted written, no further place was open for this or any other confirmatory gift.

This is not to say that miracles have not occurred since A.D. 100. They have happened and continue according to God's providence. But the medium of their accomplishment is no longer the spiritual gift of miracles: the need no longer exists to verify specific persons as channels of new revelation, for new revelation ceased with the writing of the last New Testament book. The age of miracles continues, but the age of miracle workers has passed.

The gift of "prophecy." It is surprising at first to find prophecy listed as one of the confirmatory gifts. It more frequently finds its association with gifts that pertain to the mind (cf. 1 Cor. 12:28–29; 13:2; 14:30). A possibility is that Paul chose to place it among these gifts early in chapter 12 to emphasize its dual nature, that of providing confirmation as well as revelation. This could be a very effective move in "selling" prophecy as the gift to be cultivated in the Corinthian assembly (cf. 1 Cor. 14, where the desirability of prophecy is so strongly stressed).

By separating prophecy from the words of wisdom and knowledge, Paul has no intention of denying its intimate association with them. But at this stage, he chose to emphasize the predictive element that was an indispensable characteristic of the New Testament prophet. In comparison with the Old Testament prophet, the predictive element had a much smaller place in the New Testament counterpart. Nevertheless, it is present (Acts 11:27–28; 21:10–11; Rev. 1:3). It was the ability to prophesy future happenings accurately that provided the gift with its own authenticating value.

A good question to raise is what does this gift have to do with faith? The answer is clear in Paul's response to a crisis during his voyage of Acts 27. In verse 25 of that chapter he says, "Therefore, keep up your courage, men, for I believe God, that it will turn out exactly as I have been told." Paul confidently predicted the safety of all on board the ship in spite of the imminent dangers confronting them, and he made his firm affirmation on the basis of his belief in what God had told him. By faith, he was able to speak with authority regarding the future. Prophecy, then, is another kind of faith manifestation.

Furthermore, it is important to note that the accuracy with which Paul predicted what ultimately happened made him a respected authority in his companions' eyes. This was evidenced when they began heeding his advice (Acts 27:34–36, 44).

God has not continued to bestow the predictive powers that belonged to such first-century Christians as Agabus, the daughters of Philip, and Paul. Written by the apostle John, Revelation gives notice of the termination of prophecy. It specifically states that no prophetic additions are to be tolerated (Rev. 22:18). It is quite evident in this prohibition that God incorporated into this one, great, final prophecy all the predictive elements that would be needed by the church in coming generations, until such time as these find their fulfillment in connection with Christ's second advent. Any attempt on man's part to add to the contents of the Apocalypse subsequent to its completion would constitute an attempt to add to "the words of the prophecy of this book," and hence would provoke from God plagues over and above those described in the book itself. For this reason, the wise approach is to limit prophecy to the period before John concluded the writing of Revelation at the end of the first century A.D. (For further discussion of this aspect of prophecy, see Appendix C at the rear of this volume; for further discussion of the gift of prophecy in general, see discussion at 12:28 and Appendixes A and D; for an evaluation of a recent unusual view of the gift, see Appendix B).

"Distinguishing of Spirits." The fifth and last gift in the list of faith-oriented manifestations is "distinguishing[s] of spirits." To be sure, all Christians should develop discernment in spiritual matters. That is what Paul has advocated earlier in this chapter (vv. 2–3), where he supplies tests for distinguishing the true from the false. First John 4:1 advocates the same for every believer: "Beloved, do not believe every spirit, but test the spirits to see whether they are from God; because many false prophets have gone out into the world." Yet, an additional need existed for a special class of gifted individuals who could pass immediate judgment on utterances given in a Christian assembly.

The gift of discernment filled that need for an immediate ruling on whether the words spoken originated with the Holy Spirit or with some other spirit. Paul elaborates upon the exercise of this gift in 1 Corinthians 14:29 in the words "let the others pass judgment," where the Greek verb meaning "pass judgment" is the same root as the noun translated "distinguishing" in

1 Corinthians 12:10. Such specialized discernment accompanied prophetic utterances, and herein lies the explanation of its inclusion right after the gift of prophecy. In any given instance, someone other than the prophetic speaker of the moment was to judge the source of the utterance. The wording of 14:29 indicates that the ability of discerning spirits normally belonged to those who were also prophets.

The particular need for special discernment arose in cases where the spoken message contained no direct blasphemy against Jesus as Lord and Christ. The criteria of 1 Corinthians 12:3, as well as that which came later in 1 John 2:22 and 4:1–3, tested such obvious violations. Supernatural insights were necessary, however, in cases where utterances were not so obviously wrong. For example, on the surface, the statement of the damsel in Acts 16:17 bore all the earmarks of truth: "These men are bond-servants of the Most High God, who are proclaiming to you the way of salvation." Special ability on Paul's part enabled him to recognize the source of the utterance as being "a spirit of divination" (Acts 16:16, 18) and not the Holy Spirit.

The use of "spirits" in 1 Corinthians 12:10 carries a force similar to that conveyed by the same Greek term in 1 Corinthians 14:12, which translates the word as "spiritual gifts." The sense is "spirit-manifestations." A recognition of spirit-manifestations also involves, of course, a recognition of the spirit who prompts such an utterance. In 14:12, the source is presumed to be the Holy Spirit, whereas in the present verse, the source may or may not be the Holy Spirit. It was the responsibility of the discerner to determine this. In many cases, he doubtless had to rule against the utterance when he found its source to be some other spirit, either human or demonic.

The confirmatory contribution of this gift is not immediately obvious, and it probably finds its place in the present list only because of its relationship to prophecy.

"Kinds of tongues." The last two gifts named in verse 10 constitute a third category of gifts, those that relate to the tongue. The Greek text again marks this transition by its choice of a different word for "another" in connection with "kinds of tongues." This is the same variation marking the transition to the second category at the beginning of verse 9, where the "another" connected with "faith" likewise signifies "another of a different kind." As already pointed out, the other instances of "another" in verses 8–10 are representations of a word that means "another of the same kind."

Paul, guided by the Spirit, chose to put tongues and their interpretation into a class by themselves to underscore the differences between them and the rest of the gifts. That step hopefully would counteract the disproportionate amount of attention given to tongues in the Corinthian church.

The special enabling resulting from the tongues gift meant unusual capabilities with foreign languages.[5] A person received immediate ability to speak languages that he had never acquired by natural means. This, of course, is a psychological and natural impossibility, and the ability to communicate in this manner is explainable only from the standpoint of supernatural powers. That was the nature of the gift exemplified in Acts 2, where the "tongues" of verses 4 and 11 were one and the same phenomenon as the "language" in verses 6 and 8. An atmosphere of amazement reigned on that birthday of the Christian church because here were people speaking dialects representative of widely scattered territories in the Roman Empire who could not possibly have learned those languages by natural means. "They continued in amazement" (Acts 2:12). It was the amazement that provided Peter with a large audience for his great Pentecost sermon (Acts 2:14–36). The miraculous tongues attracted a crowd of people who then heard Peter preach the gospel in Greek, a language common to them all.

The striking feature about tongues that distinguished them from the remainder of the gifts was the degree to which the mind remained in the background while the gift operated. To this same degree, tongues were an unsuitable vehicle for providing edification among Christians. This shortcoming is the burden of much that Paul says on the subject in chapter 14. He strongly expresses his personal determination that the mind and understanding be active in ministry to other Christians in 14:19: "However, in the church I desire to speak five words with my mind, that I may instruct others also, rather than ten thousand words in a tongue." Tongues were no doubt a gift that, like the others, originated with the Holy Spirit. Once bestowed, however, they were subject to misuse. Such misuse among Corinthian Christians goes far in explaining the need for a section such as 1 Corinthians 12–14.

From the use of tongues in Acts 2, it is immediately evident that the gift also lay in the realm of those that God was pleased to use for purposes of confirmation. In fact, Paul specifically categorized the gift under that heading when he later referred to its "sign" purpose (1 Cor. 14:22). The purpose of a "sign" was to arrest attention and bring about a reflection upon some spiritual lesson taught by the sign. It was, in other words, a miracle with an ethical purpose—a fingerpost of God, as it were. That tongues were successful in such an evidential way the three times they are mentioned in Acts (Acts 2; 10; 19) goes without saying.

Yet the Corinthians had cultivated a habitual use of tongues among themselves, where verification was not the prime need, if it was a need at all. Paul's plea with them in chapter 14 was to recognize the purpose and place of the gifts and to cultivate among their own number only those gifts that contributed to edification through instruction. Tongues could very well have served a useful purpose in the city of Corinth—but as a means for convincing non-Christians rather than becoming a source of confusion among Christians.

Commercially and geographically, Corinth was a city merchants and travelers visited while in transit. As an evangelistic tool in gaining a hearing for the gospel, the tongues gift could have ministered to these foreigners to very great advantage. That was the use to which Paul put the gift as he traveled about in his missionary labors (1 Cor. 14:18, 22). If one could for a moment ponder the wisdom of God in sovereignly endowing the Corinthian church so richly with this gift, it would seem to have been His intention that the gift be used in metropolitan surroundings like these.

A final note about "kinds of tongues" concerns the meaning of "kinds." A probable explanation derives from a similar phrase in 1 Corinthians 14:10, where the "kinds of languages" in essence has the sense of "different languages." This parallels the meaning of the present expression. "Different tongues [or languages]" (1 Cor. 12:10) differs from the expression "different languages" (1 Cor. 14:10) in that the former were the result of supernatural enablement, while the latter came about through natural processes of learning.

"The interpretation of tongues." As the name implies, "the interpretation of tongues" was an ability to translate into one's own native tongue from a language that had not been learned by natural means.[6] Its positioning at this point in the list grows out of its function as a companion gift to "kinds of tongues." The gift furnished the means of transforming a message unintelligible to the immediate listeners into one that could be understood, making it spiritually profitable.

The New Testament has no specific instance of the gift's use. Nevertheless, the apostle Paul argues strongly for its use among the Corinthians in chapter 14 (vv. 5, 13–19, 27–28). Only when accompanied by interpretation was the gift of tongues legitimate in any sense for use in a predominantly Christian gathering, since tongues alone could not edify or otherwise benefit those who were already Christians. Edification came only when the gift of interpretation communicated a message to their intelligence. In one sense, interpretation had a strong kinship to the gift of prophecy: through both, listeners learned divine revelation and mysteries (13:2; 14:2, 6, 30). The difference between the two lay in the interpretation's dependence upon a previous tongues utterance, while prophecy was dependent solely upon a direct inner revelation from God.

A review of the list of nine gifts in verses 8–10 is impressive in the variety that characterizes Spirit manifestations to various members of Christ's body. In the face of such variety, however, it is acutely important to recognize the unity that underlies all the gifts. So, the text in verse 11 returns once again to the theme of unity.

12:11—The common origin: one and the same Spirit. "All these things" in verse 11 means "all these manifestations" to which verses 8–10 have just referred. Many distinguishing features in the list differentiate the various gifts from each other. Each gift is, as it were, an entity in itself, and not subject to confusion with any other because of excessive similarity.

A diametric opposite to that variety comes in verse 11 through the agent who originates all the manifestations. He is "one and the same Spirit"—"one" as a contrast to the large number of members through whom the manifestations operate and "the same" as an antithesis to the variety of ways in which the gifts make their appearance. As the one and only immediate executor of spiritual ministries, the Holy Spirit stands in bold contrast to the variety of persons active in the performance of a variety of supernatural tasks. The great need among the Corinthians was for unity. What stronger foundation could Paul build upon than the oneness of the Person from whom stemmed all the gifts that so intensely interested these Christians? With them, these very gifts had come to be a cause for serious dissension, whereas a proper understanding would have bound the Corinthian church into a more cohesive unit.

The way the Spirit deals with individual members of the church also has strong emphasis. Gifts are not meted out on a mass-production basis, but "to each one individually" He gives a gift or gifts. Each individual is therefore different from every other member of the body. No carbon copies are among them. Everyone has a combination of gifts that makes him distinct from all the rest. (See Appendix F regarding "How to Discover and Use Your Spiritual Gift(s)" for an elaboration on how each person is unique.) Only the Spirit knows the need and capacity of each person and the place he is to fill in the body of Christ. Because He knows this, He can intelligently and adequately equip each one.

Closely associated with His individual attention to every Christian is the basis on which He gives all spiritual gifts. Erroneous concepts about how spiritual gifts are distributed have multiplied. Their disbursement is not on an arbitrary basis, nor on the basis of whim, whether human or otherwise. It is not in accordance with man's wishes or requests, nor do gifts come as a form of reward or recognition for human achievement, spiritual or otherwise. The one and only criterion for the Spirit's distribution of spiritual gifts is according to the words "as He wills" (v. 11; cf. "just as He desired," v. 18). Since He possesses the capacity of volition, He is capable of making determinations like this. He can and does decide what combination of gifts is best for each person and his role in the body of Christ.

It is futile, therefore, for any individual to desire some special spiritual function that he does not already possess. It may very well be that he needs to discover some capability he already possesses, but he cannot possibly attain any new spiritual ability, as the divine plan and purpose has already decided this. At the moment a Christian assumes his place in the body of Christ, he comes to possess all the spiritual gifts he will ever have (cf. discussion at 12:13). Recognition of this hard and fast guideline will be necessary to clarify commands that some have interpreted otherwise later in this section (cf. 12:31; 14:1, 13).

Chapter Three

UNIFIED NATURE OF SPIRITUAL GIFTS: A SPIRITUAL BODY

12:12–31a

A. DECLARATION OF UNITY (12:12–13)

12 For even as the body is one and yet has many members, and all
the members of the body, though they are many, are one body,
so also is Christ.

13 For by one Spirit we were all baptized into one body, whether
Jews or Greeks, whether slaves or free, and we were all made to
drink of one Spirit.

12:12—Christ, a many-membered body. Having differentiated between
spiritual gifts and non-Christian phenomena (12:1–3), and having shown the
unified origin of widely varying spiritual gifts (12:4–11), Paul now shifts the
focus to the singular organism through which spiritual gifts function. To
refer collectively to Christians under the figure of a human body is a favorite
Pauline analogy (Rom. 12:4–5; 1 Cor. 10:17; Eph. 1:23; 2:16; 4:4, 12, 16; Col.
1:18, 22). It is the body figure that dominates 12:12–31a, where the writer
teaches several important lessons regarding the duties of various members.

Creation of the body comes into view first of all (vv. 12–13), and in His
description the Holy Spirit, through Paul, makes a point of declaring the
unity of this body. Actually, the purpose of the twelfth verse illustrates the
way a group of such varied individuals (12:4–11) can constitute one organic
whole. The resolving of this seeming paradox comes from a parallel in

everyday life, the human body. Though the body is one organic whole, its various parts perform widely differing functions, so that no two parts of the body are exactly the same.

A threefold occurrence of "body" in verse 12 generates intense interest in this organism. In each case, it refers to the physical body as commonly known by everyone. This physical body is one entity despite the many components that make it up. Conversely, it is also true that all the segments of the physical frame, though they be overwhelming in number, still blend together into one structure. This visible counterpart of a spiritual reality demonstrates effectively that "oneness" does not necessarily exclude multiplicity, nor does the "many" rule out the "one." In other words, a unified spiritual company characterized by wide variety in its individual parts is a valid possibility. Christians gifted in extremely diverse ways can be, and have become, parts of one organic whole without losing their diversification.

This body unit includes all Christians, as Paul notes initially in verse 12 and confirms with assurance in verse 13. He reveals the unifying life that combines Christians of all generations and places them into one body in the closing part of verse 12: "so also is Christ." It is involvement in His personality that supplies the cohesive force to this conglomeration of individuals. But this involvement requires further elaboration.

The following aptly describes the nature of the involvement.[1] It is with Christ spiritually as it is with the human body physically. One life principle and true personality pervade each of them. Whatever affects any member of the spiritual body affects Christ, for He lives His life through the body (cf. Acts 9:5). When a spiritual gift operates through any member of the body, it is a manifestation of Christ's life at work, indwelling the collective body through the person of the Holy Spirit. In some mysterious way this organism operates in widely scattered areas from generation to generation as an exhibition of the resurrected Christ. He assuredly dwells within each individual member of the body (Rom. 8:9; 1 Cor. 6:19), but more significantly in this passage, He indwells the collective body that is His church and supplies to that body a pervading unity that nothing can destroy. This body possesses one life, and that life belongs to none other than the Lord Jesus Christ.

12:13—How the body gets members and puts life into them. Verse 13 proves the likeness of Christ to a human body stated in verse 12. Though His name is not in verse 13, the Holy Spirit, with whom He is one (cf. 12:4–5), replaces Him, as the Spirit's agency in constituting and permeating the one body of Christ is delineated. One factor is clear-cut: the same unity that pervades the physical body (v. 12) also characterizes the spiritual body ("one Spirit . . . one body . . . one Spirit," v. 13). The appropriateness of this principle as a remedy to the Corinthian schisms (1:12–17; 12:25) goes without saying.

Another feature that marks both physical and spiritual bodies is the all-inclusiveness of their scope.[2] No member is excluded from being a part in the physical body; the same must be, and is, true of its spiritual counterpart ("we all . . . we all," v. 13). Not one single person in Christ is excluded from participation in His body. Verse 13 talks about a body that is all-encompassing and universal. Religious and racial backgrounds are of no consequence when including in or excluding from this body ("Jews or Greeks," v. 13). Neither does it matter to what social stratum a person may belong ("slaves or free," v. 13). The only prerequisite is a genuine faith in Jesus Christ as Savior (cf. 1 Cor. 1:18, 21–24).

Verse 13 makes two informative statements about this body, one having to do with its formation and the other with its inner life.

1. Formation of the body of Christ: "By one Spirit we were all baptized into one body." Including himself along with his readers, Paul by this statement marks the divine action whereby all Christians at the moment of conversion become parts of Christ's body. Baptism in this instance has no direct connection with the ordinance of the same name, but looks at a spiritual act well known to both Old and New Testament traditions.[3] It has roots as far back as the words of Moses in Numbers 11:29: "Would that all the LORD's people were prophets, that the LORD would put His Spirit upon them!" The prophet Isaiah likewise looked forward to the coming of the Holy Spirit to be "poured out upon us from on high" (Isa. 32:15). He also recorded God's promise, "I will pour out My Spirit on your offspring" (Isa. 44:3). All these were promises to God's earthly people Israel.

The most notable Old Testament instance of this teaching is Joel 2:28–29 where, along with other promises, the prophet quotes the Lord God as predicting, "I will pour out My Spirit on all mankind." It was because of such written anticipations as these that various Jewish sects of the intertestamental period, such as the one at Qumran whose teachings have been discovered in the Dead Sea Scrolls, had definite expectation of a coming age of the Spirit. It was also in this light that John the Baptist by divine revelation came preaching, "He who is coming after me . . . will baptize you with the Holy Spirit and fire" (Matt. 3:11; cf. Mark 1:8; Luke 3:16; John 1:33).

The Lord Jesus also spoke frequently about a future coming of the Spirit: "This He spoke of the Spirit, whom those who believed in Him were to receive; for the Spirit was not yet given, because Jesus was not yet glorified" (John 7:39). Later, on the evening before His crucifixion in a discourse preparing His disciples for His departure and the beginning of the church on the day of Pentecost, He extended to the church some of the benefits of that promise to Israel by adding further to His disciples' expectation: "And I will ask the Father, and He will give you another Helper, that He may be with you forever; that is the Spirit of truth, whom the world cannot receive, because it does not behold Him or know Him, but you know Him because He abides with you, and will be in you" (John 14:16–17). Just a few days later, the Savior once again kindled His followers' hopes by reiterating the Baptist's promise: "For John baptized with water, but you shall be baptized with the Holy Spirit not many days from now" (Acts 1:5).[4]

A climax to these anticipations came on the day of Pentecost when Peter provided an explanation for the spiritual phenomena that people had witnessed. He proclaimed the arrival of the predicted outpouring by observing the applicability of Joel's words to the occasion (Acts 2:16–21). Such a provision was not heretofore available, but now the initial members of the body of Christ were partaking of that very provision (but not fulfilling the promise, for only to Israel was the promise made and only Israel can reap its fulfillment). It is referred to as "the promise of the Holy Spirit" (Acts 2:33, 39) and "the gift of the Holy Spirit" (Acts 2:38; cf. John 4:10, 14; 7:37–39).

Repeatedly Acts as well as the New Testament epistles refers to this baptism as a "pouring out" (Acts 2:17–18, 33; 10:45; Rom. 5:5; Titus 3:6), with a consequent "falling upon" (Acts 8:16; 10:44; 11:15) or "coming upon" (Acts 1:8; 19:6). They specifically identified the occurrence with the baptism of the Holy Spirit spoken of by John and Christ when Peter analyzed it for the Jerusalem church: "And as I began to speak, the Holy Spirit fell upon them, just as He did upon us at the beginning. And I remembered the word of the Lord, how He used to say, 'John baptized with water, but you shall be baptized with the Holy Spirit'" (Acts 11:15–16).

All these passages are but a fraction of the total number of references to the dramatic coming of the Holy Spirit at Pentecost and His coming on each occasion subsequently when a person became a Christian. Those are enough, however, to show the prominence of the baptism of the Holy Spirit in the minds of Paul and other early Christians. This prominence caused Paul to draw upon the earlier terminology of John the Baptist, the Lord Jesus, and Peter. It is as a result of this "pouring out" that a person becomes a member of Christ's body (1 Cor. 12:13). The Holy Spirit's coming to a person at conversion includes many aspects and accomplishments, but this particular one deserves special mention in the present context of 1 Corinthians.

From one perspective, the agent of this baptism is the Spirit, as seen from the words "by one Spirit" (v. 13).[5] From another perspective, Christ Himself is the baptizer (Matt. 3:11; Mark 1:8; Luke 3:16; John 1:33). Nor should the Father be omitted, as He also is ultimately involved as agent (Acts 2:33; 1 Cor. 12:18). Yet, this is not an inconsistency, as it is common in the Bible for all three Persons to be active agents in performance of the same task, for example, in the creation of the world. All three are a common source of the gifts, as already noted (vv. 4–6). So Christ is the baptizer in a remote sense, and the

Spirit is the agent of baptism in the more immediate sense. The immediate context strongly establishes His agency (vv. 8–9, 11).

Other words of clarification regarding this baptism by the Holy Spirit are in order. For example, it is important to observe that this act was not a once-for-all occurrence limited to the day of Pentecost; it also occurred in connection with the Samaritan believers (Acts 8:16), those of Cornelius' household (Acts 10:44–45; 11:15–16), and the disciples of John in Ephesus (Acts 19:6). The assertion that baptism by the Spirit was a once-for-all Pentecostal provision into which Christians enter does not satisfy terminology showing that the happening was subsequently repeated. This spiritual baptism is repeated each time a person converts to Christ. It is at that moment that the new Christian takes up his assigned position in the body of Christ and receives gifts that befit this position.

Another important aspect is that baptism by the Holy Spirit does not occur at some time subsequent to conversion and is not synonymous with the filling of the Holy Spirit (cf. Eph. 5:18). The Spirit's filling speaks of His control over the Christian life and comes about in the lives of only those Christians who yield themselves to God's will. The Spirit's baptism, on the other hand, is common to all Christians, and in this respect is distinct from the issue of whether a Christian is under the Spirit's control at a given moment. In fact, in only one case does the filling of the Holy Spirit take place in connection with Spirit baptism and that is only because of the unique character of Pentecost as the birthday of the Christian church (Acts 2:4). Throughout the rest of Acts, filling or fulness is separate from the moment of initial baptism or indwelling.

Neither was speaking in tongues an essential part of or a necessary adjunct to Spirit baptism. Speaking in tongues occasionally accompanied Spirit baptism (Acts 2:17–18, 33; 10:44–45; 11:15–16; 19:6) in the days immediately after the initial outpouring, but that was not the norm for first-century Christianity, not even for the period of the book of Acts. It is certainly not the norm for twentieth-century Christianity when the need for such evidential gifts as tongues has long since ceased to exist. Holy Spirit baptism is only one of a number of transactions that the gift of tongues verified in the book of Acts. Other accomplishments of the Spirit at conversion that this gift also verified include the regeneration (John 3:6) and sealing (Eph. 4:30) of a new believer, but tongues cannot be construed as inseparable from these. By the same token, the gift was not a necessary accompaniment to baptism of the Spirit.

In only three instances did tongues verify the Spirit's being poured out. It is far better to note that baptism by the Spirit needs no outward verification, indeed, in most instances it has had no outward sign to certify its occurrence. It was and is a purely invisible action whereby the Spirit of God places the believer in Christ into the mystical relationship known as the body of Christ. Once a part of that body by Spirit baptism, the first-century believer may or may not have exercised the gift of tongues. The will of God was determinative in this matter (see v. 11). Since the first century, when God chose to cease bestowing the tongues gift on believers altogether (see discussion of 13:8ff.), Spirit baptism has had no outward verification.

2. Inner life of the body of Christ: "We were all made to drink of one Spirit" (12:13). Associated with the momentary happening known as Holy Spirit baptism is the initiation of another relationship in which the Spirit is also prominent. At the same time He performs the inner baptismal act, He also takes up residence within the individual Christian. This residence is otherwise known as the indwelling of the Holy Spirit.[6]

The figure of being "made to drink of one Spirit" ("of" is absent from this expression in the Greek text) is in complete harmony with the scriptural custom of referring to this Person by the symbol of water. Furthermore, the way water becomes a part of man's inward physical makeup well represents His inward presence. It is in these terms that the Lord Jesus spoke concerning the coming of the Spirit, not only to baptize, but also to indwell those who believe in Him (John 7:37–39; 14:16–17).

By adding a reference to this additional function of the Spirit, Paul reinforces a dual emphasis found in the Acts history of Christianity's first thirty years. Receiving "the promise of the Holy Spirit" (Acts 2:33), receiving "the gift of the Holy Spirit" (Acts 2:38), and receiving "the Holy Spirit" (Acts 10:47; 19:2) appear in conjunction with the Holy Spirit's baptism, just as an inner reception is in the present Corinthians verse. That was part of the promise of Joel 2:28–29 that Christ extended to include the church. The spiritual baptism of a person into the body of Christ also entails God's taking up a permanent abode within that person. His coming to indwell occurs more frequently in Acts than the baptism itself (in addition to the Acts passages just cited, see Acts 1:4; 2:39; 8:15, 17–19; 8:20; 10:45; 11:17; 15:8). Paul also amplifies the indwelling ministry by frequent references to it (Rom. 8:15; 1 Cor. 2:12; Gal. 3:2; cf. Rom. 8:9; 1 Cor. 6:19).

The references to divine residence within the believer reveal that it is a relationship beginning concurrently with the Spirit baptism. For this reason, the same applies regarding a possible connection between indwelling and speaking in tongues as already stated regarding baptism and tongues: speaking in tongues is not an essential part of or a necessary adjunct to being "made to drink of one Spirit." As stated in connection with verse 10, tongues were abilities possessed by only a limited number of first-century Christians, whereas Paul emphatically notes that all Christians have been made to drink of one Spirit.

The presence of the Spirit within Christians individually carries with it

His consequent presence within the body of Christ collectively. That is the life principle of the body and explains how Christ is the body (v. 12) as its true personality. Through the third Person of the Holy Trinity, the second Person lives His life in the various members, the visible evidences of that life being its manifestation through spiritual gifts.

It is, then, because of one body with one personality that the Scripture declares in 1 Corinthians 12:12–13 a unity underlying the functioning of spiritual gifts.

B. INTERRELATION BECAUSE OF UNITY (12:14–26)

1. NEEDINESS OF LESSER MEMBERS (12:14–20)

14 For the body is not one member, but many.

15 If the foot should say, "Because I am not a hand, I am not a part of the body," it is not for this reason any the less a part of the body.

16 And if the ear should say, "Because I am not an eye, I am not a part of the body," it is not for this reason any the less a part of the body.

17 If the whole body were an eye, where would the hearing be? If the whole were hearing, where would the sense of smell be?

18 But now God has placed the members, each one of them, in the body, just as He desired.

19 And if they were all one member, where would the body be?

20 But now there are many members, but one body.

Just as cooperation among members of any human body is essential to the orderly functioning of that body's activities, so is cooperation essential in Christ's spiritual body, His church. Because of the Corinthians' need for developing this oneness, the train of thought shifts from declaring the body's existence (vv. 12–13) to discussing spiritual implications of unity in that body. Until Christians realize the important lesson of mutual dependence upon one another, they can accomplish little, no matter how impressive the array of spiritual gifts.

12:14—Necessity of variety. In proving his thesis of unity based on variety,

Paul flatly states, "The body is not one member, but many" (v. 14). Indeed, without constituent members, each one having a part of its own, no body exists. Each part has a responsibility that can be handled better by itself than by any other. No two members are exactly alike. If they were, one would be unnecessary. This is another way of saying that a maximum variety of function characterizes the physical body. Yet who would venture to say that the body is not a unit? Were it otherwise, it would automatically cease being a body. No set of circumstances can cause one member to be equated with the whole body. Variety of parts is compulsory.

12:15—Inferiority of the foot. The fifteenth verse literally reads, "If the foot says, 'Because I am not the hand, I do not belong to the body,' it does not because of this[7] not belong to the body." The principle is obvious. No member can accomplish its own removal from the human body by complaining and depreciating its own importance. Each one has a responsibility to carry out, no matter how inconspicuous it may be. The foot in verse 15 is such an inconspicuous member. The foot may compare itself with the hand and all its complex skills, realizing how far short of the hand it falls. Besides envying the hand, it may be despondent because of its own perceived unimportance and begin to feel, "I am not needed. I do not belong."

Though specific application is not made, the comparable situation in the body of Christ is obvious. Here is a Christian whose gifts are less conspicuous. Because he is never in the limelight and does not have the prominence of Christians with more spectacular gifts, he becomes discouraged over his own gift status. He may even grumble and allow himself to become discontent and jealous of those who have the more conspicuous gifts. Verse 15 very specifically declares that no amount of grumbling is sufficient to remove such a person from Christ's body.

Every member is important, no matter how hidden from view. None can be dispensed with. The body is crippled when one member is not functioning. It can be at peak efficiency only when every single part is active.

Christians need to learn this lesson. They need to be content with whatever abilities God has provided them (see vv. 11, 18) and to make it their business to operate as constantly as possible in areas where the Holy Spirit has given special aptitude. (See Appendix F, "How to Discover and Use Your Spiritual Gift(s).")

12:16—Inferiority of the ear. Verse 16 resembles verse 15 very closely, the only difference being that the writer chooses two new members to represent less favored and more favored members of the body. In this case it is the ear that becomes disgruntled. To have an ear speaking confirms that Paul has a member of the spiritual body ultimately in mind. Perhaps here as well as in verse 15, the reference is to beauty as well as functional ability. The eye is by far the more attractive to look at, and the ear might easily begrudge this comeliness in addition to envying the eye's perception.

Many indications point to jealousy in the Corinthian church, but the Corinthians were not alone in this. Christians are always inclined to selfishness and self-centeredness. This wrong spirit finds its antidote in 1 Corinthians 13, where among the other perfections of love is recorded, "Love . . . is not jealous" (13:4).

12:17—No part equal to the whole. Turning to a new aspect of the same argument, verse 17 shows that no organism can survive where only one member is involved, no matter how prominent that member. In function, the eye is superior to the organ of hearing. Yet, the normal body cannot dispense with its hearing faculty. Similarly, the organ of hearing is superior to the organ of smelling in function and appearance. Yet again, a body that has no capacity for smelling is substantially limited.

No matter how exalted may be a Christian's abilities, he cannot function as a spiritual "loner." The gifted apostle Paul was dependent upon that lowly believer with the gift of helps (cf. 1 Cor. 12:28), for an inconspicuous person endowed with only a "minor" gift could perform feats that no other could. For this reason, no child of God should underestimate his own importance as a member of the body. He need not covet the prestige of another; in God's sight his operation is just as significant. In fact, if it were left only to the more prominent members, there would be no more body, for all parts are essential.

12:18—Divine origin of the body. To summarize the body's present status and show reason for differences between members, verse 18 turns to Him who created the body. God has seen fit to create a unit that does not follow the lines of uniformity. He did not pour the members into one monotonous mold but, in accord with His own purposes, made each member different from all the rest.

"Placed," in verse 18, significantly looks to the act of divine appointment, an appointment equally meaningful both to human and to spiritual bodies. Only because God has planned it can members of the body complement one another so well. The power of vision was not self-assumed by the eye any more than the power of hearing by the ear. That a wisdom lies behind the placement and ability of each member cannot be disputed. This in itself gives unparalleled dignity to every part of the body, no matter how much or how little recognition it may receive. For a member to feel otherwise smacks of selfishness and rebellion against the supreme will that has established conditions as they are. God has made it this way for His own purposes, and the clay dare not ask the potter, "Why did you make me like this?" (Rom. 9:20).

That the divine will covers every member is clarified in the words "each one of them" (v. 18). A less-important one might readily concede that God's plan covers the more important, but in so doing he may not see how the plan can be applicable to himself. The Holy Spirit through Paul makes plain that none is excluded. "Each one" is where he is specifically because of God's placement.

Reiterating a truth already stated in verse 11, Paul in verse 18 varies his perspective and looks at the divine will from the Father's standpoint rather than from the Holy Spirit's (cf. v. 11). The will (Greek, *boulomai*, v. 11) of the Holy Spirit pictured earlier as a more passive intention is now the will (Greek, *thelō*, v. 18) of God the Father pressing this underlying intention into action. The entire Trinity is involved in distributing and operating spiritual gifts, as verses 4–6 have already divulged.

The present discussion deals with the physical body, but along with this are occasional inklings of these principles at work in Christ's body. One such implication stems from emphasizing God's part in the body's creation. A Christian does not select his own spiritual gifts, which in turn determine his place in Christ's body. God's pleasure alone determines His gifts. Human inclinations have nothing to do with the choice, and for a man to question the wisdom of the arrangement amounts to questioning what God has willed to do. No provision exists for a Christian with "inferior" gifts to be discontent. Rather, it is his place to take the gifts he has and use them to maximum advantage for the benefit of the rest of the body.

12:19—No variety, no body. The thought returns in verse 19 to uniformity as opposed to variety. A condition where no variety exists would be preposterous. No one member can account for the variety of functions necessary for a whole body (v. 17). It is thus a foregone conclusion that no body can exist composed of only one member (v. 19).

The essence of the argument lies in the absurdity of such a concept. A body with only one member would be no longer an admirable organism, but the lowest kind of animal, if even that. Every Christian must firmly grasp this principle and keep his own place and service in cooperation with other Christians in proper perspective.

12:20—Multiplicity, but unity. As a summary of verse 19 in particular and the whole paragraph in general, verse 20 picks up the section's initial thought—diversity and plurality in a body (v. 14). Variety is mandatory for any organic unit, and this is especially true of the human body and what it symbolizes.

People with widely varying capabilities compose the body of Christ. It is true that only a few have gifts that gain fame. Nevertheless, those in the background are necessary. Freedom to withdraw and form another body does not exist. There can be no plurality of bodies. The body is one and it exists only because of the many members that compose it.

2. NEEDINESS OF GREATER MEMBERS (12:21—24A)

21 And the eye cannot say to the hand, "I have no need of you"; or again the head to the feet, "I have no need of you."

22 On the contrary, it is much truer that the members of the body which seem to be weaker are necessary;

23 and those members of the body, which we deem less honorable, on these we bestow more abundant honor, and our unseemly members come to have more abundant seemliness,

24a whereas our seemly members have no need of it.

12:21—Dependence of the eye and head. Building upon the oneness of the body that closes verse 20, verse 21 initiates a new application of the body figure, an extreme opposite to that just treated. Attention has been upon the danger of underestimating one's importance, but now Paul issues a word of caution to the one who overestimates his own importance. The one cautioned is the member who possesses the more conspicuous gifts and therefore enjoys greater prominence. One who is in the limelight for a time will develop, unless he is careful, a proneness to look down on abilities that do not earn as much human recognition. Verses 21-24a were written to counteract this tendency.

When the writer speaks of the eye and the head, he refers to members that are superior to the hand and the foot. The eye's function in the body is more important, and it therefore occupies a more noble position than the hand. Likewise, the head performs the combined functions of eyes, ears, nose, and throat, and because of its complex responsibilities occupies a more exalted place than the foot ever could.

Yet, what would the eye be without the hand? It would be only a small fraction of what it is when the hand is active. Or what would the head be without the foot? It would have no means for propelling itself to a desired destination. The eye and head could make such statements as those denied in verse 21, but they could not function in the manner supposed without infinite cost to themselves and to the body as a whole.

The head sometimes typifies Christ in Pauline writings (Eph. 1:22-23; Col. 1:17-18). Here, however, Paul differs from what was to become his practice in the prison epistles. Thus, no reference to Christ's headship over the body appears in this verse, as it is unthinkable that Paul would ever think of Christ the head ever dispensing with another member. The head is just another part of the illustration in this verse.

The service of Jesus Christ is never a solo performance. No place remains for individualism. No matter how great and impressive one's abilities may be, his duty is to cooperate with other Christians. The body is one, not many, and God's plan has never been for His own to act as separate entities.

12:22—Necessity of the weaker members. After stating interdependence in a negative way (v. 21), the focus moves to the positive side of the same principle (v. 22). For the eye and head to make such arrogant claims as suggested is not representative of the true state of affairs (v. 21). But conversely, it is completely accurate to observe that the weaker members are absolute necessities (v. 22).

The truth expressed in verse 22 goes even further than that in verse 21. The more humble ("weaker") parts of the body are just as indispensable to successful activity (v. 21) as the rest (cf. "it is much truer," v. 22). Despite their seemingly secondary part, their presence and functioning are mandatory if the body is to continue.

Identification of the "weaker" members is important in grasping the total picture taught by the human body analogy.[8] Since verse 22 is a contrast to verse 21 (cf. v. 22, "on the contrary"), it is reasonable to see in verse 22 members that are weaker and even more secondary than the hands and feet (v. 21), or any others. Sensitive internal organs such as the lungs and stomach are susceptible to injury, and their only protection is what the members surrounding them afford. These internal organs, completely hidden from view, says Paul, are vital in sustaining life. Their praises are unsung. Yet they must be present and operative or there is no body.

The Corinthians had a clear preference for the gift of tongues. It attracted attention and had an aura of mystery about it. They chose to capitalize on these external features, according to the teaching of chapter 14. Their failure to be considerate of those who did not possess such spectacular manifestations necessitated the strong words in this section. The Holy Spirit through Paul informed them decisively that tongues, or any other gifts of a similar sensational character, were unable to stand alone. Gifts with glamour were completely dependent on every other gift, even those completely unnoticed by men, if the body of Christ was to function effectively.

12:23—Special attention to less honored and unbecoming members. Verse 23 mentions two more types of unsung members, as the passage continues to argue that the eye and head cannot do without the rest of the body. Rather than counting these two as dispensable, the body demands special attention for them. Designated "less honorable" and "unseemly" in verse 23, they are to be distinguished from the internal organs depicted as "weaker" in verse 22.

The former of the two, the "less honorable," are parts of the body that are less attractive in appearance. These would include, among others, the trunk, hips, shoulders, arms, and legs. We intuitively put clothing on these to render the person more pleasing in appearance. The less natural the appeal, the greater the instinct to put on some adornment.

The second category in verse 23 is not completely distinct from the first, as the "unseemly members" are also covered by clothing. Yet here more specifically are those that are covered for reasons of modesty. Whereas the "less honorable" members are only usually clothed, clothing always gives these "unseemly" members artificial attractiveness.

The course of action dictated for the body of Christ in these illustrations is self-evident. Since the habit with the physical body is to take the "behind-the-scenes" parts and devote special effort and attention to them, how much more should this be true in the spiritual body? It is a distorted sense of values when a Christian, well-known because of his well-received speaking gift, looks disparagingly at other Christians who possess no such gift. This is in direct contradiction to the principle of self-concern that characterizes any body. It is far more consistent with the principle of self-preservation that members possessing greater beauty and functional ability devote themselves tirelessly to the well-being of those not so well equipped. (See Appendix F for suggestions on practical implementation of this principle.)

12:24a—Natural beauty of honorable members. Paul closes out this theme with the first statement of verse 24: "Whereas [*but* is actually preferable to *whereas* to show a contrast indicated by the conjunction *de*] our seemly members have no need of it." The more attractive and functional parts of the body need no adornment. The total organism adjusts to the need of each member, and the self-sufficiency of these "seemly" parts means they require no special attention. The eye and the head (v. 21) have their own beauty. They do not need clothing to make them more attractive. The body's energy can best spend itself elsewhere, tending to areas where needs exist.

Prominent, gifted Christians should not draw attention to themselves. They already have all the attention they need. They should be looking instead to the less favored of their number, recognizing their own dependence upon them and their obligation to do for them what will enhance their growth and effectiveness.

3. PROVISION FOR MUTUAL CONCERN (12:24B–26)

24b But God has so composed the body, giving more abundant honor
   to that member which lacked,

25 that there should be no division in the body, but that the members should have the same care for one another.

26 And if one member suffers, all the members suffer with it; if one member is honored, all the members rejoice with it.

12:24b—Divine equalization. The "but" in the middle of verse 24 begins not only a new sentence, but also a new paragraph, as the writer takes up another aspect of his discussion. The difference in outlook from the immediately preceding discussion is twofold: (1) Verses 21–24a are in the main descriptive of what the human body takes care of by instinct, but verses 24b–26 show what God has done in forming the body. (2) Verses 21–24a, as well as verses 14–20, have dealt primarily with a functioning human organism, with only indirect allusions to the body of Christ. Beginning at verse 24b, however, the words have direct, if not exclusive, application to the spiritual organism rather than the physical counterpart to which it is analogous.

"But God" (v. 24), therefore, is indicative of a method of operation different from the system of mutual relations expressed in verses 21–24a. The focus of attention is now on God's part as He has put the body together rather than upon the concern of individual members for one another. It is not a mere natural force that has made the body what it is. God is ultimately responsible for the balance that exists between different members of the church.

The process represented by "has so composed" (v. 24) is quite descriptive. God is pictured as combining and adjusting separate members of the body into a composite unit in such a way that every part stands in equal dependence on the rest. The word for "composed" has been found elsewhere in ancient literature describing how an artist carefully mixes colors to produce the exact shade needed for his rendition. In a similar manner, God has arranged the body so that the uncomely parts are absolutely essential to the well-being of the rest. He has made it one harmonious, mutually dependent whole.

As a further definition of this tempering process, "giving more abundant honor to that member which lacked" is added at the end of verse 24.[9] In forming the body of Christ, a process spoken of earlier as a baptism by one Spirit and a drinking of one Spirit (v. 13), God has utilized an equalizing process. In the case of members who lack esteem because of inferior ability, He has made up the inferiority through the addition of "more abundant honor" (v. 24). This means that no one has a deficiency. What this person lacks in prominence because of the nature of his gifts is compensated for by way of a divinely given honor. The result, then, is an exact equality and a perfect balance among the members of Christ's body.

The Christian who is aware of his own deficiency and is prone to magnify his unimportance in his own mind can take great comfort in God's equalizing action. It means that neither he nor anyone else is called upon to take a "back seat" or be looked down upon. Equality of honor reigns within the body of Christ, no matter how great the gradation in functional abilities. It is reassuring to recall once again God's part in putting all on the same plane. Because of this, we have a basis for complete internal harmony.

12:25—Purpose of equalization. God's intention in bringing about this blend in the body is stated next (v. 25). Negatively, His intention is to remove "schism" or "division" in the body; positively, it is to create mutual concern by and toward every single member.

Schism did exist among the Corinthians. Near the outset of his letter, Paul mentions a report that there were "quarrels" ("strifes," "wranglings," 1:11) in the church. His plea has already been "that you all agree, and there be no divisions ["schisms," same word as in 12:25] among you" (1:10).

He wants them to be "made complete in the same mind and in the same judgment" (1:10), on the basis that Christ has not been divided (1:13). Further indications of dissension are seen in 3:3–4 and 11:18. In the latter reference, "divisions" is again the same word as the word in 12:25. Alienation of feelings among Corinthian Christians was indeed unfortunate, and the Holy Spirit used this means to alleviate the problem by pointing out God's intention in so constituting the body of Christ.

It takes no astute observer to discern that the divisiveness besetting the Corinthians has continued to plague the Christian church down to the present. Division among Christians is not in accord with divine intentions. Jealousy and strife can never be attributed to God's will. To be sure, differences of opinion and judgment will arise. Even Paul himself was involved in disputes (Acts 15:36–41; Gal. 2:11–14). But these should never find their basis in self-concern (1 Cor. 13:4–5).

When members "have the same care" (v. 25), they fulfill God's purpose. This is a condition of harmony, not schism. Terminology chosen by Paul in this last part of verse 25 is expressive of deep-seated feeling. This is not a superficial or casual concern, but a thoughtful or even anxious compassion for others. It shows no respect of persons. It has the same concern for every single one. The eye is not selfishly interested in its own welfare, nor does it show partiality toward a fellow prominent member such as the head; its care for the less-honorable foot is just as great because of the foot's special nobility, its additional honor bestowed by God (v. 24).

When Christians allow God's purpose to be fulfilled in their lives, their community can be characterized only by peace, harmony, and cooperation. This is a condition of loving one another as Christ loved His church and is thus in compliance with the command of Christ (John 13:34; 15:12, 17; 1 John 2:8–10; 3:23; 2 John 5). It is this theme of love that the apostle plans to develop shortly (1 Cor. 12:31b–13:13).

12:26—Results of mutual concern. As a follow-up to the purposed mutual concern of verse 25, verse 26 describes the typical outcome of such a relationship. The resulting intimacy will bring about a mutual suffering experience in all whenever just one member of the body, no matter who he is or what his position, suffers some kind of adversity. It is inconceivable for one member to be in pain and the rest not to notice. One member in adversity involves all in the adversity.

On the other side, when one member is recognized because of his usefulness or attractiveness, a common joy pervades the whole body. Unless an abnormality exists, it is unheard of for one member to begrudge the success of another. Such an analogy shows how ridiculous rivalry within the body of Christ is.

This, then, is the essence of the unity that characterizes Christ's body (12:12–13). The interrelationships of this body are so binding that believers have no alternative but to live together in harmony (12:14–26). To do otherwise is to run counter to the plan and activity of the one who has established the body. To operate in accord with these relationships, however, is to comply with the new commandment delivered by Him who is the life principle of the body (cf. John 13:34; 1 Cor. 12:12).

C. UTILIZATION FOR UNIFIED OUTPUT (12:27–31A)

27 Now you are Christ's body, and individually members of it.

28 And God has appointed in the church, first apostles, second prophets, third teachers, then miracles, then gifts of healings, helps, administrations, various kinds of tongues.

29 All are not apostles, are they? All are not prophets, are they? All are not teachers, are they? All are not workers of miracles, are they?

30 All do not have gifts of healings, do they? All do not speak with tongues, do they? All do not interpret, do they?

31a But earnestly desire the greater gifts.

12:27—Direct application of body analogy. Verse 27 provides a fitting conclusion to verses 14–26, but it is also a transition and introduction to the next paragraph, verses 28–31a. Besides the importance of body relationships just discussed, the readers need to see various gifts in their proper perspective so they may utilize them to maximum advantage within the body. Only with such knowledge are believers in a position to "earnestly desire the greater gifts" (v. 31).

The body analogy has been carried out thus far without specific statement of the readers' involvement in it. Their part was alluded to in verse 13, where the analogy was first introduced, but now the apostle turns to them directly and says, "You are Christ's body" (v. 27). In so doing, he sets squarely upon their shoulders the responsibility for implementing the lessons that have been taught. Included in these are the danger of underestimating one's contribution (vv. 14–20), the danger of overestimating one's contribution (vv. 21–24a), and the needed compassion of every member toward every other (vv. 24b–26). The Corinthians had great need of these lessons. Only by understanding them could a smooth operation of their church come about. This same requirement continues wherever people associate in the name of Christ.

For Paul to use "are" rather than "ought to be" when addressing a group so torn by internal strife is a source of amazement. This church was anything but a smoothly functioning assembly. Jealousy and bitterness were the rule rather than the exception. Yet the Holy Spirit states, "You are Christ's body," and His statement is always accurate. This is a subtle reminder that all who are in Christ enjoy an exalted position in God's sight, no matter how unfortunate their behavior may be at times. This is not an encouragement to relax all ethical restraints, but a reminder of the magnitude of God's grace. Those who so obviously were in violation of God's principles of conduct were addressed individually as "saints" (1 Cor. 1:2) and collectively as "Christ's body" (1 Cor. 12:27). The unspoken plea to them or anyone whose life is marred by such inconsistency is, "Become in your daily behavior what you have already become in God's sight" (cf. 1 Cor. 5:7, "Clean out the old leaven . . . as you are in fact unleavened").

Paul labels the Corinthians as "Christ's body," but clarification is necessary to discern the sense in which this was true. As the Greek construction shows, he does not mean that the church in Corinth was the whole body of Christ. Nor does he mean that they were one of many bodies of Christ. Rather, the Corinthian church was a miniature representation of the universal church.[10] He informs them that they, as a local group, possess the quality of the whole and should function in this light. Every local church has this obligation. Each group of believers has within itself sufficient gifts to operate in its own locality, and in that way it presents an image of the total body which, of course, is never assembled together at any one time or place. The whole body of Christ includes all believers in Christ throughout the world and from every generation of the Christian era. Those who are Christ's belong to this body because the body is Christ's. Yet, in a deeper sense, the body is not just Christ's; it *is* Christ (v. 12). He is the life principle that permeates the whole.

Another side of the picture is found in the phrase "individually members of it" (v. 27). While Christians are collectively one body, at the same time they individually constitute separate parts of that body. No one member can look upon himself as more than a small part. He is not the whole body. Yet, each one has a definite part in the life of the whole. Each has an assigned position and responsibility that differs from every other part. These several parts are now to be discussed (vv. 28–31a). A strategy that yields maximum output from the various members has been devised. That is why each one must have a proper appreciation for his own duty.

12:28—Divine appointment according to rank. In expanding upon the "individually members of it" of verse 27, Paul shows in verse 28 how the common life of the church is like the common life of the human body. One demonstrates its presence by a diversity of gifts, while the other does so by differing tasks performed by differing human organisms. The scope of verse 28 extends beyond the local representative body in Corinth to include believers wherever they were located. This broadened sense of "church" is necessary since "apostles" are included in the list. A plurality of apostles was not provided for each church, nor did every church have the privilege of even one visit by an apostle.

Echoing a note that has already sounded with great force (vv. 11, 18), Paul reiterates that placement in the body of Christ (the distribution of spiritual gifts) is the result of direct divine action. "Has appointed" in verse 28 represents *etheto*, which is the exact word translated by the "has placed" in verse 18. In the earlier verse, the more direct reference was to God's placement of members in the human body, but now it is to the spiritual counterpart. He has also placed gifted men and their functions in the body of Christ, His church. This He has done for His own purposes. Human choice to be an apostle, prophet, teacher, or possessor of any other gift is not a criterion. Placement is solely the outcome of His good pleasure (cf. "just as He wills," v. 11, and "just as He desired," v. 18).

In order to identify the gifts that would yield greater profit, Paul enumerates in verse 28 a sequence of gifts arranged in an order of descending value. That is the significance of "first . . . second . . . third . . . then . . . then." The order of listing is parallel to that in Ephesians 4:11, where gifts with higher value are also placed higher in the list.

A first reaction to ranking gifted persons and their gifts may be that of surprise, since the action comes so close on the heels of an emphasis given to equality among the members (12:24b–26). Careful consideration reveals, however, that Paul does not deny this equality at verse 28, but instead simply shifts his attention from mutual concern among various members to the profit derived from them. A local assembly does well to emphasize those gifts that produce edification rather than those that result in little or no benefit. Such a strategy does not exclude the necessary mutual compassion so strongly enjoined in verses 24b–26.

Several words of clarification are in order regarding the way Paul reflects rank in verse 28:

1. With the first three gifts, he is very specific about their standing in relation to the other five, as well as to one another. Apostles have top priority, followed by prophets, who are in turn followed by teachers.

2. With the fourth and fifth gifts, and even more so with the last three, the ranking is more general. The words "then . . . then" represent a double occurrence of *epeita*, a Greek conjunction indicating sequence. It is unquestionable that the last five gifts in the list are subordinate to the first three, but it was not feasible for Paul to continue his series with "fourth," "fifth," and so on, as he did not intend to make this an exhaustive list of gifts. Obvious omissions from Paul's other lists of gifts occur (cf. Rom. 12:6–8; 1 Cor. 12:8–10; Eph. 4:11). Nevertheless, it is doubtless that rank is still in view, though in a lesser way, in this last part of the list. The expression "the greater gifts" in verse 31 would be less meaningful if it were otherwise.

3. The positioning of tongues last in the list doubtless carries connotations of rank also. Corinth was a church that overvalued the gift, and a major purpose of 1 Corinthians 12–14 is to counteract their wrong sense of values. Tongues and their interpretation come last in the list of verses 8–10, just as they do in the questions of verses 29–30 (see also 14:26). An important lesson of 1 Corinthians 14 is the uselessness of tongues without interpretation. Whereas the Corinthians were coveting earnestly the gift of tongues, their zeal should have been for gifts in the upper echelons of importance.

The list of eight gifted men and gifts found in verse 28 names four not noticed in the list of verses 8–10 (apostles, teachers, helps, and administrations) and one that is cast in a role slightly different from the previous list (prophets; cf. v. 10). This second list includes the following gifts.

"Apostles." Apostles is the title given to a group of men who lived at a particular stage of history. What might be called "natural prerequisites" for holding this office included personal contact with the Lord Jesus while He was on earth, followed by the experience of seeing Him alive after His resurrection (Acts 1:21–22; 1 Cor. 9:1–2). In addition, it was required that an apostle have a direct appointment from the Lord Jesus to this office (Luke

6:13; Rom. 1:1). When an individual had all these, he also had the spiritual gift of apostleship.

Most likely the exact number of apostles was undefined. Had there been a specific number of which the church was aware, "false apostles" who could pass themselves off with any degree of credibility could never have arisen (cf. 2 Cor. 11:13; Rev. 2:2). Of course, there were the twelve who were apostles in a special sense (Luke 6:14–16; with Matthias substituted for Judas Iscariot after the Ascension, Acts 1:26). Two others bearing the title were Barnabas and James, the Lord's brother (1 Cor. 9:5–6; 15:7; Gal. 1:19). Lesser-known individuals such as Adronicus, Junius, and still others who are not named in the New Testament possibly possessed the gift (Rom. 16:7; 1 Cor. 15:5–7). The last person to be appointed to the apostolic office was Paul, whose induction came about under highly unusual circumstances (1 Cor. 15:8–9).

The reason for the absence of apostles from the body of Christ subsequent to Paul is obvious: the various kinds of personal contact with the incarnate Lord Jesus required for this office restrict the time for its functioning. Eyewitnesses to Jesus Christ's personal life had all but ceased to exist by A.D. 100. The apostle John, one of the twelve, died at about this time, and so far as history records, he was the last living witness of Christ's resurrection.

Leadership in the founding and early growth of the Christian church belonged to apostles. For this purpose they were granted special authority as Christ's personal representatives. This meant that when speaking or writing in certain capacities, they were mouthpieces of the Lord Himself. Their jurisdiction pertained to the church as a whole, not just to one local congregation. They were particularly instrumental in expanding frontiers of the gospel, and thus their connection with one particular locality was never more than temporary.

A person with the gift of apostleship possessed many and perhaps most of the other spiritual gifts. Sign gifts of healing (Acts 5:12–16), miracles (Acts 13:8–11), prophecy (Acts 27:25), and tongues (Acts 2:4; 1 Cor. 14:18) were given as badges of their apostleship (2 Cor. 12:12). Since they were the vehicles of revelation that eventually composed most of the New Testament books, they also must have been in possession of the gifts of wisdom and knowledge (1 Cor. 2:7, 10, 13; 2 Peter 3:15–16). As spokesmen of this revelation and as prophets of future events, they likewise possessed the gift of prophecy (Rev. 1:1–3). Instances of their special abilities in other areas of gift bestowal could likewise be adduced. One should remember, however, that apostles, though so richly endowed, were not always guarded from error in their speech and actions in the same way they were when they wrote books of the New Testament (cf. Gal. 2:11–14).

In light of the wide range of abilities and responsibilities of an apostle, it is no surprise that Paul gives this office and the associated gift of prophecy top ranking from the standpoint of benefit derived.

"Prophets." Coming second in the list of verse 28, as it does in that of Ephesians 4:11, are those with the gift of prophecy. This is the same gift referred to in verse 10. One difference between the two citations is that in verse 10 the function is in view, while this instance names the person possessing the gift. Placement of the gift in the earlier list indicates another distinction between the two occurrences. Earlier it accompanies sign-oriented gifts, but here its location emphasizes the gift's revelatory and intellectual characteristics. In company with apostles, prophets (female [Acts 21:9–10] as well as male) were recipients of new revelations from God which, of course, appealed to the mind, and which they were responsible to convey to the church (1 Cor. 14:30; Eph. 3:5). This ministry entailed an overlapping with the words of wisdom and knowledge (v. 8), as 1 Corinthians 13:2 implies. In fact, it is a point well taken that "apostles" and "prophets" in the present list replace "the word of wisdom" and "the word of knowledge" in the list of verses 8–10.

Though associated closely with apostles, all prophets were not apostles because not all had encountered personally the incarnate Christ and did not have a personal appointment by Christ. Consequently, a prophet was not authoritative in the same sense as were apostles. Their utterances were authoritative, but their authority was subject to that of the apostles (1 Cor. 14:37). Another difference between apostles and prophets lay in their geographical responsibilities. Though to some degree the prophet appears to have been, like the apostle, a minister to the church at large, on occasion, prophets did settle in one locality for ministry to a single local church (Acts 13:1; 15:32).

Great likelihood exists that prophets were a part of the congregation in Corinth. The strong case for prophecy in chapter 14 would be irrelevant were this not true. It is significant that Paul, after commanding his readers to seek the best gifts (12:31), does not use apostleship in his comparison with tongues in chapter 14; having the top-priority gift in opposition to the bottom priority would have constituted an even stronger contrast than the one he uses there. This he could not do, however, because no apostles resided in Corinth. For this reason, he substituted the number-two gift, prophecy, for apostleship in the comparison.

Another important feature grows out of the association of prophets with apostles in Ephesians 2:19–22. They closely identify with apostles as either constituting the foundation of the building that is the church, or else participating in the laying of that foundation. As even the most casual observer recognizes, the foundation is the earliest part of a structure to be erected. So it is with the spiritual building that is the church. Certain gifts were necessary in the beginning stages that ceased to be needed later on. So it is that the New Testament assigns the apostles and prophets to the earliest period of church history.

Prophecy's predictive aspect has already been seen to be a temporary part of church history (see discussion of v. 10), as has apostleship (see earlier discussion of v. 28). The proper conclusion dictated by all these avenues of consideration is that prophecy as a total gift pertained to approximately the first seventy years of church history. This was the period when the Holy Spirit chose to use direct revelation to communicate previously unrevealed truths to the body of Christ. This was vital in the absence of a written New Testament. Upon completion of a written record of "the faith which was once for all delivered to the saints" (Jude 3), further special revelations would have been superfluous and even derogatory in that they would have implied an inadequacy of the written Word.

Since the ministry of a prophet produced conviction (1 Cor. 14:24-25), edification, exhortation, and comfort (1 Cor. 14:3), some have sought to identify prophecy with activities in twentieth-century Christianity, such as preaching. Similarities between these two areas do exist, but modern preaching does not qualify completely as the biblical gift of prophecy. Preaching combines the gifts of teaching (v. 28; Rom. 12:7; Eph. 4:11) and exhortation (Rom. 12:8). These two were only part of the functions of a prophet, however. (For further treatment of the gift of prophecy, see discussion at 12:10 and Appendixes A, C, and D at the rear of this volume; for an evaluation of a recent unusual view of the gift, see Appendix B).

"*Teachers.*" An office that has not appeared in a previous list is that of the teacher. Instruction was always uppermost in the mind of Paul (1 Cor. 14:19). He considered an intellectual grasp of the truths of the faith a vital prerequisite to acceptable Christian living and service. It is not surprising, therefore, to find him and the other apostles and prophets engaged in teaching almost constantly (Acts 18:11; 19:9-10; Col. 1:28; 1 Tim. 2:7; 2 Tim. 1:11). Yet, the whole responsibility of instructing the body of Christ did not fall upon apostles and prophets alone. Another group distinct from them also engaged in this activity. Because of the premium placed upon instruction, this band ranks third in fruitfulness among the spiritual gifts in the list, taking a place just behind apostles and prophets (see also Eph. 4:11).

Teaching does not include receiving special revelation from God, but it does entail special ability to grasp these revelations, whether oral (during the first century only) or written (permanently, in the Old and New Testaments), and to communicate them effectively to listeners. This is beyond what teaching on a natural plane can accomplish, because spiritual truth is interwoven into the content (cf. 1 Cor. 2:14-15). The teacher's ministry was more oriented to one locality than were those of apostles and prophets. A usual qualification for local church leadership, in fact, was that overseers or elders be in possession of this gift (Eph. 4:11; 1 Tim. 3:2), though some elders appear not to have used the gift all the time (1 Tim. 5:17). A large part of Timothy's responsibility lay in the area of teaching (1 Tim. 4:11; 6:2). Of course, teaching was what the Lord Jesus Himself engaged in on so many occasions. It is natural that His church should carry on that emphasis. All other spiritual factors being what they should be, an instructed church is a stable and advancing church.

Without any factors to limit this gift to the revelatory period of early church history, it is proper to recognize teaching's continuing operation from the earliest moment, when the church began, down to and through the present, until finally the church goes to be with its Lord. The only variation has been that for a time teaching was based on oral transmissions from the apostles and prophets, along with the written Old Testament. After this its basis became entirely written, the books of the New Testament replacing the oral revelations.

Like many other gifts, teaching in the body of Christ is not limited to those possessing the gift. Every Christian is responsible for explaining the gospel to other people, and this is a form of teaching. A person without the gift who attempts to teach has not done wrong. In fact, some teaching must be done by the ungifted because of the unavailability of endowed teachers. Through identification and maximum utilization of those who have this as their special ability, however, the body of Christ will grow most effectively.

"*Miracles.*" Continuing the list of verse 28 and following his mention of teachers, Paul shifts his attention from persons possessing gifts to the gifts themselves. The first of these abstractions is "miracles," or "miraculous powers." This is the same gift discussed in connection with verse 10. Men specially endowed with this power in the early church consistently displayed it along with the preaching of the Word (1 Cor. 2:4; 4:20; 2 Cor. 6:7; 1 Thess. 1:5). In each case, the miracle's effect on the hearers was to create an impression of God's direct involvement in what was being said. The same word is translated "miracles" in the oft-recurring scriptural combination, "signs and wonders and . . . miracles" (Heb. 2:4; see also Acts 2:22; 8:13; Rom. 15:19; 2 Thess. 2:9).

"*Gifts of Healings.*" Another gift found in the earlier list (v. 9) comes next. The Greek usage behind the verse 28 expression is identical to that of the earlier one. As already seen, "gifts of healings" sustain a close relationship to gifts of faith and workings of miracles, as well as other sign-oriented gifts. For example, a healer was one kind of miracle worker. The goal of the gift, therefore, was verification.

"*Helps.*" Making its first appearance in the chapter at verse 28 is the gift of "helps." Derived from a word that means "to take a burden on oneself in the place of another" (cf. "help," Acts 20:35; "helps," Rom. 8:26), this term specifies help of all kinds administered to those in need. The name Romans 12:7 uses for this same gift is "ministry," or "service." In a general sense, "ministries," or "services" (1 Cor. 12:5) is a designation applicable to all spiritual gifts. But in a more specialized way, it speaks of different kinds of physical help or relief given wherever there is need. The nature of the need in Acts 6:1–3 was an equitable arrangement for table serving at meals. Other kinds of needs met by such service include those of widows, orphans, the sick, strangers, travelers, and any other case where some temporal or physical demand is present.

In contrast to the speaking gifts, which cater more to man's inner and spiritual needs, the gift of helps has more to do with outward areas. Thus "helps" are a special prerequisite for the "deacons" (a word that also means "servants") of 1 Timothy 3:8–13. People with this gift appear to have played a large part in meeting Paul's personal needs (e.g., Epaphroditus, Phil. 2:25–30; Onesiphorus, 2 Tim. 1:16–18; Onesimus, Philem. 10–13).

This activity is not such as attracts widespread attention. The Corinthians apparently were not inclined toward a gift like this because it did not cater to their ambition for public recognition, as did some of the other gifts of verses 8–10 and 29–30. Yet the Scripture placed the gift side-by-side with the more overt manifestations as a reminder that such a behind-the-scenes operation is just as indispensable as the rest. In Corinth, in fact, it was of even greater importance because of their tendency to neglect it. All too often the same lack has characterized other Christian assemblies.

The absence of "helps" posed a serious roadblock to spiritual effectiveness. It might even be said that the effectiveness of speaking and sign gifts was largely missing without an atmosphere created by such temporal ministries. In a real sense, "helps" is more directly tied to love, the vital counterpart of spiritual gifts (1 Cor. 12:31b–13:13). Only love can motivate performance of the less-noticed spiritual acts. Public recognition furnishes no incentive for these. Only an unselfish concern prompts a Christian to offer such help (cf. 1 Cor. 12:25–26). In fact, as a general rule, where love is not present, neither will there be these more inconspicuous operations. But where love is a prime force, services rendered will be the rule rather than the exception.

As is true with most of the gifts, a general responsibility applicable to all Christians lies in the area of "helps." Every member of the body of Christ should demonstrate love-evidencing help. Those with the special gift are not to render the only help in the body. Yet the existence of a special function indicates that some are more apt in this kind of service. A person with the gift can meet a specific need more effectively. If those who are especially adept can be identified and freed to perform where their gift best suits the situation, the operation of Christ's body becomes a more efficient one.

"*Administrations.*" Another gift named for the first time in 12:28 is "administrations," or "governments." This is the same gift referred to in Romans 12:8 by the expression "he who leads." This special ability includes administrative directorship of matters of external organization related to the body of Christ. The word for "administrations" in verse 28 draws upon the skill requisite in piloting a ship (cf. "pilot," Acts 27:11; "ship-master," Rev. 18:17). The notion of shrewd and wise direction is entailed. This Greek word is also the source of the English word "cybernetics," the science relating to the nature of the brain and its governing of the body.

Some within the body of Christ have special abilities in spiritual administration. They know how to organize and marshal the functional resources of a local assembly to mount the strongest possible concerted effort. These are the ones who have charge of leadership responsibilities.

The gift of government is the special need of overseers or elders (cf. 1 Tim. 5:17, where "rule" stands for the same word as "leads" in Rom. 12:8; also 1 Thess. 5:12, where "have charge over" is another way of translating this word for "rule"). It is only with this special kind of practical wisdom that Christians can provide adequate spiritual leadership (cf. Heb. 13:7, 17, 24). The gift guarantees a Spirit-given insight into how the Lord's work can operate most efficiently.

Though this gift might frequently accompany a natural ability in administrative efficiency, it is something over and above merely natural insights. This capability is supernatural, just as are all the other gifts, for the Holy Spirit is the source. A non-Christian could never function successfully in such a capacity since he is not alert to spiritual dimensions. By the same token, not all Christians have been granted this practical alertness, and it is the local church's responsibility to seek out those who have this ability of leadership. Of course, all Christians are responsible to organize their own lives and whatever Christian work they oversee. But the larger task of rulership should belong to those who are especially so gifted.

A leaderless congregation has never been, and is not, God's concept of Christ's body. Paul's obsession with doing all things decently and in order bears the Holy Spirit's endorsement (1 Cor. 14:33, 40), and such coordination is impossible without capable leaders to guide the ship. Those who can identify gifts of various members and establish an organization through which these gifts can best operate are needed in positions of control. Otherwise, duplication of effort and even conflict and confusion will come, even though well-meaning Christians attempt to use what they have to serve the Lord.

The presence of this gift in verse 28 suggests several comparisons. The authority derived from the gift is, of course, much smaller than that of apostles. By its nature, the gift will also bring some degree of recognition to the person using it. Yet it is not the same kind of admiration that accrues to the person with one of the speaking or sign gifts. In fact, much that goes into spiritual administration is thankless because it is completely unnoticed. It is thus a labor of love just as the gift of helps. To continue functioning as an organizer when no regular word of appreciation comes for excellence of service requires a high degree of unselfish devotion to the Lord and other members in the body. It means carrying on when hard feelings arise because of leadership decisions. To continue in the face of adverse circumstances requires a quality closely akin to, if not identical with, love. Paul will turn shortly to this subject (1 Cor. 12:31b–13:13).

"Diversities of Tongues." The expression "various kinds of tongues" in verse 28 is identical with the naming of the same gift in verse 10. As in verse 10, except for the interpretation of tongues, the gift again stands last. This can hardly be less than intentional in that the problem of gifts in Corinth centered in an overemphasis on this gift. As striking as it was, the Corinthians had serious need to understand the proper place and manner of exercising the gift (14:20–23). For use within the body itself, this gift was furthest from any claim of being the "greater gift" (12:31).

12:29–30—Necessity of diversity. After arranging the eight gifts of verse 28 in order of fruitfulness, Paul proceeds to a series of rapid-fire questions that establish variety as indispensable. With hammerlike impact come seven questions, each demanding a negative answer to show that no gift is possessed by all Christians.[11] This emphasis serves to reassert what is implied by the "individually members of it" in verse 27 and what is stated more pointedly in illustrative fashion in verse 14: "The body is not one member, but many." Had God bestowed all the gifts on each part of the body, each one would be a complete body in himself. That would nullify dependence on others and destroy the one-body organism. The nature of the relationship, therefore, renders it imperative that no one function be the common property of all gifted persons.

In the main, the questions of verses 29–30 pertain to gifts listed in verse 28. They omit only helps and government and add only interpretation (cf. v. 10). A further distinction between the two sets is a recasting of the last five gifts of verse 28 from the abstract into a more concrete form, with persons rather than abilities in view. That is done by the use of "all" with each gift.

The question "All do not speak with tongues, do they?" along with its associated "All do not interpret, do they?" relegates the gift of tongues to the bottom position once again. That gift more than any other placed the speaker in the forefront and directed particular attention to him. In the estimation of these Corinthian Christians, it was of paramount importance. But the Spirit-inspired writer has a radically different sense of values.

12:31a—Best strategy for growth. The apostle says, "Earnestly desire the greater gifts" (12:31). A course of action infinitely preferable to the assumption that everyone can have every gift is to see the higher value of some gifts and give more attention to the superior ones. The "greater gifts" are doubtless identified by the ranking established in verse 28. At the top stands apostleship, a gift so rich in benefit to the church that no thinking person would dare compare any other with it.

The Christians at Corinth thus received very practical advice as to how they could improve their phase of the body's operation, that is, by cultivating gifts at the top of the list rather than those at the bottom. In fact, it required more than cultivation. "Earnestly desire" calls for burning zeal.[12] If their interest in obtaining those higher services was intense enough, their practical effort to obtain them would follow as a natural consequence.

How to obtain these services is a matter that needs clarification. Since no person who had never seen the incarnate Lord Jesus could aspire to apostleship, it is clear that the command of verse 31a does not entail an individual's seeking apostleship for himself. Furthermore, the point has just been made (vv. 29–30) that no gift is available to all Christians. Such a course would also be contradictory to God's sovereign determination concerning who receives what gifts (12:11, 18). It is not for man to decide this.

So how can each be commanded to seek for himself a gift at the top of the list? Paul is encouraging a sense of values to determine the action of a whole assembly. This is a quest for men, such as those in verses 29–30—not for abstract gifts—to be added to the persons already present. These additions to a local congregation might come by conversion or through Christians coming from other localities. That system of priorities also means the Corinthians must stop placing such a premium on those who spoke with tongues and begin valuing more highly the gifts at the upper end of the spectrum.

Much of value for today comes from the principle advocated here. Apostles and prophets, in the strictest sense of the terms, are no longer available to the church as vehicles of ministry to the body. But teachers are. The congregation that gives a prime place to its teachers is steering a wise course in utilizing its personnel to promote growth most effectively in the body. The gifts available to the church are all beneficial. They cannot help but be so because they are generated by the Holy Spirit. Yet their strategic use will yield the highest return. Such strategy lends itself to the body's maximum unified output.

Chapter Four

UNQUESTIONED SUPERIORITY OF SPIRITUAL FRUIT: LOVE

12:31b–13:13

A. PREEMINENCE OF LOVE (12:31B–13:3)

12:31b And I show you a still more excellent way.

13:1 If I speak with the tongues of men and of angels, but do not have love, I have become a noisy gong or a clanging cymbal.

2 And if I have the gift of prophecy, and know all mysteries and all knowledge; and if I have all faith, so as to remove mountains, but do not have love, I am nothing.

3 And if I give all my possessions to feed the poor, and if I deliver my body to be burned, but do not have love, it profits me nothing.

12:31b—A more excellent way. Paul has not yet said all that is necessary about the most efficient use of spiritual gifts. An appreciation for the relative profit from various gifts (12:27–31a) is of great importance, but it is not the ultimate in promoting maximum benefit. Verse 31b changes the focus from what is important to what is most important: "And I show you a still more excellent way." These transitional words could go with verses 27–31a but are more of an introduction to the following subject.

"And" derives a sense of "and in addition to this command to desire the greater gifts" from the surrounding words (v. 31a). Desiring the greater gifts and an active pursuit of love are necessary complements to one another. Love is an addition to, not a substitute for, spiritual gifts. The ideal strategy for growth combines the counsel already given with the spiritual outlook about to be recommended.

Unfortunately, Paul's readers had made these two courses contradictory by their behavior. Their preference for spiritual gifts had become so strong that they had missed the weightier responsibilities of Christian living. So it is inevitable that Paul's discussion of the fruit of the Spirit that is love (cf. Gal. 5:22) takes on the nature of a comparison with gifts of the Spirit. No other way was feasible to approach the problems at Corinth.

"A more excellent way" is a path that has as its core the ideal of love.[1] It is a way that is independent of, but not contradictory to, the way of spiritual gifts. To aspire to walk in love is a more noble ambition than aspirations toward spiritual gifts. The former is to be sought more intensely (cf. 14:1). When one speaks of love, he speaks of what is first and foremost a quality that has an intrinsic value all its own and an eternal existence. Yet, this does not make love incompatible with spiritual gifts. God has projected a relationship of both love and spiritual gifts in the Christian life. But the Corinthians had made it into one of either love or spiritual gifts and had taken their stand on the side of spiritual gifts. This was the root of their problem. The Holy Spirit who produces both love and spiritual gifts cannot be in conflict with Himself. A comparison of the relative importance of these two phases of His ministry is altogether in order. This appears in 12:31b–13:13. Yet the two should never have been placed in conflict, necessitating a choice of one or the other.

Paul says, "I show you" (v. 31). This is the very thing he proceeds to do with the way of love in the verses of chapter 13.

13:1—Futility of tongues without love. First, attention in combating overemphasis on spiritual gifts naturally goes to what the Corinthians had misconstrued the most, the gift of tongues. Paul uses himself to illustrate and create a hypothetical case, one that had not and could not become actual. He pictures a situation of personally possessing the gift of tongues to the extent of being able to speak the languages of all men everywhere. He even goes beyond this and conceives of an ability to communicate in celestial languages of angels as well, whatever these languages might be (see 2 Cor. 12:4 and Rev. 14:2–3 for possible examples). Here is a case of ultimate linguistic ability that was never realized by Paul or anyone else (though Paul was richly endowed along this line, 1 Cor. 14:18). This is clearly beyond any claim the readers could make about their own facility with tongues.

A second part of the hypothetical picture, "but do not have love," is diametrically opposed to the first. Alongside the plenitude of tongues stands a paucity of spiritual fruit. Here is one whose attention to a spiritual ability has been so great that he has neglected "weightier provisions of the law" (Matt. 23:23; cf. Luke 11:42). Clearly this had not been Paul's habit. He simply uses himself as an extreme that reaches the ultimate on one side, but completely bypasses responsibility on the other.

What is the net contribution from such a life? "I have become a noisy gong or a clanging cymbal." The former, "noisy gong," was a formless piece of bronze making a clattering noise when struck. It was not musical, but instead was a reverberating sound that aggravated the eardrums. The "clanging cymbal" refers to the sound made by concave-shaped metal plates used widely in heathen worship of the Eastern world—again, a very repulsive sound. A comparison of tongues without love to pagan worship carried a stinging rebuke to the glossolalists (i.e., tongues-speakers) at Corinth. In essence, the appraisal is, "In the case supposed, I have become and remain a source of irritation instead of a source of benefit. Despite my full command of this gift, the absence of love has reduced me to a meaningless state of confusion. I have made no moral contribution at all to the body of Christ."

Paul's choice of himself as the illustration of failure is a prime example of his own love. He does not claim the virtue, but illustrates the same self-abnegation as Christ when He died in the sinner's place. This is a love for others that seeks not its own benefit but the profit of others. Its motives for doing this always exclude considerations of self. It is furthest from the one who is so preoccupied with himself and his own gifts that he is negligent of needs around him.

13:2—Futility of prophecy and faith without love. What is true of tongues is also true of another speaking gift, prophecy, and a sign gift, faith (13:2). Prophecy exceeded tongues in usefulness because it could communicate to the mind (cf. 1 Corinthians 14). Yet even this gift was insufficient when standing alone, that is, without love.

An overlapping of prophecy with the gifts of wisdom and knowledge is implicit in verse 2. The former gift in part was built upon the latter two if it be understood that "mysteries" resulted from the "word of wisdom" (cf. discussion of 12:8). This hypothetical case again involves the ultimate in endowment. When Paul says all mysteries and all knowledge, he conceives of having received the totality of divine revelation and its application to every situation that has ever arisen or will ever arise. Though Paul's office as a prophet is clear, to claim that his knowledge of God's mind was that extensive would be to equate himself with God. That is absurd. Rather, Paul has constructed another hypothesis that pictures an ultimate, though impossible, endowment.

Another case of an extreme in verse 2 is in connection with the gift of faith. "All faith" means that the full gamut of faith is under control. All degrees of faith cover all types of obstacles and miracles. This is a wonder-working faith, and not just a basic Christian trust resulting in salvation. The specific miracle selected as an illustration is one suggested by the Lord Jesus, the removal of mountains (Matt. 17:20; 21:21). From a physical standpoint this is the hardest task of all, and seemingly, the one who could accomplish that could do anything.

Yet this is not the whole story. Repeated from verse 1, the refrain "but do not have love" completes the hypothetical structure of verse 2, and again the result is failure: "I am nothing." As impressive as the gifts of prophecy and faith are, a preliminary estimate might attribute to them some slight independent value. Yet Paul does not say, "I am next to nothing." He says, "I am nothing." Apart from love, those towering gifts were without edifying value to the body of Christ, and the persons possessing them were consequently worthless.

13:3—Futility of helps without love. Verse 3 is the most difficult of all. Can a person with special ability to meet the needs of others, when he uses that ability, do so apart from love? The gift of "helps" (12:28) is particularly in view because ministries of that type have a more direct correlation with love.

The first hypothetical example of help involves surrendering all one's earthly possessions to provide food for the needy. This is total commitment of one's belongings for a worthy cause. Only with great difficulty could anyone fault that caliber of behavior. It is doubtful whether even the writer himself had gone to such an extreme.

But there is more. It is very likely that Paul's supposition of giving his body "to be burned," as the *New American Standard Bible* has it, was originally that of giving his body "that I may boast." The latter reading has better manuscript support; besides, burning as a method of persecuting Christians was unknown in the first century. In this light, the statement goes beyond surrender of an entire fortune (v. 3a) and suggests selling one's total person into slavery to have material substance to give to those in need. Historically, Paul never did this, but he says, "Suppose I had. Would not this insure benefit to others in the body of Christ?"

It would not. The purpose of the apparent sacrifice, "that I may boast," is the drawback and is sufficient to nullify whatever apparent good may come. Though one may go the limit to provide for others, his actions count for naught unless his motives are proper. The motivational deficiency in the illustration is a replacement of love with a desire for self-exaltation. That is enough to render null and void an act that otherwise would have been very fruitful in the lives of others.

The Greek words rendered "it profits me nothing" may legitimately be translated, "I on my part produce no profit" (middle voice instead of passive voice). Since the true test in 1 Corinthians 12–14 is the benefit I can bring to others (cf. 12:7; 14:6), not what I myself receive, the latter alternative may very well be the meaning of the clause. For Paul personally to be deprived of profit was of no consequence, since love is not concerned about itself (1 Cor. 13:5). But for him, not to be a channel of benefit to others through his gift of helps was tantamount to utter failure.

B. PERFECTIONS OF LOVE (13:4–7)

4 Love is patient, love is kind, and is not jealous; love does not brag and is not arrogant,

5 does not act unbecomingly; it does not seek its own, is not provoked, does not take into account a wrong suffered,

6 does not rejoice in unrighteousness, but rejoices with the truth;

7 bears all things, believes all things, hopes all things, endures all things.

By now the great importance of love is evident. With it, gifts of the Spirit are powerful tools, but without it they produce nothing. That arouses a natural curiosity: "What is love? What are some of its characteristics? You have shown how indispensable it is. Tell me more about it." This the Holy Spirit through the human author proceeds to do as He furnishes a list of fifteen perfections of love.

13:4—Two things love does and three it does not do. Love's characteristics as presented in verses 4–7 are not an exhaustive description of Christian love, though they go far in establishing outlines of such a picture. The aspects of love Paul does mention here are those needed to counter shortcomings in Corinthian conduct. In exercising their gifts, and in Christian living more broadly, they had given disproportionate attention to some phases while neglecting others. To counter the areas of neglect, the text launches into a series of exalted, bluntly phrased prescriptions. These, not the Corinthian excesses, constitute the way of love.

"Love is patient" (v. 4) refers to the temperament that patiently accepts injuries without desire for revenge. Quite literally, the word speaks of being "long-tempered." Such a long-tempered dealing with people enables the Spirit-filled Christian to endure provocations and injustices and still be in control of himself. Paul speaks of such proper character in his epistles: 2 Corinthians 6:6; Galatians 5:22; Ephesians 4:2; Colossians 3:12; and 1 Thessalonians 5:14

("patience" in each place except 1 Thess. 5:14 where the word is "patient"). In exhibiting that virtue, the Christian has no less than God Himself as a model to follow (Rom. 2:4; 9:22; 1 Peter 3:20; 2 Peter 3:9).

Love also "is kind" (v. 4). A love life puts itself at the disposal of others. It bestows benefits on others and in this sense is the reverse of long-suffering, which receives injuries from others. The word for "kind" has as its root idea "useful." Love displays a usefulness directed toward others. "Kindness" is a companion of "patience" three more times in Paul's writings: 2 Corinthians 6:6; Galatians 5:22; and Colossians 3:12.

Hard feelings toward one another have always plagued Christians. That was certainly true in Corinth. Such hard feelings and resentments are not an insuperable obstacle to genuine love, however. Love, because of its long-suffering, can take whatever the antagonist commits without responding in bitterness and, because of its kindness, can go the "second mile" to perform deeds helpful to the one who counts himself an enemy.

"Is not jealous" is the first of eight negative attributes of love—three in verse 4, four in verse 5, and one in verse 6. To have a well-rounded picture of this grace, one must know what it is not as well as what it is. The word for jealous was originally "to boil." Inner "boiling" sometimes can be the right kind of zeal in pursuing a godly life. The same Greek verb has that favorable sense of an earnest desire in 12:31 above and 14:1 below. More frequently, however, it connotes a derogatory feature, expressive of selfish passion or jealousy. The Corinthian zeal needed redirecting toward proper goals, toward a desire for gifted persons in their assembly (12:31) rather than a selfish coveting of another's gifts (13:4). The congregation was jealous, strife-torn, and carnal (1 Cor. 3:3). They needed to yield themselves to the Holy Spirit's control so that He could produce His fruit among them. By this means and this means only can any Christian gain freedom from the ravages of jealousy.

"Love does not brag" is the fourth characteristic of love and the second in the list of what love does not do. Love does not parade itself, is not ostentatious. Any effort to gain the applause of others for outstanding performance comes under this heading. The Corinthians were woefully lacking in this respect, specifically in expending themselves to "show off" their own outstanding abilities. Unfortunately, they did this at the expense of consideration for the rights and well-being of others. A constant vying for public attention pervaded their meetings: "I have a psalm, I have a teaching, I have a revelation, I have a tongue, I have an interpretation" (cf. 1 Cor. 14:26). Such disorderly competition radically violates orderly procedures of love. The activities are self-promoting and boastful and are the outgrowth of an inward pride that follows next in the list.

When Paul writes love "is not arrogant," he in effect tells the Corinthian readers they are not loving. Earlier in the letter he has made clear his own evaluation, that they are a puffed-up, arrogant people. He has written in 4:18, "Now some have become arrogant," and in 5:2, "And you have become arrogant" (cf. 1 Cor. 4:6, 19; 8:1). Now, in 13:4, he sees this condition as excluding the modus operandi of love. Inner arrogance and love cannot coexist. The proud need to submit themselves to the Holy Spirit's control and have their pride replaced by humility. Then and only then will they experience deliverance from the companion offense of self-vaunting.

13:5—Four things love does not practice. Love "does not act unbecomingly." Poor manners and rude conduct are not a part of love's repertoire. Good deportment is. Undisciplined glossolalists needed to learn that important lesson. Their conduct up till then had been unbecoming (*aschēmonei*, 13:5, literally, "unformed"); they needed to behave in a manner befitting their Christian status (*euschēmonōs*, 14:40, literally, "well-formed"). The deportment of love is always proper. It displays good manners at all times. That was a quality generally absent in Corinth. In addition to abuses caused by improprieties with spiritual gifts were the problems of women's behavior (11:2–16) and conduct in conjunction with the Lord's Supper (11:17–22). As a corrective, love is considerate enough to use good manners in the presence of others.

Love is never guilty of self-seeking ("does not seek its own," v. 5). The combination of Greek words in the second expression of verse 5 argues strongly for connecting the words with what Paul says about edification elsewhere in the epistle. Edification of others is a prime consideration in 1 Corinthians 8–10. In these earlier chapters, consideration for others in limiting one's Christian liberty meant doing only those things that would contribute to their building up (10:23). On that basis, Paul issues the injunction, "Let no one seek his own good, but that of his neighbor" (10:24; "edification," "benefit," or something similar is the idea involved in "good" in light of 10:23). This served as Paul's personal guideline: "not seeking my own profit, but the profit of the many" (10:33). Love's freedom from self-seeking also furnishes an incentive to use spiritual gifts for edifying others in the church (14:12) rather than oneself (14:4). Self-edification as a goal in itself is tantamount to selfishness, even though it may result from exercising gifts of the Holy Spirit. Love is not inclined to selfish practices of any kind.

Love "is not provoked" (v. 5). The extreme to which love does not go is an arousal to resentment that results in unfortunate incidents. Lawsuits resulting from embitterment among the readers are probably in mind here (cf. 1 Cor. 6:1–8). Paul himself was not free from experiencing provocations like this. About five years earlier he had been party to an encounter with Barnabas where hard feelings had resulted in serious repercussions (Acts 15:39, where "sharp disagreement" is from the same root as "provoked" in 1 Cor. 13:5), though Barnabas may have been the only guilty party. Provocation can, of course, be good when proceeding from worthy motives (Acts 17:16; Heb. 10:24), but the provocation that love prohibits comes from motives of self-concern.

Paul's meaning in "does not take into account a wrong suffered" (v. 5) is the concept of not holding a wrongdoer accountable for evil or injury suffered at his hand. Love does not perform the bookkeeper's task of maintaining a careful accounting of each time it is wronged. Human nature often keeps such a record with a view to future reprisals when opportunities for revenge present themselves, but love stores up no such resentment and bears no such malice. It consoles itself in the divine assurance, "'Vengeance is Mine, I will repay, says the Lord'" (Rom. 12:19). Love not only forgives; it also forgets.

13:6—One thing love does not practice and one it does. Verse 6 turns to the subject of rejoicing, to revealing legitimate and illegitimate reasons for joy. "Unrighteousness" can never be a foundation for joy in the loving heart because love has always taken and continues taking the opposite side in the eternal conflict between right and wrong. The world finds a degree of satisfaction in "successful" transgression, but love sees through the apparent triumph of the moment and recognizes it as opposition to a righteous God who is love (cf. 1 John 4:8). Love does not even find pleasure in an enemy's moral downfall, though the first human response is to rejoice over such a collapse. The moment that a violation of God's righteous standards occurs, love experiences repulsion because of the act and no longer has the faintest association with it. This may entail a degree of sternness in dealing with some situations (e.g., 2 Thess. 3:5-6, 14-15). So exalted is the moral outlook of love that it takes a strong stand against the depraved human heart, which is its diametric opposite (cf. Rom. 1:28-32, especially v. 32). Love is always staunchly positioned on the side of righteousness.

Since truth is the constant companion of righteousness, it too is the constant companion of love. Love "rejoices with the truth" because these two are "sisters." More than just the true, right way of life, this truth is the body of teaching comprising the gospel, as frequently characterized in Paul's epistles (Gal. 5:7; Eph. 1:13; Col. 1:5; 2 Thess. 2:12-13). Error is inconsistent with love, error being defined as a distortion of biblical teachings. No matter how worthy the humanitarian benefit of a deed, it can never satisfy love if associated with error because love, by definition, is always in harmony with the true doctrines of God's Word. Truth must prevail. Even the slightest compromise can nullify this fruit of the Spirit. The narrowness of love calls for sternness whenever dealing with false teaching (cf. 2 John 5-6, 10-11).

13:7—Four things love does. The final four attributes of love come in the form of hyperboles, that is, overstatements for the sake of emphasis. They must be hyperboles to be consistent with the restrictions upon love in verse 6. For example, for love to believe "all things" (v. 7) in an absolutely nonfigurative sense would amount to its adoption of blind credulity toward any and every teaching. That clearly contradicts not only love's perspective on righteousness and truth in v. 6, but also the proper responsibility of Christian discernment elsewhere advocated (1 Cor. 12:1–3; 1 John 4:1–3). Being a loving Christian does not compel one to believe that black is white and white is black. "Believes all things" instead has the sense of giving another party the benefit of the doubt. Love dictates that a person not be overly suspicious but prefer to err in the direction of trusting too much rather than too little. In light of this second expression of verse 7, therefore, other pertinent Christian responsibilities must balance each of the "all things" in verse 7.

Since the four activities of love in verse 7 fall into two pairs, the second grouped with the third and the first with the fourth, it is advantageous to consider "hopes" along with "believes" and leave "bears" to be discussed with "endures." As shown above, "believes all things" regards love as not being suspicious and distrustful. Though it does not practice indiscriminate trust, it does have the basic outlook of faith in one's fellow man. When disappointed in such present expectations, however, love turns its eyes to the future and "hopes all things." Those who frustrate trust for the present will hopefully change and become reliable objects of confidence in the future. As long as the grace of God is operative, human failure is never final. On this basis, love is optimistic about progress that can come through spiritual growth and development.

The first and fourth characteristics of verse 7 also form a pair. The root idea behind "bears all things" is that of covering up the faults of others. Love puts up with all irritations created by associates through their personality traits, ingratitude, or any other lack of consideration. It knows no such thing as a "personality conflict." It is perfectly compatible with even the most hard-to-work-with partner.

The distinction between that first expression of verse 7 and the fourth, "endures all things," is that the fourth, instead of looking to the present and having reference to one's allies, looks to the future and the return of Christ as an incentive for successful encounters with persecutions that come from one's foes. "Endures" stands for a Greek word that has a military background. It sustains its holder in the face of violent sufferings and persecutions, not just annoyances and minor grievances. It is an aggressive trait. It does not face adverse obstacles with a spirit of passivity or defeatism, but continues to press forward even when confronted with the most terrible opposition. Such an outlook is possible because of a guaranteed restitution when the Lord Jesus comes again (1 Thess. 1:3; James 5:7–8; 1 Peter 1:2–7; Rev. 3:10–11).

In his "bears-endures" combination, Paul has returned to the note on which the enumeration started, that of long-suffering or patience (v. 4). What long-suffering accomplishes toward people, forbearance and endurance accomplish toward happenings and circumstances. Since endurance looks to the future and Paul's expectation that Christians repeatedly will have to react thus to persecution (Rom. 5:3; 8:35; 12:12; 1 Thess. 1:6; 3:3, 7; 2 Thess. 1:4, 6; and many others), the question of love's relation to the future is now in the forefront. The future look constitutes a natural bridge to the next section, which deals with the objective permanence of love (vv. 8–13).

C. PERMANENCE OF LOVE (13:8–13)

8 Love never fails; but if there are gifts of prophecy, they will be done away; if there are tongues, they will cease; if there is knowledge, it will be done away.

9 For we know in part, and we prophesy in part;

10 but when the perfect comes, the partial will be done away.

11 When I was a child, I used to speak as a child, think as a child, reason as a child; when I became a man, I did away with childish things.

12 For now we see in a mirror dimly, but then face to face; now I know in part, but then I shall know fully just as I also have been fully known.

13 But now abide faith, hope, love, these three; but the greatest of these is love.

1. PERMANENCE STATED (13:8A)

13:8a—Permanence of love stated. In brief, the message of verses 8–13 is "Love never fails" (v. 8a). As though the perfections of verses 4–7 were not sufficiently impressive to echo the supremacy of this virtue, the description climbs to even greater heights in an account of love's permanence.

The more frequent translation of the word for "fails" is "fall," but at times its meaning has more the finality of "fall into decay" or "be abolished." In this respect, love is like the Scripture, no detail of which will ever change

(Luke 16:17). Temporal failure is excluded by the very nature of love because "love abides forever" (v. 13).

In one sense "never" (v. 8) carries the whole weight of chapter thirteen's final six verses. It is a time word. The Greek word for which it stands combines words that literally mean "not even at any time." The middle of verse 8 through verse 13 elaborate on this "never."

2. PERMANENCE CONTRASTED WITH TEMPORARY GIFTS (13:8B–12)

A. PASSING OF GIFTS (13:8B)

13:8b—Passing of the gifts. In contrast to the unaltered continuance of love, verse 8b presents three prominent gifts, each one introduced by an "if." These were important gifts in the early church, and Paul and his readers rightly recognized them as such. No matter how significant their contribution at that time, however, the Holy Spirit here predicted through Paul that some day their work was to end. That temporal comparison is another "more excellent" (12:31) characteristic of love.

The three gifts selected—prophecies, tongues, and knowledge—have previously received attention at 12:8, 10, 28–30. The writer selects prophecies (plural because of separate revelations that composed the gift) as one illustration because he has already recognized the gift's high rank in the total field (12:28; no apostles resided at Corinth, so he uses the gift next in rank after apostles) and because this is one of the two gifts to be discussed extensively in chapter 14. The gift, furthermore, sustains some connection with the word of wisdom (12:8, 28; 13:2), and the philosophically oriented Greeks at Corinth valued wisdom highly (cf. 1 Cor. 1:18–2:5).

"Tongues" is a second illustration chosen for obvious reasons: the readers had made this gift their prime concern. What God had established as a sign to unbelievers (14:22), they were using as a means toward selfish satisfaction (14:4). Nevertheless, the gift was from the Holy Spirit and was worthy of standing side-by-side with prophecies and knowledge. Paul will presently amplify his discussion of tongues (14:1ff.).

A third illustrative gift, knowledge, was another revelational gift in which the Corinthians had a strong interest. As heirs to the rich traditions of Greek philosophy, they had a natural inclination toward knowledge too (1 Cor. 8:1–3). The gift of knowledge consisted of more than purely intellectual pursuits, as the discussion of 12:8 has shown. Even with the gift of knowledge, however, one's degree of awareness was quite limited compared to what it will be after the consummation (13:12; cf. 13:2). These three gifts elevated their holders noticeably in respect to their own time, but in respect to durability and longevity, they had no claim to prominence alongside love.

The terminology for cessation in verse 8 deserves attention.[2] "Will be done away" in each case represents the same Greek word, *katargeō*. This word carries the idea of "make inoperative" or "put out of action," and since the cause of cessation in these two cases is outside the gifts themselves, it accurately describes the termination of revelational activity by God (though the text does not explicitly identify Him as the one doing away with the gifts). The second term ("will cease") is from a different word, *pauō*. The form lends itself to the thought of the gift's passing out of existence "under its own power," as it were. This appropriately describes the cessation of a sign gift after it had served its purpose.

B. PARTIAL NATURE OF GIFTS (13:9)

13:9—Partial nature of the gifts. The partial nature of knowledge and prophecy explains their removal (v. 9). Verse 9 has no explanatory word about tongues. The nature of that third gift did not require justification for its disappearance. Knowledge and prophecy were different, however, because they were revelatory, and clarification was necessary to tell why these two channels of divine revelation would cease to exist at some time in the future.

Paul supports his case by a twofold usage of "in part." That quantitative expression is opposed to Paul's earlier hyperbolical hypothesis that he understood "all mysteries and all knowledge" (v. 2). Verse 9 is the actual case. As rich as they were through receiving direct communications from God, the apostles and prophets could lay claim only to part of all that could be known. What they understood, and incidentally, what Christians today understand on the basis of their writings in the New Testament, is only a faint image of what will come following the Lord Jesus' return (13:12). In comparison with the full light yet to come, the gifts of knowledge and prophecy were mere glimpses.

C. REPLACING OF GIFTS (13:10–12)

13:10—Replacement of the gifts. The partial and imperfect state represented by the gifts of knowledge and prophecy (v. 9) was bound to be replaced by what is complete and perfect (v. 10). Verse 10 affirms that this doing away with the partial (same verb as "put out of action" in v. 8) coincides with the coming of "the perfect."

It is of crucial importance to grasp the significance of "perfect" in verse 10 (see n. 2). To what does Paul refer? Is it the completed canon of New Testament books? Doubtless this is involved, but this does not exhaust the term. Is it the perfect condition that will exist following the second coming of Jesus Christ? That must be part of the picture too, but it does not satisfy the total significance of "perfect." The term is a translation of *teleion*, a familiar word in New Testament writings. It draws upon the idea of "reaching an end" and sometimes means "complete," sometimes "mature," and, some would say, sometimes "perfect." A choice between the three meanings in any passage depends on the subject under discussion. The weighing of various possibilities in verse 10 points to the great likelihood that Paul's meaning is "mature," for he has already labored extensively to establish the body concept of the church (12:12–26) and will allude to the same again in the very next verse (13:11). Throughout the church age, the collective body is in the process of growing up. It is constantly entering new stages of maturity. Ephesians 4:11–16, a passage with which 1 Corinthians 12–14 has strong affinities, describes more vividly the corporate growth of the body of Christ. In part, it reads, "To the building up of the body of Christ; until we all attain to the unity of the faith, and of the knowledge of the Son of God, to a mature man, to the measure of the stature which belongs to the fulness of Christ. As a result, we are no longer to be children" (Eph. 4:12b–14a). The "mature man" of Ephesians 4:13 (*teleion* as in 1 Cor. 13:10) is one who has reached an advanced stage of development in leaving behind the characteristics of childhood (cf. "children," Eph. 4:14). As in Ephesians 4, Paul formulates a picture of Christ's body in 1 Corinthians 13:10, progressively growing up from childhood to maturity (cf. 1 Cor. 13:11).

"The perfect," therefore, is more accurately "the mature." From the standpoint of Paul's time, no one, not even the apostle himself, could speak dogmatically about how this maturity would come to the body. Paul entertained the definite possibility that Jesus Christ would return during his own lifetime (1 Thess. 4:15, 17). If such an event had transpired before he died, the body would have entered a state of absolute maturity immediately. That is the possibility for which the writer provides in 13:12.

On the other hand, Paul was aware of another phase of the church's development in which he himself was playing a major role, a phase that also bore on the church's progress in maturity. That was the writing of New Testament Scriptures to correspond with the Old Testament Scriptures with which he was so familiar. It is fairly certain that Paul was aware of his own involvement in composing God's Word (1 Cor. 2:13; 14:36–37; 1 Thess. 2:13; 5:27). About ten years later, Peter was certainly aware that Paul had written inspired books (2 Peter 3:15–16), and no valid reason exists for thinking Paul himself did not recognize this fact. Paul also knew that the writing of New Testament Scripture would not go on indefinitely. Unless it were interrupted by the return of Christ, it was some day destined for completion, just as the thirty-nine books of the Old Testament were a completed canon of books by Paul's time. The body of Christ was to continue growing, receiving revelations through prophecy and knowledge, until a fixed body of revelation would result.

Of course, at this early time no one except God knew how many books that would entail, but when consummated, the work would represent a significant step in the body's maturity. The writer alludes to this gradual accumulation of permanent revelation in his illustration of verse 11. The childhood and adolescent stages prevailed until the revelation was complete; but afterward, adulthood. (See Appendix A for further discussion of the contribution of 1 Corinthians 13:11 to an understanding of *to teleion*.)

By viewing these matters from Paul's perspective, one gains a better understanding of what he meant by "the mature." For him, the future held a twofold possibility. His prime expectation was that the body's maturity would come abruptly at the return of Christ, an event that he anticipated (v. 12). First Corinthians 1:7 verifies Paul's view of the possibility that the richness of the Corinthians' endowments would continue in operation until Christ's return. But by a sort of parenthetical illustration in verse 11 he allows for a possible delay in Christ's coming, one that would allow completion of the revelations marking the transitional period after the beginning of the first-century church. Until the time Christ does return, the body of Christ continues throughout the generations of church history to attain higher and higher degrees of maturity. The completion of the New Testament canon, marking the cessation of knowledge, prophecy, and tongues, was only one stage in the body's progressive development. Though the church continues to grow corporately, it will not reach its ultimate maturity until it is with the Lord and comes face to face with the knowledge now so incomplete (13:12).

13:11—Replacement with growing maturity illustrated. Verse 11 is parenthetical in that the continuity from verse 10 to verse 12 would be unbroken without it. But it is not parenthetical in the sense of being less important, since the Holy Spirit inspired Paul to include it at this point. An adequate interpretation of the passage must take it into account. The purpose it serves in Paul's mind is to suggest an alternate method, a means other than the return of Jesus Christ, by which the "mature" ("perfect") could arrive. An illustration derived from the writer's personal development—one that closely parallels the church's growth to maturity—tells of an alternate method by which maturity could come. "Child" in verse 11 and "mature" in verse 10 make up the same combination as is found in a companion passage, Ephesians 4:13–14. The whole design is to furnish an analogy of the collective body's growth from immaturity to maturity, that is, from childhood to adulthood, and the intermediate stages that characterize that growth.

The childhood stage corresponds to "the partial" (v. 10), the time period of tongues, prophecy, and knowledge (vv. 8–9). In fact, the threefold activity of a child is illustrative of those three gifts. "I used to speak as a child" pictures the gift of tongues, since the ill-formed words of a child often comprise sounds that are indistinguishable, just as is the case with tongues (1 Cor. 14:2). "Think as a child" represents the gift of prophecy, since the word behind "think" includes in its meaning feelings or aspirations along with mental activity. Prophecy included just such a feeling-influenced, subjective thought process (cf. Rev. 1:10, 17). "Reason as a child" stands for emotionless intellectual activity, an accurate picture of the gift of knowledge. Paul very graphically says, in effect, "Before I grew up, I used to speak, understand, and think as a child." He pointedly relegates the three gifts to early development. Nowhere in the New Testament is continuing immaturity condoned, whether it be a single immature member of the body of Christ (1 Cor. 3:1-4; Heb. 5:11-14) or, as it is here, the whole body corporately (Eph. 4:12-14). Normal human development is contrary to such a stagnant condition. Normal spiritual growth is the same.

A gradual putting off of childhood habits characterizes progress from childhood to manhood. That is the thrust of "when I became a man, I did away [same verb as 'put out of operation,' 13:8] with childish things." After childhood comes a period of adolescence, during which childhood habits decrease and ways of adulthood increase. In the illustration, childish habits portray revelational and confirmatory gifts (see n. 2).

Paul doubtless was aware of a gradual cessation of confirmatory gifts such as tongues during his own lifetime, and since confirmatory gifts and revelatory gifts were inseparable, the same would be true of prophecy and knowledge. Luke, a close associate of Paul, wrote a history of the church's first thirty years in the book of Acts. In addition to other transitional features of this period is a notable abundance "miracles, signs, and wonders" immediately after Pentecost and a gradual but marked decrease in such phenomena as history progressed. By the year 55, when 1 Corinthians was written, Acts records very few sign-gift manifestations. One of these later manifestations was Paul's encounter with disciples of John the Baptist in Ephesus three years earlier, shortly after he arrived in that city from which he was to write 1 Corinthians (Acts 19:1-7; cf. 1 Cor. 16:8). As Luke and Paul were together when Luke wrote Acts, it is inconceivable that Paul was unaware of the gradual diminishing of sign gifts portrayed in Luke's history of the early church.

Paul did not set dates for the termination of such gifts as tongues. But he did notice a diminishing frequency in the use of the gifts. They fulfilled a purpose for a limited time. The coming and going of limited periods noted for their miracle workers is a well-known aspect of Bible history. Only a few epochs have included signs and wonders granted by God through certain individuals. One was the period of the Exodus, when miraculous happenings identified Moses as God's appointed spokesman and deliverer. The crisis of that time was Israel's need to be freed from bondage in Egypt. Another such period was that of Elijah and Elisha, when God's official voices needed special identification because of a prevailing apostasy. The last such period is where Paul found himself. It was one that involved Christ and His apostles in a transition from the old economy to the new, from God's dealings with Israel more narrowly to His dealings with all men on equal terms and from a principal focus on the law to a period of emphasis on grace. Once God's authoritative message became established in a written New Testament, the need for special credentials ceased.

Since the gifts were only temporary, neither the Corinthians nor others had any business majoring on them. Only love is permanent and deserves that kind of preeminence.

It is clear that Paul's own adulthood did not illustrate the condition after Christ's coming. The difference between childhood and manhood is recognizably a very feeble way of expressing the vast difference between the church's present state and its future state when it knows fully just as it is fully known. Paul did not consider himself to have attained such perfection (Phil. 3:13–14) as would illustrate the church's state after the parousia. Neither would he say in consecutive verses, "When I became a man . . . I know in part" (1 Cor. 13:11–12), if his own manhood served to illustrate a condition after the consummation. Instead, he portrays by his adulthood the possibility for continued growth of the church through as many generations as might elapse until the unknown time of Christ's second coming. (See Appendix A for a further discussion of the contribution of 1 Cor. 13:11 to its context.)

13:12—Replacing with absolute maturity explained. Verse 12 is a further explanation of the "mature" of verse 10. Here Paul turns to discuss an event he loved, the appearing of Jesus Christ (2 Tim. 4:8). The illustration of verse 11 does not exhaust the meaning of "mature" since it covers the life of the church only under conditions of the present age. Beyond the present, beginning with the return of Jesus Christ, a changing maturity and growth will not mark the church's state, but finalized maturity will. That will be a time of completeness when the partial characteristics of the present economy become things of the past (see n. 2).

"We see" and "I know" refer to the gifts of prophecy and knowledge, respectively. A "mirror" in ancient times gave very imperfect and distorted reflections, the reflected image being quite inferior to direct gaze. So to see by means of "a mirror" furnishes an apt comparison to present spiritual vision. What one sees, one sees only darkly or obscurely. Figuratively, this is the "in part" nature of prophecy's message (cf. 13:9).

Paul does not specifically identify the object of prophetic vision or the sequel that will replace it, the "face to face" encounter (13:12). It would be safe to conclude, nevertheless, that the object is the vision and knowledge that will become complete after the parousia. The inward picture within the prophet's mind at the time of his vision was only a vague and incomplete outline, but at the future moment of believers' joining together with Christ, vision will be unobscured. Reference to the gift of knowledge in verse 12b carries over the "in part" expression from verses 9–10. Knowledge resulting from the word of knowledge under those conditions was at best only fragmentary, but, in describing what it will be in the future, Paul expresses himself more emphatically: "I shall know fully just as I also have been fully known [by God]" (v. 12b). That pictures completeness of future illumination. Assimilating all knowledge at the moment of the imminent consummation (cf. 1 Cor. 15:51–52) is a certainty. Very boldly Paul depicts this future fulness of knowledge in terms of what God Himself knows. No greater heights remain to ascend in this description of the church's ultimate maturity (cf. v. 10).

The "now . . . then" contrast in both parts of verse 12 pointedly refers to conditions before and after the coming of Christ. The gifts belonged to the period before, a period Paul hoped would be terminated during his own natural lifetime (cf. Phil. 3:20–21; Titus 2:13–14). As church history has turned out, however, Paul's lifetime and the period of prophecy and knowledge came to an end hundreds of years ago, and Christ has not yet returned. Yet, the body continues to grow (v. 11), and will do so until the glorious moment of His appearance. Until that time, the church must make the best use of partial prophecies and knowledge derived from Paul and his contemporaries and recorded in the twenty-seven books of the New Testament. The New Testament along with the Old Testament is God's completed revelation to His church, but when compared to post-Advent conditions, even this inspired collection will be seen as only a small fraction of all God knows. It is only when the Savior returns that the body of Christ will be permitted to exceed the wisdom and knowledge of God's Word.

3. PERMANENCE CLARIFIED (13:13)

13:13—Permanence of love clarified. The "but" that begins verse 13 indicates a contrast between the first half of the verse and the temporary gifts discussed in verses 8b–12. Faith, hope, and love occupy the entire present age, whereas the aforementioned three gifts continued only until the church had a completed written revelation (cf. v. 11). The Greek words for "now" in verses 12 and 13 are different, but they still encompass the same time span, the time up to the advent of Jesus Christ. The three Christian attributes have a guaranteed permanence, a guarantee that did not apply to the three gifts of prophecy, tongues, and knowledge (see n. 2).

This trio of Christian attributes occurs frequently in the New Testament (Rom. 5:2–5; Gal. 5:5–6; Col. 1:4–5; 1 Thess. 1:3; 5:8; Heb. 6:10–12; 10:22–24;

1 Peter 1:21–22). They seem to have constituted a good, succinct summary of the Christian life for early Christians. Of course, "faith" in verse 13 is not to be confused with the gift of faith mentioned in 12:9 and 13:2. Here it is the more general trust common to all Christians, whereby they have been saved (1 Cor. 1:21), and the principle according to which they govern their Christian lives (2 Cor. 1:24). Hope is the outlook that enables a Christian to endure persecutions (1 Thess. 1:3) in light of the assured deliverance that will come with the return of Christ. Love has received a full definition earlier in the chapter. Along with the other two attributes, it continues without interruption and is indispensable to the ongoing "body life" of the church's earthly existence. Well-ordered Christian lives that make up the corporate life of the body of Christ are impossible without them and the spiritual resources they furnish.

It is not so with the gifts that furnished initial revelation and confirmation to the body. These were indispensable to early phases of development, but they have long since completed their task of furnishing the church with a marked-out set of scriptural writings. Their contribution has been made and the body continues to grow because of what they furnished while they were actively functioning.

One further distinction remains to be made. It comes as a final contrast: "but the greatest of these is love" (v. 13b). Somehow a line of demarcation separates faith, hope, and love on the one hand, and love alone on the other. The distinction must lie in time relationships, since time is paramount from the paragraph's beginning (v. 8) up to these very last words. Faith, hope, and love are superior to the three gifts under discussion in that they continue throughout the era of the church. But love individually is superior to the faith-hope-love triad because it alone will survive and continue beyond the coming of Jesus Christ for His church (see n. 2). Second Corinthians 5:6–8 shows that the gathering together of believers into Christ's presence will result in faith, being replaced by sight. Romans 8:24–25 similarly notes that the moment hope is fulfilled by sight, it ceases to exist. So faith and hope will be no more after Christ's return. The only surviving member of the trio will be love. That is the only one that possesses eternal duration because it is the only one that God Himself experiences (1 John 4:8).

Building on this clearly established uniqueness and superiority of love, the Spirit-inspired apostle proclaims, "The greatest of these is love." In so doing, he returns to the note sounded as the paragraph began, "Love [and only love] never fails" (v. 8). On this ground also, the case for love as "a more excellent way" (12:31) than the way of gifts comes to a forceful conclusion.

Chapter Five

UNIFIED PURPOSE OF SPIRITUAL GIFTS: EDIFICATION

14:1–36

It is now time to descend from the pinnacle to which the discussion of love in chapter 13 has ascended. A suitable foundation is in place for the writer to attack a very difficult agenda: governing criteria for practice of the speaking gifts, prophecy and tongues. The ranking of the gifts just completed in 12:27–31a is not specific enough. Paul must also show that the prime consideration in using any gift is edification of other parties in the church. Love dictates that it must be this way.

A. EDIFICATION THROUGH PROPHECY: UNCONDITIONAL (14:1–5)

1 Pursue love, yet desire earnestly spiritual gifts, but especially that you may prophesy.

2 For one who speaks in a tongue does not speak to men, but to God; for no one understands, but in his spirit he speaks mysteries.

3 But one who prophesies speaks to men for edification and exhortation and consolation.

4 One who speaks in a tongue edifies himself; but one who prophesies edifies the church.

5 Now I wish that you all spoke in tongues, but even more that you would prophesy; and greater is one who prophesies than

one who speaks in tongues, unless he interprets, so that the church may receive edifying.

14:1—The best and the better. Bridging back to the subject of 12:31, Paul uses two directives to clarify relative values attached to love and spiritual gifts. The two imperatives are "pursue" and "desire earnestly" (14:1). The former command means to follow with persistence, a strong and unrelenting pursuit. Philippians 3:12 and 14, where "press on" represents the same word, pictures the straining intensity of a runner as he presses toward the finish line of his race. The concept of following or pursuing blends well with the idea of love as a route to be traveled (12:31). Vigorous pursuit is a favorite metaphor of Paul for describing spiritual effort (cf. Rom. 9:30–31; 12:13; 1 Thess. 5:15; 1 Tim. 6:11; 2 Tim. 2:22; in the NASB all the cross-references translate the same Greek word with "pursue" except Rom. 12:13, where it is "practicing," and 1 Thess. 5:15, where it is "seek after").

The second imperative in 14:1, "desire earnestly," stands for the same Greek as "earnestly desire" in 12:31 and "desire earnestly" in 14:39. It depicts a strong desire, a desire with intensity. Spiritual gifts constitute a prominent motive for Christian life and service. Yet, in comparison to the degree with which love is to be pursued as the supreme way, this motivation belongs to a lesser category. Gifts are less important than love. But that does not mean they are of no importance and therefore not to be sought. Anything generated by the Holy Spirit through an obedient vessel is bound to be profitable.

The same word as in 12:1, "spirituals," is the nomenclature here for gifts of the Spirit in general. The functions are activities clearly distinguishable from love. Paul proceeds to provide guidance for the strong desire for these gifts, hinted at in 12:31.

The concluding words of verse 1, "but especially that you may prophesy," say in effect, "Your desire to exercise the gift of prophecy should be more intense than that for other gifts of the Spirit." That sentiment harmonizes with the gift's high ranking among the rest (12:28). Had apostleship been an option for the Corinthians, Paul doubtless would have written instead of "prophesy," "function as apostles." But the readers did not meet natural prerequisites for the gift of apostleship; they were not eyewitnesses of Christ's resurrection, neither did they have a direct appointment from Him. Hence the most effective service open to them was prophesying. And "the greater [best] gift" (12:31) available to them was the one they should cultivate in their local gatherings. The superior benefit derived from this gift lies behind much that is found in 14:1–25. More specifically, verses 1–5 point out prophecy's unconditional guarantee of edification to the church.

14:2—Reason for tongues' low rank. Verses 2 and 3 expand the reason for preferring prophecy, verse 2 expressing the inadequacy of tongues and verse 3 the sufficiency of prophecy.

In handling the immediate problem of the Corinthian church, Paul points out that a tongues speaker communicated nothing to his companions in a Christian gathering. The foreign tongue utilized in their presence made it impossible for them to understand what he was saying.[1] The medium of communication was strange to their ears, and he would have done far better using a language with which they were familiar. The listeners heard the sound, but were unable to distinguish the words. The "no one" of verse 2 is, of course, limited by the surrounding discussion of chapters 11–14. It means that "no one" in the local gathering was of the particular linguistic background represented by the tongues message.[2] Acts 2:1–13 is a case where appropriate linguistic audiences were present. The Acts 2 episode, however, differed from the Corinthian circumstances in that the gathering consisted of people with varying linguistic backgrounds, not of people with the same native tongue.

In Corinth, no one was present to understand except God Himself, and it was useless to address Him with an inspired tongues message, for He was the source of the message in the first place. Neither this spiritual gift nor any other had the purpose of communicating with God, so, to speak to God rather than man through tongues was improper. The "groanings too deep for words" of Romans 8:26 have no connection with verse 2. In Romans 8, the subject is the Christian's private prayer life, and the context has no correlation with spiritual gifts. The Spirit-led prayers of Romans 8 are the duty of all Christians, not just those with a certain gift, and such prayers are unrelated to the gift of tongues. It is not to "groanings too deep for words," but to a supernaturally produced linguistic ability that 1 Corinthians 14:2 refers. That is not to say that the Christian's prayer life is not also dependent upon the Holy Spirit (Rom. 8:26–27); it very definitely is. But the Spirit's ministry is not limited to this one area, as His part in producing spiritual manifestations (1 Corinthians 12–14) clearly evinces.

"But in his spirit he speaks mysteries" (v. 2b). The activity of speaking with tongues has long been misunderstood because of the gift's long-standing dormancy. The words that close verse 2, however, permit a slight glimpse into the nature of the gift. By means of his spirit-manifestation (i.e., "in his spirit," verse 2, where "spirit" stands for the same Greek noun and has the same sense as "spiritual gifts" in 14:12),[3] the tongues speaker uttered "mysteries." Everywhere in Paul's writings "mysteries" were truths about God and His program that for a time remained hidden, but were at that moment revealed through the inspired writer (Rom. 11:25; 16:25; 1 Cor. 2:7; 13:2; 15:51; Eph. 3:3–4, 9; 5:32; Col. 1:26). The divine mysteries making up the content of tongues messages were the same as divine revelations and prophecies referred to in 14:6, the only difference being that in the present case successful communication did not transpire because of a language barrier. Direct revelation such as that provided through the word of wisdom (cf. 12:8) was at times involved in the gift of tongues, but it was a revelation that was never received unless someone present was of the same linguistic background as the tongues message (Acts 2:1–13), or unless someone present possessed the spiritual gift of interpretation (cf. 12:10; 14:27). In other words, tongues in themselves under normal circumstances of Christian worship were helpless to communicate their own messages, even though those messages were important revelations from God. Truths from God that otherwise could have been known remained hidden in that case. The speaker alienated his listeners from the substance of his message by his decision to use tongues rather than somehow speaking to their understanding. That was the deficiency of tongues in a Christian gathering and the reason for its low place in the list of 12:28.

14:3—Reason for prophecy's superiority. The prophet, like the tongues speaker, was a spokesman of divine mysteries. Yet, one important distinction separated them: one spoke in an understandable language; the other did not. Prophesying was an activity eminently more desirable than tongues because it communicated effectively with listeners in the assembly and in the process produced edification in their lives (14:3).

"Edification" is another way of saying "building up." Romans, 1 and 2 Corinthians, and Ephesians often describe growth of the church in that terminology, whether it be the church as a building (1 Cor. 3:9–17; Eph. 2:19–22) or the church as a body (Eph. 4:11–16, as it is here (cf. 1 Cor. 12:12–26). Impartation of additional insight into God's truth is most often the means of building up the body of Christ. Through His truth comes spiritual fortifying of the individual and hence of the corporate church. Because the human mind is an indispensable medium in the process of edification, prophecy (v. 3) and not tongues (v. 2) was the preferred gift for Christian worship. Paul will have much to say in the following verses to demonstrate that edification of the total group must be the prime consideration in choosing spiritual gifts (cf. 1 Cor. 14:4–5, 12, 17, 26).

Verse 3 specifies two avenues toward edification, exhortation and consolation.[4] The former exists as a distinct spiritual gift (Rom. 12:8), but it was also a function of prophecy. An exhortation addresses itself to the human will and moves people to action by strengthening their determination to attain a goal (cf. 1 Thess. 5:11). The latter element, "consolation," contributes to edification by means of soothing or consolation brought to the troubled heart (cf. 1 Thess. 2:11 and Phil. 2:1, where roots of the same two words appear together again). Yet, the two do not exhaust all the ways to edify. Verse 31 includes instruction as an important means. Indeed, instruction furnishes the foundation for and gives meaning to the exhortation and comfort listed in verse 3. Through instruction, listeners gain added understanding of God's truth. Without it, words of exhortation and comfort are empty and unproductive.

What the gift of prophecy did for the early church, the gifts of teaching (Rom. 12:7) and exhortation (Rom. 12:8) have done since the completion of written New Testament revelation. Modern-day teachers and exhorters take truths from the written Word that have come to man through the gift of prophecy, and make good use of them in the ongoing growth of Christ's body.

14:4—Possible objects of edification. Verse 4 describes two kinds of edification, self-edification and church edification. Self-edification was the most that could happen through one who spoke with a tongue. A tongues message left the church devoid of any benefit. On the other side, since prophecy communicated to the understanding, it had an edifying effect upon the whole group, including the speaker himself. Prophecy was, therefore, to be regarded as having higher value for Corinthian worship.

Can anything good be said about tongues and self-edification? The tongues speaker apparently had a limited understanding of the general nature of his own utterance. Otherwise, he himself could have received no edification. Yet, to the extent that he insisted on using up the meeting time with his tongues message, he was demonstrating his own selfishness and thereby violating at least one of the "perfections" of love that "does not seek its own" (13:5).

Is it possible, then, that the total effect of one whose goal is self-edification is nothing beneficial? Very probably it is, because tongues without love was completely unproductive (cf. 13:1).[5] This means that certain kinds of edification or building up are not constructive because of improper goals. That is certainly true in 1 Corinthians 8:10, where the conscience of the weak one was "strengthened" (lit., "built up," the same word as "edifies" in 1 Cor. 14:4) to eat things at the expense of offending his own conscience. Such destructive edification is a sin against the weaker brother and Christ Himself (1 Cor. 8:12). Even so worthy an instrument as a gift from the Holy Spirit can become detrimental when the motivation of love is absent (cf. 1 Cor. 8:1). That is what 1 Corinthians 14:4a specifies. Verse 4a cannot be a use of tongues in private, for spiritual gifts were and are by their very nature open manifestations designed not for the gifted one himself but for others whom he serves (cf. 1 Cor. 12:5, 7). Paul was emphatic in not advocating tongues or any other gift for the purpose of private use or self-edification. The edification for which the loving member of Christ's body seeks is that of the other members (cf. 14:12). The child of God is not to seek his "own profit" but that of the other party (1 Cor. 10:23–24, 33).

The one who, prompted by love, takes the message of prophecy and uses it to teach, exhort, and comfort, does this very thing and is a profitable servant to the rest of the church (14:4b).

14:5—Relative value of prophecy and tongues. In verse 5, Paul summarizes the picture he has painted in verses 1–4, that of prophecy's preference. He opens the verse with a hyperbolic concession: "I wish that you all spoke in tongues." However, that is a wish doomed to impossibility of fulfillment (just as is his wish of 1 Cor. 7:7). It was not God's will that all have this gift (cf. 1 Cor. 12:11, 30). The words are hyperbolic, for an inspired writer would never wish for anything contrary to divine principles. The reason Paul expresses himself in such an unusual way is to allay any false impressions that he undervalued the gift of tongues. He has already admitted its importance as a manifestation of the Holy Spirit (12:7, 10), and subsequently he will show his own possession and extensive use of the gift (14:18). At this point, he simply inserts a hyperbolic concession to balance his earlier strong statements (vv. 2, 4) asserting the gift's inferiority. The gift itself was perfectly valid and valuable when used for the right purpose (14:22). It was misuse of it that brought damage.

When Paul adds his "but even more" (v. 5), he shows his clear preference for prophecy in the church. His intention throughout the chapter is not to depreciate tongues completely but to exalt prophecy and point to areas where it is superior to and the antithesis of tongues. Significantly, Paul does not say, "that *all of* you prophesied." He has dropped the hyperbole of the previous clause. It was not the divine purpose that every individual possess the gift of prophecy but rather that prophecy might dominate their assemblages as a church.

In the strongest terminology thus far, Paul explicitly adds in the latter half of verse 5, "Greater is one who prophesies than one who speaks in tongues." As the preceding words of the paragraph have made clear, his strong prejudice in favor of prophecy grows out of its superior communicative ability and hence its greater usefulness for purposes of edification (14:3–4).

Yet, one circumstance presented a possibility for the tongues speaker to equal the prophet in value, and that came when interpretation accompanied his tongues message. In this manner, his foreign utterance could become intelligible, and therefore, profitable for edification and on an equal plane with prophecy. The "mysteries" (v. 2) spoken in tongues could become palpable to the listeners. When that happened, the church experienced edification, and tongues in a Christian meeting became legitimate (14:27). When no interpretation could follow, however, the only course for the tongues speaker in the church was to keep silent (14:28). The deciding factor for Paul at all times was, "Will the church be edified?" If the answer was yes, a gift's exercise was proper and desirable.

It is this "exception" of verse 5, the necessity for interpretation to accompany tongues, that the writer develops next.

B. EDIFICATION THROUGH TONGUES: CONDITIONAL (14:6–19)

1. THE PROFITLESS USE: WITHOUT INTERPRETATION (14:6–12)

6 But now, brethren, if I come to you speaking in tongues, what shall I profit you, unless I speak to you either by way of revelation or of knowledge or of prophecy or of teaching?

7 Yet even lifeless things, either flute or harp, in producing a sound, if they do not produce a distinction in the tones, how will it be known what is played on the flute or on the harp?

8 For if the bugle produces an indistinct sound, who will prepare himself for battle?

9 So also you, unless you utter by the tongue speech that is clear, how will it be known what is spoken? For you will be speaking into the air.

10 There are, perhaps, a great many kinds of languages in the world, and no kind is without meaning.

11 If then I do not know the meaning of the language, I shall be to the one who speaks a barbarian, and the one who speaks will be a barbarian to me.

12 So also you, since you are zealous of spiritual gifts, seek to abound for the edification of the church.

14:6—Profitless tongues. Paul draws a highly significant lesson in verse 6 from his own experience in effective teaching. His readers rightly expected a personal visit from the apostle to bring their local church considerable edification. Yet, the first part of the verse suggests a hypothetical visit that would be utterly fruitless, one in which he would come to them speaking only with tongues. Even one of apostolic rank speaking with tongues could not edify Christians. The Corinthians could accept that principle only with great difficulty, for they valued the gift independently, without applying the test of edification. For that reason, Paul softens the sixth verse, a word of indirect rebuke, with his term of endearment, "brethren."

The profit of tongues in building up Christians was dependent solely upon the presence of its companion gift, interpretation. That is the thrust of the "exception" clause at the end of verse 5.[6] When interpreted into a familiar language, the "mysteries" (14:2) of the tongues utterance produced understandable revelation, knowledge, prophesying, and doctrine. It was only through making the mysteries understandable that Paul felt his coming with a tongues message could profit the church. An overlap existed, therefore, between interpretation on the one hand and the gifts of wisdom, knowledge, prophecy, and teaching on the other. In fact, the gift of interpretation was a practical equivalent of prophecy and teaching. The only difference was its dependence upon a previous tongues speech (cf. Acts 19:6).

Of the four parallel terms in verse 6b, the first two were inward in nature, "revelation" being connected with the word of wisdom and "knowledge" with the word of knowledge. The last two were outward, the "prophecy" based on a "revelation" received and the "teaching" finding its basis in the divinely imparted "knowledge." The richness of the interpretive gift is therefore apparent, in spite of its secondary character as dependent on tongues. Here and here alone was the key to benefit if tongues were to be productive in a setting where the Corinthians insisted on using them. Without interpretation, a glossolalist—even Paul himself—accomplished nothing constructive for the church.

14:7—Futility of indistinct musical sounds. Verse 7 embarks upon a series of illustrations that graphically portray disadvantages of uninterpreted tongues. First of all, the writer compares them with two musical instruments, a wind instrument—a "flute"—and a stringed instrument—a "harp." The two were the most common instruments at banquets, funerals, and religious ceremonies of the day. Those soulless (i.e., "lifeless things," v. 7), inanimate instruments were in most cases known for beautiful music and the moods of joy and sorrow created by them. Another use was possible, however, one that made no distinction in tone and rhythm. Sounds might come, but the listener would hear no recognizable melody and so would be at a loss to react to what was played on either instrument. Consequently, no benefit was forthcoming. The analogy of the situation to uninterpreted tongues is obvious.

14:8—Futility of a vague trumpet signal. To confirm the indecisive outcome of using musical instruments in an indistinct way, verse 8 provides a second and stronger illustration. The military trumpet was the loudest and clearest of all musical sounds, but the same limitation pertains to it as to the flute and harp. When rendering a straightforward signal, the trumpet dictates a clear meaning and course of action. Yet, no soldier, however alert, will make battle preparations in response to confusing or indefinite blasts. The same futility prevailed with uninterpreted tongues, as verse 9 goes on to state explicitly.

14:9—Corresponding futility of an uninterpreted tongue. The Corinthians needed to apply the principle just illustrated in their own circumstances, as "so also you" (v. 9) shows. The gift of tongues could be just as unsuccessful at communicating as a meaningless flute, harp, or trumpet.[7] A tongues message was rendered "clear" when accompanied by interpretation, but it remained unintelligible without translation. It is with regard to the last instance that the writer asks, "How will it be known what is spoken?" (v. 9). The only conceivable answer is that it cannot be known. Without doubt, "what is spoken" will not be understandable at all. Here is a practice comparable to "speaking into the air" (v. 9). With no human ear attuned to a given language form, the only possible receptor is the atmosphere surrounding the speaker. That graphically portrays the utter uselessness of the Corinthian glossolalists who were not careful to provide for an interpretation of their messages. They had no audience except the air they breathed.

14:10—Intrinsic meaning of the world's languages. Having made an effective point about the uselessness of tongues without interpretation (vv. 6–9), a reader might expect Paul to turn to a new phase of the subject. He does not, however. As though fearful that somehow he had not made the lesson clear enough, he picks up at verse 10 the same line of thought and proceeds to illustrate it further (vv. 10–11) before applying the principle a second time (v. 12). Paul's zeal in pursuing the need further is intense, highlighting the matter's importance. It is imperative that Christians understand the necessity for communicating an intelligible message. Without intelligibility no edification can result.

Verse 10 lays the foundation for an illustration culminated in verse 11. It looks at the vast number of languages spoken throughout the world: "There are, perhaps, a great many kinds of languages in the world." "Kinds of languages" is equivalent to "different languages."[8] Paul does not specify an exact number. He did not know, nor has anyone yet discovered, the precise total of languages spoken in the world. But all agree the number is very great.

The last half of verse 10 adds the obvious truth that none of the languages is "without meaning." No language was, or is, inarticulate. Every language has an essence that makes it an effective medium of communication. Otherwise it would not be a language.

14:11—Frustration of foreignness. Continuing the illustration begun in verse 10, verse 11 envisions a situation where a language's meaning is unintelligible to a listener because he has not experienced that linguistic orientation. Verse

10 has established that no language is unintelligible in itself. Unintelligibility results from foreignness, not from a deficiency in the language. The problem is with the hearer, not the speaker.

By injecting himself into the picture once again (v. 11), Paul portrays a condition under which he did not know "the meaning of the language." From his perspective, this speaker was a "barbarian," or "foreigner" as the word denotes in a more modern sense. Reciprocally, as the speaker perceived that Paul did not grasp the meaning of his words, Paul became a foreigner to him.

"Barbarians" was a general designation for those of the first-century world who were ignorant of the Greek language. The city of Corinth abounded with such visitors. Thus, the illustration was full of meaning for the city's residents. Most of them doubtless were familiar with the frustration of encountering another intelligent person with whom it was impossible to converse. Visitors from other linguistic backgrounds could not comprehend the Corinthian speech any more than the Corinthians understood theirs.

Paul's plea through this illustration was for the exclusion of such barriers from their public meetings. Though the gift of tongues differed in origin from the languages of verses 10-11, the resultant problem was the same—an inability to communicate efficiently and intelligently with a listener who had no knowledge of the language used. No spiritual ministry was successful with such a limitation. No edification resulted.

14:12—An enlightened zeal for spiritual gifts. "So also you" (the same Greek expression as in v. 9) leads into a second application. A principle in the case just cited (v. 11) corresponds to a problem in their public meetings. In essence verse 12 says, "Since distinct language is necessary to being understood, be careful to choose spiritual gifts that make your speeches intelligible to the rest of the church. Otherwise, you will be like foreigners, unable to communicate with one another."

The verse does not fault the Corinthians for being "zealots of spirits" (the literal meaning of "zealous of spiritual gifts," v. 12). "Zealots" represents the same root word as "earnestly desire" in 12:31 and "desire earnestly" in 14:1 and 14:39. "Spirits" refers to diverse manifestations of the Holy Spirit through the channel of spiritual gifts (cf. the same word used the same way in 14:2, 32). A zeal for spiritual gifts is commendable, and Christians who have little or no interest in spiritual abilities should match the fervency of these Corinthians.

What the Corinthians lacked was application of this zeal toward the right purpose: "seek to abound for the edification of the church" (v. 12). They needed diligence in using their gifts more purposefully to enhance the church's growth, not their own personal growth (cf. 14:4a). It is the course of love not to seek its own, but the good of another (1 Cor. 10:24; 13:5). With a motivation such as this—one completely devoid of selfish interests and totally committed to benefiting others—problems of rivalry and disorder would soon disappear.

When Christians of any generation have been able to take their eyes off themselves and look to the needs of the rest of Christ's body, they have witnessed remarkably rapid growth of the body. When unselfish devotion prevails, the lost are won and Christians are strengthened. Such evidence of love is an unmistakable badge of Christ's follower, and it inevitably results in wholesome fruit. "By this all men will know that you are My disciples, if you have love for one another" (John 13:35).

The point made repeatedly by example and illustration in verses 6–12 is the ineffectiveness of tongues without interpretation. The paragraph has concluded by recommending a general course of action that will correct this problem.

2. THE PROFITABLE USE: WITH INTERPRETATION (14:13–19)

13 Therefore let one who speaks in a tongue pray that he may interpret.

14 For if I pray in a tongue, my spirit prays, but my mind is unfruitful.

15 What is the outcome then? I shall pray with the spirit and I shall pray with the mind also; I shall sing with the spirit and I shall sing with the mind also.

16 Otherwise if you bless in the spirit only, how will the one who fills the place of the ungifted say the "Amen" at your giving of thanks, since he does not know what you are saying?

17 For you are giving thanks well enough, but the other man is not edified.

18 I thank God, I speak in tongues more than you all;

19 however, in the church I desire to speak five words with my mind, that I may instruct others also, rather than ten thousand words in a tongue.

14:13—Interpretation the goal. Paul next applies the general purpose of edifying the church (v. 12) specifically to a well-known practice in Corinth, praying with a tongue.[9] It was possible for a person to speak with tongues publicly and still benefit the church if he did so solely for the sake of the interpretation that would result. A guided zeal for using the gift demanded that its use be with interpretation as the objective. Stated negatively, the tongues speaker could not with propriety embark upon a tongues prayer unless assured in advance that an interpretation would follow.[10] This is also the clear directive of 14:27. The tongues prayer was not to be the end in view, in other words. The goal was rather the interpreted prayer that would result. That and only that would bring benefit to the church (cf. 14:12) because through this process tongues would convert into prophecy or teaching.

That the prayer of verse 13 is a tongues prayer and not a prayer intelligible to the listeners is a necessary conclusion. A conscious prayer for the gift of interpretation, or any gift for that matter, would contravene the divine prerogative of determining who is to receive what gift (cf. 1 Cor. 12:11, 18). Making verse 13 a conscious prayer rather than one in tongues would also run counter to the remainder of the paragraph beginning in verse 14, where prayer with a tongue is the predominant thought. Were verse 13 to be taken as a conscious request for the gift of interpretation, it would loom as a possible contradiction to the directive of verse 28 as well. In that last portion, the absence of an interpreter is a call to silence, not one to seek an additional gift. With no interpreter present, a tongues message was automatically not permissible in public worship.

It is far more harmonious with the preceding verses as well as the verses to follow, therefore, to understand "pray that he may interpret" in verse 13 in the sense of "pray with a tongue in order to generate an interpretation of that prayer." In other words, the only justification for uttering a tongues prayer in a Christian assembly was the interpretation that would result from it.[11] The translated prayer was the end product sought, and the tongues prayer was only a means to that end. The tongues speaker's settled aim was to produce a body of interpretation that would issue from his prayer in a tongue; that interpreted data would in turn build up the church. Such is the outlook throughout chapter 14 (cf. 14:5, 28).

It is this means of deriving benefit for church edification based on the gift of interpretation, as suggested in verse 13, that is the unifying thought of verses 14–19.

14:14—Fruitlessness of tongues prayer without interpretation. In explaining why the speaker in tongues should pray for the sake of the resultant interpretation, verse 14 notes that a tongues prayer without interpretation was ineffective in producing benefit in the lives of others. Paul once again used himself as an example of the principle taught. He continues as the prominent figure throughout the section (cf. vv. 14–15, 18–19).

In verse 14, his example is hypothetical and negative. "What if I were to pray in a tongue only, and not follow my prayer with an interpretation?" he seems to ask. The result would have been a praying spirit but an unfruitful understanding. It is uncertain what Paul meant by "my spirit" and "my mind" (v. 14), but the following commends itself as most plausible.[12] When Paul wrote "my spirit," he was picking up the same meaning for the "spirit" as he has used in 14:12. It was his "spirit-manifestation," or "spiritual gift." The general meaning of "spirits," or "spiritual gifts," in verse 12 narrows down to one specific gift, the gift of tongues, in the expression "my spirit" in verse 14. This latent spiritual ability possessed by the apostle was in action whenever he uttered a tongues prayer.

Yet, the tongues ability was only part of his spiritual equipment. He refers to another part by "my mind." Here is a spiritual gift that lay dormant as long as the tongues were uninterpreted. The "mind" is another way of referring to the gift of interpretation, which is so prominent beginning at verse 5, but is especially important in the immediately preceding verse (v. 13).[13] The only way to bear fruit in the lives of others is to communicate with them through their intellects. That was possible by following up a tongues utterance with a translation into the listeners' native languages. If the sequel gift remained inoperative, only one verdict was possible: "unfruitful." For Paul to refer to the interpretive gift as "his mind" is not surprising in light of his preference for spiritual gifts that catered to the mind (1 Cor. 12:8, 28). As far as he was concerned, nothing had been accomplished, spiritually speaking, until listeners had assimilated data via the intellect (1 Cor. 14:19). Such a transaction from mind to mind was possible in conjunction with tongues only through the medium of interpretation.

When Paul passes the verdict "unfruitful," he has reference not to the speaker but to the listeners.[14] The speaker's understanding produced no fruit in others because it did not communicate anything comprehensible to them. Benefit to others is the overriding criterion throughout chapter 14. This is especially so in the immediate section (vv. 12, 16–17, 19). To bring profit and edification to the rest of the church is the ultimate objective of all spiritual gifts (12:7; 14:5–6, 26, 31). That is why verse 14 represents an unsatisfactory state of affairs. The church did not receive benefit in such a situation.

14:15—Both tongues and interpretation the answer. Continuing with himself as an example in verse 15, Paul asserts his own determination never to allow his tongues prayer or song to fall on unappreciative ears. Because of the unfruitfulness of isolated tongues (v. 14), he had made up his mind never to transmit a message without assuring it would be understood by the recipients.

The writer's choice of prayer and singing shows that public worship is still in view, as it has been since 1 Corinthians 11:2. The two activities were prominent in Christian public worship from earliest times. Since Paul personally possessed the gift of interpretation, he could guarantee that, in his own case, any time he spoke a tongues message, its interpretation would follow if needed. "The mind," which in his own case was an indispensable counterpart to tongues, suitably represents the interpretive gift in view of the gift's capacity to formulate matters with the mind and communicate them to others (see n. 13). It was this unique ability that an interpreter possessed.

In this respect, interpretation differed from tongues. The tongues speaker did have a general and limited understanding of his own utterance (cf. 14:4).[15] Otherwise, he could not have distinguished a prayer of thanksgiving (14:16) from other kinds of prayer. Yet the glossolalist's understanding was limited. The interpreter, however, had a precise, detailed grasp of what the tongues speakers, either himself or some other, had said, and could communicate the substance of the message effectively to whatever listeners were present. Paul was determined in his own practice to be content with no less than a combination of the two gifts. That was the only profitable use of tongues among Christians.

14:16—Exclusion of the ungifted by noninterpretation. The "otherwise" of verse 16 is an abbreviation for, "If you do not pray and sing with the mind as well as with the spirit" (cf. v. 15). By this means, verse 16 returns to the same general case as set forth in verse 14. A tongues message came to the congregation without benefit of a subsequent interpretation. In verse 16, Paul drops his personal example and addresses an unspecified individual. In addition, a "blessing" (emphasizing the element of praise) or "giving of thanks" (emphasizing the content of thankful prayer) in verse 16 replaces the more general prayer of verse 14.

Verse 16 describes the listener as "the one who fills the place of the ungifted." By careful comparison of this verse with verses 23–24 below, this "ungifted" person must be anyone ignorant of the language used.[16] Here was a Christian seated in a public worship service of his local church, hearing sounds that proceeded from a speaker's lips, but unable to connect any meaning with those sounds because he himself was ungifted in interpreting, and no other person was performing that function for him. The nature of the proceedings forced the person into the role of an *idiōtēs* (note a relationship to the English word "idiot"), an unlearned or ungifted one. He "filled the place" (v. 16) or "played the part" of that kind of individual, being compelled to do so by the speaker's insistence on using a language he did not understand.

Placed at such a disadvantage, the listener was at a complete loss to affirm his agreement with and concurrence in the speaker's word of thanksgiving. The "amen," as in earlier Jewish worship, became in Christian worship also a means for adding "so let it be" to the word spoken by another party. It was a vocal approbation of a statement just made and indicated the listener's affirmation that those were his sentiments, too. Yet, such vocal concord was impossible when one uttered his thanksgiving in a foreign tongue. "He does not know what you are saying" (v. 16) precluded acknowledged agreement with the speaker.

Paul's avowed purpose was never to be involved in that kind of situation. He recommended the same restraint as the only sane course for his readers to follow. Blind emotional worship was contrary to his goals, and remains contrary to the will of God as revealed in His written Word.

14:17—Benefit restricted to self. The text once again guards against completely robbing tongues of their significance. Benefit comes to the user of any of God's gifts, and coming from the Holy Spirit, tongues could never be called valueless. The question is: Who receives the value (cf. v. 4)? Directing the gift toward improper goals brings an associated loss that cancels the value for everyone.

The first half of verse 17 singles out the tongues speaker and in effect says of him, "You, considering yourself alone, give thanks in a beautiful manner. In taking God's gift and deriving profit from it for yourself, you have performed an artistic act." An element of irony or sarcasm resides in the "well enough." It pictures an elegant production appreciated in full by the artist himself, but falling upon stone-deaf ears that are unable to grasp even the most basic elements of the work's comeliness. A vast gulf separated the profit derived by the speaker from the condition forced upon the listener. With the latter, not even the faintest glimmer of edification materialized. "The other man" (v. 17), "the one who fills the place of the ungifted" (v. 16), never received edification through a speaker he did not understand.

14:18—Legitimacy of tongues. Returning to his own experience, Paul, in verses 18–19, confirms what he has been saying about the public use of tongues among believers. Initially, in verse 18, he counters possible opposition that might claim his animus against tongues grew out of personal jealousy over not having the gift himself. Following up the hint of 13:1 and the stronger implication of 14:6, 14, and 15, he now explicitly states that he personally possessed the gift. In fact, he exercised the gift to a greater degree than the Corinthians themselves, and out of that background he derived his evaluation of it.[17]

When Paul wrote in verse 18, "I thank God," he maintained a continuity with verses 16–17 where thanksgiving comes in the form of tongues utterances. In other words, Paul also utilized tongues prayers for thanksgiving.[18] He by no means had disdain for the gift. Yet, this was not the only form his tongues utterances took, for he goes on in the verse to use a general expression covering all forms when he says, "I speak in tongues." He did not limit his tongues messages to prayers of thanksgiving. They came in other forms as well. He used this gift in many connections, to a greater degree than even the Corinthians, who placed such a premium on the gift.

What was this more frequent use by Paul? Certainly it was not in Christian meetings, as verse 23 will point out. Nor was it in private, for this section of 1 Corinthians (chaps. 11–14) has to do with public matters. Furthermore, it is the nature of spiritual gifts that they render benefit to persons other than the one exercising the gift (1 Cor. 12:7, 25; 13:5–6; 14:12, 19, 26). In light of that emphasis, Paul would hardly have set himself up as an example of claimed superiority on the basis of his own selfish use of one of the gifts. That was the very thing he was combating among the Corinthians. The private use of something intended for others is certainly nothing to boast about. Tongues' purpose was a public one, as 14:20–25 will shortly show (especially, v. 22).

It must, then, be in connection with a public ministry of some kind that Paul found occasion to exercise his own deep endowment of tongues. As the missionary apostle to the Gentiles, he frequently encountered new linguistic groups in his travels. Authenticating signs accompanied the ministry of one such as he (Rom. 15:18–19; 2 Cor. 12:12), and tongues was one of the signs. Upon hearing a foreigner speak their own language without ever studying it, the listeners would perceive the apostle's miraculous demonstration and be ready to give attention to his divinely verified presentation of the gospel (cf. Acts 2:1–13). It was for this purpose that Paul found ample room, even an indispensable place, for tongues. He used the gift extensively in this way (1 Cor. 14:22). That, however, was far different from the Corinthian habit of exhibiting their linguistic talents among themselves as a source of selfish satisfaction.

14:19—Greatest effectiveness in the church. As opposed to his extensive use of tongues in other kinds of public gatherings, Paul's strong preference when addressing a Christian assemblage was to speak intelligibly to his listeners.[19] This he could do only by using their native language.

Two conflicting ways of public ministry stand side by side in verse 19: "five words with my mind" and "ten thousand words in a tongue." A superficial response to these two would be that the latter is of much greater value because of the extremely large number of words ("ten thousand") in that case, compared to the few ("five") in the other. After all, what can one say in just five words? Nevertheless, the opposite is true. Five comprehensible words are far superior to ten thousand in a language foreign to the listeners.

As it is throughout the paragraph, beginning at verse 13 when he uses "my mind" (cf. vv. 14–15), Paul's reference is still to the gift of interpretation when he uses "my mind" in verse 19.[20] He gave constant attention in public ministry to speaking in a realm where his listeners' intelligence was operative. Interpretation was the only means by which he could do this when exercising tongues. In his estimation, the accompanying translation was of infinitely greater value, no matter how limited its length, than a tongues message of great length.

The difference between the two approaches lay in the goals sought. "That I may instruct others also" points out the route to edification of the church. Instruction was and is of prime importance in building Christian lives. Without it, spiritual anemia results, as was happening in Corinth (1 Cor. 3:1–4). With it, the body of Christ constantly takes strides in its growth to maturity. The great apostle was never interested in the momentary sensation. Through insight given him by the Holy Spirit, he understood clearly that the only real progress is made over long periods through a process of patient instruction. The gift of tongues was usable toward that end, but only when combined with the gift of interpretation.

C. Proper Places for Tongues and Prophecy (14:20–25)

20 Brethren, do not be children in your thinking; yet in evil be babes, but in your thinking be mature.

21 In the Law it is written, "BY MEN OF STRANGE TONGUES AND BY THE LIPS OF STRANGERS I WILL SPEAK TO THESE PEOPLE, AND EVEN SO THEY WILL NOT LISTEN TO ME," says the Lord.

22 So then tongues are for a sign, not to those who believe, but to unbelievers; but prophecy is for a sign, not to unbelievers, but to those who believe.

23 If therefore the whole church should assemble together and all speak in tongues, and ungifted men or unbelievers enter, will they not say that you are mad?

24 But if all prophesy, and an unbeliever or an ungifted man enters, he is convicted by all, he is called to account by all;

25 the secrets of his heart are disclosed; and so he will fall on his face and worship God, declaring that God is certainly among you.

Up to this point in chapter 14, the writer has laid down guidelines showing what will and will not bring edification. In brief, sounds made up of intelligible speech that triggered the mind and brought the Word of God to the listener in a form digestible to the understanding were beneficial to the church, but sounds that were unfamiliar to the listener could appeal only to the emotions and resulted in no profit to the congregation. At verse 20, the inspired writer shifts the tempo of his discussion somewhat, seizing upon a key element in verse 19 and developing it in more detail. The words "in the church" (v. 19) allude to location or kind of audience, a feature of crucial importance in appropriating the chief values of tongues and prophecy. Verses 20–25 settle the issue of where and with whom to use tongues and prophecy.

14:20—Childhood and adulthood in malice and understanding. With "brethren" tenderly preparing the way once again, verse 20 turns to address the readers directly in commands that are pregnant with stinging implications. Here were people who prided themselves in their intelligence. Telling them they were still children in understanding was bound to produce a strained relationship. Yet, that did not deter Paul from lovingly asserting that they had not come to understand the first elements about the primary purpose of tongues.

"Do not be children in your thinking" (v. 20) is more precisely, "stop being children in understanding." The Corinthians had already become guilty of childishness by their undue attention to the tongues gift in church. Their craving for what was amusing rather than useful, for the glittering and spectacular rather than the solid, was a token of their shallow understanding. The disposition that is pleased with trifles and puts a false estimate upon them has not begun to comprehend the true essence of spiritual progress. Termination of such a state of affairs was the apostle's clear mandate.

Whereas a childlike quality is reprehensible in using the mind, it is perfectly legitimate and even strongly preferable in the sphere of moral evil: "yet in evil be babes" (v. 20). "Babes" in verse 20 represents a different word from "children" and denotes an even lower age than the first. Infancy rather than childhood in malice or maliciousness is worth cultivating. No experience or development in an evil disposition is desirable. Christian growth proceeds at a much healthier pace without it. The middle portion of verse 20 echoes an earlier command of Paul to these people that they purge themselves of "the leaven of malice" (1 Cor. 5:8). They had been maturing where they should not have been (i.e., "in malice") and not maturing where they should have been (i.e., "in understanding").

By pitting the adulthood stage against childhood, Paul reverts once again to one of his favorite comparisons (cf. 1 Cor. 2:6 and 3:1; 13:10–11; Eph. 4:13–14). A "grown-up" use of the intelligence in place of a childish use is what he advocates: "In your thinking be mature" (v. 20). Though it is perfectly proper to remain an infant in evil moral attitudes, it is wholesome to advance as quickly as possible to manhood in matters of the mind. This the Corinthians had failed to do, and one of the epistle's primary purposes was to encourage them to overcome that defect. Making the necessary progress meant they needed to learn certain basic purposes of the tongues gift.

14:21—Old Testament counterpart of tongues. To understand tongues' basic nature requires an understanding of God's dealings more broadly. The Old Testament prophet Isaiah ("Law," v. 21, denoting the whole Old Testament) had quoted the Lord centuries earlier concerning His handling of Israel during one of the nation's rebellions. The particular occurrence involved God's speaking "By men of strange tongues and by the lips of strangers" (v. 21 with Isa. 28:11). The "foreign tongues" and "stammering-lipped" people in Isaiah were the Assyrian conquerors, and the "tongues," therefore, refers to the language of these foreigners. The foreignness of the Assyrian tongue is analogous to the gift of tongues, of which the Corinthians had become so fond, though in their case the foreign language had not been learned by natural processes.[21]

Because of the Israelites' rebelliousness, God found it necessary to adopt an extraordinary means of communication. He had previously sought in vain to bring them back through the prophets' words. Had they responded, God would never have needed to use the strange tongues. But Israel responded to the message of Isaiah and others by saying, in effect, "We are not children who require such elementary teaching" (Isa. 28:9–10), thus rejecting the prophets' message of repentance. So God did something more complex, something they could not understand, by sending them foreign-speaking masters (Isa. 28:11–12).

Paul's main reason for introducing the historical analogy lies in the quotation's last line: "and even so they will not listen to me" (14:21). Another rendering is, "and not even thus will they listen to me." The emphasis is on "not even thus" because Paul wants to show the extraordinary character of a foreign-language gift and the one who uses it.[22] The statement views the Assyrians as God's spokesmen whom He validated as such in a very special way. He adopted a special means to attract listeners who would not respond to those speaking their own language. Tongues in Isaiah's day were a proof of divine presence and activity. The provocative nature of this sign was designed to arrest attention and identify God's spokesmen.

The same characteristic belongs to tongues, as verse 22 will show.

14:22—Purposes of tongues and prophecy. To discern where tongues and prophecy were appropriate required a clear comprehension of the purpose of each. It is on the note of purpose that the apostle climaxes his citation of Isaiah 28:11–12 by stating specifically the purposes and realms of these two gifts.

Paul derives his conclusion from the last line of the Isaiah quotation (v. 21), first of all pointing to the purpose of the tongues gift: "Tongues are for a sign" (v. 22). That is obviously not an elaboration upon the gift's failure, as was the use of strange tongues in Israel's history, but a presentation of the gift's constructive objectives (see n. 22). Foreign languages supernaturally spoken were an evidence of divine presence and activity, designed to attract those who were estranged. It was so with the Assyrian language in Isaiah's day; it was likewise true with the gift of tongues in Paul's day.

"Sign" translates the Greek word *sēmeion*. The word's predominant use throughout the New Testament is to designate a miracle with an ethical purpose. A *sēmeion* was, as it were, a "fingerpost" of God, an authenticating (Rom. 4:11; 2 Thess. 3:17) and in most cases miraculous (Acts 2:19, 22; 14:3; Rom. 15:19; 1 Cor. 1:22; 2 Cor. 12:12) pointer. In the bulk of instances it pointed to God, but on rare occasion it indicates the enemy of God (2 Thess. 2:9). As was true with the other sign gifts, tongues had an evidential value (cf. 1 Cor. 12:9–10). Certain critical phases in God's program down through history have required special evidence, and the transitional phase represented by the period of Christ and His apostles was most certainly one of these. Those who had been steeped in Judaism all their lives needed elements of tangible proof that the new movement founded by Jesus Christ was genuinely of God. Those whose background was exclusively heathen also needed that kind of help. The God of the Old Testament was completely strange to them, as was the new message brought by missionaries such as Paul. Divinely produced credentials were certainly in order, for example, tongues and the other sign gifts.

But for whom were these signs intended? "Not to those who believe, but to unbelievers," Paul said (v. 22, see n. 22). Those who had already converted to Christianity were not the target of these signs, for they needed no proof of the message's divine source. They were already convinced of the veracity of the message. Yet, the Corinthians insisted on giving major attention to one particular sign gift in their public meetings. That was wrong; it was immaturity on their part (cf. v. 20). The mature mind realized the proper place for tongues was among unbelievers to play a confirmatory part in their conversion experience. This certainly was the use of tongues in Acts 2:1–13. Acts 10:44–48 and 19:1–7 also involved unbelievers, though in a slightly different way. In the latter two cases, though the new converts themselves became channels for the tongues gift, the net result was still evidential. A unique linguistic ability was proof to them and others present that God's seal of approval rested upon the message given.

In contrast to tongues, "prophecy" was for a different constituency, "those who believe" rather than "unbelievers" (v. 22). It is the thrust of chapter 14 to demonstrate this. Prophecy produced edification among Christians; tongues did not. The principal end of prophecy was instruction, the very thing needed by those already converted. For nonbelievers, however, instruction was not the prime need. Conversion through being persuaded to trust Christ was necessary first. An evidential sign such as tongues rather than prophecy facilitated that. The distinction was of utmost importance in knowing where to use each gift most effectively.

It is significant that the Greek text refrains from calling prophecy a sign (in the NASB, "for a sign" is in italics in v. 22b because of its absence from the Greek).[23] It might have done so since prophecy found a place among the sign gifts in 12:10, but it could not provide instant verification as did the other sign gifts. Furthermore, the dominating characteristic of prophecy was not its accrediting function but its content of instruction, exhortation, and comfort. That combination of characteristics made it more suitable for a Christian audience.

14:23—A tongues-dominated church gathering: sterile. An important key for understanding verse 23 in light of the principle just laid down (v. 22) lies in the nature of the audience. Here it is "the whole church . . . assembled together." The inappropriateness of devoting all or most of such a meeting to the gift of tongues was extreme, since the listeners were for the most part believers. Paul has just established that tongues were not for believers. To take the gift and use it thus was contrary to its primary purpose as an evangelistic tool (see n. 22). Even a visiting, ungifted unbeliever could judge that fact and pronounce the verdict, "You are mad" (v. 23).

Although Paul referred to a believing person as "ungifted" in verse 16, in verse 23, he designates unbelievers in the same way (see n. 16). The thing the two kinds of people had in common was their inability to receive any meaning from what was spoken. Conspicuous impropriety prevailed when adult persons behaved this way in the company of others (cf. v. 20), and even unbelieving outsiders could verify the impropriety. It was to the discredit of the believing group that they allowed such confusion to reign among them.

When explained in such a way, verse 23 is the natural conclusion about the state of affairs in Corinth in light of the principle of verse 22. What might appear to be a contradiction between the two verses, that is, that unbelievers are repelled by the gift of tongues (v. 23) and that tongues are a sign for unbelievers (v. 22), is hereby resolvable. Reconciliation of the two verses comes by identifying the place where unbelievers witnessed the gift in use. What might have been and often was an instrument in bringing them to conversion in a secular setting became an object of disdain when used improperly among those gathered for Christian worship. To Christians who let the gift get out of hand and become a showpiece, the unbeliever's verdict was, in essence, "You are out of your senses. You are carrying on a kind of conversation that no one around you understands" (v. 23). Yet, to the missionary who brought them the gospel in a non-Christian setting during the rapidly expanding era of first-century Christianity, their response was, "I see indisputable evidence that you have a special linguistic ability from God, and I am interested in hearing the message that God has given you to share with me" (cf. Acts 2:1–13).

14:24—A prophecy-dominated church meeting: fruitful. The effect of a Christian gathering upon a visiting unbeliever was the exact opposite, however, when all the speakers in the meeting utilized prophecy rather than tongues (v. 24). Instead of passing a negative judgment on the undignified proceedings, the "ungifted" visitor would understand the message of each prophet, which would then produce a "conviction" and thorough inner scrutiny ("called to account"). Of the two, the former, "he is convicted," represents the Holy Spirit's work in reproving or convicting the world of sin, righteousness, and judgment (John 16:8); the latter, "he is called to account," is the capability for accurately examining spiritual persons and things (1 Cor. 2:14–15). The inspired prophetic speakers were agents of the Holy Spirit in bringing the visiting unbelievers to a conviction of their sinful condition and putting them on trial to reveal the details of their state in the light of God's Word.

This is a far cry from the result reaped when the message of each speaker came in tongues (v. 23). That prophecy could have such a positive effect on unbelievers at first appears incompatible with the guideline of verse 22. Again, however, the location of the prophetic message—i.e., in the Christian assembly—explains how verse 24 coincides perfectly with the principle that prophecy is for "those who believe" (v. 22). The orderliness of the proceedings impressed the visitor, as well as the loving way Christians conducted themselves toward one another in an unselfish teaching of divine truth. In that atmosphere the Word of God thrived in their lives.

14:25—Illumination and conversion. A third step in the spiritual experience of exposing an unbeliever to a prophetic Christian meeting was the revealing of "the secrets of his heart" (v. 25; cf. the first two steps, "convicted" and "called to account" in v. 24). After conviction and a detailed investigation of his lost condition, his own conscience discovered the findings. Up to this point in the process, the inclinations of his inner life were unknown to anyone, including himself. But now he could see himself as he really was, as God saw him.

On the basis of this new discovery—in fact, through the process of it—he was now ready to "fall on his face" and "worship God" (v. 25). Falling upon one's face was symbolic of self-condemnation and self-abhorrence. It was a complete renunciation of dependence upon human righteousness and strength and a humbling of the soul before God. That was and is an absolute prerequisite before coming to Jesus Christ for reconciliation (cf. Luke 17:16; 18:13). Verse 25 speaks of the reconciliation in terms of "worship[ing] God." Here is the soul's approach to favor and fellowship with God. Because of what the listener had heard from the prophet's lips, he was ready to become a Christian.

Yet, his spiritual development did not stop there. He would go on to report "that God is certainly among you" (v. 25) to all, a far cry from his saying "you are mad" (v. 23). So vital was this in his own experience that he could not keep it to himself (cf. Rom. 10:10). God's dwelling among His people when thus assembled locally would become a well-known fact. It was evident to all that this was His spiritual temple (cf. 1 Cor. 3:16) when orderliness prevailed. The testimony of a meeting composed of prophetic utterances was therefore the diametrical opposite of the testimony issuing from a tongues meeting (cf. v. 23).

Verses 24–25 set forth an excellent example for Christian worship in all subsequent generations. Indispensable elements include a loving and self-giving attitude that is genuinely interested in the spiritual progress of the rest and a message based squarely on the written revelation of the Old and New Testaments and understandable to the listeners. These are ideal not only for inducing edification of those who are already Christians but also for reaching the lost.

D. Proper Procedures with Tongues And Prophecy (14:26–33a)

Verses 1–25 of 1 Corinthians 14 have drawn together a number of theoretical principles based largely on hypothetical situations, illustrations, and personal examples. The opening "what is the outcome then" of verse 26 draws these principles together and applies them generally to the circumstances at hand (v. 26). The section then applies the principles to tongues (vv. 27–28) and prophecy (vv. 29–33a) in more detail.

1. General: Edification, Not Confusion (14:26)

26 What is the outcome then, brethren? When you assemble, each one has a psalm, has a teaching, has a revelation, has a tongue, has an interpretation. Let all things be done for edification.

14:26—*Edification, not confusion.* The affectionate "brethren" in verse 26 again signals upcoming words of sternness (cf. 12:1; 14:6, 20). A brief but vivid picture of a typical Corinthian meeting occupies most of the verse. On any given occasion these Christians arrived for worship with a predetermination to have a speaking part on the program for the day. It may have been something prepared in advance, as in the case of "a teaching" (v. 26) or something improvised on the spur of the moment, such as "a tongue" (v. 26). Whether it was something given through an advance working of the Spirit or the product of His simultaneous working, each spokesman appeared with the eager purpose of exercising his own gift. The inevitable consequence was a display of competition and rivalry in the church meeting.

The accounts of Moses and Miriam (Exodus 15); Balaam (Numbers 23–24); Deborah (Judges 5); and Mary, Zacharias, and Simeon (Luke 1–2) provide biblical illustrations of improvised psalms (v. 26). Christians used psalms to exhort and encourage one another (cf. Eph. 5:19–20; Col. 3:16). Under normal circumstances they were not tongues utterances but words spoken in a language native to the listeners, as evidenced by the separate mention of "a tongue" later in verse 26. As an avenue of exhortation (cf. Rom. 12:8), a psalm properly given was beneficial in building up a congregation. But when used in a disorderly manner, as was apparently the case in Corinth, it was just another confusing distraction.

The gift of teaching also found its place among the ambitions represented at Corinth. To have "a teaching" (v. 26) means that some had doctrines or teachings they felt needed expounding before the whole church. Paul never underestimated the importance of clear and exact instruction, as the surrounding verses show (14:19, 31). Yet, even this important activity was susceptible to degeneration if performed in a disorderly way.

The "revelation" is such as was given to prophets (14:30). It was the Holy Spirit's unveiling of a mystery and incorporates an implementation of the word of wisdom (1 Cor. 2:6–7; 12:8; 13:2). The gift involved immediate inspiration of a prophet. Such revelations were of extreme importance, more important than "teaching" or "doctrine." Correct teaching and doctrine found their basis in revelation given during the foundational days of Christianity. Yet, despite their importance, even those could be a detriment in a Christian meeting if they contributed to chaos, rivalry, and competition. Restrictions upon prophets pertained also to "revelations" (vv. 29–32).

"A tongue" in verse 26 is obviously the gift so prominent throughout these three chapters. The presence and use of the gift among the Corinthians surfaces repeatedly in the context. Yet, this does not imply that Paul endorsed the manner in which they used it. On the contrary, he strongly disapproved of the place (14:23) and manner (14:27–28) they had adopted for it. Once again, the tongues gift along with its companion, interpretation, comes last in a list of gifts. This is the fourth time the writer has selected this order, a feature indicative of its lower appraisal (cf. 12:8–10, 28, 29–30).

The counterpart to tongues, "interpretation," closes the series of possibilities. In light of interpretation's strategic importance (vv. 6–19), it is somewhat surprising to find it, too, as a possible instrument for creating confusion. Yet, the worthwhileness of the gift was not the issue. The crux of the matter centered in the spirit behind the gift. If the translation came from a loving consideration for others—their rights and needs—then it could hardly fail to benefit. Nevertheless, the picture emerging in the present verse is one of selfishness and self-assertion. In such an atmosphere the inherent value of any spiritual gift disappeared (1 Cor. 13:1–3).

Individualism that drove separate members of Christ's body in different directions instead of toward a common goal needed to be replaced by a desire to edify others. That is the meaning of "Let all things be done for edification" (v. 26). This general rule serves as a guide for all gifts and all circumstances in a local gathering. Such a rule does not prohibit participation by any single member but regulates appointments to speak at a given meeting in light of the spiritual growth the remainder of the church might derive.

2. *Tongues Regulated (14:27–28)*

27 If any one speaks in a tongue, it should be by two or at the most three, and each in turn, and let one interpret;

28 but if there is no interpreter, let him keep silent in the church; and let him speak to himself and to God.

14:27—Procedures for using tongues. Verse 27 spells out specific guidelines for tongues dictated by considerations of edification. It fixes three regulatory principles.

1. The first limited the number of allowable glossolalists at one session. The ideal number was two, but an absolute maximum was three. This precaution prevented the gift from monopolizing the whole meeting and kept a reasonable balance between tongues and the other speaking gifts.
2. The second restriction regulated the order to be observed. At no time were two or more persons to speak simultaneously. No competition between speakers trying to outdo each other was allowable, but each in turn was to have his fair share of time.
3. The third regulation fixed the mode of tongues speech. It was always to be followed by an interpreter. One interpreter per session was the rule. The gifted interpreter could in some cases be one of the tongues speakers, but never were two or more interpreters to be active at the same gathering.

The detailed discussion of 14:1–25 lays the groundwork for the absolute necessity of an interpreter's presence to translate. No edification for the

Corinthians could occur when they did not understand the message. The limitation of not having more than one interpreter also had practical advantage. It was a safeguard against profitless discussion that might have usurped time from the more useful prophetic messages.

Verse 27, then, outlines the three conditions under which there could be a profitable use of the tongues in a Christian assembly. When they followed these to the letter, the readers could expect edification to result.

14:28—Tongues forbidden. Having pointed out three governing procedures that would ensure edification through the gift of tongues, the text in verse 28 turns to a condition where the third criterion was not enforced, that is, when no interpreter was present. Neither the speaker with tongues nor any other in attendance possessed the gift of interpretation in the case supposed. The tongues speaker had only one option, that of remaining silent. His tongues gift did not compel him to speak on every occasion. It was within the realm of human choice to refrain from utilizing this gift or any other gift, particularly so if considerations of love and edification required nonparticipation. The general principle, "Let all things be done for edification" (v. 26), dictated in this particular circumstance that tongues were not to be a part in the service because no edification would result (cf. 14:6–11).

The last half of verse 28 explains how the tongues speaker was to keep silent in church. The suggestion that "speak to himself and to God" deals with private activity is not plausible in a context devoted to public worship, which is the general theme of 11:2–14:40. Particularly, 14:28 itself is regulatory of activities in the church, not of those in private. The meaning of verse 28b is thus, "Let him keep silent in the church, and let him do this by means of speaking to himself and to God only."[24] This required the tongues speaker to meditate quietly on what his own mind could grasp of the tongues message that he might otherwise have given publicly—had an interpreter been present—thereby deriving for himself whatever edifying benefit he could. "Speaking to oneself and to God" was a proverbial expression for meditation. The guideline calls upon the would-be tongues speaker, out of consideration for the rest of the congregation, to engage in such a contemplative activity rather than speak up in the absence of an interpreter and do something that had no benefit whatever for anyone else in the audience. Paul has devoted extensive discussion earlier in the chapter to the fruitlessness of tongues apart from interpretation (vv. 6–11, 14, 16–17), and in verse 28, he is explicit in ruling out tongues under such conditions.

3. PROPHECY REGULATED (14:29–33A)

29 And let two or three prophets speak, and let the others pass judgment.

30 But if a revelation is made to another who is seated, let the first keep silent.

31 For you can all prophesy one by one, so that all may learn and all may be exhorted;

32 and the spirits of prophets are subject to prophets;

33a for God is not a God of confusion but of peace.

14:29—Number and testing of prophetic messages. Before verse 26 (cf. "revelation"), Paul gives almost no hint of the possibility of the abusive use of prophecy. Earlier he describes the gift only in glowing terms (14:1, 3–5, 24–25). Yet, even this high-ranking gift had to be under surveillance of the general guideline of verse 26: "Let all things be done for edification." For even prophecy was worthless apart from considerations of love (13:2). Thus, in verses 29–33a, he lays down governing principles for prophecy similar to those already considered for tongues. Verse 29 gives two principles.

1. The maximum number of prophets to speak at a single meeting was "two or three." The difference between this limitation and that for tongues (v. 27) is the absence of "at the most" from verse 29. In other words, Paul accepted three prophetic utterances more readily than he did three messages with tongues. Despite the slight difference, however, he still placed a definite limit on the number of speaking prophets at each service.

2. Prophecies were to be subjected to the judgment of discerning persons within the congregation before being validated and recommended for acceptance. In the absence of a written New Testament and a fully delineated body of doctrine, the gift of discernment (cf. 12:10) was a necessary counterpart to prophecy. Only that gift could supply a means of verification. Discernment was a necessary adjunct to prophecy, just as interpretation was to tongues.

"The others" (v. 29) who discerned were none other than the prophets themselves.[25] While one prophet spoke, the rest listened and ruled upon the source and accuracy of his message. From this it is evident that those who possessed the gift of prophecy also possessed the gift of discernment. They were the "others," the only ones qualified to judge prophetic utterance. No other means were available for checking the truthfulness of an alleged prophecy; that is, no authoritative written source existed with which to compare it besides the Old Testament. Thus, God provided gifted people with special insight to guard the church from being led astray during this period. To conduct a meeting without "discerners" present apparently excluded prophecy from the proceedings. Corinth seems to have been blessed with a good number of "prophet-discerners," but interpreters seem to have been relatively scarce.

14:30—When to terminate a prophetic message. A third principle regulatory of prophecy impinges upon the message's length. Verse 30 makes it compulsory for the initial speaker to stop when told of another prophet with a fresh revelation.[26] No one messenger, not even a prophet, was to dominate the entire session. Another prophet's receipt of fresh inspiration was an indication that the speaker was in danger of going beyond what had been revealed to him. Undelayed delivery of the new message took precedence over continuing the old. For that reason, the first speaker was obliged to terminate his message, recognizing that to go on would deprive the congregation of superior benefit from a new voice. No one prophet in a first-century congregation had a "corner" on all special revelations. It was a privilege and responsibility shared by numbers of persons in the congregation, and it was not permissible for any individual to consume the whole time.

14:31—Maximum learning and encouragement. Verse 31 stipulates specifically how the prophets' willingness to yield to one another would result in greater benefit to the church. When conditions were such that permitted all prophets to speak, the whole congregation, including the prophets themselves, received more instruction and encouragement.

"You can all" is the same as "you are all able" (v. 31). What was expected of the prophet in verse 30 was not an impossibility. It lay within his power to fulfill it. By following the prescribed procedure it was possible for "all" the prophets to participate at some time or another. All of them could not, of course, take part in a single meeting unless not more than three were present. That does not seem to have been true in Corinth, as this was a church with a good number of prophets. It was envisioned that all would have their chance over a period of time.

A fourth regulatory principle for prophecy appears in the expression "one by one" (v. 31). Just as with tongues (v. 27), two or more could never speak simultaneously. Decency and order (v. 40) were to prevail with this high-standing gift, just as with all gifts below it on the scale (cf. 12:28).

The last two *alls* in verse 31 encompass not just the prophets, but the whole congregation. The edification derived by the entire group lay in the areas of learning and exhortation, or comfort. The assembly's need of intellectual help was basic (cf. v. 19). Teaching was part of the prophetic gift and could meet this need. The will and emotions also benefited from prophecy. "Exhorted" (v. 31) represents a Greek word broad enough to include both the persuasive element and the aspect of encouragement to the troubled soul. It is derived from the same source as the word translated "exhortation" in 14:3. Through these channels, prophecy had the highest potential for edifying the whole church (v. 26; cf. v. 4).

14:32—Provision for containment. Verse 32 furnished further justification for expecting the first prophet to "keep silent" (v. 30). It lies in the prophet's capability of controlling his own gift. "Spirits" (v. 32) means the same as the identical Greek expression in 14:12, which translates the same word by "spiritual gifts." These are spirit-manifestations of the prophets (cf. also 12:10; 14:2, 14–15).[27] As a spirit-manifestation, prophecy could be used or not used in a given situation, according to the prophet's own determination. The ideal case cited was the one where love motivated the prophet with a desire to do what was best for the congregation. That meant in some cases putting an early end to his remarks to clear the way for another.

Heathen oracles did not have that kind of control (cf. 1 Cor. 12:2). Speakers felt compelled to go on speaking until the impulse left them. No true prophet of God could claim a prolonged hearing on that ground. No such compulsion existed whereby he lost control of himself and was unable to contain his inner urge to speak. Such lack of self-restraint was to be blamed on himself, not on his prophetic gift.

14:33a—The God of peace. Because of the nature of God, Paul can say what he has just said about the spirits of the prophets. God is not a God of commotion, but a God of peace (v. 33). The gifts from Him are, therefore, capable of being controlled. People who disturb the peace and order of the church service by insubordination or some other abuse are either deluded or impostors. They cannot trace their inspiration to God, for it can never be said that He is on the side of disorder and turbulence. He is the God of love and, as has already been noted, love "does not act unbecomingly" (1 Cor. 13:5).

The contrasting pictures presented by "confusion" and "peace" in verse 33 were relevant to the conditions and needs for the peace of the church in Corinth. Self-assertiveness and personal rivalry had resulted in a state of disorder and unsettlement. A whole series of disorderly acts brought about a chaotic state whenever they assembled for worship. The nature of God, however, demanded that these be replaced by harmonious acts producing a condition of peace. Only in this way could God's presence among them be evident (14:25b; cf. 14:40).

E. WOMEN IN WORSHIP (14:33B–36)

33b   as in all the churches of the saints.

34   Let the women keep silent in the churches; for they are not permitted to speak, but let them subject themselves, just as the Law also says.

35 And if they desire to learn anything, let them ask their own husbands at home; for it is improper for a woman to speak in church.

36 Was it from you that the word of God first went forth? Or has it come to you only?

At this point in his delineation of standards for spiritual gifts in worship, Paul turns to an aside that does not relate directly to spiritual gifts (vv. 33b–36). Worship is still in view, but Paul's thoughts are parenthetical here, not having to do with spiritual gifts exclusively.

Established criteria for orderly behavior by the charismatically endowed were not the only needs in Corinth. In this city as elsewhere, proper worship also involved observances based on distinctions between the two sexes. The writer, therefore, proceeds to speak about the proper conduct of women in worship services (vv. 33b–36).

14:33b—Universality of observance. A change in the NASB punctuation of verse 33 supplies a more plausible understanding. It is preferable to put a period instead of a comma after "peace," to begin a new sentence with "As in all the churches of the saints," and to place a comma instead of a period after "saints." A new sentence and a new paragraph thus begin in the middle of the verse.[28]

"As in all the churches of the saints" forewarns that the regulation appearing next was not one confined to Corinth. In whatever cities and locations groups had convened in the name of Christ to constitute local churches, this was standard practice in worship. Where Paul dealt with women's behavior earlier in 1 Corinthians, he also invoked a statement of universal ecclesiastical custom (1 Cor. 11:16). The role of women in disrupting Christian meetings may have never become an issue in all churches as it did in Corinth (though see 1 Tim. 2:11–15), but the principle still held true for the apostle wherever he went, according to his testimony of 14:33b.

14:34—Silence and submission of women. The universal standard "in all the churches of the saints" (v. 33) prescribes woman's nonvocal participation in worship services: "Let the women keep silent in the churches" (i.e., church meetings; v. 34). The extent to which this restriction was and is to be applied is not easy to establish. Various possibilities are: (1) it is not meant to cover all occasions, but only occasions where abuse occurred, as in Corinth; (2) it refers only to women speaking with tongues or prophesying, in accordance with the contextual emphasis of chapter 14; (3) it refers only to a woman assuming an authoritative role in a local church, not to her actual speaking in public; (4) it refers to a restriction against women giving spoken criticisms of prophecies uttered during a church service; and (5) it is an absolute rule permitting no exceptions.

Possibility (1) is highly unlikely because of the prefaced words "as in all the churches of the saints" (v. 33b), as well as because of the appended word about universality in verse 36. Possibility (2) is not good because in the following verse (v. 35), questioning her husband at home could hardly be a substitute for her use of tongues or prophecy in public worship. Possibility (3) has the same difficulty as (2), in addition to giving insufficient weight to the explicit statement that speaking and silence are in view, not an authoritative position in the church. Possibility (4) also faces the same objection as (2), because questioning her husband at home could hardly replace vocal criticisms of prophecies in a church service.

Suggestion (5) is the most probable meaning of the words.[29] That is the viewpoint that best accords with the plain sense of the language, that is, that it was Paul's ideal for public services of the church to have exclusively male leadership. He is not denying women the use of their speaking gifts (cf. Acts 21:9), but he is saying they should use them in circumstances other than meetings of the whole local assembly. Paul recognized the severity of this restriction. He was aware that the Corinthians would not readily accept it, and made provisions in case women chose to go on taking part in the services (cf. 1 Cor. 11:5–6). But as far as he was concerned, for them to continue doing so was only second best. To the inspired writer, the orderly worship service was one in which the women refrained from speaking. It is impossible to substantiate that Corinth was a special circumstance, different from all others (cf. v. 36).

Reinforcing the command of silence, Paul explains, "They are not permitted to speak." That is the governing principle standing behind the previous injunction. It remains constantly in force, allowing for no exemptions.

The words "let them subject themselves" (v. 34) tell what the women's duty is. The act of speaking publicly was the very opposite of the duty. For a speaker to address an audience was tantamount to his (or her) assuming authority over those who listened. The role was contrary to the divinely established relationship of woman to man. Submission did not dictate female silence in the home (v. 35), but in the local church it did (cf. 1 Tim. 2:11–15).

It is a badly mistaken idea that submission of female to male is synonymous with women's inequality or inferiority. It is the same between woman and man as between Christ and God the Father (cf. 1 Cor. 11:3). The Son is constantly in submission to the Father's will (Matt. 26:39; Heb. 10:7), but never for a moment has the Son ceased being equal with the Father (John 5:17–18; 10:30; 14:9; Phil. 2:6). God's order fixes relationships of headship and subjection in many realms, but none of these entails the least bit of inferiority of one party to the other. Though commonly misunderstood, it is nonetheless true that submission and equality can coexist without even the slightest contradiction.

"As the Law also says" alludes to the scriptural foundation of this ruling about women. "Law" in verse 34 points to the first five Old Testament books instead of the whole Old Testament (as in v. 21). The apparent reference of Paul's statement is to Genesis 2:20–22 (cf. Gen. 3:16). God created Eve to be a helper suitable for Adam, and that order of role relationships has prevailed ever since. Such decorum is the only one that accords with the will of God. Subordination with equality is what He has prescribed (cf. 1 Cor. 11:3).

The requirements for female Christians in verse 34 are stringent. Many a woman in her zeal to contribute to the work of the Lord has sensed a strong compulsion to speak up in a Christian worship service where she felt she could make a definite contribution. Many sisters in Christ have been and are well-taught biblically and are quite capable of communicating their learning to those around them. It is doubtless their responsibility to do this very thing, but in the proper setting. A service where the whole church meets is not that proper setting, according to 14:35. In the wisdom of God, that is not orderly procedure. The order of creation (Genesis 1–2) and consequences of the Fall (Genesis 3) establish a divine mandate for conduct in the Christian assembly: only the male members are to engage in leading the service. In the interest of love and becoming conduct (1 Cor. 13:5), women are to refrain from speaking.

14:35—Questions from women. Woman's part continues as the subject in verse 35, but she appears in a slightly different capacity—that of a questioner rather than a speaker (v. 34). This change in role represents a definite gradation, verse 34 saying, "Woman is not to participate as a speaker," and verse 35 adding, "She is not even to ask questions in the public service of the church, but is to wait until she is at home alone with her husband."

Verse 35 does not say or even imply that the desire of women to learn should be stifled ("if they desire to learn"). Rather than allowing the desire to be frustrated, it should be encouraged. Women have faculties for acquiring knowledge just as men and have a right to use those faculties. In spiritual matters, however, prescribed guidelines are to be followed.

1. Location of the learning is quite explicit: "at home" (v. 35). She, of course, profits much from what takes place in the public meeting of the church, but a desire to supplement public instruction must take the form of questions asked at home. Female questioning must be in private, possibly as a guard against self-assertion and independence by the woman in a mixed audience. This restriction presupposes that occasionally a simple question or the manner in which it is phrased may sow seeds of dissension and undercut

the speaker's authority. To avoid this danger, she should limit such questioning to the privacy of the home.

2. The source from which women are to supplement their learning is also limited. It is to be from "their own husbands" (v. 35). From church leader to husband to wife is the ideal flow of instruction. "Their own husbands" highlights the exclusiveness of the source, that is, the wife is to seek this information from no one else. If her husband does not know the answer to her question, he must seek it in public or elsewhere. But the channel of her learning aside from instruction received in public meetings is her husband.

The assumption, though it is not explicit, is that women who have no husbands are still under subjection to a father, brother, or guardian, so that they too have a source who can properly satisfy their curiosities. Also, without doubt there were women living in Corinth whose husbands were not Christians. Some special provision for answering their questions was also necessary, whether through another member of the family or a selected male member of the congregation.

Paul closes verse 35 with a word in support of this channel of questioning. The general conviction of antiquity had been that it is inconsistent with modesty and reserve for women to speak in a church service, in that it is out of keeping with their submissive status. "Improper" (v. 35; cf. 11:6) is more graphically translated "shame." This communicates the scandalous nature of women being heard in the congregation. Paul's advice rests on that ground (cf. vv. 34–35).

14:36—Corinth versus the rest of the churches. A strong reaction to the strict guidelines laid down for women is anticipated by verse 36. An untranslated word for "or" opens the verse and leads to another alternative in case the Corinthians were unwilling to accept the option just given (vv. 34–35). "Or, if you are unwilling to accept the rightness of what I have just said," is the implied connotation of "or."

The alternative presented in verse 36, however, is actually no alternative at all. It is rather a tool of Paul's biting sarcasm to pit the Corinthian church against Christian churches in every other place. It poses the ridiculous possibility of Corinth being authoritative over and independent of Christians elsewhere. That Paul would resort to this extreme is strong indication that women in Corinth were playing an undue part in the services. The only conceivable justification for their improper behavior would be for the Corinthian church to set itself up as the mother church, whose example all other churches were to follow. To do this would be impudence on their part. The whole assumption was absurd.

"The word of God" (v. 36) is practically equivalent to "the gospel" as preached and taught (cf. 2 Cor. 2:17; 4:2; Phil. 1:14; Col. 1:25). The Corinthians had felt free to move out in new directions and set their own standards based only on their own local understanding of the gospel message and its implications. That was presumptuous on their part. "Was it from you that the word of God first went forth?" asks if they were the source of the gospel. They obviously were not. "Has it come to you only?" asks if Corinth was the sole destination of this message. In other words, "Was it to you alone that it reached?" The clear-cut answer is again negative.

In effect, what Paul has done in verse 36 is to return his readers' thoughts to the consideration with which he began the paragraph, namely, the universal custom in the churches (v. 33b). For Corinth alone among all the churches to grant women freedom to speak in worship services amounted to erecting double standards, one for Corinth and another for the rest of Christendom. It was the height of arrogance on the part of this church (cf. 1 Cor. 13:4) and was inexcusable. The suggestions of verse 36 need no reply, and are flatly rejected because of their sheer absurdity. No option remained but for the readers to comply with the standards of verses 34–35.

Chapter Six

UNIFIED PERSPECTIVE OF SPIRITUAL GIFTS: ORDERLY CONDUCT

14:37–40

Returning to the main theme in 1 Corinthians 12–14, Paul has two elements to treat in summarizing and concluding his extended remarks. One is the authority on which he bases his directives (vv. 37–38), and the other, orderliness in carrying out the directives (vv. 39–40).

A. DIVINE AUTHORITY (14:37–38)

37 If any one thinks he is a prophet or spiritual, let him recognize that the things which I write to you are the Lord's commandment.

38 But if any one does not recognize this, he is not recognized.

14:37—Written commandments of the Lord. The question of whether Paul, a writer of inspired Scripture, was aware of his own authority while writing receives its specific answer in the explicit statement of verse 37. In the verse he makes acknowledgment of his writing's authoritative character a criterion for testing the genuineness of "a prophet or spiritual" person. A person's estimation of himself and his own spiritual gift is in focus in verse 37. "Prophet," of course, alludes to a conception of oneself as possessing the gift of prophecy. "Spiritual" refers to a self-evaluation of one having the capacity of a tongues speaker. That Paul would take "spiritual," which has had a general sense in 12:1 and 14:1, applying to spiritual gifts of all kinds, and give it in 14:37 a sense restricted to the gift of tongues, marks a continuation of his sarcasm from verse 36.[1] The readers were inclined to view the gift of tongues as the spiritual gift par excellence because of their pagan background. Hence, Paul in an ironic tone concedes their evaluation by referring to the gift in terms of its spiritual source. The prominence of prophecy and tongues as the sole topic earlier in this chapter (14:1–5, 20–33a) verifies that tongues only is in view in the term "spiritual." The two continue to be featured subsequent to verse 37 (cf. v. 39). Any pretense to possessing either of the two gifts was measurable only by a willingness to concede Paul's position as an apostle, prophet, and author of inspired Scripture (cf. 12:28). Through him came the word of wisdom and the word of knowledge (cf. 12:8) recorded in permanent form for the church of all generations. In effect, Paul presented to the Corinthians his own gift status as a means for measuring their own.

Paul is uncompromisingly dogmatic in declaring that it was the Lord who originated the commandments he had written, not himself. As a divine appointee to the apostolic office, he was absolutely certain that he wrote the words as the mouthpiece of Christ Himself (cf. 1 Cor. 2:16; 7:40; 2 Cor. 13:3; 1 Thess. 2:13). It was imperative that a prophet or spiritual person fully recognize Paul's infallible authority if he was to verify his own legitimacy as a divine oracle. In essence, verse 37 pits authority against authority, Paul against those in Corinth who might be unwilling to accept the strictness of regulation set down in 1 Corinthians 12–14. Paul's willingness to stake his own reputation and status on the accuracy of his written words discloses the degree of importance he attached to them. His readers had to accept the words as binding or else label him an impostor. Only the former course was feasible because of the countless evidences of Christ's commissioning of and presence with this apostle to the Gentiles.

14:38—Consequence of ignorance. An unwillingness to accept the apostolic leadership advocated in verse 37 was tantamount to ignorance, according to verse 38. "If anyone does not recognize this" (v. 38) hypothesizes a staunch refusal to accept Christ as the source of Paul's rulings on spiritual gifts. This was more than just innocent ignorance, of course. It was a willful ignorance, a rebellion against divinely constituted authority.

Verse 38 builds around an interesting play on words. With the best documented reading in the last part of the verse, English could represent the Greek terms by "If any man be ignorant, he is ignored"; or, "If any man does not know, he is not known"; or, "If any man does not recognize [this], he is not recognized."[2] The connotation of "he is ignored" or "he is not recognized" is that such a person was not recognized as a prophet or spiritual one. He was to be ignored by the church because of his failure to recognize an apostle of God. That kind of ostracism did not necessarily estrange him from the church's fellowship (cf. 1 Cor. 5:1–5), but it did exclude him from exercising his speaking gifts in public services. For him to go on speaking would have created a dilemma of conflicting authority, Paul's against his own. More of such confusion was the very thing Corinth did not need.

B. DECENT APPLICATION (14:39–40)

39 Therefore, my brethren, desire earnestly to prophesy, and do not forbid to speak in tongues.

40 But let all things be done properly and in an orderly manner.

14:39—Proper perspective of prophecy and tongues. The final two verses of chapter 14 offer a summary of the main points discussed in chapters 12–14. The appearance of "brethren" in verse 39 signals Paul's return to an affectionate tone following his sarcastic and severe censure of the readers (vv. 36–38). He tenderly reminds them once again of the proper balance between prophecy and tongues. The words "desire earnestly" (cf. 12:31; 14:1) and "forbid not" portray well the marked preference for prophecy over tongues in a Christian gathering. The chapter has repeatedly featured this comparison (14:1–5, 20–25). Prophecy was one of the "greater gifts" (12:31), and one that would in Christian worship bring greater benefit to saint (14:1–5) and sinner (14:20–25) alike. The value of tongues under such conditions was relatively small. Yet, Paul has not expressed hostility toward the latter gift or those who used it, unless they insisted on using it apart from his clear-cut rules of procedure (14:27–28). Value from tongues, as from prophecy, could come to such a first-century congregation if the church rigorously applied specified stipulations, but they could assure edification through prophecy with a much higher degree of certainty. Therefore, instead of being simply not forbidden, prophecy was to be zealously sought for the building up of the congregation.

14:40—Beauty and order in worship. The final point in summary is a regulative principle to govern all parts of public worship: "Let all things be done properly and in an orderly manner" (v. 40). Reaching back to where the larger section begins at 11:2, the words exceed the scope of spiritual gifts, not only explaining the summary instruction of 14:39 but encompassing also all that Paul has written regarding Christian meetings. He recommends two general guiding principles as the chapter and section draw to a close: decency and order.

"Properly" is a term of beauty. It literally means "well-formed," and carries the connotation of comeliness. In Christian worship, a pleasing impression on all the right-minded attendants is the desirable object. Ecclesiastical decorum ought always to be beautiful and harmonious, not unseemly (cf. 13:5). Though not without application to spiritual gifts (1 Cor.

12–14), the former word is especially appropriate to matters discussed earlier in reference to the dress of women and celebration of the Lord's Supper (1 Cor. 11).

The word translated "orderly manner" is of military origin. A well-disciplined military force puts every man in his proper place with a knowledge of his particular responsibility. He knows how to perform his task at the proper time and in the proper way. A condition of tumult such as characterizes an unreasoning mob should not characterize church worship any more than it does the well-ordered military unit. The need for order in connection with chapter 11 is clear, but the need was especially prominent in relation to spiritual gifts (1 Corinthians 12–14).

Though differing from the Corinthian picture in some details, modern church worship does well to adopt the same twofold criterion of beauty and orderliness in conducting its worship services. It is through this balance that the most effective job can be done in building up the saint and converting the sinner wherever Christian churches convene.

Appendix A

FIRST CORINTHIANS 13:11 REVISITED: AN EXEGETICAL UPDATE

In 1974, I proposed an interpretation of 1 Corinthians 13:10 that assigned *to teleion* the meaning of "complete" or "mature" instead of the more frequent rendering of "perfect."[1] At least three developments show that the subject needs a renewed look: (1) a misconstruing or confused statement of my view by others;[2] (2) a continuing claim that biblical exegesis yields no explicit indication of the termination of some spiritual gifts;[3] and (3) a growing personal realization that explanations of the passage have overlooked the important contribution of 1 Corinthians 13:11 to the meaning of *to teleion*. A renewed discussion of the issue can probably do little to remedy whatever it is that causes (1) above, but perhaps a focused treatment of the exegetical nuances related to 1 Corinthians 13:11 and their impact on the meaning of *to teleion* in 13:10 will contribute to a recognition that (2) is wrong in light of the oversight named in (3).

Farnell has conveniently summarized the five main viewpoints regarding the meaning of *to teleion* in 1 Corinthians 13:10: (1) the death of a believer when ushered into Christ's presence, (2) the eternal state, (3) the completed New Testament canon, (4) Christ's second advent, and (5) the maturing of Christ's body through the course of the church age.[4] Positions (2) and (4) assign the meaning "the perfect" to *to teleion* largely because of the neglect of important factors in 1 Corinthians 13:11. With respect for those who interpret differently, I offer the following as some of those factors.

REASONS WHY *TO TELEION* CANNOT MEAN "THE PERFECT" IN 13:10

The most common definitions of the English word "perfect" applied to 1 Corinthians 13:10 would probably include:
(a) being entirely without fault or defect[5]

(b)   corresponding to an ideal standard or abstract concept
(c)   the soundness and the excellence of every part, element, or quality
       of a thing frequently as an unattainable or theoretical state.[6]

Either of these three or a combination of them is the usual notion the average person attaches to the word. All three are qualitative in nature, a characteristic that renders them unsatisfactory renderings of *to teleion*. Four reasons demonstrate this:

(1)   No other use of *teleios* in Paul can possibly mean "perfection" in the sense of the absence of all imperfection. In fact, the meaning of "perfection" in Greek philosophers—that of a "perfect" man—is absent from the New Testament.[7] Utopian perfection was a philosophical notion, not a New Testament idea, for this word.[8] Elsewhere in Paul the adjective is figurative and refers almost exclusively to a grown man (cf. 1 Cor. 2:6; 14:20; Phil. 3:15; Eph. 4:13; Col. 1:28; cf. also Heb. 5:14).[9] One other time, in Colossians 4:12, it means "mature" in the Old Testament sense of wholeness and obedience to God's will, and picks up on his ambition for every man as stated in Colossians 1:28.[10] So six of the other seven times Paul uses the word, it means "mature." The remaining use is in Romans 12:1 where its meaning is "complete."[11]

       This pattern of usage establishes a strong probability that the word includes the sense of maturity in 1 Corinthians 13:10, especially since its other two uses in 1 Corinthians have that sense.

(2)   In the immediate context of 1 Corinthians 13:8–13, a qualitative word such as "perfect" is unsuitable in light of the apodosis of the sentence in 13:10. "Perfect" is not a suitable opposite to *ek merous* ("partial"). A better meaning would be "whole" or "complete" as antithetical to *ek merous*.[12]

(3)   The terminology of 13:11 is most conclusive because it is an analogy with the stages of human life (i.e., *nēpios* ["child"] and *anēr* ["man"]).
       (a)   The analogy directly impacts the meaning of *to teleion* in 13:10 because it sets up a *teleios/nēpios* antithesis in verses 10–11 that is relative, not absolute, and therefore incompatible with the concept of perfection. The difference between childhood and adulthood is a matter of degree, not one of mutually exclusive differentiation.
       (b)   The *nēpios/anēr* antithesis in verse 11 has the same contextual effect of ruling out the notion of an ideal state as denoted by the translation "perfect."

(4)   The terminology of 13:12 requires an allusion to degrees of revelatory understanding, not perfection or freedom from imperfection. The verbs *blepomen* ("I see") and *ginōskō* ("I know") correlate with the

gifts of prophecy and knowledge and their limited insights compared with the complete understanding that will prevail in the future. This is quantitative, not qualitative, so *to teleion* must have the same quantitative connotation.

Hence, both etymological and contextual considerations argue emphatically against the meaning "perfect" for *to teleion*.

REASONS WHY *TO TELEION* MUST MEAN "COMPLETE" OR "MATURE"

Corresponding to the reasons for not translating "the perfect" in 1 Corinthians 13:10 are four considerations pointing toward the meaning "complete" or "mature" for *to teleion*.

1. The idea of totality, wholeness, or completion controls the New Testament usage of *teleios*. In the present connection, totality takes on an added dimension: "Yet in the main the feeling of antiquity . . . was that only an 'adult' can be a 'full' man; hence these senses can overlap in Paul."[13] The thought behind the overlap of "complete" and "mature" in this word's usage is that in the minds of the ancients, adulthood represented a degree of completeness not present during childhood. If ever a clear case for this overlap in meaning existed, 1 Corinthians 13:10 is that case. The background of *teleios* not only allows for the overlap; the circumstances of the context also require the dual concept of "complete-mature."[14]

2. Another reason for this meaning is the consistent sense of the *teleios/ nēpios* antithesis in Paul, the New Testament, and all Greek literature. Whenever in the proximity of *nēpios*, as it is in 1 Corinthians 13:10–11, *teleios* always carries the connotation of adulthood versus childhood (1 Cor. 2:6 and 3:1; 14:20; Eph. 3:13–14; cf. Heb. 5:13–14).[15] In 1 Corinthians 2:6 Paul speaks of imparting wisdom to *tois teleiois* ("the mature"), but he encounters an obstacle because, according to 1 Corinthians 3:1, his readers are *nēpiois* ("infants"). In 1 Corinthians 14:20, his command to the Corinthians is to be children (*nēpiazete*) in malice but adults (*teleioi*) in understanding. In Ephesians 4:13–14, his goal is for all members of Christ's body to attain to the unity of the faith and of the full knowledge of the Son of God, i.e., to a *teleios anēr* ("mature man"), so that they be no longer *nēpioi* ("children"). The writer of Hebrews echoes this antithesis in 5:13–14 when he compares elementary teaching to milk that is suitable for a *nēpios* ("child" or "infant") with solid food that is suitable for *teleiōn* ("the mature").

3. First Corinthians 12–14 has many parallels with Ephesians 4:1–16, a passage that teaches the gradual maturing of the church through the present age. That correspondence is all the more instructive in light of Paul's presence in Ephesus while writing 1 Corinthians. He was probably teaching the Ephesian church the same principles he penned in the Corinthian letter. Then about five years later, as he wrote back to the Ephesian church, he found it necessary to reemphasize and develop the same truths about growth in the body of Christ that he had instructed them about while present with them. The similarities between the two contexts include the following:

a. All seven unifying influences listed in Ephesians 4:4–6 are present in 1 Corinthians 12–14 (1 Cor. 12:4–6, 13; 13:13; 14:22). Particularly noticeable are one body, one Spirit, one Lord, one baptism, and one God and Father of all.

b. Emphasis on unity in the body (1 Cor. 12:4–6, 11–13, 24–26; Eph. 4:3, 13) along with the diversity of the body's members (1 Cor. 12:14–26; Eph. 4:11, 16) pervades each passage.

c. The noun *meros* ("part") in both passages depicts individual members of Christ's body (1 Cor. 12:27; Eph. 4:16).

d. Corporateness of the body (1 Cor. 12:27a; Eph. 4:15–16) combines with an individualistic focus (1 Cor. 12:27b; Eph. 4:4, 7, 16) as a ruling consideration in both places.

e. The general subject under discussion in Ephesians (Eph. 4:7, 11) is spiritual gifts as it is in 1 Corinthians 12–14.

f. The figure representing the church in both passages is the human body, as it is always when Paul talks about spiritual gifts (1 Cor. 12:12–27; Eph. 4:4, 15–16; cf. Rom. 12:3–8).

g. Edification of the body of Christ is the stated objective in both sections (1 Cor. 14:12, 26; Eph. 4:12, 16).

h. Growth from childhood to adulthood is portrayed in Ephesians 4:13–14 as it is in 1 Corinthians 13:11.

i. The *nēpios/teleios anēr* antithesis is found in Ephesians as it is in 1 Corinthians 13:10–11 (Eph. 4:13–14).[16]

j. Love is the overarching quality in the growth process in both passages (1 Cor. 13:1–13; Eph. 4:15–16).

Since Ephesians 4:1–16 offers a distinct picture of a gradually developing and maturing body of Christ,[17] the probability is strong that Paul intends to convey the same in 1 Corinthians 13:11. Though he may not say explicitly "the complete or mature body" (i.e., the complete or mature body with reference to revelatory activity) in 1 Corinthians 13:10, he had doubtless taught them verbally at some time during his extended eighteen–month residence in Corinth (as he did the Ephesian church) regarding this analogy so that it was perfectly clear to them what he was talking about. It remains for the interpreter to clarify what he meant by resorting to another of his writings quite relevant to 1 Corinthians.

4. The illustration of 13:11 is hardly suitable to refer to the difference between the present and a period after the parousia.[18] So, the analogy of verse 11 must be supplying data supplemental to what is in verse 12.

   a. To say that the parousia is in view in verse 11 is to see Paul as using his own adult status to illustrate a perfection that follows the parousia. Yet, in Philippians 3:12, he views himself as incomplete in his current state as an adult (*teteleiōmai* ["I am brought to completeness"], a perfect tense; cf. *gegona*, 1 Corinthians 13:11, which has a present force: "now that I am a man"[19]). In fact, in the very next verse, 1 Corinthians 13:12, he disclaims such a completed state by noting that currently he is among those whose present state is that of conspicuous limitations.[20] This state of incompletion in Paul as an adult negates any possibility that he intends his adulthood of verse 11 to correspond to the state of ultimate completion in verse 12. It is also contrary to Pauline Christian humility as reflected elsewhere in the apostle's writings that he would choose such an illustration (e.g., 1 Cor. 15:9; Eph. 3:8; 1 Tim. 1:15).

   b. The nature of the transition from childhood to adulthood is not sudden as will be the change at the parousia. It is a gradual process.[21] Adolescence is a transitional period between childhood and adulthood.

   c. By nature, the process described by *katērgēka* ("I render inoperative") in 13:11 indicates an altered condition that continues. It is a dramatic perfect.[22] It indicates "a change of state which still continues; the emancipation from childish things took place as a matter of course, . . . and it continues."[23] If Christ did not return before a permanent body of New Testament revelation was finished, a degree of completion would arrive that would render unnecessary a continuation of the process involving the revelatory gifts.

   d. The difference between childhood and manhood is a feeble illustration of the vast difference between the Christian's present state and that which will exist after the parousia.[24]

Reasons Why 13:8–13 Requires the Completion-Maturity Concept

1. The purpose of the paragraph of 1 Corinthians 13:8–13 is to establish the eternality of love. The beginning ("love never fails," v. 8) and end ("the greatest of these is love," v. 13) of the paragraph prove that.

2. Between the two points the writer shows the eternality of love by two sets of contrasts: (a) one between the duration of revelatory gifts that may or may not extend until Christ's return (13:10–11) and the triad of faith, hope, and love that will definitely extend to the time of Christ's return (13:13a), and (b) one between the triad of faith, hope, and love that continue until Christ's return (13:13a) and love alone that will remain after Christ's return (13:13b).

3. The two sets of contrasts emphasize the secondary character of the revelatory and confirmatory gifts from a temporal standpoint, and the supreme importance and lasting character of love because of its eternality. Love lasts longer than these gifts; it even lasts longer than faith and hope to which it so closely relates until Christ's second advent.

Objections to the Completion-Maturity Explanation

The objections to this position seem to be about six in number, though no extensive response to the completion-maturity view has yet appeared:[25]

1. *Objection:* Verse 11 is merely an illustration or an analogy and an explanation of its meaning must draw upon the meaning of verse 12, which refers to Christ's second coming.[26]

    Response: If verse 11 says something different from verse 12, it must be allowed to have its distinctive contribution. Fee acknowledges that the analogy of verse 11 is "ambiguous at best."[27] That is because his interpretation of "the perfect" has no room for the inclusion of the verse's meaning. Paul was not just padding his discussion when he inserted verse 11. To interpret verse 11 in light of the meaning of verse 12 is to rob the verse of its distinctive contribution, thereby robbing Scripture of an aspect of its meaning.

2. *Objection:* Verse 12 has *tote* ("then") to link it with *hotan* ("when") of verse 10.[28] Verse 11 has no such temporal indicator.

Response: Verse 11 does have temporal indicators, i.e., the two occurrences of *hote* ("when"). Such a temporal indicator picks up the *hotan* of verse 10 even more specifically than the *tote* of verse 12, which does not limit the temporal reference of the *hotan* in verse 10, but is antithetic to the two occurrences of *arti* in verse 12.

3. *Objection:* The idea of the maturity of the body of Christ is nowhere present in the context.[29]

Response: Maturity is in the context in 13:11. See also 14:20 where individual maturity is in view. In 1 Corinthians 2:6 and 3:1 individual maturity is also in focus. It is not a matter of maturity being absent from the context; it is rather a question of the maturity of what, individuals or the corporate body? Verse 11 most naturally refers to corporate maturity because of the singular number used in the analogy of verse 11 compared to the plurals in verses 9, 12. Paul has a proclivity for going back and forth between the corporate aspect of the body of Christ and the individual members of that body. He does the same in the broader context here (12:12, 27; cf. Eph. 4:13–14).[30] The presence of maturity in the context forces a choice between individual and corporate maturity. The nature of the discussion and the added input from Ephesians 4:1–16 tips the scale in favor of corporate maturity. The criticism of this maturity view, which notes that the context does not speak about the immaturity of individual believers,[31] rests on a misunderstanding of the view. The view looks at the immaturity of the total body during its earlier years, not explicitly that of individuals. It was these gifts' temporary nature that marked the infancy of the body of Christ, not of single members of that body. Maturity is also implied in the emphasis on edification of the body in 1 Corinthians 14:12, 26 (cf. 12:7). Edification equates with building up, which is equivalent to growth—the same as maturing according to Ephesians 4:13–16. So, maturity shows itself contextually in yet another way: through the emphasis on edification that appears in 1 Corinthians 12–14. It *is* a factor in the passage under study.

4. *Objection:* The context says nothing about the completion of Scripture.[32]

Response: Here is another superficial objection. Completion is in the context. Note the four occurrences of *ek merous* that require an opposite—"completion": 13:9 (twice), 13:10, and 13:12. It is not a matter of completion's absence from the context; it is rather a question of the completion of what. The completion spoken of in verse 12 is unobscured cognitive sight to replace the limited prophetic revelations and unlimited knowledge to replace partial revelations through the gift of knowledge. Those partial revelatory gifts were the means used by the Spirit in bringing the New Testament Scriptures—among other revelations—to the church. So a termination of revelatory gifts coincided with the completion of the New Testament. Verse 12 does not speak of seeing God face to face,[33] which would be a qualitative condition inappropriate to this context. This would break the continuity of the earlier part of the paragraph where revelatory gifts are in view. Verse 12 must refer to unlimited prophetic sight and knowledge. What is not in this context is a contrast between perfection and imperfection. It is not talking about a qualitative set of conditions, but a quantitative one.

5. *Objection:* The idea of completion or maturity replaces the reference to Christ's return that is clearly in the context.[34]

   Response: The maturity concept does not replace Christ's return; it supplements it. It adds to it another possible eventuality. Uncertain as he was about the time of Christ's return, Paul left open the possibility that before Christ's return the body of Christ might reach the requisite stage of maturity where the revelatory and sign gifts were no longer necessary (13:11). But he also indicated the possibility of Christ's advent before the church reached that stage (13:12).

6. *Objection:* It is a misguided emphasis to focus on verse 11 to explain the meaning of *to teleion*. It is letting the tail wag the dog to allow an analogy to dictate the meaning of the argument as a whole and the plain statement of verse 12b.[35]

   Response: The completion-maturity explanation does not focus on verse 11 alone, but it does give the verse its deserved place as part of the explanation. An unwillingness to let 13:11 have its natural sense leads inevitably to viewing the analogy to human development as ambiguous.[36] It will obviously appear ambiguous if it means something other than what the interpreter wants it to say. By allowing verse 11 to inject the element of maturity into the discussion, one has not allowed the analogy to have precedence over the argument as a whole. He has rather taken into account an indispensable ingredient of the argument. Just as it would be wrong to let the analogy of 13:11 exclude the reference to the Second Coming in 13:12, it is also wrong to let the reference to the Second Coming exclude the graphic analogy that expresses another possibility regarding the cessation of prophecy, tongues, and knowledge. Verse 11 cannot be treated as excess baggage getting in the way of a preconceived interpretation.

The maturity-completion view stands without an unanswerable objection because the proposed weaknesses of the view rest on misunderstanding or consist of invalid criticisms.

PAUL AND THE FUTURE OF PROPHECY, TONGUES, AND KNOWLEDGE

Paul knew of an earlier period when God spoke directly to His prophets. That period had come to an end with the prophets Haggai, Zechariah, and Malachi, and was followed by the four hundred silent years (cf. Matt. 23:35, 37; Heb. 1:1–2). He also knew that the close of the Old Testament canon coincided with the cessation of Old Testament prophecy (e.g., Luke 24:44) long before the first advent of Christ.[37] He was conscious that he was now in the midst of a new period during which God was speaking directly to His apostles and prophets, resulting in inspired utterances, part of which were taking their place alongside the Old Testament canon as inspired Scripture (cf. 1 Cor. 14:37; 1 Thess. 5:26; 2 Peter 3:15–16). One possibility he foresaw was that this period of prophecy could come to its conclusion before the second advent of Christ just as Old Testament prophecy had come to its conclusion four hundred years before the First Advent. Such a cessation would resemble the gradual development from childhood to manhood. When the church reached an appointed stage, it would no longer need revelatory and sign gifts. It would come to a close with the completion of a new canon of an unknown number of writings that would result from New Testament prophecy to serve as a companion to the Old Testament canon. (See Appendix D, "Correlation of Revelatory Spiritual Gifts and New Testament Canonicity.) But because of Paul's strong anticipation of Christ's imminent coming, that was a secondary expectation and was added in verse 11 according to the mode of customary Pauline digression.

Paul also knew the possibility that Christ's second coming could be very soon, even within his own lifetime (1 Cor. 15:51–52; 1 Thess. 4:15–17). Had this happened, the period of New Testament prophecy would have halted abruptly as members of the body of Christ were transformed immediately into the image of Christ (cf. 1 John 3:2). That would automatically culminate a new completed body of Scripture to serve future generations because the body of Christ would no longer be on earth to receive more revelation. This principal expectation is reflected by the *gar* that connects 13:12 with 13:10.[38]

The apostle did not know which of these would occur first, a stage of relative completeness marking adulthood in comparison to childhood or a stage of absolute completeness that would characterize those in the immediate presence of Christ. So, through inspiration of the Spirit, he portrayed his uncertainty by choosing terminology and illustrative material that were compatible with either possibility. He knew that the partial would be replaced by either the mature or the complete, and perhaps by first one and then the other.

The best he could do was to emphasize the eternality of love with a double contrast:[39] (1) a contrast between revelatory and sign gifts that may or may not characterize the entire church age on the one hand, and on the other, the qualities of faith, hope, and love that definitely would characterize the entire period; and (2) a contrast between the triad faith, hope, and love that continue to the parousia on the one hand, and on the other, love alone that will survive and continue following the parousia.

It is interesting to compare the ways Paul states the disappearance of faith and hope at the parousia. In 2 Corinthians 5:6–8, faith is juxtaposed with sight, and one is associated with being absent from the Lord and the other with being present with the Lord. Faith will be replaced by sight when Christ returns. According to Romans 8:24–25 the Christian awaits what he hopes for, but once it arrives, hope has no further place. When Christ the believer's hope appears, hope will have no further function.

The disappearance of the revelatory gifts is described in terms that are very different. "They will be rendered inoperative" (*katargēthēsetai*, vv. 8 [twice], 10) in the same way as adult maturation has rendered inoperative and keeps on rendering inoperative (perfect tense, *katērgēka*) the characteristics of childhood (v. 11). That is hardly an exclusive reference to the parousia as is the case with the disappearance of faith and hope. Prophetic sight and knowledge will infinitely increase at that time so that they are no longer partial. This will be the prevailing state. If the revelatory gifts were unquestionably to extend to the parousia, no rendering inoperative of those gifts would happen; universal knowledge for all would simply replace them.

Regardless of what the future would hold, Paul was confident of one thing: "Love never fails . . . and is the greatest of these." It will stand the test of time and eternity.

That overarching "fruit of the Spirit" is the supreme quality, for which sensible Christians are very thankful. They may differ in their interpretations of this or that passage, but they have the privilege of continuing to love one another, no matter what. I am grateful for this opportunity of once again expressing in love what I deem to be the truth about an important text of the New Testament: *to teleion* in 1 Corinthians 13:10 refers to maturity in the body of Christ, and consequently furnishes a good exegetical basis for concluding that revelatory and sign gifts granted to the body of Christ ceased functioning in early church history.

Appendix B

PROPHECY REDISCOVERED?

A Review of *The Gift of Prophecy in the New Testament and Today*

Notoriety has come to Wayne A. Grudem's book, *The Gift of Prophecy in the New Testament and Today*.[1] No doubt that is partly because the Kansas City Fellowship with its Kansas City "prophets" and John Wimber, founder of the Vineyard Church Fellowship and leader of the Signs and Wonders movement, have used arguments from the book to support their "prophetic" practices.[2] Grudem, a professor at Trinity Evangelical Divinity School and an attender of a Vineyard-affiliated church at the time of this writing,[3] has based the book largely on his 1978 doctoral dissertation at Cambridge University.[4]

Undertaking a review of Grudem's book entails a degree of apprehension because of this reviewer's high esteem for its author both as a scholar and as a friend and because of the prestigious credentials afforded the work through its acceptance by the Cambridge University faculty.[5] Yet, a concern to promote the well-being of the body of Christ through correcting the book's misrepresentations outweigh that apprehension.

MERITS OF GRUDEM'S BOOK

In his well-written and persuasive work, Grudem sees certain characteristics of spiritual gifts in proper perspective. For instance, once a person has become a member of the body of Christ, his gifts remain the same, since members of the spiritual body of Christ are analogous to parts of a human body (1 Cor. 12:12–26).[6] Another point well taken is the potential for developing and sharpening one's spiritual gifts as advocated in the New Testament.[7]

In contradicting recent critical theories, Grudem also is to be commended for showing the appointment of local-church elders and deacons to have occurred during and not after Paul's missionary labors.[8] Further, the author is correct in holding that no postascension prophecies from Jesus have been read back into the gospel accounts, as though Christ had spoken them before His ascension.[9]

Grudem also correctly attributes to the New Testament prophets the abilities to perceive the thoughts and background details of another person[10] and to predict future events,[11] though neither of these is necessarily the primary function of the gift. He also correctly observes that the purpose of prophecy is edification of the church.[12] Furthermore, the book allows for the temporary nature of the gift,[13] though, as will be shown later, his explanation of the duration of the gift of prophecy leaves much to be desired.

CONFLICTS IN GRUDEM'S VIEW OF THE GIFT OF PROPHECY

A characteristic that makes Grudem's definition of New Testament prophecy[14] so intriguing is its novelty.[15] He acknowledges that an understanding of the gift as he describes it has eluded the church since the second century.[16] He attributes this to the church's failure to make a fine distinction between degrees of authority involved in prophetic utterances.[17] This reviewer, however, cannot put such blame on the early church for dropping the gift because of its alleged lack of ability to perceive its true nature. The collage of New Testament prophecy offered in Grudem's book is confusing. Some of the conflicting characteristics suggested by Grudem are as follows.

UNLIMITED VERSUS LIMITED NUMBER-OF-PROPHETS CONFLICT

Based on Numbers 11:29 and Joel 2:28–29, the expectation of all God's people was that everyone would prophesy,[18] but God has appointed only a limited number to be prophets.[19] The idea that Christians should seek the gift as though it were available to all is misleading if it is available only to a restricted number of Christians.

NONDOCTRINAL VERSUS DOCTRINAL CONFLICT

Unlike the gift of teaching, the gift of prophecy, according to Grudem, did not impart "doctrinal and ethical standards,"[20] but it may have included the divine disclosure of doctrinal material[21] or the knowledge of a future event.[22] But how can prophetic content be both doctrinal and not doctrinal?

NONETHICAL VERSUS ETHICAL CONFLICT

Prophecies did not convey ethical standards for the church,[23] but they provided guidance in Christian living[24] through their practical application (of ethical principles) to the lives of the hearers.[25] What is guidance in Christian living if it is not a setting forth of ethical standards to be followed?

MORE BENEFICIAL VERSUS NONAUTHORITATIVE CONFLICT

Prophecy, Grudem states, is more beneficial to the church than teaching,[26] but teaching is authoritative while prophecy is not.[27] This means that teaching had to be obeyed, but prophecy did not.[28] How can prophetic content—whatever it is—whose acceptance is optional be more edifying than authoritative teaching with its binding obligations?

TRUTH VERSUS ERROR CONFLICT

Prophecy originates in a revelation from the God of truth who cannot lie,[29] but in the process of human transmission the prophecy may degenerate to a mistaken or erroneous report of that revelation.[30] Yet, how can God who is without error involve Himself in a revelatory process that He allows human imperfection to spoil?

ONE-GIFT VERSUS TWO-GIFT CONFLICT

The work depicts the gift of prophecy as one gift,[31] but throughout his 1988 work, Grudem distinguishes between authoritative "apostolic prophecy" and nonauthoritative "local-church prophecy."[32] However, for a gift to be both authoritative and nonauthoritative is self-contradictory. The difference between the two requires that there be two gifts.

CESSATIONIST VERSUS NONCESSATIONIST CONFLICT

The revelatory gift of apostleship ceased about the end of the first century A.D.,[33] but, according to Grudem, other revelatory gifts (e.g., prophecy) and the signs confirming their revelations (e.g., miracles, signs, and wonders that served to identify apostles; 2 Cor. 12:12) continue until the second coming of Christ.[34] However, after the beginning years of the church, direct revelation with its accrediting signs either ceased or did not cease. It could not do both.

If Grudem's view of New Testament prophecy, with these conflicts, had been the concept of prophecy transmitted to the second-century church, the church did right in putting it to sleep. It would otherwise have brought untold confusion to Christians at a time they needed no more confusion. In addition to these conflicts, Grudem's interpretations of key relevant passages are revealing.

GRUDEM'S TREATMENT OF KEY PASSAGES ON THE GIFT OF PROPHECY

In a discussion on prophecy, Grudem surprisingly makes little mention of *to teleion* in 1 Corinthians 13:10. Apparently he assumes, as do many, that it means "the perfect";[35] he does not support that meaning, nor does he discuss the more likely view that it refers to either "the complete" or "the mature."[36] Nor does he elaborate on the view that *to teleion* may refer to a maturing of the body of Christ.[37] In addition, in his extended discussion of 1 Corinthians 14:20–25, he does not refer to a significant possible interpretation of the section, one based on the dominant New Testament usage of *sēmeion* ("sign," 14:22).[38]

Two key passages Grudem discusses are Ephesians 2:20 and Acts 21:10–11. In discussing the former passage, he argues primarily for the existence of nonauthoritative prophecy[39] and in the latter for mistaken prophecy.

EPHESIANS 2:20

Ephesians 2:20 refers to "the foundation of the apostles and prophets" (*tō themeliō tōn apostolōn kai prophētōn*). Grudem discusses four possible interpretations of the phrase.[40] Two of the four place the New Testament prophets on the same plane of authority as the apostles, a tenet he says is unacceptable.[41] He offers seven reasons why this cannot be so.[42] Only the first two reasons have serious exegetical significance. One of these two is a grammatical observation that notes the possible reference of "the apostles and prophets" to one group (apostles-prophets) rather than two.[43] That is not cogent evidence, however, because it only notes the *possibility* of such an interpretation of the Greek construction. The grammar allows for other possibilities too. Besides this, he does not mention obvious contrary evidence in Ephesians 4:11, which clearly distinguishes the prophets as a group separate from the apostles.[44] The foundation of the church is the inspired teaching ministries of two groups of people, apostles and prophets.[45]

Grudem's second significant objection to understanding two groups in Ephesians 2:20 rests on his claim that the subject under discussion in Ephesians 2:11–3:21—the inclusion of Gentiles in the church on an equal basis with Jews—was a revelation only to apostles and never to prophets.[46] In support of this he lists thirteen passages in which that revelation came only to apostles. However, nine of the thirteen passages were written by Luke, who was not an apostle and did not possess what Grudem would call the gift of "apostolic prophecy" (cf. Luke 24:46–47; Acts 1:8; 10:15, 34–35, 46–48; 11:2–18; 15:6–29; 22:21; 26:17–18). By the standards Grudem himself has set for mere prophecy, the gospel of Luke and the book of Acts, if viewed as works of a prophet, could not have been authoritative.

In Appendix B of his work, Grudem lists Luke and Acts among the New Testament books that were authoritative though written by nonapostles.[47] Those were included in the New Testament canon because they contained God's words.[48] Thus, by the admission of Grudem himself, here was another means or gift, one other than apostleship, for transmitting *authoritative* divine revelation. Luke, a nonapostle, had the gift that in all probability was prophecy, and it made him a vehicle for inspired Scripture.[49]

If that is the case, then the inclusion of Gentiles in the church on an equal basis with Jews was a revelation through prophets who were not apostles, at least through Luke, and the force of Grudem's second argument against two groups in Ephesians 2:20 is without force.

Grudem's awareness of the dubious nature of his arguments for making apostles and prophets "one group" is evident when he adds a brief section offering an alternate view. It suggests that the "two-group" interpretation is reconcilable with his presupposition of a nonauthoritative gift of prophecy.[50] In brief, the reconciliation consists of conjecturing a third prophetic gift, authoritative prophecy, to add to apostolic prophecy and local-church (nonauthoritative) prophecy. That attempt to sustain his view that the New Testament gift of prophecy was sometimes nonauthoritative lacks cogency.[51]

ACTS 21:10–11

The prophecy by Agabus in Acts 21:10–11 is the classic example of a prophecy that is in error, according to Grudem's theory. He says this prophet distorted his God-given revelation in saying that the Jews would bind Paul and would turn him over to the Gentiles. Neither of these details was accurate, Grudem says, because Agabus erred in his attempt to transmit to others the inerrant revelation he had received. Grudem points out that the Romans, not the Jews, bound Paul after rescuing him from the Jews (Acts 21:32–33).[52]

Grudem's analysis of that prophecy is unacceptable for two reasons.

1. He is not only accusing Agabus of error; he is making the same accusation against the Holy Spirit because in the inspired record Agabus introduced his prophecy with the words, "These things says the Holy Spirit." Grudem tries to circumvent this difficulty by viewing the introductory formula as only a vague claim regarding content, not an indication of a direct quotation: "This is generally (or approximately) what the Holy Spirit is saying to us."[53] Yet, the same introductory expression, *tade legei* ("these things he says"), introduces

the exact words of the Lord Jesus seven times in another prophecy, Revelation 2–3 (cf. Rev. 2:1, 8, 12, 18; 3:1, 7, 14). Acts 21:10–11 records the very words of the Holy Spirit uncontaminated by any human mistakes of Agabus.

2. Grudem's conclusion that Agabus' prophecy was mistaken overlooks other statements in the book of Acts. As stated in Acts 28:17, Paul agreed with the latter detail of Agabus' prophecy when he viewed his transport to Caesarea while bound as being "delivered over from Jerusalem," the headquarters of the Jewish hierarchy, into Gentile hands at Caesarea, the headquarters of the Roman governor of Palestine. The Jews through their plot against Paul's life forced him to be moved to the Gentile city (Acts 23:12–33).

The former detail about his being bound by the Jews recalls Acts 2:23 in which Peter attributed the crucifixion of Christ to the Jews (also see 3:13–15; 5:30; 7:52). Actually Roman soldiers crucified Christ, but the Jews were the prime instigators of the crucifixion (4:25). In the same vein, the Jews were the ones who bound Paul, that is, they were the instigators of his binding. It is common to speak of the responsible party or parties as performing an act even though he or they may not have been the immediate agent(s).[54] For example John 19:1 states that Pilate scourged Jesus. That means that he had Him scourged, that is, Pilate was the instigator of the scourging. The Jews were the ones who put Paul in chains just as Agabus predicted.

The prophecy of Agabus (and the Holy Spirit) was absolutely accurate. The Jews did put Paul in chains and turn him over to the Gentiles. When God revealed the future to His prophets, He also provided for the accurate reporting of those revelations to the prophets' listeners. Acts 21:10–11 is an instance of this.

CORRECTIVES IN 1 CORINTHIANS 12–14

The following suggestions provide corrections to a few selected interpretations from 1 Corinthians 12–14, a passage basic to Grudem's interpretive decisions throughout the New Testament. The reader may refer to a more extensive exposition of the section appearing earlier in this volume.[55]

1. The gift of discernment (1 Cor. 12:10) is a companion gift to prophecy, and 1 Corinthians 14:29 refers to its functioning.[56] The gift of discernment served to identify true prophecy and to dismiss nonprophecy as unworthy of congregational attention. Discerning the worthiness of a prophetic utterance was not an opportunity open to the entire congregation. That was the function of other prophets alone.

2. The "others" of 1 Corinthians 14:29 who judged the validity of

prophecies were the other prophets.[57] "Others" does not refer to the entire congregation and their being allowed to form subjective opinions about the prophecies.[58] Nor does the evaluation of prophecies by others imply the presence of both true and false elements in the prophecy.[59] It simply enables the congregation to detect whether the message was a prophecy from God.[60]

3. New Testament prophets spoke divinely inspired words, not "merely human words" toward which the congregation could adopt a "take it or leave it" attitude.[61] Prophecy would have been an exercise in futility if recipients of its message had the choice of accepting or not accepting its stipulations.

4. Divine revelation to a prophet carried the guarantee that the prophet would report it accurately to his listeners and not weaken its authority through human mistakes.[62] Hence it was binding that the hearers (or readers) submit to the doctrinal and ethical standards of the revelation.[63]

5. First Corinthians 12:31 does not command Christians to seek additional gifts (including prophecy) for themselves individually, as Grudem contends, but tells them to seek the greater gifts for their local congregation.[64] The quest was to be for additional gifts that would benefit the whole group the most, not for additional gifts to be given to individuals.

6. Faith and hope do not continue beyond the second coming of Christ (Rom. 8:24–25; 2 Cor. 5:6–8).[65] Herein lies their contrast to love, as stated in 1 Corinthians 13:13, for love is eternal.

7. The gifts of prophecy, tongues, and knowledge served their useful purpose during the same period as the gift of apostleship, and they ceased functioning after the period of the apostles and direct revelatory activity (1 Cor. 13:8–13).[66] Miraculous signs necessary to confirm spokesmen of divine revelation were purposeless after the conclusion of the period during which God was granting special revelation.

A PREFERRED VIEW OF PROPHECY

Other corrective recommendations for Grudem's work are possible, but instead, an alternative to Grudem's view of prophecy, one more in line with the view of the second-century church, will alleviate some confusion.[67]

Persons possessing the gift of prophecy shared with the apostles the privilege and responsibility of being channels of direct divine revelation. They had insights into the "mysteries" of God (1 Cor. 13:2; Eph. 2:20; 3:3, 5) as did the apostles. Yet, one with the gift of prophecy did not necessarily have the gift of apostleship also. It seems that the converse was the case—all apostles were prophets—but most prophets did not meet the criteria required to be an apostle. Consequently prophets did not have the same broad authority in the body of Christ as did apostles. Yet, New Testament prophets were still vehicles of authoritative divine revelation (cf. 1 Cor. 14:29), some of which passed into written form and gained a place in Scripture (e.g., the Epistle to the Hebrews; see Appendix D). The very words of their prophecies, being based on and inseparable from divine revelation, were inspired and therefore authoritative. That was an indispensable element of prophecy. Without direct revelation from God, someone who promoted edification through exhortation and comfort had to base his message on the inspired words of others and was exercising the gift of exhortation (cf. Rom. 12:8) or teaching (cf. 1 Cor. 12:28), not the gift of prophecy. This explanation of modern-day preaching is preferable to the view that equates preaching with the gift of prophecy. Through their receiving of special revelations from God, the prophets were authoritative, though not in as general a sense as the apostles.

Another distinction between apostles and prophets is in their sphere of responsibility. Whereas the apostles' responsibility was to minister to the church at large and to extend its borders, those who were prophets only usually served in settled situations, being attached to a single local church (Acts 13:1; 15:32).

The prophets' special function was to provide edification to the body of Christ by exhorting and comforting the saints through the revelations granted them (1 Cor. 14:3, 29–30). Most of these revelations were temporary and local in application, and were not needed for the body of Christ in other generations and localities. Those of permanent value were in written form, preserved as part of the New Testament canon.

Another element of prophetic ministry was the ability to predict future happenings (Acts 11:27–28; 21:10–22; 1 Tim. 1:18; Rev. 1:3). As far as can be determined from the New Testament, the predictive element of prophecy for the body of Christ was not as extensive as it was in the prophetic ministry to the people of Israel in the Old Testament. Yet, Old Testament prophets were more closely parallel to New Testament prophets, not to New Testament apostles.[68] Though prediction was not the major element in New Testament prophecy, it was an indispensable part of it.

Because of future predictions and their fulfillment, the prophetic gift appears among the "confirmatory" gifts in 1 Corinthians 12:10. The fulfillment of a prophet's prediction gave him the credentials of divine authority in the eyes of those to whom he spoke. That was the way with Paul on His voyage to Rome (Acts 27). In a terrible storm and against overwhelming odds, he predicted there would be no loss of life among the 276 people on board the ship (27:22-24, 34). When later they all came to land safely (v. 44), Paul's authority as God's spokesman grew immeasurably in the eyes of the rest of ship's passengers. The respect of the crew for Paul, probably in large part because of his prophecy, seems to have grown even before the final prophesied deliverance came about (vv. 31-36), but the fulfillment of his prophecy was God's visible vindication of Paul as His prophet.

Females in the early church also had the gift of prophecy, as indicated by the four virgin daughters of Philip (Acts 21:9). Presumably these functioned in roles within the guidelines Paul set for the conduct of Christian worship. Paul's preference was for them not to prophesy to the whole congregation (1 Cor. 14:34-35), but if they insisted on doing so, it was to be with a sign of authority on their heads (1 Cor. 11:5-6, 10).

With the completion of the last book of the New Testament, the gift of prophecy became obsolete. Jesus pronounced a severe penalty on anyone who attempts to add to the prophecies of the Apocalypse (Rev. 22:18). Since the book of Revelation covers events occurring from the time John wrote it until the eternal state, any alleged prophecy subsequent to that book is counterfeit.[69]

The canon of the New Testament is God's completed revelation for the body of Christ. No more direct divine revelation can come subsequent to the completion of that collection. Prophets in the future will minister to people of Israel and the world at large during the seventieth week of Daniel, after the rapture of the church (Joel 2:28). They will not be the prophets described in relation to the gifts of the Spirit bestowed on members of the body of Christ because the church will no longer be on earth during that period.

CONCLUSION

Grudem has sought to present a concept of prophecy that is not so restrictive (i.e., authoritative) as to exclude charismatically inclined people or so loose (i.e., nonrevelatory) as to repel the noncharismatic.[70] He evidences that in several places. After alluding to the charismatic and noncharismatic positions, the author writes, "Can a fresh examination of the New Testament give us a resolution of these views? Does the text of Scripture itself indicate a 'middle ground' or a 'third position' which preserves what is really important to both sides and yet is faithful to the teaching of the New Testament? I think the answer to these questions is yes."[71] In the same vein he writes, "So I wonder if there may be room for more *joint* theological reflection on this area."[72]

A desire for unity is commendable, but the compulsion to obtain unity should not be so strong that it necessitates mishandling the New Testament text. Second-century Christians rightly valued the survival of the truth over the establishment of a unity that would have encompassed Montanist teaching. If they had sought a middle ground with the Montanists' error regarding the gift of prophecy, that would have seriously retarded the progress of the church. They did the right thing in labeling the movement as unorthodox in that phase of its doctrine, thereby preserving the right perspective regarding the true nature of New Testament prophecy.

The desire to bring Christians together should not be based on a premise that is less than faithful to the New Testament standards. The New Testament picture of the gift of prophecy remains undistorted, namely, the spiritual ability to convey authoritative and inerrant revelatory messages from God in the church up to the time of the completion of the New Testament canon for the edification of the body of Christ. The description of this gift in *The Gift of Prophecy in the New Testament and Today* falls short of that standard.

Appendix C

THE SPIRITUAL GIFT OF PROPHECY IN REVELATION 22:18

I. DESCRIPTION OF THE SPIRITUAL GIFT OF PROPHECY

Recent attempts have sought to define prophecy so as to cover all kinds of prophecy, including New Testament prophecy.[1] These definitions are helpful in pointing out some of the leading characteristics of Christian prophets— that is, those with the spiritual gift of prophecy—but a description rather than a definition facilitates more comprehension of all that the gift entails.

A. CHARACTERISTICS OF THE GIFT OF PROPHECY

In the following listed properties of prophecy the purpose is to represent a general consensus of current opinions. Because of the objective here of dealing with the gift in the apocalypse of John, certain assumptions are necessary. These assumptions have been effectively developed elsewhere as noted. (1) The gift involved immediate divine inspiration of the spokesperson or writer.[2] (2) The gift provided exhortation and encouragement.[3] (3) Another aspect of prophecy was its element of teaching.[4] (4) The gift of prophecy incorporated prediction.[5] (5) The gift entailed a degree of authority less than that of the Old Testament prophets and the New Testament apostles, but some kind of authority was present.[6] (6) A further characteristic of New Testament prophecy was its inclusion of an ability to discern the validity of other prophecies.[7] (7) Gifted prophets had an ability to perceive the thoughts and motives of other persons (cf. Luke 7:39; John 4:19; Acts 5:3-4; 8:21ff.).[8] (8) Exercise of the gift was occasionally accompanied by symbolic acts.[9] (9) Another phenomenon was that most often prophets were residents in a single locale, but some were also itinerant.[10] (10) Additionally, most New Testament prophecy was oral, but some was written.[11] (11) Prophetic language was characterized by a variety of literary forms.[12] (12) Another characteristic of prophecy was its dependence on the Holy Spirit.[13] (13) Another observation calls attention to the gift not being an office in the church but rather a regular ministry to the church.[14] (14) A further point is that the gift entailed the prophet's being in a special state, usually called "ecstasy."[15] (15) This New Testament gift provided for a "charismatic exegesis" of traditional material.[16] (16) A last characteristic is that the spiritual gift was described as in some sense temporary.[17]

From the above characteristics one must conclude that not all prophecy is the same as the spiritual gift of prophecy. For instance, there are differences between this gift to the body of Christ, on the one hand, and prophecy as practiced in the Old Testament and in Judaism, on the other.[18] The New Testament prophet did not enjoy unlimited authority as did the Old Testament prophet. He was a member of the community, not an authority figure over it.[19] The Apocalypse appears to be an exception to this, until one remembers that here apostolic authority is represented, not just prophetic authority.[20]

Because of this and other differences, in the words of Aune, "Christian prophecy is most adequately treated as a distinctively Christian institution."[21] It is a gift intended only for the body of Christ, and like the body of Christ, it has temporal limitations in regard to its appearance in history.

B. UNFOUNDED IDENTIFICATIONS OF THE GIFT OF PROPHECY

At times unfounded ideas regarding the gift of prophecy have been advanced. One of them is that prophecy is another name for preaching.[22] To equate preaching with the spiritual gift of prophecy is wrong.[23] Preaching is a merging of the gifts of teaching and exhortation.[24]

It is also significant to note that prophecy is not an ecstatic frenzy of some sort.[25] Whatever terminology is chosen to designate their state, New Testament prophets never lost control of their senses.[26] The English word "ecstasy" has many meanings, but whatever meaning it has in connection with New Testament prophecy, it cannot denote that the prophet lost his composure.[27]

The notion that there were two gifts of prophecy in the body of Christ also needs to be dispelled. That there could be one gift through which the words were inspired and another through which only the general gist of the prophecy was inspired[28] presses for nonexistent distinctions. The major support for such a distinction rests on differentiating prophecy in 1 Corinthians 12–14 and prophecy in Ephesians 2:20; 3:5.[29] But whenever the New Testament describes prophetic revelatory activity it always uses the same terminology.[30] To bear this out, Paul's prophetic gift is included in both the above sections (1 Cor. 13:9; 14:6; Eph. 3:1–5).

Another wrong idea advocates that the gift of prophecy was a means of reading back into the life of Jesus words uttered long after His ascension. J. Jeremias has written, "Early Christian prophets addressed congregations in words of encouragement, admonition, censure and promise, using the name of Christ in the first person. Prophetic sayings of this kind found their way into the tradition about Jesus and became fused with the words that he had spoken during his lifetime."[31]

Such reasoning is faulty. The prophetic utterances cited in support of that notion are known to this day to be words of the risen Lord, not words given to New Testament prophets after His ascension. They offer no basis for attributing to the historical Jesus words of the exalted Christ spoken to the prophet through the Spirit.[32]

II. THE APOCALYPSE AS A PRODUCT OF THE GIFT OF PROPHECY

For the sake of clarity it is well to point out specifically that the Apocalypse is the result of the spiritual gift of prophecy. Its character is primarily that of a prophecy rather than Jewish apocalyptic and that of New Testament rather than Old Testament prophecy.

A. APOCALYPTIC VERSUS PROPHECY

Revelation was the first book to be called an "apocalypse," being so labeled on the basis of the first word in its Greek text (Rev. 1:1). Since 1822, the term has become widely used to describe a distinctive literary genre of works that resemble the apocalypse of John in both form and content.[33]

Since John's apocalypse is the source of the terminology, one might be inclined to call it apocalyptic rather than prophecy. That is inaccurate. The work differs from the usual apocalyptic pattern in a number of important respects, such as its lack of pseudonymity.[34] This and other differences bolster the book's claim that it is a prophecy (1:3; 19:10; 22:7, 10, 18–19), and it must be accepted as such even though it has a number of features in common with apocalyptic.[35]

B. OLD TESTAMENT PROPHECY VERSUS NEW TESTAMENT PROPHECY

Similarities between the Apocalypse and Old Testament prophecy are observable.[36] Yet, evidence is available to offset these similarities and to show John to be representative of, if not typical of, early Christian prophets.

Like other Christian prophets, John received divine revelation that he relayed to his prophetic colleagues in the churches.[37] He exhorted and encouraged. He also taught and predicted the future. He claimed authority, more so than the typical prophet because he was an apostle. The seven messages of chapters 2–3 reflect his insight into the inner lives of the people in the churches. Symbolic acts accompany his prophecy. Though he did not deliver his prophecy orally in a local church setting, he directed that it be read there. His prophecy was the message of the Holy Spirit. He received his visions while "in the spirit," probably a reference to an ecstatic state of some kind. He interpreted traditional material, particularly the Old Testament, with the charismatic exegesis typical of a prophet.

Since John was a member of the body of Christ and since his prophecy was overwhelmingly similar to the spiritual gift of prophecy, the conclusion must be that John produced this prophecy through the use of that gift.

III. THE RELATIONSHIP BETWEEN THE END OF NEW TESTAMENT PROPHECY AND REVELATION 22:18

A closer look at Revelation 22:18–19 lessens further any lingering doubts about whether the Apocalypse is prophecy: "I testify to everyone who hears the words of the prophecy of this book: If anyone adds to them, God will add to him the plagues that have been written about in this book; and if anyone takes away from the words of the book of this prophecy, God will take away his part from the tree of life and from the holy city, which have been written about in this book." Käsemann and Aune have cited the literary form of these statements as evidence of the prophetic nature of the book.[38]

A. A PROPOSED PURPOSE: TO ASSURE ACCURACY

Aune sees these verses as typical of the effort of prophets to insure the accurate transmission of their writing. H. B. Swete and Caird note other writers who followed the same practice of giving scribes added incentive to copy their works carefully.[39] This kind of warning was particularly characteristic of the Jews in their view of the inviolate nature of Scripture (cf. Deut. 4:2; 12:32).[40]

The idea that the purpose of Revelation 22:18–19 was primarily to assure accurate transmission is open to serious question. The admonition is not addressed to potential copyists but, as 1:3 states and 22:18 confirms, to listeners at church gatherings in the seven cities to which John sent the Apocalypse. For them, adding and subtracting could hardly come by way of altering the text that the public reader held in his hand.[41] The listeners had no control over that written document. Besides this, if the purpose of the warning was to assure accurate transmission, it has signally failed because today no other book of the New Testament has such an uncertain text.[42]

B. A PROPOSED PURPOSE: TO ASSURE OBEDIENCE TO COMMANDS

If accurate transmission was not the goal of the warning, then what was it? Others have noted that its purpose must coincide with the purpose of the book as a whole: to obtain higher moral behavior.[43] Eliminating soft-pedaling of the book's teachings would uphold its high ethical standards and jealously guard its spirit. No distorting thought to evade the required behavior was allowable. That was the thrust of Moses' similar injunction in Deuteronomy.

Such a purpose as this for the whole book is undeniable, but it hardly fits the wording of 22:18–19. "Keeping the things written" in the words of this prophecy was John's way of speaking of obedience in 1:3. That is very clear, but much manipulation is necessary to make the warning in 22:18 mean that. The prohibition pertains to the content, not to the hearers' moral response to the content. In Deuteronomy 4:2, Moses was zealous to preserve intact the commands he had written. He wanted the log of commandments retained without any alteration. Compliance by way of obedience was certainly the purpose of the Pentateuch, but Deuteronomy 4:2 pertained to the source document itself. So the same must be true of 22:18, and that rules out this purpose of the warning.

C. THE CONDITION OF THE CHURCHES OF ASIA

Before consideration of a final possibility, a closer look at the situation in the churches will facilitate discovery of how they would have understood such a warning.

The Christian communities to which John wrote were distinctly prophecy conscious.[44] Apostleship was disappearing, and Christians were searching for new leadership authority. John was one of a larger group of prophets who ministered to these seven churches. According to 22:6 "the God of the spirits of the prophets" sent John to make this revelation, and according to 22:9 the angel was also "a fellow slave of John's brothers, the prophets." The role of these gifted prophets was to mediate divine revelation to the churches (cf. 1:1, 3).[45] The warning in 2:20 to Jezebel, who claimed to be a prophetess, further confirms the focus on prophecy. The words of 22:18 must be understood in light of a wider prophetic ministry that was active in the churches.

The Johannine epistles also attest widespread prophetic activity in Asia during the last decade of the first century. First John 4:1 reflects a major problem created by the multiplication of prophets: "Many false prophets have gone out into the world." Very likely, those were the secessionist deceivers who posed so great a problem for the readers of 1 John.[46] For this reason, John proposed a testing of the spirits to determine whether they were of God.[47]

They were claiming prophetic authority superior to that of John, so John challenged his readers to test them.

John was coping with a growing wave of false prophecy. People of this type undermined the position and authority of genuine prophets.[48] The same problem is reflected in 2 and 3 John.[49]

The Apocalypse needs to be understood against a backdrop of competition for authority and leadership in the churches of the area, including a struggle among competing prophets. The *Didache* and the *Shepherd of Hermas*, which originated a few years later, reflect the growing numbers of false prophets.[50] Regarding this period, Friedrich writes that "false prophets are abroad and these undermine the authority and repute of true prophets."[51]

Evidence of prophetic conflict is present in the Apocalypse itself. John saw the behavior of Jezebel (2:20–24) and the Nicolaitans (2:6, 15) as contrary to Christian norms and therefore deserving of condemnation.[52] He also took issue with the doctrinal basis of this behavior. Mention of the teaching of the prophet Balaam in conjunction with the Nicolaitan heresy (2:14–15) commends the view that novel emphases of the movement were supported by prophetic utterances.[53] John's commendation of those in Thyatira who had not known "the deep things" (*ta bathea*) of Satan (2:24) evidences a revelatory activity whose source was devilish. These revelations were counterparts of the revelations from God to Christian prophets that enabled them to know "the deep things" (*ta bathē*) of God (1 Cor. 2:10). Also the false apostles rejected by the Christian community at Ephesus (Rev. 2:2) probably represented a claim to divine authority in support of the Nicolaitan teaching.[54]

Opposing ideologies had arisen, all of which supported their positions by alleged prophetic utterances. The author of the Apocalypse represented only one of those who sought to prevail against the others.[55] His warning in 22:18 as well as the strong emphasis on his prophetic call in 1:9–20 was an attempt to settle this authority crisis once for all.

D. THE EFFECT OF THE WARNING ON OTHER PROPHETS

How would the warning have affected other prophets and the willingness of the churches to hear them? To them, it was not a restriction on false prophecy only. This had been tried earlier in dealing with Jezebel and the Nicolaitans. Nor was it an effort to keep other prophets from tampering with the contents of the Apocalypse. It was not change that was forbidden in verse 18 but addition—the warning of 22:19 deals with change. The warning was probably understood as prohibiting additional prophetic activity.

A slight distinction in phraseology in the warning's two parts is significant. In 22:18 the sequence is "the words of the prophecy of this book," the greater emphasis lying on the prophecy, and in 22:19 it is "the words of the book of this prophecy," which puts more focus on the totality of the book composed of prophecies.[56] So when John[57] warned against adding to the words, the principal item in mind was additional prophecy.

It is reasonable that he was forbidding any further prophecy. Two circumstances show this: (1) John had tried unsuccessfully to deal with false prophecy by warning against it. Jezebel is a case in point. He had given her a chance to repent, and she refused (2:21). No way is available for knowing about the success of his warning against false prophecies in 1 John 4:1-6, but judging by the continuing encroachments of related false doctrines about the person of Christ in the early second century, it was at best only partially successful. By the time he wrote the Apocalypse, John may well have decided that the only solution was to have no more prophecy of any kind. (2) The comprehensive scope of the Apocalypse also commends the all-inclusive nature of the prohibition of 22:18. The book is comprehensive in its inclusion of both the words of encouragement and parenesis (Rev. 2-3) and the predictive elements of prophecy (Rev. 4-22). If nothing additional is allowable in these two areas, that in essence spells the end of the gift. The book is also comprehensive in what it professes to cover. Regardless of which interpretive approach one follows, it claims to span the entire period from John's time through history into eternity future, from the death and resurrection of the Lamb to the Parousia and after.[58] Any prohibition about adding to a book of that scope is tantamount to cancellation of prophetic activity for the church altogether.

The anticipation of this strong warning is that the book's message will be unpopular, especially with other prophets. Certainly this was true for the false prophetess Jezebel and her followers (2:20ff.), the propagators of Nicolaitanism (2:6-7), and the Jewish slanderers in Philadelphia (3:12).[59] John did not warn about potential mistakes of judgment in interpreting the book but about deliberate distortions by others who claimed prophetic authority.[60]

Incipient Gnosticism was gathering momentum in his day. This kind of warning was needed to head off such works as the *Gospel of Thomas*, which presented the teaching of Jesus so as to make Him into a Gnostic. A little later, Marcion's edition of Luke depicted Jesus as not having a real body. He also promoted antinomianism. Tatian's *Diatessaron* had a heretical bias in selecting the passages to include. According to Tertullian, Valentinus perverted the text of the whole New Testament by additions and changes.[61]

Another indication that John saw the need to terminate prophecy is visible in his choice of the "canonization formula" of Deuteronomy 4:1ff. as a model for Revelation 22:18-19.[62] Though consistently viewed as applying primarily to the Pentateuch, the words from Deuteronomy came to be applied by extension to the Old Testament in defense against any further additions to it. In essence, then, John claimed canonical authority for his writing.[63] In so doing, he indicated that there were to be no more inspired messages.

E. THE RESPONSE TO THE WARNING

If the tentative conclusion is that the meaning of 22:18 entailed the termination of the spiritual gift of prophecy, what was the impact upon the seven churches of Asia? History has not preserved a detailed answer to that question. The churches could have responded with complete compliance and the prophets in the churches ceased their prophesying immediately. In light of the difficulties that John had already encountered with these prophets,however, a unanimous response of this type seems unlikely. What appears more probable is that compliance with the warning was gradual, with prophetic messages diminishing slowly over a long period of time.

A survey of second-century Christian writings supports the probability of the latter type of response. John's words originally went directly to the seven churches of Asia and, in effect, attempted to shut off prophecy in those churches. It was not long, however, until the authority of his warning spread more widely. The second-century Muratorian Canon records, "For John also, although in the Apocalypse he wrote to seven churches, nevertheless speaks to all."[64] The seven churches were understood as representative of all churches everywhere. Instructions given them were universally binding.

History describes the second century as a crisis period for prophetism in Christian communities.[65] Various scholars acknowledge that New Testament prophecy did in fact undergo a gradual decline through the course of the second century A.D. Aune notes that prophets are conspicuous in their absence from a statement in the *Shepherd of Hermas* that mentions apostles, bishops, teachers, and deacons. In the same quotation, apostles are a thing of the past.[66] A similar omission occurs in at least three other places in the *Shepherd*. Aune suggests that the omission may be designed to discredit the kind of prophecy with which the author was familiar.[67] He also proposes that certain characteristics of the true prophet in that work indicate that revelatory experiences described in the *Shepherd* were literary fiction and not based on actual revelatory events.[68] The *Didache* apparently implies that the number of prophets was dwindling at the time of its writing.[69] Not all Christian communities had resident prophets, indicating that a prophet was no longer essential to the life and worship of the church.[70] Early in the third century, Hippolytus, an opponent of a number of heresies including Montanism, held the apostle John to be the last of the prophets.[71]

F. REASONS FOR THE DECLINE OF NEW TESTAMENT PROPHECY

Most cite the Montanist movement as marking the termination of the gift.[72] Hitherto, recent suggestions unrelated to Revelation 22:18 have been forthcoming to explain this termination. Five major reasons have been cited, three explaining the decline sociologically and two theologically:[73] (1) The presence of false prophets, which eventually undermined the authority of genuine prophets.[74] This opinion coincides with the growing problem faced by the author of the Apocalypse. Eventually the church dealt with it by ruling out prophecy altogether. (2) The repudiation of Montanist prophecy.[75] Montanism looked upon itself as a "new prophecy." It was indeed new because it represented a total break in the significance of prophecy for early Christianity.[76] Reaction against the Montanists caused the church to deal decisively with prophecy. This reaction cannot be the whole explanation, however, because a trend was evident before Montanism arose. (3) Increasing authority of the official ministry in an institutionalized church.[77] Evidence indicates that the prophet, like the apostle, was never integrated into the organizational structure of the local church.[78] Intramural conflict developed between prophets and the established leadership composed of elders and deacons, and prophets were the eventual losers.[79]

The presence of this conflict is undeniable, but one cannot help asking how the first-century church handled this circumstance without a power struggle. The two realms of authority coexisted then in reasonable harmony without major confrontation. Hence, that reason is too superficial to be primary.

The last two proposals are theological: (4) The proper transmission of apostolic truth.[80] Revelation that had come through the apostles was most highly regarded. Hence recent prophetic revelations were viewed with suspicion.[81] (5) The foundational nature of the prophetic gift.[82] The mention of prophets as part of the foundation of the church in Ephesians 2:20 suggests that once the church was established the gift would be discontinued.[83]

Two additional contributing influences in the decline and end of New Testament prophecy are plausible: (6) The close association of the gift with that of apostleship. Prophets are repeatedly found alongside apostles in the New Testament (1 Cor. 12:28–29; Eph. 2:20; 3:5; 4:11; Rev. 18:20). Apostleship was a thing of the past to second-century writers. An analogous end of its companion gift was certainly a live option. This close association of the two gifts is verified by the *Didache,* Ignatius, and the Muratorian Canon.[84] The last-named work looks back to the end of prophecy by saying the number of prophets was complete (see Appendix D of this volume for further elabora-tion). (7) Analogy with the end of Old Testament prophecy. Whether Old Testament prophecy ended, leaving a period without prophetic activity be-fore the beginning of New Testament prophecy, is debated. Guy, Peisker, and Hill say that it ended with Haggai, Zechariah, and Malachi.[85] Aune and Meyer question that conclusion.[86] Yet, amid their questioning, they admit that Ju-daism in the time of Jesus held that prophecy had ceased with the close of the Old Testament canon. They also admit that prophecy, as they define it, underwent radical changes after Malachi. Aune goes so far as to speak of "a period when the canon was virtually closed and prophetic inspiration had ended."[87] Without investigating details of the debate, a sound conclusion is that a major change occurred, even if Old Testament prophecy as some define it was not terminated, strictly speaking.

Early Christian leaders knew the opinion of Judaism on the issue. If they viewed Old Testament prophecy as having ended, they must also have entertained the same possibility for New Testament prophecy.

In summary, significant factors in the decline of the spiritual gift of prophecy were, sociologically, the threat of false prophecy and, theologically, the preservation of apostolic truth, the foundational nature of the gift of prophecy, the close association of prophecy with apostleship, and the model provided by the cessation of Old Testament prophecy.

G. The Purpose of Revelation 22:18

The part played by the warning of Revelation 22:18 in this decline and cessation should not be overlooked, however. That was perhaps the most basic reason of all. The warning must be understood in light of the prophetic focus of the times. Ample reason existed for John to conclude that no more prophecy was needed. Over a century ago, Bishop Wordsworth approximated this opinion about the warning: "Here is a prophetic protest against spurious Revelations forged by false Teachers in the name of the Apostles. . . . Here is also a Prophetic Protest against all *additions* to the words of Holy Scripture; whether these additions be made by unwritten traditions, or by Apocryphal books, as of equal authority with Holy Scripture."[88]

Heretofore this essay has approached Revelation 22:18 as the words of John the prophet, which they surely were.[89] In addition, there is the basic exegetical issue of whether they are an editorial comment of the prophet or a quotation of the words of Jesus Himself. Very good reasons exist to choose the latter option. Notably, the first-person subject of *martyrō*, "I testify," in 22:18 is identified in 22:20 where the participle of the same verb is used in the statement, "The one who testifies these things says, 'Yes, I come quickly.'" The warning must be a direct quotation of Jesus.[90]

If this is true, the profundity of the warning's implications for the spiritual gift of prophecy is even more striking. It was not merely a human desire of John to end competition. Here is a divine proclamation terminating use of the gift. This thought is sobering, though ultimately it carries no more authority than the words of John as Christ's prophetic spokesman.

IV. CONCLUSION

The conclusion of this investigation accepts the inevitability of connecting the decline and cessation of the spiritual gift of prophecy to Revelation 22:18. Compliance with, indeed universal knowledge of, this warning was not immediate. Nevertheless the divine intention behind the warning necessitated that it eventually be recognized and that the body of Christ move into new phases of its growth without dependence on the foundational gift of prophecy.

Appendix D

CORRELATION OF REVELATORY SPIRITUAL GIFTS AND NEW TESTAMENT CANONICITY

In three of his epistles—Romans, 1 Corinthians, and Ephesians—the apostle Paul speaks of God's building the body of Christ through spiritual gifts He bestows on individual believers. Among the eighteen gifts Paul mentions are several that provided for special revelation to the church, revelation that would complement the inspired data available to early Christians in the Old Testament. The following discussion will explore how those revelatory gifts related to books of the New Testament canon that the church eventually identified.

First will come a brief explanation to identify the New Testament revelatory gifts of the Spirit, particularly those in addition to apostleship. A follow-up section will discuss several New Testament examples of revelatory gifts in action in the New Testament. After this will come a listing and discussion of tests of canonicity applied by the early church in its recognition of the New Testament canon. The second and third of these sections will focus on the importance of the gift of prophecy.

REVELATORY SPIRITUAL GIFTS

The obvious starting point in correlating revelatory spiritual gifts and New Testament canonicity is the New Testament gift of apostleship. Apostolic authorship is the most widely cited test of canonicity, with some scholars going to the point of asserting that it is the only criterion. Harris has stated, ". . . The test of canonicity applied by the early church was apostolic authorship."[1] He concludes,

The view of the determining principle of the canon expressed previously may be summarized by saying that the canonicity of a book of the Bible depends upon its authorship. If the book was in the Old Testament, the people of the day accepted it because it was written by a prophet. If it was part of the New Testament, it was recognized as inspired if it had been written by an apostle—either by himself or with the help of an understudy or amanuensis.[2]

He cites extensive evidence from the New Testament itself to demonstrate the authoritative role of apostles.[3] He concludes his discussion with these statements: "The Lord Jesus did not, in prophecy, give us a list of the twenty-seven New Testament books. He did, however, give us a list of the inspired authors [i.e., the apostles]."[4] One can hardly debate the major role of the apostles in penning books of the New Testament and the recognition of the early church regarding the importance of that role in pinpointing books to take their places alongside the Old Testament canon as authoritative Scripture.

Yet to limit the determination of canonicity to apostolic authorship alone is precarious. In speaking about Ephesians 4:11 and 1 Corinthians 12:28, Harris notes the first rank of apostles and the second rank of prophets, and says, "The gift of prophecy was one which all Christians were to desire; the apostolate came directly from God."[5] He observes later in comparing New Testament prophecy with Old Testament prophecy that New Testament prophets held a lower status in the area of divine authority, indicating that tests of fulfilled predictions and miracles did not apply to them.[6]

This representation of the gift of prophecy is seriously misleading. For one thing, though the New Testament prophet did not have to pass tests of fulfilled predictions and miracles, he did have to pass the test of discernings of spirits in the presence of his fellow prophets (1 Cor. 12:10; 14:29).[7] Also, the context of 1 Corinthians 12 and 14 shows quite clearly that God sovereignly bestows all gifts of the Spirit according to His will and not according to human quests and desires. First Corinthians 12:11 describes the source of gifts this way: "But one and the same Spirit works all these things, distributing to every single person just as He wills." And 1 Corinthians 12:18 confirms, "But now God on His part has placed the members, each one of them, in the body just as He desired." Prophecy was not "up for grabs" among the members of Christ's body. Harris apparently has mistakenly understood 1 Corinthians 12:31 to convey that sense, but the command to be zealous for the greater gifts was a command for the corporate local body to seek the greater gifts for itself, not for each individual Christian to do so for himself or herself. First Corinthians 14:29–31 clarifies that only a limited number had that gift in the Corinthian church. The last passage also shows that whatever authority the prophetic gift possessed was subject to the authority of Paul, who as an apostle had the authority to direct its usage.[8]

Apostleship was not the only revelatory gift among those named in Pauline epistles. Prophecy was another, along with two others that seemed to have overlapped or to have been somewhat interchangeable with apostleship and prophecy. These are the word of wisdom and the word of knowledge (1 Cor. 12:8).[9] The replacement of wisdom and knowledge by apostleship and prophecy at the head of the lists of 1 Corinthians 12:28–29 furnishes strong implications regarding close relationships between the two pairs of gifts.[10] Several lines of reasoning affirm the revelational character of these three nonapostolic gifts: prophecy, the word of wisdom, and the word of knowledge.

(1) Prophecy's close association with apostleship requires its inclusion in the revelational category. Twice in 1 Corinthians 12:28–29 the gift follows immediately after the apostolic gift as being the second-most profitable in edifying the church. In Ephesians 4:11, it again takes second place after apostles in a listing of gifted persons who contributed to building up the body of Christ. Perhaps most interesting of all is the inclusion of prophets with apostles in Ephesians 2:20–21 as having a significant role in laying the foundation of the spiritual "holy temple" of the church.[11] Contextually, the foundational role includes the reception and transmission of previously undisclosed "revelation" (Eph. 3:3, 5) regarding the fellow heirship and joint membership of Gentiles and Jews in the body of Christ (Eph. 3:6). Regarding that new revelation, Paul speaks of information "which in other generations was not made known to the sons of men as it has now been revealed to the saints through His apostles *and prophets* through the Spirit" (Eph. 3:5, emphasis added). The prophets along with the apostles were recipients of special divine revelation, according to the apostle.

In the context of Ephesians 2:19–3:10, another characteristic emerges. That is the appearance of a certain technical vocabulary pertaining to divine revelatory activity. The terms include *apokalypsin* ("revelation") in 3:3, *mystērion* ("mystery") in 3:3 and *mystēriō* in 3:4, *apekalyphthē* ("has been revealed") in 3:5, *mystēriou* in 3:9, and *apokekrymmenou* ("hidden") in 3:9. All are words that frequently assume a technical revelatory significance. When used together, they portray God's activity in making known to His special servants hitherto unrevealed information relating to the outworking of His program in the world. The clustering of such words in a given context is indicative of direct revelatory activity such as provides for divine inspiration through His spokespersons and, in the case of the New Testament, writers. In this type of setting *gnōrizō* ("I make known,"), also used in that Ephesian context (3:3, 5, 10), takes on a special meaning of an immediate proclamation of the divine will.[12] Added to the technical terms is, of course, the noun *apostolos* ("apostle") in 2:20 and 3:5, a designation applied by almost everyone to special authoritative appointees of Christ who received direct revelation for the church.

The appearance of prophets alongside the apostles in such a strongly revelatory context, and their role in conveying previously unrevealed data (Eph. 3:5), supplies a pointed indication that prophecy, too, was a revelatory gift. Nor should it escape notice that another gift-related term, *sophia* ("wisdom," 3:10), appears here with the rest of the revelatory terms. It designates new information received through apostles and prophets. This appearance of "wisdom" directs attention to another passage where it is prominent.

(2) Paul wrote much about wisdom in his first epistle to Corinth, especially in 1 Corinthians 2, another context where revelatory terms are frequent. That passage provides readers with what is probably the best New Testament picture of regular Christian revelatory activity.[13] Technical words there include *mystērion* in verses 1[14] and 7, *apokryptō* in verse 7, *apokalyptō* in verse 10, and *sophia* in verses 1, 4, 5, 6 (twice), 7, and 13. In addition, Paul graphically describes the hiddenness of what God has revealed in a conflation of quotations from Isaiah 64:4 and 52:15 (v. 9) and uses a technical expression for secrets of God, *ta bathē* ("the deep things,"[15] v. 10), that the Spirit has revealed to Paul and other special divine messengers.

Amid this strongly revelatory context, the apostle emphatically designates the Holy Spirit as the immediate agent of revelation and climaxes his description of the process thus: "which things we also speak, not with words taught by human wisdom, but with [those] taught by the Spirit, combining spiritual [thoughts] with spiritual [words]" (1 Cor. 2:13). Charles Hodge renders the last three Greek words of that verse, "clothing the truths of the Spirit in the words of the Spirit," and continues:

There is neither in the Bible nor in the writings of men, a simpler or clearer statement of the doctrines of revelation and inspiration. Revelation is the act of communicating divine knowledge by the Spirit to the mind. Inspiration is the act of the same Spirit, controlling those who make the truth known to others. The thoughts, the truths made known, and the words in which they are recorded, are declared to be equally from the Spirit.[16]

The way special agents of divine revelation operated was to receive input from the Spirit in their inner consciousness and through the Spirit to transform that input into inspired words they communicated to others. They may have delivered those words orally as in a prophet's communication to a local congregation in Corinth, or they may have done so in writing as in the first epistle of Paul to the Corinthians. The purpose of the former type was to meet needs of that particular congregation for a time. The ultimate purpose of the latter, after meeting the doctrinal and practical needs of the Corinthian congregation, was to minister in the same way to the body of Christ throughout the present age. Divine revelation had divine inspiration as its necessary sequel.

Sophia is prominent throughout Paul's discussion of the process of revelation and inspiration, a factor that attaches to the term a technical revelatory significance. It may in some contexts refer generally to wisdom available to all believers, but in this kind of setting it has its more restricted sense of referring to "the deep things of God" communicated to agents of special revelation. The latter is its connotation when Paul speaks of "the word of wisdom" in 1 Corinthians 12:8. That was a gift to a limited number that enabled them as apostles and prophets to receive, assimilate, and communicate "mysteries" to others.

(3) The gift of "the word of knowledge" takes on a revelatory connotation because of its use alongside prophecy in 1 Corinthians 13:2: "And if I have [the gift of] prophecy and know all mysteries and all knowledge, and if I have all faith so that I move mountains, but do not have love, I am nothing." If knowledge results from prophetic revelations as do mysteries, it, too, must be revelatory in nature. As the word of wisdom pertained to newly revealed data, the word of knowledge apparently pertained to an inspired application of that data to new situations, as illustrated in 2 Peter 3:1–3 and Jude 17–18.[17]

If the New Testament names more than one revelatory gift—as it apparently does—that opens the possibility that writings by nonapostles could be inspired.

EVIDENCE OF REVELATORY GIFT ACTIVITY IN THE NEW TESTAMENT

The New Testament itself illustrates the use of revelatory gifts to produce inspired utterances and writings.

(1) The spoken ministry of Agabus is an example. As one of the prophets from Jerusalem who came to the church of Antioch, he predicted a widespread famine that would happen during the reign of Claudius (Acts 11:27–28). The famine occurred as predicted and became the occasion of the "famine visit" by Barnabas and Saul of Tarsus to Jerusalem with an offering to relieve the church in Judea (Acts 11:29–30).

How was Agabus able to foretell the future? God revealed to him, as a possessor of the gift of prophecy, an event soon to occur, which revelation he transformed into spoken words so as to communicate it to fellow Christians. That inspired message provided the basis for the Antiochan church to act by way of providing for their fellow believers in Judea.

Scripture never calls Agabus an apostle, but it does call him a prophet. The gift of prophecy was a sufficient credential to receive special revelation to convert into an inspired message.

Acts records another prophecy and fulfillment of Agabus in Acts 21:10-11:

> And while we remained many days, a certain prophet named Agabus came down from Judea, and after he came to us and took Paul's belt and bound his own feet and hands, he said, "The Holy Spirit says these things: 'The man whose belt this is, the Jews will bind thus in Jerusalem and deliver him into the hands of the Gentiles.'"

Acts later records the literal fulfillment of this prophecy too (21:33).[18] Here is another instance of revelation to a nonapostle who possessed the gift of prophecy and of the inspired utterance resulting from that revelation.

(2) Acts records a prophetic message by Paul and its fulfillment just as it does for Agabus. Acts 27:22 gives Paul's prediction that no loss of life would come to those on the storm-tossed ship. That resulted from a message given him by an angel of God, one that he believed (27:23-25). The prediction even included the grounding of the ship on an island (27:26). Each detail of Paul's prophecy came to fulfillment (27:41-44).

Notable are the parallels of this prophecy and fulfillment with those of Agabus. Yes, Paul was an apostle who would be the expected recipient of revelation to transmit to others as an inspired message. But so was Agabus, a nonapostle.

Probably all the apostles received the gift of prophecy, but not all the prophets were apostles, of course.

(3) Harris has written, "No New Testament book claims authorship by a prophet,"[19] but with his documentation offers a qualified correction to that statement when he acknowledges Revelation to be such a book.[20] Bruce has more correctly noted a New Testament writer who bases his work solely on prophetic inspiration:

> The Apocalypse is called 'the book of this prophecy' (e.g., Rev. 22:19); the author implies that his words are inspired by the same Spirit of prophecy as spoken through the prophets of earlier days: it is in their succession that he stands (Rev. 22:9). . . . Whether the seer of Patmos was the son of Zebedee or not, his appeal throughout the Apocalypse is not to apostolic authority but to prophetic inspiration.[21]

The last book of the Bible conspicuously demonstrates the revelatory nature of the New Testament gift of prophecy. The author bases the book's authority on his prophetic role, not on his apostolic gift. Harris is correct in observing the importance of apostolic authorship in the early church's recognition of the book's canonicity, but within the book itself, John sees the work's prophetic character as furnishing its determinative stature.

He uses *prophētēs* or its cognates eighteen times in the twenty-two chapters.[22] In a number of ways, John puts himself into the category of the Old Testament prophets.[23] He experienced an inaugural vision that gave him a divine endorsement (1:9–20). He used symbolic acts such as devouring the little scroll (10:10). He employed oracular formulas in the messages of chapters two and three (2:1, 8, 12, 18; 3:1, 7, 14). The primary if not exclusive focus in 10:7 is on Old Testament prophets, but just a few verses later, he refers to his own New Testament prophetic gift (10:11). The first three references to prophecy in chapter 11 are probably to Old Testament prophecy (11:3, 6, 10), if Moses and Elijah are those witnesses.

In 11:18, however, *tois prophētais* ("the prophets") probably includes both Old Testament and New Testament prophets. The linking of the prophets with the apostles in the similar passage of 18:20 and the angel's reference to the prophets as John's brothers in 22:9 require inclusion of a reference to New Testament prophets.[24] The writer's reference to prophets in 10:7, however, quite definitely referred to Old Testament prophets. So this must be a book where John regularly groups New Testament prophets with the prestigious company of Old Testament prophets.[25] Several have suggested a reason for such an elevation of New Testament prophets: by the time John wrote Revelation, the death of all the apostles but John had thrust prophecy into the limelight.[26] That such an authority shift occurred toward the close of the first century is quite conceivable in light of John's focus on prophecy in his epistles and in Revelation.[27] Jezebel's claim to the prophetic gift (2:20) is further recognition of the elevation of this gift.

The entity known as Babylon is apparently responsible for the deaths of "saints and prophets" in Revelation 16:6 because 17:6 speaks of that harlot as being drunk "from the blood of the saints and from the blood of the martyrs of Jesus." From the link between the two passages, one would judge that the prophets of 16:6 are Christian prophets. Otherwise, they and their companion "saints" could hardly be martyrs of Jesus. The same observation applies to 18:20, 24. Use of *prophētai* alongside *apostoloi* in verse 20 necessitates a reference to Christian prophets, as does the fact that they suffered persecution for Jesus' sake.[28] In 19:10 once again, exclusively New Testament prophecy is in view. Though the preincarnate Christ was the channel of revelation to the highly regarded Old Testament prophets (1 Peter 1:11), their testimony did not center on the testimony of Jesus. Only New Testament prophets by virtue of being vehicles of Jesus' words could qualify for the definition, "The testimony of Jesus is the spirit of prophecy" (19:10). Of interest in 19:10 is the elevation of the New Testament prophet's revelation to the level of angelic revelation. In response to John's attempt to worship him, the angel identified himself as a fellow slave of John and other Christian prophets, an indication of prophetic inspiration's authority. According to that statement, the prophets had the same part as angels in bearing the witness of Jesus.

The last six references to prophecy are in Revelation 22 (vv. 6, 7, 9, 10, 18, 19) and relate to John's prophetic ministry in writing the prophecy of Revelation. Of special relevance to the present survey is the inclusion of other Christian prophets as "fellow slaves" with the revealing angel (22:9). The verse shows that the prestigious role of the prophet John in 19:10 was not limited to him. It belonged to his contemporaries who also possessed the gift of prophecy.

Of course, as I have suggested elsewhere, 22:18-19 announces the termination of New Testament prophecy.[29] In practice, the church of the second century did not respond immediately to that warning. The decline of prophecy during the second century was gradual, but by the time of Hippolytus[30] and Chrysostom,[31] the gift of prophecy in the church was recognized as a thing of the past.

The discussion above shows the New Testament to speak of four revelatory gifts, apostleship, prophecy, the word of wisdom, and the word of knowledge. The last two overlap with the first two and are not as prominent. None disputes the revelatory character of apostleship, so this discussion's main attention has gone to developing the revelational nature of New Testament prophecy.

TESTS OF CANONICITY

If that is true of New Testament prophecy and if revelation resulted in inspired utterances and inspired writings, it is appropriate to investigate tests applied in the early church to ascertain which books belonged in the canon.

TEST OF INSPIRATION

In light of 2 Timothy 3:16, the test to prove a book's canonicity would be its inspiration: "All Scripture is inspired by God." If inclusion in Scripture involves being "God-breathed" (theopneustos), canonization entailed that same qualification because books of the New Testament canon constitute New Testament Scripture just as books of the Old Testament canon constitute Old Testament Scripture. Some recent scholars have suggested that canon does not equal Scripture, that human elements—the doubts, the debates, and the delays—of the canonical process are a part of the definition of canon.[32] Canon, they say, is a theological construct that belongs to the postapostolic period, but Scripture speaks of the intrinsic quality of inspiration and is devoid of the ideas of delimitation and selection that canon entails.

That definition of canon falters, however, in not conceding that New Testament writers, who were conscious that they were penning Scripture,[33] were also conscious of closed Old Testament canon their works supplemented,[34] creating a new canon that would eventually close if Christ did not return before such a body of literature was complete. If the idea of canon existed this early, it is not legitimate to view canon as a "theological construct" arising in the postapostolic period. It seems better to follow Harris and Warfield in concluding that the test of canonicity is inspiration.[35]

The early church did not apply this test directly and exclusively, however. Gamble notes, ". . . In the deliberations of the ancient church about the authority of its writings, we nowhere find an instance of inspiration being used as a criterion of discrimination."[36] Early second-century Christians lived in an environment of many inspired utterances, some of them a spillover from the apostolic period[37] and some of them allegedly originating in the second century and onward. They apparently applied 2 Timothy 3:16 terminology freely, using words related to "inspiration" to refer to postapostolic writings.[38] Use of "inspiration" to apply to writings from the second century and later is attributable to a lack of discernment among the early fathers.

But to view spill-over sayings from the apostolic period as inspired is most probably valid in many cases. It is likely that early Christians possessed sayings of Jesus not found in the canonical gospels. Such was the case of Paul's citation of Jesus' words in Acts 20:35. In addition, some whose lives spanned from the apostolic period into the postapostolic period likely remembered prophecies of local and temporary application delivered to various congregations. Such were not necessary for the long-term health of the larger body of Christ, however, and were lost to later generations.

So, the task of the second-century church was that of sifting through mounds of inspired sayings and writings—some legitimate and others counterfeit—to come up with those that would benefit the growth of the church until the Lord Jesus' return. The method they used was not to rule out as noninspired all noncanonical writings, but rather to decide on those whose inspiration was unique in that they exhibited special authority with long-lasting and universal value, value that matched the authority of the Old Testament canon.[39] What were their criteria for doing so? It appears that they had a sort of "grid" that writings had to pass through in order to gain that recognition, a grid composed of the following tests.

TEST OF APOSTOLICITY

The first criterion was that of apostolicity or apostolic authorship. Since Jesus Christ left no writings of His own, the special representatives whom He appointed held the highest authority for His followers. Harris presents a thorough case to demonstrate the importance of apostolic authorship to second-century Christian writers.[40] Even in cases where an author was not an apostle, patristic tendencies argued for an apostolic influence. The fathers claimed Peter's apostolic authority for Mark and Paul's apostolic authority for Luke and Hebrews.[41] It is indisputable that a book's relationship to an apostle was an important factor as early Christians sorted among many allegedly inspired writings.

But was apostolicity ultimately determinative? Bruce concluded, "The patristic idea that his [Luke's] Gospel owes something to the apostolic authority of Paul is quite unfounded."[42] Did the early church make a mistake? Was, then, the church's selection based on erroneous criteria? Stonehouse says no, the church did not receive Mark and Luke because of their apostolicity but because of their inspiration.[43]

Harris attempts to defend apostolic authorship as the only criterion, claiming that Mark and Luke followed the teachings of their masters, Peter and Paul, and that Paul wrote Hebrews using a secondary author.[44] He is undecided on the authorship of James and Jude. He holds them to be apostolic either because they were written by the James and Jude, who were among the twelve, or because they were written by James and Jude, the half-brothers of the Lord, who as witnesses of His resurrection became apostles in a special sense.[45]

In defending apostolicity as the sole test, Harris writes, "But rather remarkably, there is no hard evidence for lost writings of the apostles."[46] Later he adds, "Efforts to prove that there were some books that have been lost have not been successful."[47] Yet, statements by Paul in his extant epistles provide substantial indication that he wrote letters that have not survived. The most conclusive evidence of a lost epistle lies in 1 Corinthians 5:9–11 where it is evident to most that Paul refers to a letter to the Corinthians earlier than 1 Corinthians. Philippians 3:1 also offers a strong implication to that effect. About the latter, Lightfoot wrote, ". . . In the epistles of our Canon we have only a part—perhaps not a very large part—of the whole correspondence of the Apostle [Paul], either with Churches or with individuals."[48] Perhaps 2 Corinthians 3:1 in referring to "epistles of recommendation" implies that much correspondence of the nature of 3 John circulated among early churches to provide personal letters of introduction. If apostles wrote some of those, they, too, are now lost.

The assumption that apostolicity was the sole criterion of canonicity falters also in its position that Christ's authoritative apostles were inerrant in all their utterances and writings. Peter's behavior at Antioch in refusing to have table fellowship with Gentiles should suppress any thought that they were (Gal. 2:11–14). Paul's confrontation with him over that issue proves that apostles made mistakes even after being commissioned by Christ to serve as

His authoritative representatives. So, apostolicity as the only test of canonicity is insufficient in another regard.

The New Testament books not written by one of the twelve or Paul are Mark, Luke, Acts, Hebrews, James, and Jude.[49] If one grants that James and Jude became apostles by Christ's appointment—Galatians 1:19 indicates James was such and 1 Corinthians 15:7 strongly implies it—that leaves four books without apostolic authorship. That the apostolic circle was wider than just the twelve and Paul seems likely in light of 2 Corinthians 11:13. Paul's opponents at Corinth could hardly have disguised themselves as apostles if that group consisted of only thirteen people who were well-known.

That leaves the apostolic authorship of four books unaccounted for. The defenders of a one-test criterion argue for the *apostolicity* of these four, if not the apostolic authorship. As noted above, Harris contends that an understudy or an amanuensis of an apostle wrote them, thereby giving the books apostolic authority.[50] That theory is insubstantial, however, because apostleship was a nontransferable spiritual gift. An apostle had no authority to bestow the gift or its revelational ability on another. For a book to possess apostolic authority, it must have an apostle as its author, not someone he designates. God alone could bestow apostolicity (1 Cor. 12:11, 18)—or any other spiritual gift for that matter—and that only on those who had witnessed Christ's resurrection. Mark may have been a witness of Christ's resurrection, but Luke and the writer to the Hebrews were not (Luke 1:1–4; Heb. 2:1–4).

So apostolicity cannot account for the inspiration of all the books the church eventually recognized as part of the New Testament canon. Gamble agrees: "Widespread and important as this criterion [i.e., apostolicity] was, it must still be said that no New Testament writing secured canonical standing on the basis of apostolicity alone."[51] Some books did not come from an apostle, so some other gift must explain the inspiration of the remaining four.

TEST OF PROPHETICITY

The other speaking gift that provided a basis for inspired communication was the gift of prophecy. The discussion above has shown conclusively how John claimed nothing more than prophetic authorship for his Apocalypse. It has also disclosed that he freely intermingled New Testament prophets and their prophecies with Old Testament prophets. With that setting of the stage for the second-century church, how did early Christians respond to the possibility of prophetic origin as a proof for inspiration?

The Muratorian Canon values prophetic origin quite highly in that regard.[52] This list of canonical works approves the Apocalypse very strongly and even uses that book's authority to verify the catholicity of Paul's epistles:[53]

... The blessed apostle Paul himself, following the example of his predecessor John, writes by name to only seven churches. . . . It is clearly recognizable that there is one Church spread throughout the whole extent of the earth. For John also in the Apocalypse, though he writes to seven churches, nevertheless speaks to all.

By making Paul dependent on John in this way, the list's compiler shows his preference for prophetic inspiration even over apostolic authorship. Bruce has written:

This making Paul follow the precedent of John is chronologically preposterous; it probably indicates, however, that for the compiler the primary criterion of inclusion in the list was prophetic inspiration. In the early church as a whole the predominant criterion appears to have been apostolic authority, if not apostolic authorship; for this writer, however, even apostolic authorship evidently takes second place to prophetic inspiration.[54]

Paul's patterning of his seven epistles after John's seven messages in Revelation 2–3 demonstrates the intention that those epistles reach the church in every place. The precedence granted the Apocalypse in that statement reflects the compiler's high ranking of the book among the rest of the books he lists. Bruce is correct in recognizing the Muratorian author's high esteem for prophetic inspiration, which is also the basis of the Apocalypse's self-claim of authority.

The author's view of prophecy's importance should affect the interpretation of a later statement in his Canon:

But the *Shepherd* was written by Hermas in the city of Rome quite recently, in our own times, when his brother Pius occupied the bishop's chair in the church of the city of Rome; and therefore it may be read indeed, but cannot be given out to the people in church either among the prophets, since their number is complete, or among the apostles for it is after (their) time.

Both Bruce and Metzger refer this statement to the Old Testament prophets,[55] but plenty of contextual merit favors the interpretation that the number of *New Testament* prophets is complete.[56]

First, the compiler's preferential ranking of John's Apocalypse among the recognized books makes at least a partial reference to New Testament prophets probable. Second, he makes no mention of the Old Testament elsewhere in the extant portion of the list.[57] It devotes exclusive attention to books eventually recognized as the New Testament canon, so why at this point should the list abruptly inject a reference to Old Testament prophets? Third, the compiler could hardly suggest that the *Shepherd* might have been read among the *Old Testament* prophets, because that work is a distinctly *Christian* writing. In his discussion of the New Testament-related writings, he would hardly have negated the possibility of reading a Christian work among writings of Old Testament prophets. Fourth, the relatively recent date of the *Shepherd's* composition furnishes the compiler of the list a reason for excluding it from books to be read in church. This factor may well imply that the period of normative New Testament revelation had passed not too long before its writing.[58] It would hardly be suitable if the relatively recent date was a ground for exclusion from the Old Testament prophets who had completed their work over four centuries earlier.

If the writer does in fact state that the number of New Testament prophets is complete and that is his reason for not recommending the reading of the *Shepherd* in church, it furnishes another strong indication of his recognition of prophetic inspiration as a foundation for inclusion in the New Testament canon.

A number of other early fathers and writings manifest a high respect for prophetic inspiration in relation to canonical recognition. The *Didache* blends together New Testament prophets with apostles and Old Testament prophets and emphasizes the need to distinguish between true and false prophets or apostles:[59]

> Let every apostle that cometh to you be received as the Lord. But he shall not remain *except* one day; but if there be need also the next; but if he remain three days, he is a false prophet. And when the apostle goeth away, let him take nothing but bread until he lodgeth; but if he ask money, he is a false prophet. And every prophet that speaketh in the Spirit ye shall neither try nor judge; for every sin shall be forgiven, but this sin shall not be forgiven. But not every one that speaketh in the Spirit is a prophet; but only if he hold the ways of the Lord. Therefore from their ways shall the false prophet and the prophet be known. . . . And every prophet, proved true, working unto the mystery of the Church in the world, yet not teaching *others* to do what he himself doeth, shall not be judged among you, for with God he hath his judgment; for so did also the ancient prophets (*Did.* 11. 4–8, 11).

Note the free interchange of apostles with prophets as spokespersons of inspired utterances.

Ignatius also lifts the gift of prophecy when he instructs his readers to hear Christian prophets because the prophets had "lived according to Jesus Christ" and were "inspired by His grace" (*Magn.* 8.2; cf. 9.2). He adds that Christians should love not only the gospel and the apostles but also the prophets because they had announced the advent of Christ and had become his disciples (*Phld.* 5.2).[60] Clement of Alexandria cites "the prophetic spirit" as the source of a number of New Testament as well as Old Testament portions of Scripture (*The Instructor* 1:5). Since he included nonpredictive parts of the New Testament in this designation, he most probably had in mind the prophetic inspiration that lay behind all books of the Bible. Justin Martyr wrote about Abraham: "For as he believed the voice of God, and it was imputed to him for righteousness, in like manner we, having believed God's voice spoken by the apostles of Christ, and promulgated to us by the prophets, have renounced even to death all the things of the world."[61] He defended the existence of prophetic power in the Christian church.[62]

In the third century, Dionysius of Alexandria, a pupil of Origen, wrongly thought that John the Apostle did not write Revelation but nevertheless accepted the book's inspiration.[63] Though arguing vigorously against apostolic authorship of the Apocalypse, he said, "But for my part I should not dare to reject the book" (Eusebius *The Ecclesiastical History* 7.25). Dionysius' willingness to embrace the authority of the Apocalypse without apostolic authorship indicates his recognition of a nonapostolic source of inspiration that was most probably the gift of prophecy.

At least three other early fathers echo from the Muratorian Canon a relationship between Paul's epistles to seven churches and John's seven messages in Revelation 2–3. They are Cyprian, Victorinus of Pettau, and Jerome.[64] The two former leaders point out the relationship between Paul's churches and those of John, indicating an ongoing tradition of Paul's dependence on John's prophecy as a pattern.

Granted, these early voices do not speak as loudly or as frequently about prophetic inspiration as they and others do about apostolic authority, but they do speak. In light of such early words, Gaussen's reasoning based on New Testament revelation has merit:

> And since St Luke and St Mark were, amid so many other prophets, the fellow-workers chosen by St Paul and St Peter, is it not clear enough that these two apostolic men must have bestowed upon such associates the gifts which they dispensed to so many besides who had believed? Do we not see Peter and John first go down to Samaria to confer these gifts on the believers of that city; this followed by Peter coming to Cesarea, there to shed them on all the Gentiles who had heard the word in the house of the centurion Cornelius (Acts viii. 14, 17)? Do we not see St Paul bestow them abundantly on the believers of Corinth,

on those of Ephesus, on those of Rome (Acts xix. 6, 7; 1 Cor xii. 28, xiv; Rom i. 11, xv. 19, 29)? Do we not see him, before employing his dear son Timothy as his fellow-labourer, causing spiritual powers to descend on him (1 Tim iv. 14; 2 Tim i. 6)? And is it not evident that St Peter must have done as much for his dear son Mark (1 Peter v. 13), as St Paul did for his companion Luke (Acts xiii. 1, xvi. 10, xxvii. 1; Rom xvi. 21; Col iv. 14; 2 Tim iv. 11; Philem 24; 2 Cor viii. 18)? Silas, whom St Paul had taken to accompany him (as he took Luke and John, whose surname was Mark), Silas was a prophet at Jerusalem (Acts xv. 32). Prophets abounded in all the primitive churches. Many were seen to come down from Jerusalem to Antioch (Acts xi. 27); a great many were to be found in Corinth (1 Cor xii. 19, 20, xiv. 31, 39); Judas and Silas were prophets in Jerusalem. Agabus was such in Judea; farther, four daughters, still in their youth, of Philip the evangelist, were prophetesses in Cesarea (Acts xi. 28, xxi. 9, 10); and in the Church of Antioch, there were to be seen many believers who were prophets and doctors (Acts xiii. 1, 2); among others Barnabas (St Paul's first companion), Simeon, Manaen, Saul of Tarsus himself; and, finally, that Lucius of Cyrene, who is thought to be the Lucius whom Paul (in his Epistle to the Romans) calls his kinsman (Rom xvi. 21), and whom (in his Epistle to the Colossians) he calls *Luke the physician* (Col iv. 14); in a word, the St Luke whom the ancient fathers call indifferently Lucas, Lucius, and Lucanus.

From these facts, then it becomes sufficiently evident that St Luke and St Mark ranked at least among the prophets whom the Lord had raised up in such numbers in all the Churches of the Jews and the Gentiles, and that from among all the rest they were chosen by the Holy Ghost to be conjoined with the apostles in writing the sacred books of the New Testament.[65]

Gaussen erred in believing that apostles had the authority to bestow gifts on men but was correct in the sense that apostles did have the discernment to recognize what gifts others had received from God. He correctly reads the New Testament in allowing for an abundance of people with the prophetic gift in the first-century church and in acknowledging that Mark and Luke composed their gospels by virtue of revelation received through their gifts of prophecy. In essence, Paul verified Luke's prophetic gift in 1 Timothy 5:18 when he calls Luke 10:7 "Scripture." Though the New Testament never applies the term "prophet" to either Luke or Mark, no other satisfactory explanation of canonical recognition for their works has been forthcoming. The same is true of the Epistle to the Hebrews. By his own confession, the writer was neither a personal witness of Christ's life and resurrection nor an apostle (Heb. 2:1–4), so he must have possessed the gift of prophecy in order to receive special revelation and produce an inspired product.

The test of propheticity was subject to one further qualification. Application of the test must keep in mind the authority of apostles over prophets as illustrated in Paul's regulation of the Corinthian prophets (cf. 1 Cor. 14:29–32). That explains the pronounced inclination of the early Christian fathers to connect books written by prophets with apostles. They related Luke, Acts, and Hebrews with Paul in one way or another, and Mark with Peter. New Testament prophets did not work independently of apostolic oversight.

The first test a work had to pass to gain recognition as inspired, then, was either apostolicity or propheticity. Conceivably, however, early Christians had in their possession numerous inspired messages that met one of these two criteria. How did they proceed beyond this point? Bruce suggests the additional tests of antiquity, orthodoxy, catholicity, and traditional use.[66]

TEST OF ANTIQUITY

A work that originated after the period of the apostles and prophets, though possibly considered inspired by some, could not be canonical. The Muratorian Canon compiler had a high regard for the *Shepherd of Hermas,* but it came too late to merit being read in church. The apocalypse of Peter had merit in some circles, but being written by someone other than Peter at a later time, neither did it possess the authority to gain universal acceptance, according to the compiler of the Muratorian list. The test of antiquity, then, was nothing more than a verification of the tests of apostolicity and propheticity.

TEST OF ORTHODOXY

Second-century churchmen applied the criterion of orthodoxy to writings that were inspired or claimed inspiration to determine their worthiness for inclusion among the canonical Scriptures. This test appealed to the doctrines set forth in the undisputed apostolic writings and maintained by churches founded by apostles.[67] These churchmen lived in a climate of developing heresies such as Docetism and Gnosticism, so when imitation Gospels and Acts began to appear in the name of apostles, they had to apply criteria that would distinguish their teachings from what the apostles had taught. That teaching had remained consistent through a regular succession of elders in those original churches and was summed up in the churches' rule of faith or baptismal creed.[68]

That rule of faith answered Marcion in declaring that the Bible included more than one gospel and ten epistles of one apostle. It included four gospels and thirteen epistles of Paul as well as Acts, which gave a background for those epistles.[69] That was the beginning of the definition of the apostolic tradition, so any other books that belonged alongside those writings had to coincide with their teachings. In a sense, apostolic tradition helped determine what was Scripture, and in turn, the earliest recognized books helped determine the extent of the New Testament canon.[70]

Central among those teachings was what a book said about the person and work of Christ. Does it identify Him as the historical Jesus of Nazareth, crucified and raised from the dead, and ascended to the Father's right hand?[71] Any writing that did not maintain a true picture of Him as its central figure was unacceptable (cf. 1 Cor. 12:3). If it questioned His full humanity throughout His life, as did Gnostic writings, it could not be canonical (1 John 4:2–3). The same was true of any that questioned His deity and physical, bodily resurrection.

Yet, some works that were quite orthodox in their teaching had to be ruled out because of pseudonymity. These included ones such as the *Acts of Peter*, the *Acts of Paul*, and the *Apocalypse of Peter*,[72] writings that also failed the "Test of Antiquity."

Some early works remain that could pass the tests of inspiration, apostolicity or propheticity, antiquity, and orthodoxy, works that were "impeccably 'orthodox,'" but did not gain final canonical recognition.[73] Two further considerations remained, the tests of catholicity and traditional usage.

TEST OF CATHOLICITY

To become a part of the New Testament canon, a work had to be beneficial on more than a local scale. The church as a whole had to endorse it. The Western church was slow to accept the Epistle to the Hebrews, but eventually did accept it so as not to be out of step with the rest of the churches.[74]

Though from a modern perspective some might rule out some of Paul's canonical epistles such as Galatians and the two Corinthian epistles because of their localized emphases, early leaders deemed them useful to all churches because Paul wrote epistles to seven churches just as John sent messages to seven churches in Revelation.[75] Every document started with local recognition, but the acceptance of only the canonical ones spread throughout the early church.

TEST OF TRADITIONAL USAGE

The criterion of traditional use did not come into play until the third and fourth centuries. Origen and Eusebius in particular tried to discern whether a writing had been in public use from early times in the churches,[76] as did Jerome and Augustine a little later.[77] Unlike the other tests of apostolicity or propheticity—antiquity, orthodoxy, and catholicity that related more to internal characteristics of a writing—traditional usage took particular note of a book's place in the practice of churches.[78]

Traditional use was in no way a major criterion, however. Some documents that occasionally found places in public reading did not eventually find their places in the New Testament canon, works such as *Shepherd of Hermas*, *1 Clement*, and the *Didache*. Conversely, other works that lacked long-standing and broad usage—works such as James, 2 Peter, and 2 and 3 John—did gain canonical status, even though it was late in coming.[79] The test simply corroborated conclusions reached on the grounds of other tests.

These tests, then, were the means earliest Christians used to decide which books were inspired and therefore deserved places of authority alongside the Old Testament canon: Did the writing come from an apostolic or prophetic source? If so, it was inspired and remained in the running. If not, it could not be inspired. Did the inspired writing come from antiquity, i.e., from the apostolic era? If so, it was still a candidate. Was it orthodox or, in other words, in accord with the doctrines of the apostles? If so, it remained a possibility. Was it catholic in its message so that all the churches would benefit from it? If so, it could still become canonical. Did it have a history of traditional usage in the churches? If so, that sealed the work's place among the books of the New Testament canon.

This is not to say that every test applied to every writing, nor is it to say early Christians applied the tests in the suggested sequence. Gamble observes, "It should be clear that the principles of canonicity adduced in the ancient church were numerous, diverse, and broadly defined, that their application was not systematic or thoroughly consistent, and that they were used in a variety of combinations."[80] Testing for apostolicity or propheticity was indispensable, but ultimately, the providence of God determined how and when the early church applied the rest of the tests.

But it should also be clear that without the avenue of special revelation resulting in direct inspiration, no writing could have attained such an exalted status. That is why the gifts of apostleship and prophecy—along with their attendant gifts of the words of wisdom and knowledge—are indispensable considerations in discussions of New Testament canonicity. Without inspired utterances and writings originating during the first century, no New Testament canon could have come into being. Those gifts were the vehicle—apart from the oral teachings of Jesus Christ—that God chose to communicate His new covenant message to the church and future generations. No writing was canonical apart from their use.

SUMMARY OF THE CASE

The four revelatory gifts of the Spirit to the body of Christ were apostleship, prophecy, the word of wisdom, and the word of knowledge. The last two are varying perspectives on the first two, which have far more prominence in the New Testament. Nonapostles as well as apostles received the gift of prophecy (as illustrated in the ministry of Agabus), allowing them to receive special revelation and transmit inspired communications.

The early church valued products of apostles most highly in their recognition of authoritative writings to take their places alongside the Old Testament canon because they had direct appointments from Christ as His authoritative representatives. But apostolic authorship alone could not settle the issue of canonicity, so the early church also had a high regard for New Testament prophets as producers of inspired writings to be recognized as canonical. In the last decade of the first century, John emphasized a high view of prophecy by claiming prophetic inspiration as the basis of authority for the Apocalypse and by placing the New Testament prophet on a plane with Old Testament prophets and angels as channels of divine revelation. The Muratorian Canon took its cue from that in its special focus on prophetic revelation. Then followed the *Didache,* Ignatius, Clement of Alexandria, Justin Martyr, and others.

From among the inspired writings of apostles and prophets, the consensus of early Christians selected twenty-seven writings worthy of canonical recognition to compose New Testament Scripture. They did so with divine guidance, selecting from among many inspired writings that survived the first century A.D. by applying tests of antiquity, orthodoxy, catholicity, and traditional usage.

Appendix E

THE EIGHTEEN SPIRITUAL GIFTS

The New Testament designates eighteen spiritual gifts, though it nowhere says that other gifts do not exist. The eighteen are of such a nature, however, that they appear to cover the field of possible gifts quite thoroughly. No one has ever suggested an additional gift of the Spirit that does not come under the heading of one or more of the eighteen. For example, the gift of being a missionary is the same as the gift of evangelism, or the gift of preaching is a combination of the gifts of teaching and exhortation. Were someone to suggest the gift of singing as a spiritual gift, the correct response would be that singing is a natural gift, not a spiritual gift. That natural gift is often used in conjunction with the gift of exhortation to sway people's wills, but singing is not a spiritual gift. The conclusion must be that the eighteen gifts designated in the New Testament are the extent of the special spiritual abilities through which God purposed to build the body of Christ.

It is helpful to discuss the gifts in four groups. The first two groups were operative only during the infancy phase of the body's growth, and the last two belong to the entire life of the body of Christ, from the day of Pentecost to the day when Christ returns to take His bride, the church, to be with Himself.

GROUP 1: THE REVELATORY GIFTS

The first five gifts which helped start the church growing were gifts that provided revelation of previously unrevealed truths and an accompanying ability to communicate those truths in inspired messages. Four of those gifts were wisdom, knowledge, apostleship, and prophecy. As indicated in the earlier exposition, apostleship and prophecy in the lists of 1 Corinthians 12:28–30 replace wisdom and knowledge that appeared in the list of 1 Corinthians 12:8–10. Wisdom and knowledge probably focus more on inward revelations to persons so gifted, while apostleship and prophecy probably look more at the inspired utterances that resulted from those revelations.

Because of its connection with the gift of prophecy, a fifth gift, the distinguishing of spirits, belongs in this first category also. Its revelatory aspect lay in the ability of one so endowed to distinguish a genuine prophecy from a message that did not originate with the Holy Spirit.

A look at each gift individually divulges further details regarding the five.

THE GIFT OF APOSTLESHIP

Possession of the gift of apostleship—a gift that was also an office in the early church—required several natural qualifications. The first was that an apostle must have had personal contact with Jesus during His thirty-three years on earth. Acts 1:8, 21–23 points out the necessity of one's having been a witness of Jesus' earthly ministry if he was to be a candidate for the apostolic vacancy created with the suicide of Judas Iscariot. The second was that he had to be an eyewitness of Jesus' resurrection from the dead. Along with Acts 1:21–22, Luke 24:48 and 1 Corinthians 9:1–2 certify that to be an apostle a person must have seen the risen Christ with his own eyes. Those two qualifications, as essential as they were, were not enough to constitute one an apostle. All who saw Jesus before and after His resurrection were not apostles. One further criterion had to be met: that of having a direct appointment to this office by Jesus Himself. Luke 6:13–16 reveals that part of the requirement. Only some, not all, of Jesus' disciples received such an appointment.

Some would add a fourth requirement, i.e., that a person had to perform the signs, wonders, and miracles that were emblematic of apostleship (cf. Rom. 15:15–19; 2 Cor. 12:12). That is hardly a natural qualification, however, since the Spirit bestowed such supernatural abilities as gifts at the same time as He imparted the gift of apostleship to a person. At times, people have suggested that *apostle* is just another name for a missionary. On that basis they have argued that the gift of apostleship has been available throughout the centuries of the Christian era. This definition of *apostle* does not rest on biblical evidence, however. Unquestionably, *apostle* was a technical and narrow term in the New Testament and in the early church. The dominant scriptural use of this name refers it to a select group of Christian leaders who met the three criteria stated above. In light of the first two criteria, the gift was available to members of the body of Christ only as long as eyewitnesses of Jesus' life and resurrection were alive. Paul's fulfillment of those criteria came under somewhat unusual circumstances, as he states. He was the last person to be appointed an apostle (cf. 1 Corinthians 15:8–9). The last apostle to die was probably John, in about A.D. 100. With his death, the gift of apostleship ceased to function in the body of Christ.

A further clarification is also necessary. Was the gift of apostleship limited to the Twelve (or to the Twelve and Paul), or was it more widely disseminated? Since the New Testament specifically mentions a direct appointment by Christ only in connection with the Twelve and Paul, some have concluded that there were only twelve or possible thirteen apostles. Yet, the New Testament seems to use "apostle" in its technical sense as applicable to a larger group. First Corinthians 9:1, 5–6; 15:7; and Galatians 1:19 apparently apply the title to Barnabas and James, the brother of the Lord. Romans 16:7 and 1 Corinthians 15:5, 7 perhaps so name Adronicus, Junias, and others. It would appear from 2 Corinthians 11:13, which decries apostolic impostors, that there must have been an indefinite number of apostles. Otherwise, it would have been impossible for anyone in deception to pass himself off as an apostle.

Whether twelve or thirteen apostles or more, it is certain that they possessed the highest authority in the first-century church because they were Christ's immediate representatives. When they spoke, it was as though He was speaking. Their influence extended to the body of Christ as a whole, not just to a church in one location. By virtue of this gift and associated revelatory gifts, the ones so gifted were recipients of direct divine revelation which they were responsible to transmit to other Christians. Their credentials for the office consisted in various supernatural feats accomplished through the confirmatory gifts of the Spirit that they also possessed (cf. 2 Corinthians 12:12). The gift of apostleship and related gifts provided recognition to the books of the New Testament as authoritative writings.

Acts 8:14–17 illustrates the authority of the apostolic office. Without the presence of such a gifted person, God chose to refrain from imparting the Holy Spirit to the Samaritans who had believed in Christ. When Peter and John arrived, however, and condoned the ministry of Philip and the response of the Samaritans, the Holy Spirit came upon the new believers just as He had the apostles and other believers in Jerusalem on the day of Pentecost. That was because of the divinely given authority of the two apostles. To them belonged the prerogative of extending the frontiers of the gospel to include new groups during those early decades of the Christian church.

Another illustration of apostolic authority comes from 1 Corinthians 14:36–37. Paul realized that he was Christ's spokesman, and challenged the Corinthian readers with the impossibility of concluding otherwise. The only alternative presented to them was to think of themselves as the ultimate authority in revelation, an utterly ridiculous assumption.

To these men (so far as we know, there were no female apostles, unless "Junia" were to be read and understood as a female numbered among the apostles in Rom. 16:7) belonged the task of laying the foundation of the Christian church (cf. Eph. 2:19–22). Once their job was done, they passed the baton to leaders who were gifted in ways that we shall discuss presently.

Their authority was not equivalent to infallibility, however. Galatians 2:11–14 reflects the possibility of unwarranted vacillation and/or mistaken judgment on the part of some of the apostles at times. We must presume, however, that whenever apostles functioned as channels of special divine revelation, the possibility of their erring disappeared. For this reason, the books of the New Testament composed by them were without error.

All that the apostles wrote by virtue of their spiritual gift(s) did not find its way into the New Testament canon. It is certain, for example, that an epistle of Paul to the Corinthians, written before our 1 Corinthians, has been lost (cf. 1 Corinthians 5:9). Though such a lost epistle may very well have been the result of divine revelation, its contents were of such a nature that necessitated only a local application to that first-century situation. Hence, the New Testament canon did not preserve it. We may suppose that many other inspired utterances and writings originated during this foundational stage of the body of Christ, writings that are not extant in the twentieth century. They served their purpose in helping the body get started, and in the providence of God, are not available for other generations of Christians.

We learn a good bit about spiritual gifts in general from a consideration of the gift of apostleship. In a true sense of the word, it was the "king" of the gifts in that it provided such a great contribution to the growth of Christ's body (cf. 1 Corinthians 12:28). Perhaps one of its more significant characteristics is that it served its function at the very beginning of the church and then passed from the scene.

THE GIFT OF PROPHECY

Persons possessing the gift of prophecy shared with apostles the privilege and responsibility of being channels of direct divine revelation. They had insights into the "mysteries" of God (cf. 1 Cor. 13:2; Eph. 2:20; 3:3,5) as did the apostles. Yet, everyone with the gift of prophecy did not have the gift of apostleship. It does appear that the converse was true—that all apostles had the gift of prophecy—but most prophets could not meet the three criteria necessary to be an apostle. Consequently, prophets did not possess the same authority in the body of Christ as the apostles did. Yet, prophets were still vehicles of divine revelation, some of which passed into written form and is a part of Scripture. To the degree that a prophecy was valid, being based on divine revelation (cf. 1 Cor. 14:29), a prophet spoke inspired and therefore authoritative words. The authority of apostles was of a more general and ultimate nature than that of the prophets, however (cf. 1 Cor. 14:37).

Another distinction between apostles and prophets lay in their sphere of responsibility. Whereas the apostles' responsibility was to minister to the church at large and to extend its borders, those who were prophets only, while they may have been available more broadly, usually served in more settled situations, each being assigned to a single local church (cf. Acts 13:1; 15:32).

The prophet's special function was to provide edification to the body of Christ by exhorting and comforting the saints through the revelations granted to them (cf. 1 Cor. 14:3, 29, 30). Most of those revelations were temporary in application, not needing to be preserved for the body of Christ in other generations. Those that were of permanent value went into written form and became part of the New Testament canon (see Appendix D of this volume).

Another facet of the prophetic ministry was an ability to predict future happenings (cf. Acts 11:27–28; 21:10–11; 1 Tim. 1:18; Rev. 1:3). The predictive element of prophecy for the body of Christ was apparently not as extensive as it was in connection with the prophetic ministry to the people of Israel in the Old Testament. Yet, Old Testament prophets still find their closest parallel to New Testament prophets, not to New Testament apostles. Though prediction was not the major element in New Testament prophecy, it was an indispensable part of it. Without that aspect, for example, someone who provided edification through exhortation and comfort would be exercising the gift of exhortation (cf. Rom. 12:8) or teaching (cf. 1 Cor. 12:28), not the gift of prophecy. That is what modern-day preaching does; it is not the gift of prophecy.

Because of the ability to predict the future, the prophetic gift is among the "confirmatory" gifts in 1 Corinthians 12:10. The fulfillment of his prophecy provided the prophet with credentials in the eyes of those to whom he sought to minister. It was this way with Paul on his Acts 27 voyage to Rome. In the midst of a terrible storm and against overwhelming odds, he predicted that there would be no loss of life among the 276 people on board the ship (Acts 27:22–24, 34). When they all came through the ordeal safely (Acts 27:28), Paul had greater credibility among them. The respect of the crew for Paul, probability in large part because of his prophecy, seems to have grown even before the final deliverance became reality (cf. Acts 27:31–33), but the fulfillment of his prophecy was God's visible vindication of Paul as His prophetic spokesman.

There were female prophetesses, as proven by the four virgin daughters of Philip (Acts 21:9). Presumably they functioned in roles within the guidelines set by Paul for the conduct of Christian worship (cf. 1 Cor. 11:5–6; 14:34–35).

With the completion of the last book of the New Testament, the gift of prophecy became obsolete. Revelation 22:18 pronounced a severe penalty on anyone who attempts to add to the prophecies of the Apocalypse (see Appendix C of this volume). Since Revelation purports to cover the entire period from the time John the apostle wrote it until the eternal state, any alleged prophecy subsequent to that is counterfeit.

The completed canon of the New Testament is God's completed revelation for the body of Christ. No more direct divine revelation for the church has or will come subsequent to that time (see Appendix B of this volume). The prophets of the future spoken of by the prophet Joel (Joel 2:28) will have a ministry to the people of Israel and the world at large during the Tribulation after the Rapture of the church. They will not be prophets with the gifts of the Spirit bestowed upon members of the church, the body of Christ.

THE GIFT OF THE DISTINGUISHING OF SPIRITS

As implied by its position immediately after the gift of prophecy in 1 Corinthians 12:10, distinguishing of spirits—also referred to as discerning of spirits—is a companion gift to prophecy. Persons with this gift—who according to 1 Corinthians 14:29 also possessed the gift of prophecy—could pass immediate judgment on prophetic utterances given in the Christian assembly. Someone other than the prophetic speaker needed to render an immediate opinion about the validity and source of a prophet's message after completion of the message. That someone had the gift of the distinguishing of spirits.

Spirits in the name of this gift refers to spirit manifestations or spiritual gifts, a meaning that the same word has in 1 Corinthians 14:12. The discerner was responsible to determine whether the utterance came from the Holy Spirit or from some other spirit, whether human or demonic. If it was the latter, he had to rule against the authority of what the prophet had said. If it was the former, he could authenticate the validity of the prophetic message.

The New Testament has no illustration of this gift in action in a Christian meeting, but Paul's encounter with a young woman in Philippi illustrates how the gift must have worked. The woman gave what appeared to be a truthful word: "These men are bond-servants of the Most High God, who are proclaiming to you the way of salvation" (Acts 16:17). Paul through his special ability recognized, however, that the source of her words was "a spirit of divination" (Acts 16:16, 18), so he proceeded to cast the evil spirit from the woman (Acts 16:18).

Paul describes the functioning of the gift of distinguishing of spirits in 1 Corinthians 14:29. There he points out that prophecies, whenever uttered, were subject to the judgment of certain discerning persons. No complete New Testament was available to test the truthfulness of what was spoken, so a special gift was necessary to validate the true prophecies and recommend their acceptance. "The others" (14:29) who passed judgment were the other prophets in the congregation who were listening. Those able to distinguish spirits were God's provision for guarding the church from being led astray during the period awaiting the completion of the New Testament.

The existence of specially gifted discerners did not relieve all Christians from developing discernment in spiritual matters. In 1 Corinthians 12:2–3, Paul had told the whole church how to the distinguish the true from the false. John did the same in 1 John 4:1–3. Those were tests that were more objective and useful for any believer. But situations for applying those tests were different from having to judge immediately the genuineness of what someone had just uttered, something that may not have been blatantly wrong but still did not originate with the Holy Spirit. Discernment in other than this special sense is an ongoing responsibility of all in the body of Christ.

THE GIFT OF (THE WORD OF) WISDOM

Since the gifts of apostleship and prophecy replace the gifts of wisdom and knowledge (1 Cor. 12:8) in later lists (1 Cor. 12:28–29), there is rationale for including wisdom and knowledge with revelatory gifts. The association of prophecy and an understanding of mysteries with the gift of knowledge (1 Cor. 13:2; cf. 1 Cor. 13:8, 9, 12) confirm such a classification of the two gifts. "Mysteries," of course, is a technical term related in the New Testament to the disclosure of divine secrets not previously divulged. So, the gift of wisdom closely relates to the gift of prophecy.

The definition of the gift of wisdom is a special ability to receive and pass on to others a disclosure of God's mysteries during the period when He was granting direct revelations to members of the body of Christ. The distinction between this gift and the gift of prophecy is that it focuses more attention on the reception of the revelation from God while prophecy puts more emphasis upon communicating to others what has been received. Perhaps the most enlightening discussion of the functioning of wisdom and prophecy is in 1 Corinthians 2:6–13. Here is a discussion of wisdom as the Spirit impressed it upon the inner consciousness of Paul and other prophets, a direct revelation that they in turn transmitted to the churches to whom they ministered. They spoke the "wisdom" of God in a "mystery" which had been "hidden away" (1 Cor. 2:7). God "revealed" it to them through the Spirit who drew upon "the depths of God" in order to do so (1 Cor. 2:10). Having received "the things freely given to us by God" (1 Cor. 2:12), the prophets spoke with "words . . . taught by the Spirit, combining spiritual [thoughts] with spiritual [words]" (1 Cor. 2:13). In some way unknown to us moderns, the Spirit put into the minds of people who were so gifted the revelation that had been, until that time, hidden. They "converted" their revelatory impressions into a form that they could articulate and communicate to God's people either in speech or in writing. In 2 Peter 3:15, Peter acknowledges Paul's use of the gift in composing his epistles: Paul wrote, says Peter, "according to the *wisdom* given to him" (emphasis added).

God granted the special revelations during the infancy of the body of Christ, as part of the foundation of the church (cf. Eph. 2:19–21). The infant church was in need of such to supplement what they already had in the books of the Old Testament. Some of the revelations were of a temporary and local application, but others were of permanent validity and found their way into the books of the New Testament. An example of the latter is found in Ephesians 3:3–6. By "revelation" the "mystery" was made known to Paul (Eph. 3:3). That "mystery of Christ" (Eph. 3:4) was unknown to earlier generations, but "now it was revealed to the saints through His apostles and prophets by the Spirit" (Eph. 3:5). The mystery consisted of the Gentiles' being fellow heirs and fellow members of the body and fellow-partakers of the promise in Christ Jesus through the gospel (Eph. 3:6). Paul's mission was to bring to light "the stewardship of the mystery which had been hidden away" that he might make known "the manifold wisdom of God" (Eph. 3:9–10).

A revelatory connection is the correct understanding of the gift of (the word of) wisdom. A clear distinction exists between this gift and the general practical wisdom available to all members of the body of Christ. James speaks of a wisdom from God that any child of God can claim when he encounters circumstances that test his faith (James 1:5). Wisdom in knowing how to encounter those situations is most certainly distinct from the wisdom connected with the spiritual gift. The general practical wisdom is available to all as a means for living a profitable Christian life, but the gift of wisdom was a special ability restricted to a select few in the early days of the Christian era.

THE GIFT OF (THE WORD OF) KNOWLEDGE

Several considerations show that the gift of knowledge is revelatory in nature. One of these is its connection with the gift of (the word of) wisdom in 1 Corinthians 12:8, where it stands in the same category with wisdom. When apostleship and prophecy (12:28, 29) replace it and the gift of wisdom (12:8–9) in subsequent lists(12:28, 29), further indication of this revelatory nature surfaces. Then in 1 Corinthians 13:2 it connects with prophecy and the understanding of mysteries. It relates to prophecy and tongues in 1 Corinthians 13:8, 9, 12. That is the beginning of a good case for the revelatory character of this gift.

More specifically, what is this revelatory gift? It is a special ability to grasp objective data that results from special revelation connected with the word of wisdom to systematize it and extend its implications to new situations. It consisted of a revelatory aptitude to comprehend the logical nature and relations of truths revealed through the companion gift and to state the application of these in an inspired and inerrant fashion.

To discuss the gift more fully, we need to note the association of *gnōsis* ("knowledge") with a certain "word cluster." A number of words that we have encountered already in our discussion of revelatory gifts group themselves together whenever a writer is talking about revelatory activity. That cluster includes *apostolos* ("apostle"), *prophētēs* ("prophecy"), *mystērion* ("mystery"), *apokalypsis/apokalyptō* ("revelation/I reveal"), *sophia* ("wisdom"), *apokryptō* ("I hide"), and *gnōrizō* ("I make known"), among others. We have already seen this phenomenon in Ephesians 2:19–3:10. Another good example is Colossians 1:26–2:3. Among the words used in the latter passage is *gnōsis* (2:3), which occurs side-by-side with *sophia* as it does in 1 Corinthians 12:8. This again confirms an occasional use of this word with revelatory connotations.

Second Peter 3 illustrated what results from the use of the word of knowledge. In verse 2 Peter asks his readers to "remember the words spoken beforehand by the holy prophets and the commandment of the Lord and Savior spoken by your apostles." The reference is to revelation that had come earlier through the word of wisdom. Then in verse 3 the writer goes on to apply the earlier revelations to a new situation that had arisen at the time of the writing of 2 Peter. That application constituted an inspired extension of previously revealed "mysteries" to the new situation and represented an exercise of Peter's use of the gift of knowledge. The same type of thing occurs in the epistle of Jude, as shown in Jude 17–18.

Another illustration of the difference between direct revelation and inspired application is seen in 1 Corinthians 7:10–12. In verses 10–11, Paul conveys what he had directly from the Lord, but in verses 12 ff. he relates what he has deduced by extension of certain principles to situations not covered by direct revelation. The latter would be the word of knowledge (cf. 1 Cor. 7:40).

The difference between this application of principles and the application of scriptural principles made by Christians in everyday life lies in the matter of inspiration. The gift of knowledge guaranteed the inerrancy of the application, but in mere human application through the Spirit's illumination much room for error remains.

Several distinctions should be emphasized. One of them is to reemphasize that the word of knowledge does not pertain to knowledge obtained through the use of reason and instruction on a natural level. As with other gifts, this one operates on a supernatural plane.

Another fact to remember is that the gift of knowledge is distinct from the knowledge available to all Christians through the illuminating work of the Holy Spirit. Such enlightenment comes through the study of the Scriptures, and is indeed "supernatural," but is separate from the special revelatory ability to apply previous divine revelation in an inspired way.

Since this gift was revelatory in nature and intimately related to the gifts of apostleship and prophecy, it had no further usefulness after completion of the period of special revelation. With the completion of a written revelation, it no longer had a function.

GROUP 2: THE CONFIRMATORY GIFTS

Gifts used by God to confirm His inspired messages during the first century include faith, healing, miracles, tongues, and the interpretation of tongues. A secondary function of prophecy whereby a prophecy's fulfillment confirmed prophetic revelation shows prophecy's kinship with confirmatory gifts, but prophecy's primary function was revelatory. It therefore belongs most closely to Group 1. Similarly, a secondary function of tongues was revelatory—if someone interpreted the tongues message—but because its primary function was as a sign gift, tongues most properly belongs with Group 2. Interpretation of tongues is with the same group because of its connection with the gift of tongues.

Confirmatory gifts supported the revelatory gifts. Without them, those listening to inspired messages had no visible means of knowing whether a spokesperson and his message were from God or not. Miracles, signs, and wonders were the credentials of the apostles and prophets just as they were for Christ before them (cf. Acts 2:22). They emphatically signaled to observers that the miracle worker was from God and had a message that they needed to heed.

A closer look at the confirmatory gifts will reflect how the gifts attracted that kind of attention:

THE GIFT OF FAITH

In 1 Corinthians 12:9–10, the gift of faith is first in a category of gifts that includes—besides itself—healing, miracles, prophecy, and the distinguishing of spirits. In that list, those gifts provide various means for confirming revelations from God to the first-century church through the gifts of wisdom, knowledge, apostleship, and prophecy. Faith is the broadest of the gifts in its category and, in a sense, lends itself to providing a common thread for the rest of the confirmatory gifts. They all operated on the basis of the special faith exhibited by the gifted one.

Paul speaks again of the gift of faith in 1 Corinthians 13:2: "if I have all faith, so as to remove mountains." He in all probability had in mind Jesus' references to "faith as a mustard seed" as a means for removing mountains (Matt 17:20) and to faith without doubting as sufficient to cast a mountain into the sea (Matt 21:21; Mark 11:23). Faith was the means Jesus used to overcome obstacles to His ministry. The gift of faith was the means certain members of the early church used to overcome obstacles to their ministries for Christ.

That gift consisted of a special ability to believe God to the point that He would miraculously remove particular hindrances in the spread of the good news. Sometimes He did it through healing, sometimes through other miracles such as the blinding of Elymas (Acts 13:11–12). But the gift of faith operated in still other ways.

Paul told his companions on the voyage to Rome, "I believe God that it will turn out exactly as I have been told" (Acts 27:25; cf. 27:34). God, through an angel, revealed to him that the terrible storm they were experiencing would not take the life of anyone on board the ship (Acts 27:22–24). Paul through his gift of faith accepted that message as true, even though it was humanly unreasonable to do so. On the basis of that faith, he uttered the prophecy regarding their deliverance from the storm. The hindrance to Paul's mission was the inclination of the sailors to do something foolish that could have threatened Paul's safe arrival in Rome for a ministry there (cf. Acts 27:30). Paul's steady faith through this threatening situation, along with his fulfilled prophecy, gave credibility to him and his message in the eyes of those aboard the ship with him.

Of course, faith in Christ is what saves an individual. Faith in Christ should be the rule of life for every child of God. But faith in Christ for salvation and Christian living is not the gift of faith. The gift of faith was operative in the early church during a period when direct revelation to apostles and prophets resulted in inspired messages that stood in need of some type of conspicuous supernatural confirmation. That gift passed from existence with the other confirmatory gifts, but faith for salvation and Christian living is an ongoing condition for people to have a right relation to God.

THE GIFT(S) OF HEALING(S)

That the gift of healing belongs in the category of gifts highlighted by the gift of faith is apparent because the exercise of this gift rested on a basic confidence in God to heal in an unusual way. It does not cover the entire scope of gifts in this category, however, since it was limited to the sphere of sickness and disease.

This gift did not eliminate the need for the human science of effecting healing through medicinal and surgical methodologies. Luke, a companion and fellow laborer with Paul, was a physician and probably served Paul in a traditional medical capacity. Yet, the gift of healing was distinct from Luke's professional activity. It featured physical cures that were accomplished through spiritual power working upon bodily maladies. The plural "gifts" and the plural "healings" is indicative of the wide variety of illnesses against which this supernatural power was operative.

Healing was one of the gifts that a person so gifted could not exercise indiscriminately. It had to be accompanied by a consciousness of harmony with the will of God in any given instance. It was God's will that the lame man at the door of the temple be healed by Peter (Acts 3:6 ff.), but it was not God's will that Paul be relieved of the eye disease that plagued him (2 Cor. 12:8-9).

In cases where it was God's will to heal, spectacular recoveries occurred. The healing of the lame man in Acts 3:6-8 was a very public event, evoking much amazement and attracting much attention. It was this very feat that gained for Peter an audience as "all the people ran together to" him and John after seeing the well-known cripple restored to wholeness (Acts 3:11 ff.). That act of healing became Peter's credential with the listeners. They reasoned, "Anyone who can perform a marvelous deed like this must surely be God's spokesman, and his message to us must be precisely what God wants us to hear."

So it was on other occasions when the apostles healed people miraculously. The same was true of the life of Jesus. He was "accredited" in the eyes of men through the miracles and signs and wonders that God did through Him (Acts 2:22). It is quite evident, then, that the purpose of this gift was to attract attention, to center that attention on the agent of healing, to identify him as God's spokesman, and to attest God's approval of the message he brought. Such a purpose was very evident on the occasion of the first use of the gift in Acts (cf. Acts 3:8, 9, 11, 12, 13; 4:1, 2, 9, 10, 14, 16).

Too often people have misunderstood the purpose of the gift of healing. They have erroneously assumed that the gift was primarily to give people good health. If this had been the gift's purpose, it was surely a failure, because it was used on only a small fraction of the people who were sick and even those who were healed eventually died. Good health was only an incidental benefit from the gift. Its principal purpose was that of authentication.

Such authenticating gifts were necessary because of the drastic changes involved in the conveyance of New Testament revelation. Some means was necessary to identify the true message from God in the midst of many counterfeit messages. Without such dramatic means, no radical departure from the past would have been possible. God chose to use that kind of means at other critical periods of biblical history, such as in the time of Moses and Aaron and in that of Elijah and Elisha. Such a special concentration of miraculous activity had biblical precedent.

The gift should not be confused with the promise of healing in answer to the prayers of God's people, spoken of in James 5:15. The New Testament speaks of three types of physical healing: (a) natural healing, as in 1 Timothy 5:23; (b) supernatural healing in answer to prayer, as in Philippians 2:27; and (c) charismatic healing, as in 1 Corinthians 12:9. The second type represents the privilege and responsibility of every Christian to pray for physical healing. It has nothing directly to do with the gift of healing. It brings glory to God, but it authenticates no divine messenger or message the way the gift does. It is still a day of divine healing in answer to such prayers, but the period of divine healers as accredited spokesmen of direct divine revelation is past. Spoken messages in the contemporary body of Christ receive their accreditation through the written word of God. Therein lies their means of verification.

Whatever is represented in this day and time as the gift of healing has several possible explanations: psychosomatic cures, hoaxes, Satanic deceptions, or healings in answer to prayer. None of those qualifies as the gift of healing as exercised during the days of the infant church.

THE GIFT OF THE EFFECTING OF MIRACLES

The "effecting [or working] of miracles" is another of the confirmatory gifts (1 Cor. 12:10). It covers miracles other than those accomplished through the gift of healing. This was another way the gift of faith manifested itself. Bringing a person back to life (e.g., Acts 9:40) was a miracle that is not, strictly speaking, in the category of healing.

Paul exercised the gift when he produced the blinding of Elymas (Acts 13:8–11). That was his credential to gain a hearing for his message (Acts 13:12). Miracles like the other confirmatory gifts served the purpose of validating God's spokesmen and their messages. Such miracles, signs, and wonders provided verification of the inspired messages that came through the revelatory gifts such as apostleship and prophecy. They occurred frequently in the early days of Christianity. The Greek name for this gift is the word *miracles* that appears in the combination "miracles, signs, and wonders" attributed to Jesus in Acts 2:22. It is the same word that attributes miracles to Jesus in the Gospels (cf. Matt 11:20–21, 23; 13:58; Mark 6:2; Luke 10:13; 19:37) and to the apostles and other early Christians in Acts and the Epistles (cf. Acts 8:13; 19:11; 2 Cor. 12:12; Gal. 3:5; Heb. 2:4).

The exclusive purpose of the gift was to provide authentication for God's spokesmen and their message. No document was available as a standard for measuring the truthfulness or authority of what they said. The gift provided a special means for attracting the attention of listeners, giving them a basis for trusting the message, and thereby expediting the spread of the gospel during the days of the church's beginning. Once God's inspired revelation to the church was complete, such confirmatory gifts had no further purpose to fill.

The termination of the gift to the body of Christ does not rule out God's providential purpose in accomplishing miracles since that time. Miracles have happened and continue to happen since the completion of the New Testament. Yet, God has not been pleased to use miracle workers the way He did while He was in process of revealing new covenant truth. The age of miracles continues, but the age of miracle workers has ceased.

THE GIFT OF TONGUES

The following is a description of the spiritual gift of tongues. The discussion divides into three parts: the nature of the gift of tongues, the purpose of the gift of tongues, and the duration of the gift of tongues.

THE NATURE OF THE GIFT OF TONGUES

As part of the building of the infant church, the gift of tongues consisted of a special capability to speak a foreign language that had not been learned by the natural and usual method. The tongues referred to in Acts 2:4, 11 were identified on that occasion as being languages by the use of the term *dialektō* ("dialect") in verses 6 and 8. That word is definitive because *dialektō* can mean nothing else but a human language.

Since the miracle on that occasion, the day of Pentecost, was not a miracle of hearing, it must have been a miracle of speaking. The gift was not given to the unbelieving listeners to facilitate their ability to listen; it was given to the believing remnant on that great day to enable them to speak other languages. The position that the gift of tongues consisted of inarticulate utterances is hardly tenable. The crowds in Jerusalem on the day of Pentecost would hardly have given a second notice to people who were simply producing sounds that they could make nothing of. Undoubtedly there was recognition of meaningful sentences in their own language along with languages they could not comprehend, and that is what provoked their attention, raised the question of whether the speakers were drunk, and gave Peter an audience for his sermon.

Some, though freely admitting that tongues in Acts were foreign languages, question whether they were the same in Corinthians. They try to build a case for a difference in the book that was written twenty-five years later than the day of Pentecost. Assigning a different nature to tongues in Corinthians is impractical, however. There is not the slightest indication that the nature of the gift changed in the intervening quarter century. Furthermore the book of Acts, which was written as a record of the day of Pentecost, was written some seven years after 1 Corinthians, indicating that the terminology even at that late date was still a reference to foreign languages. The nature of the gift as foreign languages fits quite well in all contexts of 1 Corinthians that refer to the gift.

The special ability hypothetically extended to the facility of speaking the angelic language (1 Cor. 13:1) if the occasion had ever arisen. It is doubtful, however, that such ever happened. In 1 Corinthians 13:1, Paul was simply speaking of an ultimate in linguistic ability and counting it as nothing without the presence of love.

THE PURPOSE OF THE GIFT OF TONGUES

First Corinthians 14:22 states implicitly the purpose of the gift of tongues: "Tongues are for a sign, not to those who believe but to unbelievers." The word translated "sign" in this verse is a widely used word throughout the New Testament. It speaks of a miraculous happening with a deeper spiritual or symbolic significance. It is the same word used earlier in the New Testament along with the words meaning "miracles" and "wonders" when outstanding and surprising feats happened as an indication of God's presence and endorsement. In Peter's Pentecost sermon (Acts 2:22 ff.), he described Jesus the Nazarene as a man approved, identified, accredited, confirmed, and dedicated from God or by God to the Jewish people by means of miracles and wonders and signs that God did through Him in the midst of these same people. Such supernatural feats were what proved the apostles and prophets to be from God and demonstrated the divine origin of the message they spoke. As it was with Jesus the Nazarene, so it was with the apostles whom He appointed and with the prophets whom He also inspired.

In Acts 14:3, this same word for sign or signs is used in conjunction with the ministry of Paul and Barnabas in Iconium on their first missionary journey. There they bore witness to the Lord and to the word of His grace while God was granting signs and wonders to be done through their hands. The supernatural deeds were indicators to the Jews and Greeks to whom they ministered that they were God's authoritative spokesmen.

The gift of tongues was a special ability God gave to perform signs to authenticate an inspired message that the spokesman generally delivered in the Greek language, the *lingua franca* or the common language throughout the Mediterranean world at that time. The gift of tongues was the badge of the household of Cornelius in Acts 10:44–46 to demonstrate to Peter and his fellow Jewish Christians that God had granted to those Gentiles the same experience of the new birth and the reception of the Holy Spirit as He had granted the Jews in Acts 2:14 ff. In Acts 19:5–6 the gift of tongues was the evidence of the disciples of John at Ephesus to Paul and his associates that they now had received the Holy Spirit on the basis of the fuller message given them through Paul. Though tongues is not explicitly mentioned, the believers at Samaria received some visible evidence of their reception of the Holy Spirit, probably by way of the same gift of tongues because Simon the magician witnessed what happened to them and requested the gift of the Holy Spirit (Acts 8:17–18).

This primary function of the gift of tongues explains why Paul could inform the Corinthian readers that he had spoken with tongues to a greater degree than all of them (1 Cor. 14:18b). As an apostle to the Gentiles, he used his gift among many linguistic groups in a legitimate way in proving to his listeners upon his arrival in a given city that he was God's true representative, when he immediately spoke fluently the language of the local populace. The Corinthians had not used their gift nearly to this degree and, of course, they used it for a wrong purpose, not to reach new language groups but rather to derive their own personal satisfaction.

As elaborated upon in 1 Corinthians 14, the gift of tongues appears to have had a secondary purpose also. First Corinthians 14:2 says that tongues-speakers spoke mysteries. The usual meaning for *mysteries* in the New Testament—and there is no reason to see an exception here—was to identify new and fresh revelation that had hitherto been unrevealed until the time disclosed through God's representative. The message in a foreign language delivered through the gift of tongues apparently had substance to it, content that could be appreciated fully only through use of the gift of interpretation (1 Cor. 14:5b, 13). The reason why interpretation had to accompany tongues in a Christian assembly is that the cognitive content of the new revelation derived from tongues was available to listeners only through the gift of interpretation. Tongues with interpretation, in fact, was a counterpart of the gift of prophecy (cf. Acts 19:6). Clearly, however, prophecy was a more efficient way to receive the inspired utterance in that it came directly in the language of the people addressed.

The mention of tongues alongside prophecy and knowledge in 1 Corinthians 13:8–11, then, is indicative of its role as a gift for confirming two revelatory gifts, the gifts of prophecy and knowledge. When in God's sovereign purpose He was pleased to terminate revelatory activity through prophecy and knowledge—because the infant body of Christ had now reached a stage where it had sufficient permanent revelation to insure its growth without this heavenly input from without—the gift of tongues as the confirmation of such revelation terminated of its own accord in that it served no further useful purpose (1 Cor. 13:8). In 1 Corinthians 13:10, "perfect"—better translated as "mature" or "complete"—represents that point of growth in the body of Christ. The identification of that stage of the maturity of the body of Christ belongs to a discussion of the duration of the gift of tongues to follow.

The concept of confirmatory gifts such as tongues as being temporary has posed a difficulty for some. Perhaps a review of biblical history more broadly would help remove the difficulty. The history of mankind as recorded in the Bible tells of three periods when miraculous feats multiplied, and each time it was for a specific purpose. A great surge of the miraculous happened under the leadership of Moses and Aaron when God sought to bring His people out of bondage from Egypt. The purpose of miracles in that case was to convince Pharaoh of God's presence with His people and to make Pharaoh willing to let them go.

The second concentration of miracles came under the leadership of the prophets Elijah and Elisha. Theirs was a time of great of apostasy in Israel and miracles fulfilled the need of giving credentials to the true prophets of God. Many false prophets were in circulation and the people in their confusion did not know who was speaking for God. That set of miracles identified Elijah and Elisha as those true spokesmen.

The third period of miraculous activity came through the ministry of Christ and His apostles. The period served to bridge the very difficult gap of God's dealings with the nation Israel exclusively to his dealings more broadly with a spiritual body composed of both Jews and Gentiles called the church. The message was a rather startling addition to the revelation God had given in the Old Testament, and some special indicators were necessary to prove to listeners that God's hand was in it.

The gift of tongues was only one of those confirmatory signs, but it was a very significant one during the period when the gospel was going to new language groups within the framework of the Roman empire.

THE DURATION OF THE GIFT OF TONGUES

Previous discussion has hinted about the limited duration of the gift of tongues. The possibility of some spiritual gifts being only temporary and designed for the earliest stages of the Christian church is evident and convincing in the earlier discussion of the gift of apostleship. No one could have the gift of apostleship after the generation of eyewitnesses of Jesus' resurrection had died. That point arrived in about A.D. 100 with the death of John the apostle. It is quite plausible that the gifts of confirmation should have the same duration as one of the gifts of revelation, the gift of apostleship. The two types of gifts are companions; both belong to the period of the laying of the foundation of the church (Eph. 2:20). Once the foundation is in place, the work then proceeded to the next stages of building upon that foundation.

The temporary appearance of confirmatory signs at various points in biblical history must furnish a partial explanation of "the mature" (as "the perfect" is more properly rendered) in 1 Corinthians 13:10. As Paul wrote those words about the termination of revelatory and confirmatory phenomena, he was certainly aware that things like this had come and gone at special points in the past. On this basis, he must have known that the use of tongues, along with the other two gifts—prophecy and knowledge—was subject to termination once God's revelatory purposes had been completed. Furthermore, he was aware of a completed Old Testament canon that had seen no additions to it in over four hundred years. Based on such factors, he could confidently assert that the body of Christ, about which he had written so extensively in 1 Corinthians 12, would reach a point of maturity where these initial phenomena would no longer be a part of the body's growth. It was gradually approaching a point where the features of its infancy would be dispensable. In amplification of this line of possibility, Paul compared the body's growth to his own personal growth in 1 Corinthians 13:11. It was a gradual growth from childhood or infancy into adulthood. As a developing human being, he had passed through stages of preadolescence, adolescence, and others before he became an adult. The characteristics of his childhood had dropped by the wayside one by one and disappeared completely by the time he became a man. He envisioned a similar development for the body of Christ. One of the characteristics of childhood was the continuing need of direct input from the heavenly Father to get the body of Christ started. Once that input had become a sufficient, self-contained entity, the body was at a stage that it did not require such direct revelation and confirmatory gifts to continue its growth.

Yet another line of possibility loomed in Paul's thinking. He also foresaw that Jesus might return before such a self-contained entity became a reality. He allowed for that possibility in 1 Corinthians 13:12. In this case, the maturity of the body of Christ would happen instantaneously in conjunction with the return of Christ, as all those in Christ would ascend to meet the Lord in the air. At that point, the gradual growth of the body would immediately culminate by being conformed to Christ, fully mature (Eph. 4:13).

Gifts in general, and these three gifts in particular, are therefore temporally inferior to love according to 1 Corinthians 13:8–13. Perhaps, the gifts of prophecy, tongues, and knowledge will not last as long as faith, hope, and love (13:13a) because this triad of qualities will definitely continue until the coming of Christ. Love, however, stands out even among this triad because it will remain even beyond that point after faith and hope are no longer necessary because of the personal appearance of the Lord.

Hence, the duration of tongues extended only to about one hundred and the gift disappeared from the scene about the same time as did the revelatory gifts that it supported.

THE GIFT OF THE INTERPRETATION OF TONGUES

The gift of interpretation of tongues was an ability to translate into one's own language from a foreign language that had never been learned by natural means. It was a companion gift to the gift of tongues. By virtue of this gift, a message in a foreign language that was unintelligible to immediate listeners could become immediately intelligible and therefore spiritually profitable.

The New Testament has no specific illustrative use of the gift, but Paul speaks extensively about its proper use in 1 Corinthians 14. In that chapter, he devoted seven verses to portraying how unprofitable tongues without interpretation was for the Christian assembly (vv. 6–12) and seven verses to show how profitable tongues with interpretation was for the same group (vv. 13–19). In fact, tongues with interpretation was equivalent in value to prophecy because it was a revelation of the mysteries of God (cf. 1 Cor. 14:2) and therefore resulted in edification. Interpretation differed from prophecy, however, in that it was dependent on a previous tongues utterance. Prophecy depended solely on a direct inner revelation from God.

The gift of interpretation and that alone legitimized the use of tongues in a Christian gathering. Otherwise, tongues was completely out of place when Christians assembled together.

GROUP 3: THE SPEAKING GIFTS

Group 3 turns its attention to gifts that benefited the church not only in its infancy but also in its continuing growth until Christ's second advent. Four of those gifts involve communication through speech—though they can also communicate through the written page: evangelism, teaching, pastor-teaching, and exhortation. All four presuppose a direct revelation as their basis. Ever since the first century ended, that direct revelation has been in the form of the completed New Testament canon.

The speaking gifts contribute to the growth of Christ's body in several different ways. They add members to the body through evangelism, instruct members in the truths of doctrine, provide shepherdly instruction, and persuade believers to conform to the principles of God's Word that they have learned.

The speaking gifts lead the way in imparting edification to the body as a consideration of each gift indicates:

THE GIFT OF EVANGELISM

In Ephesians 4:11, Paul names "evangelists" in third position in his list of gifted persons. That mention indicates the existence of a gift of evangelism.

The New Testament calls one person an evangelist. That is Philip who was one of the first seven deacons (Acts 21:8; cf. Acts 6:5). Like the rest of the seven, he was probably a Hellenist, i.e., a Jew who had adopted the Greek language and a Hellenistic culture and perspective. That allowed him more freedom than Hebraist Christians to go and share with the Samaritans and other non-Jews the good news of Jesus the Messiah.

Acts 8 gives a record of his evangelistic successes. Verses 4–25 are an account of his leadership in bringing many Samaritan people to Jesus as their Messiah and Savior. Verses 26–39 are a description of how he brought an Ethiopian eunuch to salvation by identifying for him the Suffering Servant of

Isaiah 53. Verse 40 is a summary statement that tells of his evangelization of other cities and his ultimate arrival in Caesarea. He apparently remained in this last city, one that had a strong Roman element, and engaged in planting a church there.

A number of characteristics of the gift of evangelism are fairly evident from the scriptural data. It is primarily a ministry of conversion. It consists in an unusual ability to persuade lost people to place their trust in Christ, and hence directs its attention primarily toward the will of the person receiving its benefit. People possessing this gift have special persuasive powers so that when they convey the gospel facts to lost people, the lost come to the point of making the crucial decision to trust Jesus Christ and become Christians.

The evangelist will not necessarily have 100 percent success in his efforts, but he will have a much higher "batting average" than one who does not have the gift. The strategy of channeling the energies of such a person as much as possible into that area of endeavor, therefore, goes without saying.

The gift of evangelism may function in two different ways. As in the case of Philip, the evangelist may be effective with public evangelism as happened in Samaria, or he may be effective in personal evangelism as was true with the Ethiopian eunuch. Presumably, if a person has the gift, he may use it in either way or in both.

Another factor to be noted regarding the gift of evangelism is that the evangelist's work did not end with conversion. He was responsible for helping a local church get started too, after he had won people to Christ in a given location. To some extent, his work paralleled that of apostles who were primarily responsible for extending the frontiers of the church. The evangelist apparently came on the scene and functioned within a new frontier after an apostle had opened the door. When appropriate, signs accompanied his spoken message (Acts 8:6) until he had other credentials he could furnish, such as an inspired written revelation. At any rate, in some situations he organized a local body of believers into a church after he had won them to Christ. In this regard, he functions as what is called in modern times a missionary.

In this connection, an additional dimension of this gift is relevant. Though primarily directed toward the will and seeking to persuade people to make a decision, the gift appeals to the minds of recipients of this ministry also. Telling a person what he needs to believe to be saved is an aspect of teaching. Then, too, church planting involves a certain amount of teaching. The evangelist, therefore, does not limit his ministry strictly to powers of persuasion. He has an ability of instructing also.

Billy Graham is a conspicuous example of a twentieth-century evangelist. His ministry is mostly in mass evangelism, but he himself emphasizes that without personal evangelism, his city-wide campaigns would never be successful. Bill Bright is another good example of the contemporary use of this gift. His emphasis has been on personal evangelism, and the impact of his ministry directly and through others whom he has trained has been phenomenal.

In the case of the latter of these two examples, a very significant impact on growth in the body of Christ has been made by helping people to discover that they have the gift of evangelism. Many Christians have the gift but do not realize it because they have never tried to win a lost person to Christ. One of the benefits of the Campus Crusade program is that it forces people to try their hand at witnessing and sharing with people the four spiritual laws. In the process of such an exercise many have discovered to their amazement their own unusual abilities of persuasion.

Normally one would expect this gift to be bestowed on people with outgoing types of personalities. In a secular realm, they would be good salespeople. But that is not always the case. Sometimes people who are quiet introverts turn out to be very effective evangelists. So, the gift does not necessarily correlate with natural gifts, though most of the time natural abilities can probably serve as guidelines in discovering one's gift(s).

The gift of evangelism is extremely important. Without the functioning of evangelists, numerical growth in the body of Christ is severely limited. If people are not coming to Christ, teachers will have no one to teach. Here is an all-important lesson: the body must function as a unit or it does not function at all. Were it not for the great work done by evangelists of this generation, our theological seminaries would face shrinking enrollments.

A very special precaution is in order, however. The presence of evangelists in the body of Christ does not release the rest of the members of the body from the responsibility of witnessing to and winning the lost. That is part of the great commission left to every Christian. Even those without the gift must "do the work of an evangelist" (2 Tim. 4:5). Our percentages of success may not be as phenomenal, but we still must be busy sowing the seed. "The fruit reaped is in proportion to the amount of seed sown," so all of us must be constantly giving out the gospel.

THE GIFT OF TEACHING

Compared with the gift of evangelism, the gift of teaching appeals more to the human intellect than to the will. Because of this, it produces more direct benefits in Christian edification. The New Testament makes it quite clear that the enhancement of a believer's understanding is the normal route followed in the process of spiritual growth.

Teaching, or its product, doctrine, is the essence of Christianity. In the gospels, references to Christ's teaching ministry outnumber those to His preaching ministry by about one-third. The Gospels refer to Him by the title "teacher" between forty-five and fifty times, but never once is He called "preacher." Acts mentions teaching or doctrine about twenty times, and in the epistles references to the two number around sixty.

What then is the gift of teaching insofar as the body of Christ is concerned? It consists of an ability to grasp, arrange, and present revealed truth effectively and in an organized manner so that recipients have an enhanced understanding of the Scripture under consideration. A teacher must be able to understand the text, systematize his understanding of it in an appropriate way, and communicate it to others in a meaningful manner. The result of his teaching will be a class, congregation, or audience that leaves his teaching session with a better comprehension of this particular part of the Bible than what they had before hearing the lesson.

This differs from the natural gift of teaching. Some who have special ability in teaching secular subjects may have little ability in teaching the Bible. The converse is also true: a person who is not a teacher in the natural realm may be a very good teacher of Scripture.

Paul exemplifies the functioning of a teacher. He settled in among the Corinthian Christians for eighteen months, "teaching the word of God among them" (Acts 18:11). This was probably done largely in public meetings. An example of private teaching comes a little later in the city of Ephesus. Acts 18:26 records how Priscilla and Aquila took Apollos aside "and explained to him the way of God more accurately."

Teaching is the lifeblood of the Christian faith because without doctrine Christianity is nonexistent. The subjective element of trusting Christ for salvation and obeying Him in service is also essential to being a Christian, but without doctrine a person knows nothing of what to believe in or how to obey. Doctrine is the rock-bottom line, and teaching is the God-chosen method for transmitting that doctrine.

The New Testament reminds us numerous times of the importance of the mind in Christian living. Romans 12:2 points out the place of "the renewing of the mind" in the ongoing process of transformation into the image of Christ. First Peter 1:13 reveals the need to "gird up the loins of your mind" if you want to live a life of holiness pleasing to God.

The sole basis of teaching is the sixty-six-book collection that we call the Bible. While books of the Bible were in process of being written, teaching had to rely on revelation available up to that point, but now that the collection is complete, a teacher has the whole of the Old Testament and New Testament on which to base his instruction. Human observation and experience, as important as they are in their places, cannot replace the Bible as the basis for teaching. The revelation of God that we have in nature is also important in its realm, but it does not furnish an adequate foundation for the spiritual gift of teaching. The others may offer illustrations and secondary confirmations of what Scripture says, but they cannot replace Scripture as the authoritative support for what the teacher says.

During the church's foundational days in the first-century era, prophecy furnished its own basis for instruction through direct revelations from God to the prophet. But those direct revelations are no longer happening, so the only existing basis of authority is Scripture, which has already been revealed.

All that we have stated about teaching underlines the importance of a Sunday school teacher or a Bible class teacher in a local church. He or she may be the most influential person in the congregation because of the potential for strengthening the personal growth of people taught in the class. Efforts to impart the essence of biblical thought, otherwise known as Christian doctrine, should permeate everything a local church does.

Several words of precaution regarding the gift of teaching are in order:

1. Everyone does not have the gift of teaching, but occasions arise when every Christian must do the work of a teacher. One such occasion is filling a need in a local church situation when a gifted person is not available to teach an existing class. Another is witnessing to a lost person—telling him the facts of the gospel so that he has something to believe is a form of teaching. Another situation is the parental responsibility of teaching children the Bible in the home. These are duties that belong to all Christians whether they have the gift of teaching or not.

2. Though every Christian does not have the gift of teaching, every Christian has the capability of grasping doctrine. Very often, people with a good understanding of Scripture but without the gift of teaching will function well in some administrative role such as superintendent of a Sunday school department. They will know good teaching when they hear it, yet acknowledge that they themselves do not possess the special capability of organizing their knowledge in a way to communicate it to others effectively.

3. The gift of teaching focuses mainly on the human intellect, but it does not exclude the will and emotions from its domain. Though in a "minority role," the Christian's decision-making function and feelings are bound to be touched by teaching that is truly biblical. That is because of the nature of biblical content. The Bible's claim upon people's lives forces them to the point of making some kind of decision.

THE GIFT OF PASTOR-TEACHING

The gift of pastor-teaching (Eph. 4:11) is related to the gift of teaching, but is broader. Add to the service accomplished through teaching the element of shepherdly concern, and you have the gift of pastor-teaching. Yet, the two are not separate. Pastor-teaching is the expression of a pastoral care for the sheep of God, the most prominent element of which is the feeding of the sheep.

This gift incorporates the instruction of the flock, but it does more. It more broadly concerns itself with other areas of need among the people over whom the oversight extends. Paul charged the elders in the church of Ephesus with such a broad responsibility: "Be on guard for yourselves and for all the flock, among which the Holy Spirit has made you overseers, to shepherd the church of God which He purchased with His own blood" (Acts 20:28). This is an ongoing necessity in the body of Christ until the time when the body is caught up to meet Christ in the air.

The New Testament applies the name "elders" to those who exercise this gift for the good of the body. First Timothy 3:2 is explicit in naming the ability to teach as one of the qualifications of elders, but feeding is only a part of the total responsibility of caring for the people of God. A Christian has temporal needs from time to time that only the leadership of a local body of believers can meet. A person may lose his job and have to look elsewhere for help temporarily. He may be beset by some prolonged physical illness, creating a need for personal encouragement from close brothers in the body of Christ. He may lose a loved one and need someone to stand by him during his adjustment to a new situation. He may have to struggle to overcome some lingering sinful habit and need constant reminders of His dependence on the Lord. Shepherds may come to the rescue in countless ways and provide the necessary spiritual backup for any situation.

That kind of care is what all of us should be showing for each other, but each local congregation needs a number of "specialists" in this area to provide leadership for the whole group. Call them "elders" or something else, they should be specially adept through a spiritual endowment to care for the sheep in such a way. The gift can function at other echelons of church life besides the leadership of a whole local body. A Sunday school teacher, for example, may and should exercise shepherdly concern for members of his or her class. Functioning of this gift need not stop at the highest levels of church leadership. It should spread its benefit throughout an entire local body of believers.

This is the same responsibility with which Jesus charged Peter in a thrice-repeated command: "Tend My lambs" (John 21:15), "Shepherd My sheep" (John 21:16), and "Tend My sheep" (John 21:17). It is the same duty that Peter passed on to leaders in the churches addressed in his first epistle: "shepherd the flock of God among you" (1 Pet. 5:2).

It is a special ability given to some in the body of Christ. Without the full benefit of this gift, the body is incapacitated.

THE GIFT OF EXHORTATION

The fourth and last speaking gift in operation in the church is the gift of exhortation (Rom. 12:8). It is a gift where persuasion of believers looms largest. It is geared to the will of the believer, just as the gift of evangelism is geared to the will of the unbeliever. The element of imparting information to the mind is not entirely lacking in this gift, but that is not its main function. Persuasion through the gift of exhortation may be of two kinds:

1. It may seek to induce a correct moral choice. Here is a Christian who has grown indifferent to spiritual concerns or has allowed some other sin to gain a foothold in his life. One with this gift has a special knack in showing him the biblical perspective and convincing him of the need to get his life back into adjustment to God's will. Carnal Christians are an all-too-frequent commodity in today's churches. Someone with this special ability needs to confront them with the seriousness of their carnality and bring them back to a close walk with the Lord.

2. The persuasion may come by way of persuading a grieving person to find reassurance in the Lord. Looking on trying circumstances in the right way will often help alleviate a difficulty. A person with the gift of exhortation can help bring about a decision to view a trial properly.

First Thessalonians 3:2 tells of Timothy's use of the gift: "that he might strengthen you and exhort you concerning your faith." This was probably exhortation by way of encouragement to the persecuted Christians in that city. First Thessalonians 2:12 tells of Paul's use of the gift to induce correct moral choices: "exhorting you ... that you might walk worthily of God." Later Paul told Timothy to "reprove, rebuke, exhort with all longsuffering" (2 Tim. 4:2).

We all should be performing this service to fellow members of the body of Christ, but the fact remains that some of us have been specially endowed for that sort of thing. The gift is critical for the body's growth, but it has limitations. Its use must be in conjunction with the gift of teaching, and a proper balance between the two is vital. Preaching that is all exhortation and devoid of instructional content wears thin very quickly. The benefits from it are very short-lived. That is why the New Testament never speaks of a "pastor-exhorter" the way it does of a "pastor-teacher."

Barnabas whose name means "son of exhortation" (Acts 4:36) furnishes a good example of one with the gift of exhortation. We read of his encouraging the Christians at Antioch to remain true to the Lord (Acts 11:23). He also joined Paul in encouraging the new Christians in three cities of South Galatia to continue in the faith in the face of adversity (Acts 14:22). It is no wonder that Paul wrote Timothy to pay attention to exhortation as he ministered to the saints in Ephesus (1 Tim. 4:13).

This is one gift that finds effective use in conjunction with music. Often music will sway people's wills as they hear a genuine servant of the Lord minister to them in song. Yet, we are not to conclude that music is a spiritual gift. It is not the music itself; it is the gift of exhortation that channels its persuasion through the music.

GROUP 4: AUXILIARY GIFTS

Yet, just as the eye cannot say to hand, "I do not need you," the speaking gifts cannot say to the last group of gifts, "I do not need you." Speaking gifts need a wide variety of supporting services, services provided by the auxiliary gifts. Supporting gifts number four: helps, showing mercy, giving, and administrations. Without those kinds of support, the body would be crippled, rendering the speaking gifts of little or no value.

Here is how each of the auxiliary gifts furnishes its support:

THE GIFT OF HELPS (OR MINISTRY)

An auxiliary gift is one that supports the speaking gifts to make them more effective. The gift of helps (1 Cor. 12:28) or—as Paul calls it in Romans—ministry (Rom. 12:7; also called "service") certainly had the broadest scope of any of the auxiliary gifts. It functions wherever temporal or physical needs arise in connection with the church's ministry.

In a general sense, "ministry" or "service" applies to the functioning of all spiritual gifts, but this gift performs that service in more specialized ways. It refers to many different kinds of physical help or relief administered wherever a need exists. A New Testament example of the gift's use is in Acts 6:1-6 where the church needed persons to set up an equitable arrangement for serving tables at mealtime. The apostles and the people chose seven men to fill that role, presumably men with the gift of helps. That gift is an obvious prerequisite for anyone who would serve in the office of deacon—a word whose root idea is "servant"—in a local church (cf. 1 Tim. 3:8-13).

A large segment of the body of Christ needs that kind of service, people such as widows, orphans, the sick, strangers, travelers, and any others with needs of a temporal type. By rendering help to such, the church prepares the way for more effective use of the speaking gifts: teaching, pastor-teaching, evangelism, and exhortation.

Paul knew from personal experience the vital role played by people with the gift of helps. He profited from the special ministries of such men as Onesiphorus (2 Tim. 1:16–18) and Onesimus (Phile. 10–13). Had he not mentioned them in his writings that became a part of the New Testament canon, such men would have gone unrecognized for their service. Most in the body of Christ who have rendered that type of service never receive outward recognition. That is the nature of the gift: it is an unsung service. It is not because this is any less vital to the healthy functioning of the body of Christ. Such behind-the-scenes activities are just as indispensable as teaching, evangelism, and exhortation. The body is crippled without them.

Two observations apply to those whose gift of ministry functions effectively:

1. They, more than people with the conspicuous speaking gifts, must act from motivations of pure love. They will not enjoy the satisfaction of having their deeds publicly appreciated by others. What they do, they must do because of unselfish concerns to see others benefited.

2. The gift consists of an unusual ability to know how people's temporal needs are best met and of an unusual skill in meeting those needs. Not every Christian has that know-how and skill.

On the contemporary scene, opportunities galore for implementing the gift of helps exist. The way someone prepares a Christian meeting place—with flowers, cleanliness, appropriate furniture, etc.—makes a world of difference to some who will attend to hear the preaching and teaching of the Word. They will be open to hear what is spoken much more readily if they find themselves in attractive and comfortable surroundings. The person who meets them at the door and ushers them to their seats can accomplish great things for God by a warm and cheerful greeting. Those are different areas of help.

On occasions of church suppers, some have special abilities to function in the church kitchen in preparation of the meal. Others have special abilities in washing dishes and cleaning up after the meal. Those are aspects of the gift of helps in that they prepare the way for a cordial reception of the Word at a later time. People whose gift includes skill with their hands are very important on church work days, when the flock gathers to fix up the premises of the local church. Others have ability in the church office in keyboarding or typing, doing other clerical jobs, and duplicating material to be used in Bible classes or church services. Those are opportunities for special applications of the gift of ministry or service.

As is true with other gifts, the gift of helps represents a general area of responsibility in which all Christians should function whether they have the gift or not. Those with the special gift are not the only ones who should administer love-evidencing help. That is one of the general responsibilities that belongs to all Christians (Gal. 5:13). Every Christian when called upon should be willing to help in the best way he or she can. God will honor that effort.

Yet, those with the gift of helps are more apt in rendering that kind of service. A person with the gift can meet a need more efficiently and effectively. By identifying those with the gift and freeing them from other responsibilities, a local church can operate more efficiently.

THE GIFT OF SHOWING MERCY

Romans 12:8 mentions the gift of showing mercy. To show mercy is a specialized form of the gift of helps that directs itself in particular to those experiencing some kind of distress, misery, pain, anxiety, or something of that sort. The gift consists of special skill in relieving that distress, misery, etc. The right actions and/or the right words at times of that kind of emergency can effectively relieve a crisis through which a victim is passing. Those are the ways that a gifted person shines the brightest in support of others in the body of Christ.

Dorcas of Joppa exhibited the benefits reaped through a person possessing the gift of showing mercy. She abounded "with deeds of kindness and charity, which she continually did" (Acts 9:36). The church in Joppa was that much richer because of the exercise of her gift. When she herself became sick and died, the church summoned Peter who came and exercised his gift of miracles in raising her from the dead (Acts 9:37–41). That miracle gave Peter credentials that he apparently needed for a long ministry in Joppa, a ministry through which many came to believe in the Lord (Acts 9:42–43).

The side-by-side use of two gifts—the gift of showing mercy and the gift of miracles—in that setting provides an excellent example of their effectiveness. Undoubtedly, the conspicuous nature of the miracle performed by Peter—bringing a dead person back to life—attracted much wider attention because of its spectacular appeal. Yet, the supportive effect of Dorcas' deeds of mercy made the ground that much more fertile for the preaching and teaching of Peter and others in that city. Widows and others who had benefited from the good works she had done in the name of Christ (cf. Acts 9:39) were undoubtedly more receptive to the message preached by those with one of the speaking gifts. Many came to faith in Christ not only because of Peter's miracle but also because of Dorcas' acts of mercy. Both supported an expanding outreach.

Epaphroditus was apparently another person gifted with showing mercy.

The crisis that he was called upon to relieve was the hardships Paul faced while under house arrest in Rome. The church at Philippi wanted to serve Paul in some way during his confinement, so they selected Epaphroditus to represent them in ministering to Paul's need. He was their "messenger and minister to my need" (Phil. 2:25), and the church sent him "to complete what was deficient in your service to me" (Phil. 2:30), writes Paul. Epaphroditus must have been so gifted, or the church would not have chosen him.

His exercise of the gift exhibits another important lesson about using any spiritual gift. It entails hard work and unselfish service. Epaphroditus risked everything, even his own life, to be of service to Paul and meet his need. "He came close to death" (Phil. 2:30) to render service to Paul for the sake of Christ. Exercise of the gift puts oneself into the background and considers only the positive value it can impart to others.

"Showing mercy" is a special "know how" in consoling the mourner, relieving the sufferer, accomplishing acts of various kinds of assistance, or something of that sort for the benefit of distressed people. It is a service to be rendered with cheerfulness, according to Romans 12:8. In the contemporary scene, the world is full of distressed people, which means many open doors for service by Christians with the gift of showing mercy. Some believers have just the right words to speak when comforting bereaved relatives of a person who has just died. They know intuitively just how to assist and just the right demeanor at such times. Often they will prepare meals to serve just after funeral services. That can be a great encouragement to those who otherwise would be preoccupied with how much they will miss their loved one who is no longer with them.

At times of injury or debilitation, people need others to reassure them of their genuine concern. When one has borne the brunt of unjust treatment at the office or elsewhere in social interaction with unbelievers, that person needs others to come alongside with words that will provide strength for weathering the crisis.

Countless types of occasions provide opportunities to show mercy in the name of Christ, thereby creating an environment in which the spoken word of the gospel will have greater effectiveness. That is the function of the gift of showing mercy just as it is for all the auxiliary gifts. People in a local congregation with that gift should be "freed up" and not allowed to get bogged down with other responsibilities for which they may not have as much spiritual endowment as they do in showing mercy.

Yet, they are not the only ones responsible to demonstrate the quality of mercy toward distressed persons. Even though they may not possess a special ability in knowing what to do or say, the Bible requires all Christians to show mercy to others when they find themselves in tumultuous circumstances (Jude

22–23). They are to match the compassion of Jesus who was so deeply moved when the saw the multitudes as sheep having no shepherd (Matt. 9:36). Mercy is a positive attribute that should be present in every Christian life (cf. James 2:13; 3:17).

THE GIFT OF GIVING

Giving is a gift listed among other gifts in Romans 12:8: "he who gives, with liberality." The gift consists of a specialized ability to invest material substance in spiritual undertakings so as to reap the maximum spiritual dividends. Most often, we associate the gift with those who have large material resources, and that is often the case. But people with more limited resources can possess that skill, too, as they use wisely what God has put into their hands.

Giving is another specialized form of the gift of helps. Paul refers to it in 1 Corinthians 13:3 when he speaks of giving all his possessions to feed the poor and of delivering his body "that I may boast" (a reading of the text preferred over "to be burned"). Paul suggests the possibility of using all his earthly belongings for the benefit of the poor but goes beyond that to suppose that he might sell himself into slavery in order to have even more to give for charitable purposes. In that verse, though, he notes the uselessness of it all if love is not the moving force behind such generous giving.

A biblical example of the gift of giving is that of Barnabas in Acts 4:36–37. As one of a larger company in the early church at Jerusalem who were selling property and giving the proceeds to help their needy fellow Christians (cf. Acts 4:34–35), Barnabas—whose name means "Son of Encouragement"—was an outstanding example. He sold his tract of land and brought the proceeds to the apostles to distribute, with a view to relieving the needs of others. That type of skillful giving was what created a wholesome atmosphere for the preaching of the Word in those early days. Such sensitivity and openness drew early believers close together and undoubtedly helped in recognizing Ananias and Sapphira whose giving to the church did not spring from such pure motives (cf. Acts 5:1–11).

God has been pleased to bestow the gift of giving on a good number of individuals around the turn of the twenty-first century. Without their generosity, many evangelical ministries would not have grown to the degree that they have. People such as R. G. Letourneau and Dewey Lockman have benefited a number of outreach ministries by donating most if not all of their accumulated wealth to support Christian works of various kinds. Unfortunately, others with the same gift have shared in the support of Christian churches, schools, literature projects, mission endeavors, and the like, but because their resources have been more limited, they have not received the acclaim that their richer fellow believers have. Yet, their role is nonetheless important. God has gifted them in this way, and they have used their gift faithfully.

Those with the gift of giving have made possible the expansion of the gospel both nationally and internationally. Their resources have supported people in full-time vocational Christian ministry, built church facilities and college and seminary campuses, printed Bibles and Christian literature in English and other languages of the world, and in various other ways expedited gospel outreach in such a way as would not have been possible otherwise. The auxiliary role of the gift of giving is so apparent as to need no elaboration. Just as Paul acknowledged to the church at Philippi—"[I] have received everything in full, and have an abundance; I am amply supplied, having received from Epaphroditus what you have sent, a fragrant aroma, an acceptable sacrifice, well-pleasing to God" (Phil. 4:18)—giving by God's people enables a person with one of the speaking gifts to keep preaching the gospel without taking time out to support himself. People with that special gift play a large role in such support.

Yet, those with the special gift are not the only ones who must give. Giving is the responsibility of every Christian. Paul directs the words, "Each one must do just as he has purposed in his heart; not grudgingly or under compulsion; for God loves a cheerful giver" (2 Cor. 9:7), to all Christians, not just to those with the gift of giving. Those with the gift cannot and should not be expected to shoulder the whole financial responsibility for the work of Christ. It is a charge given to the whole body of Christ. The rest who do not possess the special skill at giving must act as wisely as they can with their resources in supporting the Lord's work.

THE GIFT OF GOVERNING (OR RULING)

What Paul calls the gift of "administrations" or "governments" in 1 Corinthians 12:28, he calls the gift of "leading" or "ruling" in Romans 12:8. With it in the latter reference, he urges the quality of "diligence." This is a special ability in leadership and is also a necessary prerequisite for the office of elder (1 Tim. 3:4–5). Paul reasons, if a husband and father cannot lead effectively in his own family, how can he do so in the church of God? The same word designates the ruling function in both Romans 12:8 and 1 Timothy 3:4–5.

This gift consists of a special skill in administrative direction that enables the gifted one to steer the flock of God into channels of most effective service. It has to do with matters of external organization and calls upon resources of shrewd and wise direction—as in the piloting of a ship—that harnesses the maximum potential of a local body of believers. Some within each local church have that ability. Their church should draw upon that ability. Many times, a church has been full of talented and spiritually gifted people, but they all have been "doing their own thing" without contributing to a concerted effort of the whole body in a certain direction. Skilled leadership can take that variety of gifts and organize it into a united front in accomplishing a specified task or tasks.

The gift of ruling is definitely not a type of tyrannical dictatorship in which one person dominates. It is the combined wisdom of a team whereby a group of people who are so gifted pool their skills and reach a decision about how to steer the body into its most efficient efforts. No single person has all the right answers. Leadership is a team effort.

A number of New Testament passages refer to the function of leadership: 1 Thessalonians 5:12; 1 Timothy 5:17; Hebrews 13:7, 17, 24; 1 Peter 5:2-3. The passages furnish guidelines for leaders and for the proper treatment of leaders by those being led. In general, leaders should exhibit genuine, unselfish concern for the flock, and the flock should reciprocate by showing the highest respect for their leaders.

One of the functions of leadership is recognizing the gifts of individuals within the flock. The elders at Timothy's church publicly recognized his spiritual gift (1 Tim. 4:14) and appointed him to an appropriate sphere of service in light of that gift. That should be a common occurrence in local churches, i.e., the leadership taking an inventory of what gifts people have and organizing them in a way to derive maximum spiritual benefit from those gifts.

That is only a fraction of the responsibilities that fall upon leaders, however. The tasks for which they must give an account are many (Heb. 13:17), yet their diligent work goes unnoticed most of the time. What they have to do involves a sacrificial giving of themselves for the sake of the flock. Rarely do they receive public recognition for their services. Nevertheless, without them the ship could never stay upright and on course.

Every believer needs to follow the example of wise leaders. Though his leadership decisions may involve a group smaller than the whole church, such as a Sunday school class, his own family, or even himself alone, he still has a responsibility before God to make wise choices regarding the direction of his life and ministry for Christ. He needs to cultivate the utmost in spiritual discernment.

Governing or ruling is another gift of the Spirit that is indispensable in the smooth functioning of the body of Christ. It serves in support of the speaking gifts to make them more effective by arranging a cooperative effort on the part of the other members toward a common goal. With the gift of governing in place, a body of believers can achieve that goal much sooner and with greater satisfaction.

Appendix F

HOW TO DISCOVER AND USE YOUR SPIRITUAL GIFT(S)

HOW TO DISCOVER YOUR SPIRITUAL GIFT(S)

Discovering one's spiritual gift(s) entails following nine rather distinct steps. Knowing the biblical possibilities of the gifts is one thing; identifying what one's own spiritual abilities are is another. This is a discovery that relatively few Christians seem to have made. A theory regarding the gifts is of little practical value unless that theory becomes practical in individual lives. The following process, if followed carefully, should lead a Christian to an understanding of what his or her gift or gifts are.

1. The first step in the process of learning what one's gift(s) is involves reaching the settled assurance that every Christian has at least one gift. Each context where spiritual gifts receive specific mention in the New Testament strongly emphasizes this fact (cf. 1 Cor. 12:7, 11; Rom. 12:3; Eph. 4:7; 1 Peter 4:10). In every one of those verses, the Greek word *hekastos* ("each") occurs. The word individualizes each member with his specific gift. First Corinthians 12:11, in addition to *hekastos*, uses *idios* ("its own"), which makes the expression more emphatically individualistic. The operation of spiritual gifts is not merely for certain parts of the body; it is for the whole body, every single individual member. To the extent that even one member does not function in his or her proper role, that member cripples the whole body. Every part needs to be equipped and be in operation if the body is to have its full effectiveness.

2. The second step toward the discovery of one's spiritual gift(s) is an awareness of the possibilities and the purposes of the gifts. A discussion of the gifts in Appendix E has outlined what the eighteen gifts are. Speaking as twentieth-century Christians, we can conclude that eight gifts are currently operative in promoting continual growth in the body of Christ. They include the speaking gifts (Group 3 in Appendix E) and the auxiliary gifts (Group 4 in Appendix E). The speaking gifts are evangelism, teaching, pastor-teaching, and exhorting. The auxiliary gifts are helps or ministry, giving, showing mercy, and governing or administration. The speaking gifts strengthen the body of

Christ both numerically and qualitatively. Evangelism adds new members to the body of Christ, and pastor-teaching, teaching, and exhorting help the already existing members to walk in service to the rest of the members. The auxiliary gifts in various ways make the speaking gifts more effective, and without them the speaking gifts could have little impact on the growth of the body.

God specifically designed the remaining ten gifts for the infant church, the body of Christ, in the days of its beginning, each one with specific purposes as outlined in Appendix E.

3. The third step toward discovery is the step of prayer for enlightenment regarding one's gift(s). Though not explicitly named in connection with learning about gifts, prayer sustains an unquestionable connection with zeal for spiritual gifts for which Paul commends the Corinthians. First Corinthians 14:1 commands a zeal for spiritual gifts, even though that zeal is secondary to the pursuit of love in the same verse. The zeal is still there and indicates a degree of intensity in one's quest for spiritual gifts. This, without a doubt, involves prayer toward that end. First Corinthians 14:12 presents the zeal of the Corinthians for spiritual gifts in a favorable light. Their zeal seems to have been misdirected as to its purpose, but that same zeal with a corrected purpose is desirable. Prayer is involved wherever Christian zeal is involved. It must be.

4. The fourth step leading to the discovery of spiritual gifts is a consideration of one's natural abilities, circumstances, and resources. Such a consideration is not determinative in the final analysis because gifts do not always fall into line with a person's natural background. However, it seems that most of the time, the Spirit chooses to match one's spiritual gifts to one's natural situation.

A conspicuous example of the association of a spiritual gift with natural circumstances is the gift of apostleship. No one could receive such a gift without being an eyewitness of the ministry and resurrection of Christ. Hence the bestowment of the gift presupposed a certain series of personal experiences in the past. An example of the association of one's spiritual gifts with one's natural resources is in the gift of giving. While not an absolute necessity, it presupposes that a person has a significant amount of substance to give. Surely Christians can have very limited means and still make very wise investments of what they have in the Lord's work, so they may still possess the gift of giving. But the most conspicuous examples of those with the gift of giving seem to be the ones who have been well endowed with material things. In regard to natural abilities, a person with significant difficulty in communicating by speech would hardly receive the spiritual gift of teaching. That is not absolutely true in every case, however, since a person can teach by other means, such as writing. But most often, the gift of teaching will presuppose a substantial natural ability to communicate orally.

5. The fifth step in this sequence is probably the most difficult of all, yet in a sense it is the most crucial. Experimentation is essential if someone wants to discover his or her gift(s). Believers must try their hand at every possible gift before they can know with certainty whether they have the gift or not. When we speak of experimentation, we are not speaking of one brief attempt to function in a given capacity. We are referring, rather, to a prolonged and extended effort in a given area during a period of four to six months at least. The discoverer must delve into each of the eight areas of possible giftedness.

That suggestion may seem rather bold and even ill-advised. Someone may ask, "What if I try my hand in a particular area and turn out not to be gifted in that area? Have I not presumed upon the Lord? Have I not plunged into an area of expertise I have no business entering?" The answer is flatly, "No, you have not." Every one of the eight gifts represents a general Christian responsibility, a ministry where every Christian is responsible to God to be active, whether he or she has that gift or not. If you turn out not to be gifted in a given way, you have not sinned, you have simply obeyed God in trying to have a positive effect on the growth of the body of Christ through carrying out duties every Christian should be performing. It is no sin to witness to a lost person and seek to win him to Christ if you do not have the gift of evangelism. You have simply obeyed the Great Commission given to every Christian. You have not sinned by trying to comfort a bereaved brother or sister in Christ without having the gift of showing mercy. That is a service you should perform anyway, whether you have the gift or not. The same is true throughout the list of eight operative gifts. Each is a duty every child of God needs to carry out even without that specific specialized ability. In the process of trying out the gifts one by one, you will not only discover your gift, but you will fulfill the will of God for your life as a Christian.

Getting people to experiment is very difficult. It is hard to experiment; it takes courage. Dozens of objections to undertaking this part of the process will arise, yet it must be done. It is crucial. No amount of spiritual-gift surveys can replace this. Experimentation is the proving ground where actual discovery comes. The acknowledged difficulty will disappear if a person possesses the zeal spoken of in 1 Corinthians 14:1, 12. If your desire to know your gift(s) is strong enough, you will go out on a limb, take that hardest of steps, and try to function in each of the eight ways.

6. The sixth step in the process of discovering these special abilities is the stage of self-evaluation. When a person experiments in one or more of the eight areas, he or she will sense an inner satisfaction not found in the others, a satisfaction consisting of knowing the special worthwhileness of the activity in which he or she has just engaged.

First Corinthians 14:4 observes that a person who speaks in a tongue edifies himself or herself. The self-edification spoken of in the verse is not a wholesome thing. It is an action contrary to the principle of love in 1 Corinthians 13:5, that love does not seek the things of itself. It is edification for selfish purposes that is not commendable nor is it to be condoned. Edification of oneself is not a high Christian ideal. We know from 1 Corinthians 8:10 that negative edification can even be a factor in tearing down the body of Christ.

Yet, 1 Corinthians 14:4 does highlight another characteristic of spiritual gifts. When you use your gift for the right purpose, that of building up other members of the body of Christ, as a by-product you, yourself, will experience a degree of edification. Edification of yourself is not your goal in what you do, but you will experience it as a secondary effect of serving others. That is the inner satisfaction that you become aware of in performing functions in areas where you are gifted. For example, there is great satisfaction in preparing a lesson from Scripture and teaching it to others. Though that is not his purpose, the teacher himself experiences growth in the faith. He experiences a subjective awareness that in building up others, his own edification has resulted. This is the satisfaction for which one should be alert in the step of self-evaluation.

7. The seventh step toward the discovery of one's own spiritual gift(s) is to seek out the reaction of others who are mature and respected Christians. The ultimate test of our ministry for Christ is its impact upon other people. In 1 Corinthians 14:19, Paul points out his preference for having a positive impact on the lives of others. Though the quantity of his ten thousand words in a tongue far exceeds his five words with understanding, the five words with understanding far exceeds the ten thousand words in importance. Why? Because other people receive benefit by way of Christian growth. The importance of seeking the opinion of others is consequently quite apparent.

First Corinthians 14:29 is a further illustration of the value of soliciting the reaction of others. For a prophet's utterance to have been accepted as valid, fellow prophets had to judge it. If their opinion was negative, the church disregarded the speech. The words had not been a true prophecy.

We need the responses of other people. At the point of self-evaluation (step 6), we have some help, but our conclusions may be so subjective that we have evaluated wrongly. One thing or another may be present in our lives to create a blind spot. Double-checking our own opinions is vital; hence we need the confirmations of respected, mature Christians. After engaging in an act of service, seek out these Christians and ask them questions such as, What degree of benefit to others did you detect? What degree of benefit to you was there in my service? Evaluation must be part of the learning process in researching your own spiritual gifts.

8. The eighth step in this sequence must be the allowance that a person

may discover more than one gift, even a combination of gifts. That is one feature that keeps two members of the body of Christ from being identical with each other. Paul had the gift of apostleship (1 Cor. 9:1); he also had the gift of tongues (1 Cor. 14:18). Probably the apostles had all the gifts. Such plentiful bestowment will not characterize our lives, but most Christians will discover more than a single gift, more than a single special ability to perform in the service of the other members of the body of Christ.

Lines of distinction between gifts that are found in combination are next to impossible to draw. The gifts are usually overlapping in nature. For example, the gift of showing mercy and the gift of pastor-teaching have many characteristics in common. Compassion and sensitivity to the needs of others must be present in both cases. One should not be too concerned whether at any given moment one is exercising the gift of pastor-teaching or the gift of showing mercy. That person should simply be conscious in a general way of the presence of both gifts. What is true of these two gifts by way of overlapping is true of other combinations of the eight gifts under discussion.

9. The ninth step is recognition of degrees of giftedness. Among those with the gift of teaching, for example, there will be a range of ability. Some will be better than others. Because one is not as effective a teacher as some bright person who is highly endowed with communicative skills, that person should not conclude necessarily that he or she does not possess the gift. That person may have effectiveness, though it is not nearly as profound as that of another.

At the same time, however, remember that there is a great gap between those who are in the range of giftedness and those who fall far from that range. The latter group may function as they should in teaching regarding matters that are the responsibility of all Christians, but those without the gift of teaching cannot in reality attain the range of ability that characterizes those with the gift. The same is true of all the gifts in regard to whether persons possess gifts to a greater or lesser degree.

The presence of the range of abilities is another factor that makes for variety in the body of Christ. No two members are the same; no two have identical degrees of ability. The variation in degrees of giftedness combined with the variation in combinations of gifts (see step 8) is ample provision for the absolute distinctiveness of every individual member of the body of Christ.

HOW TO USE YOUR SPIRITUAL GIFT(S)

Discovery of one's spiritual gift or gifts is only the beginning of the process, not the end. There are five practical lessons or principles of Christian living derived from Scripture that one must apply to use gifts to their utmost effectiveness.

1. The first principle is the lesson of development. In 1 Timothy 4:13, Paul tells Timothy to give himself to reading, to exhortation, and to teaching. The last two of these, exhortation and teaching, were areas in which Timothy was apparently gifted. In verse 14, Paul tells Timothy not to neglect the gift of God that is in him. The gift spoken of in the singular is apparently a combination of all the gifts possessed by Timothy, including exhortation, teaching, and whatever other gifts were his. Paul's direction to him is that he not neglect them but that he pay close attention to them with a view to sharpening and developing them into greater and greater effectiveness.

In 2 Timothy 1:6, Paul tells his younger associate to kindle afresh, or build a fire under, the gift that he has. He was to do everything in his power to enhance that gift. He was to study ways that the gift could become more effective. He was to practice and practice and practice until the gift developed into a very smooth technique. Over the passage of time, the gift would increase in effectiveness, its value and contribution toward the growth of the body of Christ becoming greater and greater.

A theological seminary and a Christian or Bible college cannot dispense spiritual gifts to its students. Only God dispenses the gifts. First Corinthians 12:11 clarifies that the sovereign will of God the Holy Spirit determines who in the body of Christ will have which gifts. First Corinthians 12:18 teaches that God the Father's sovereign will determines the distribution of gifts. In other words, when God decides on the placement of members in the body of Christ, He determines who will have what gifts. Training institutions and theological institutions have the responsibility of helping students discover—if they do not know them already—and develop their gifts. Generally those whom God calls to study in such a place know their gifts or else they are open to discovering them as soon as possible. In the school environment, they can sharpen those gifts through study, through practice, and through exchange with faculty and other students. They also have internship opportunities in which to try out the gifts and find ways of making them more effective. Institutional training can help the development of the gifts, but it cannot give them.

Even after training, servants of God must continue developing their gifts. They must constantly seek improvement, always looking for ways to enhance their gifts and make them more profitable for people whom they serve. Ongoing development is of prime importance in the use of our spiritual gifts.

2. The second guideline for using spiritual gifts to the best advantage is to assure that they are in harmony with the fruit of the Spirit. According to Galatians 5:22, the fruit of the Spirit is love. The supreme importance of love is the reason for the inclusion of 1 Corinthians 13, the love chapter, between two chapters dealing with spiritual gifts. The Corinthian readers missed that most basic point. They received Paul's strong rebuke for erring regarding such a basic standard. They had devoted their exercise of gifts largely to personal

pleasure derived by the users themselves. Paul impressed upon them this shortcoming in an indirect and gentle way in 1 Corinthians 12:31b–13:13. He described the quality of Christian love in general terminology as it was most applicable to the Corinthians' need. Then in 1 Corinthians 14, he applied the implementation of love more specifically in reference to the gifts of prophecy and tongues.

In 1 Corinthians 13, it is justifiable to label love as the *fruit* of the Spirit for reasons that may not be so apparent. The listing of the qualities of love in 1 Corinthians 13:4–7 shows an amazing correspondence to the fruit of the Spirit listed in Galatians 5:22–23. The list begins with love, and all the following fruits really describe and define what love is. In Galatians love is defined by *joy;* 1 Corinthians 13 says love *rejoices* with the truth. In Galatians love has *patience* or *longsuffering;* 1 Corinthians 13 describes love as *patient* or *longsuffering.* Galatians includes *kindness* in the list headed by love; 1 Corinthians 13 describes it by the adjective *kind.* Galatians says that love is *self-control;* 1 Corinthians 13 says that love *does not act unbecomingly.* The rest of the two listings match each other in a similar way. All the qualities are what Galatians 5:22–23 calls the fruit of the Spirit.

That same love is an indispensable element in the functioning of spiritual gifts. In 1 Corinthians 13:1–3, the Holy Spirit through Paul talks about the preeminence of love. In verse 1, he speaks of one who possesses the ultimate degree of linguistic ability through the gift of tongues, an ideal but not an actual case for anyone. He says that even if one had such a rich gift, it would amount only to a sounding gong or a clanging cymbal if not accompanied by love. In verse 2, he speaks of the maximum of the gifts of prophecy and knowledge, possibly including the gift of wisdom as referenced in understanding all mysteries. In the same verse, he refers to the ultimate measure of the gift of faith. Such bountiful endowments as these are useless if not exercised in conjunction with love. In verse 3, he refers to the gift of helps or showing mercy, or perhaps even the gift of giving. He speaks of giving all his possessions, which Paul, incidentally, never did; he kept enough to support his own ministerial efforts. He adds the possibility of even selling himself into slavery so as to have additional means to help the needy. But all of this giftedness avails nothing and produces no profit for the rest of the body of Christ, unless a motivation of love lies behind its implementation. That love, in turn, is attainable only through a person's being controlled by the Holy Spirit. The believer walking in harmony with the Holy Spirit loves; one out of harmony with the Holy Spirit cannot love. The fruit of the Spirit is essential in the fruitful use of spiritual gifts.

The major problem in Corinth was the absence of love. The Christian congregation there had rich measures for outstanding spiritual gifts (cf. 1 Cor. 1:7), but they were using their gifts for the wrong purposes. People were insisting on their right to show off their gifts whenever they chose because of the selfish satisfaction they derived from it (cf. 1 Cor. 14:4). A constructive harnessing of gift potential in submission to the needs of other people was absent.

That love teaches us to subserve our own interests in order to cater to the interests of others is the essence of what Paul teaches in 1 Corinthians 13:4, 5, and 7. Those qualities bring out the submissiveness of love. Patience or longsuffering does not fly off the handle quickly at the shortcomings of others or ill treatment by other people. Love is kind; the basic force of the word for kindness is usefulness. Love does what is useful on behalf of other people. Love is free from jealousy. It is glad for, rather than envious of, the success and prosperity of other people. Love does not vaunt or promote itself; it does not insist on a place in the limelight. It does not have to be the center of attention. The reason for its freedom from such tendencies is that love is not puffed up or arrogant; it does not create the settled assurance of being number one in importance or ability. The verse adds that love does not behave itself unbecomingly. The Corinthians had demonstrated very bad manners, even at the time of their "love feasts" (1 Cor. 11:20–22). Love does not seek the things of itself, no matter how positive those qualities may be. It does not even seek its own edification (cf. 1 Cor. 10:23– 24, 33). The profit that is the purpose of spiritual gifts (1 Cor. 12:7) is not the profit of the gift's possessor, but the profit of other members of the body for whose benefit the gift functions. Love is exclusively outgoing and other-directed. Love is not provoked to anger in response to the faults of others. It takes it on the chin and does not fight back. It is able to keep a cool head and not lose its temper. Remaining free from anger does not violate the principle of Ephesians 4:26, which allows wrath in a limited sense of being angry at the things that anger God. The provocation that love shuns in 1 Corinthians 13 is a provocation for selfish reasons because another violates a person's personal rights. A further description of love in the list shows that love does not keep a permanent record of the evil or wrong that it experiences. It does not keep a long-term record with a view to future revenge.

The submissive qualities of love continue in verse 7. Love "bears all things," in other words, it puts up with personality differences that would normally irritate. Personality clashes do not occur in relationships among loving Christians. Love "believes all things." It is not suspicious. It takes people at their word and accepts at face value their statements and promises. To be sure, often people do not fulfill their word and they break promises. When this happens, love "hopes all things." It looks to a future time when that other person will solve the spiritual problem that has made him or her unreliable and will become a truthful person who is trustworthy. Lastly, love "endures all things." It holds up under suffering inflicted by enemies of the cross. Persecution comes and creates hardship, but hardship and suffering do not obstruct love. It goes on loving in spite of all negatives, just as Stephen, when his oppressors were afflicting him, prayed for their forgiveness. That response evidenced love.

The Corinthians were in desperate need of such qualities. Rather than submitting to the best interests of others, they were using every opportunity to take advantage of others. Also needed among them, however, was another side of love, love's strictness, of which verse 6 speaks. They needed to recognize that love has its boundaries. When an action bypasses the righteousness of God, love does not rejoice; it grieves. No matter how humanly worthy a purpose may seem to be, if it violates God's righteous standards, it is not Christian love. Neither does love set itself against the truth of God; rather it rejoices only in fellowship with the truth. Doctrinal error, such as a wrong view of the resurrection that Paul corrected in 1 Corinthians 15, cannot join hands with Christian love. Strict confines set by God's truth are boundaries beyond which love does not operate.

All the qualities described above, both those pertaining to submission and those pertaining to strictness, are relevant to the proper use of spiritual gifts. Those qualities are necessary to exercise gifts to their maximum benefit. Christians can use their gifts while in a carnal state, and with *apparent* benefit. Real benefit will come, however, only if they keep themselves under the control of the Holy Spirit in demonstrating the fruit of the Spirit.

3. A third guideline to be followed in the use of spiritual gifts requires that the gift be regulated in the light of stronger Christian duties. This involves a consideration of the effects of its use upon others. A set of circumstances may arise where harm will come rather than good in the use of your gift. Sometimes you must refrain from using your gift even when you feel you are more gifted than another whose gift is functioning in the church, or even when you feel that you could bring more benefit to the body of Christ than the one who is currently under appointment to fill the given role. You may detect a jealous spirit on the part of another or others in the assembly. Your use of your gift under those circumstances would only aggravate and enhance that jealousy. Granted such jealousy is wrong and needs to be corrected, yet for the time being it is better to wait to use your gift until the spiritual atmosphere has cleared.

The congregation may have a duly appointed or elected official to perform a given task that another gifted person knows he or she could perform far more effectively. It is that person's place to recognize God's sovereign oversight of that appointment and to respect the position and authority of the one who rightly discharges that responsibility.

First Corinthians 14:30 furnishes an instance of this. In the middle of a prophetic utterance, a prophet found himself interrupted by another who had received a revelation from God. His duty was to stop speaking and yield the floor to the new prophet. That was the right and orderly way to proceed.

In such a way, prophets were able to prophesy consecutively and not simultaneously for the benefit of the whole congregation (1 Cor. 14:31). An orderly procedure accords with the will of God, who is not a God of confusion but of peace and order (1 Cor. 14:33).

Those stronger Christian responsibilities that limit the exercise of spiritual gifts mean that a person will not exercise his or her gift constantly. In fact, considerable periods of time between usages may occur. This is an important consideration in the light of love and taking into account what is of benefit to others in the body of Christ.

4. The fourth principle to be observed in the use of spiritual gifts is avoiding pride. Here is another specific application of love in connection with spiritual gifts. It is quite evident in other parts of 1 Corinthians that the Corinthian Christians were a proud people (cf. 1 Cor. 4:18). Such arrogance is contrary to love (1 Cor. 13:4). They were also puffed up about their possession of some of the more sensational spiritual gifts. It is quite easy and natural to become proud when one has special abilities that other people admire, especially those abilities that are flashy and attract attention. People with such gifts easily begin believing compliments that people give them about how outstanding they are. Self-centeredness is natural in those situations. God says that this ought not to be.

First Corinthians 12:21 uses the illustration of the human body where the eye, with its marvelous capabilities, could become self-centered and tell the hand that it is not necessary. The verse also poses the case of the head doing the same with the foot. In picture form, that is an indication of pride. It is a highly gifted one looking down on those with lesser gifts and telling them they are not necessary. That is arrogance, which has absolutely no place in the exercise of spiritual gifts.

5. The fifth guideline in the use of spiritual gifts is to remember that each member of the body of Christ is needed. It is true with the body of Christ as it is true with the human body. If any individual member of the human body fails to function, it cripples the human body. The body cannot operate at its maximum efficiency and effectiveness without that member. So it is in the body of Christ. Every single member is absolutely necessary for the smooth operation of the spiritual body. Every gift, no matter how apparently insignificant, is vital to the effective functioning of the body of Christ. Paul points out in 1 Corinthians 12:15–16 that no member of the body can look at itself and say, "I am not needed." Variety is necessary; *all* functions must be operative (1 Cor. 12:17). An individual contribution may appear to be quite small, but its absence initiates a chain reaction of hindrances and far-reaching losses in the growth of the body. Never in this life will a time come when we can sit back and assume that the church no longer needs our gifts. We must continue contributing our part, even though it may seem very small in comparison to the contribution of others.

ENDNOTES

1. (p. 18) Another explanation for the *de* of 12:1 is to make it adversative ("but"), introducing a contrast to the final statement of chapter 11 (11:34) (Godet, 1886, 2:177–78). The resultant sense is, "There is nothing pressing about setting the rest in order. I will do it personally when I come, but there is one more matter that cannot wait, and that is the matter of spiritual gifts [or persons]. I must instruct you about these right now." In favor of this meaning is the possibility that Paul in 12:1 continues a series that had begun with *prōton men* ("in the first place") in 11:18, with the *de* of 12:1 marking a second member in the series of items relating to public worship (Hodge, 1959, 239). A contextual factor also lends credence to this understanding: a common subject closely binds chapters 12–14 to chapter 11, that of proper behavior in public worship. Evidence favoring a transitional meaning for the *de* ("now") in 12:1 seems stronger, however. Recurrence of *peri de* as a customary formula to introduce answers to questions throughout the epistle (7:1, 25; 8:1; 16:1; cf. 11:2) is sufficient to outweigh the evidence for seeing a primary connection between 12:1 and 11:34. Spiritual gifts were a subject distinct from the rest, and about which this congregation had queried Paul in their letter to him (Parry, 1916, 174; Morris, 1958, 166; Fee, 1987, 570; Mare, 1976, 261; Kistemaker, 1993, 412). This conclusion does not deny a relationship between the subjects of chapter 11 and chapters 12–14, nor does it deny that this relationship has a part in influencing the sequence in which treatments of the two are arranged. But it does claim that the primary function of chapters 12–14 was not to insert something that Paul had initially intended to postpone, as the adversative force of *de* would require.

2. (p. 18) Instead of interpreting *pneumatikōn* (12:1) as a neuter to refer to "spiritual gifts," some see it as a masculine referring to "spiritual persons" (Parry, 1916, 174; Godet, 1886, 178). With this understanding, chapters 12–14 explain the spiritual qualifications requisite in a person in order for him to have the right to speak in the worship service. The masculine usage of this same adjective in 1 Corinthians 2:15; 3:1; 14:37, and Galatians 6:1 supports this understanding. Advocates of this approach also point out that persons are prominent in the remainder of the present paragraph (second person plural subject of *ēte* ["you were"], 12:2; *oudeis* ["no one"], 12:3), as well as in the paragraph to follow (*hekastō* ["each one"], 12:7). Some have explained this alternative by making spiritual persons the sole possessors of spiritual gifts (e.g., Barrett, 1968, 278; Bruce, 1971, 116–17).

The viewpoint that makes *pneumatikōn* neuter, on the other hand, has enough in its favor to override the masculine possibility. The usage of the same adjective in 1 Corinthians 14:1 in a context very similar to 12:1 is also neuter. Further, persons possessing spiritual gifts in these three chapters have them, not because of their desirable spiritual traits, but despite their inferior spirituality (e.g., *schisma* ["division"], 12:25; cf. 1:10–13; 3:3–4; 11:18). In fact, the majority of gifted persons in Corinth seem to have been unspiritual. Possession of the gifts is not tied to spiritual qualifications but to the sovereign will of God (1 Cor. 12:11, 18).

That the neuter understanding is proper receives further confirmation by noting that chapter 12 as a whole deals more with the gifts than it does with people who exercise them, whether spiritual persons or not. It is not a discussion of Christians and their need to become spiritual persons, as is true of 1 Corinthians 2:14–3:4 (Hering, 1962, 122–23; Godet, 1886, 178–79; Hodge, 1959, 239; Kistemaker, 1993, 412–13; Fee, 1987, 575, though Fee wants to combine the two views loosely). The *charismatōn* of 12:4, therefore, explains more precisely the neuter adjective standing alone in 12:1. The correct connotation is "spiritual gifts." An interesting variation of the neuter explanation limits *pneumatikōn* to "gifts of inspired perception, verbal proclamation and/or its interpretation," while referring *charisma* to all the gifts (Ellis, 1974, 129). It is certainly true that such gifts of utterance are prominent in 1 Corinthians 12–14. A good case for this meaning exists. Yet, to have nonspeaking gifts incorporated into 12:9–10, 28–30 points to a more general meaning for *pneumatikōn*, one covering the same ground as *charisma*.

    3. (p. 20) The identity of the first "no one" in 12:3, and the circumstances under which he made his statement, "Jesus is anathema," have proven so puzzling that a variety of explanations has arisen.

    First, some have suggested that these were Christians involved in worship who did not know what they were saying because of the state of ecstasy in which they found themselves. This observation aligns with the known practice of ecstatic heathen worship alluded to in 12:2 (Bittlinger, 1968, 16; Barrett, 1968, 280). In such a condition of extreme excitement, a Christian conceivably could have distorted the truth of Galatians 3:13 regarding Christ's becoming a curse for us (cf. Deut 21: 23) (Morris, 1958, 168). Yet, it is inconceivable, unless other factors are involved, that Christians seated in the meeting would have been prone to attribute such a heathenlike statement to inspiration by the Holy Spirit (cf. Schmithals, 1971, 125–27). A test such as 12:3 provides would have been completely unnecessary in a case like that.

    A second explanation places the words in question in the mouth of an unbeliever attending the Christian service. This would explain the antagonism toward Jesus that is expressed in the words. It takes into account that unbelievers sometimes were in attendance at Christian gatherings (1 Cor. 14:23–24) (Bittlinger, 1968, 16). This viewpoint's insufficiency, however, lies in its inability to answer the question: "How could the Corinthian Christians ever have attributed an utterance from a non–Christian to the Holy Spirit?" The test suggested by Paul in 12:3 becomes superfluous in this case. Even a state of ecstasy on the unbeliever's part would not be sufficient ground for supposing him to be a mouthpiece of the Spirit.

    A third viewpoint drops the aspect of ecstasy and makes these words the statement of a backslidden Christian or apostate. Apart from a parallel situation found in an ancient letter of Ptolemy regarding backsliders from the Serapis cult (Bittlinger, 1968, 17), this view has little plausibility. The former Christian posture of such backsliders would hardly be sufficient warrant for connecting such an antagonistic statement with a source like the Holy Spirit. In fact, the person's apostate condition would be reason for doing the very opposite.

    A fourth explanation of the identity of the former spokesman in 1 Corinthians 12:3 is that he was a Jew. The Jewish origin of *anathema* and the curse pronounced by Deuteronomy 21:23 upon anyone who was hanged (e.g., on a cross) give good support to this fourth idea (Bittlinger, 1968, 17). Jewish opposition to Jesus is a well-known aspect of biblical history (Acts 13:45; 17:6; 26:11), and for Jews to have infiltrated Christian assemblies and made such statements in the midst of such a frenzied atmosphere as the Corinthian worship is a distinct possibility. The question is, however, whether the Corinthian Christians would not have recognized a speaker's unbelieving background and restrained him from uttering derogatory statements about Jesus in their meetings. Certainly their sense of values had not left them so far as to allow such a statement coming from such a source to be attributed to the Holy Spirit (cf. Schmithals, 1971, 125).

A fifth way of identifying speakers in the category under consideration is to relate them to a doctrinal viewpoint under which "Jesus is accursed" and "Christ is Lord" are not contradictory statements. Roots of Gnosticism, with its teaching that separated the historic Jesus from the pneumatic Christ, began to surface prior to the end of the apostolic era, as seen from 1 John 2:22 and 4:2–3 (Schmithals, 1971, 127; Bittlinger, 1968, 18). One later Gnostic sect, the Ophites, would admit no one to fellowship who had not cursed Jesus (Godet, 1886, 186–87; Schmithals, 1971, 128; Bittlinger, 1968, 18). It is suggested by proponents of this view that Gnostic elements, if not a full-blown Gnosticism, had already made inroads into the Corinthian church by the middle fifties, when this epistle was written (cf. Bruce, 1971, 21, who admits this but does not support this view). The existence of the "Christ party" in Corinth (1 Cor. 1:12) (Bittlinger, 1968, 18), the presence of people who did not love the Lord (1 Cor. 16:22) (Godet, 1886, 185–86), and the arrival of false teachers who preached "another Jesus" (2 Cor. 11:3–4) (Godet, 1886, 185) are considerations that have been summoned to support this doctrinal explanation of why the Corinthians permitted Jesus to be cursed in their services and even were willing to attribute the statement to the Holy Spirit. In the face of some plausible elements, nevertheless, the view encounters difficulty in explaining the statement on a purely doctrinal ground. It is suggested that such doctrinal aberrations as this did not appear until some fifty years later (Robertson and Plummer, 1914, 261). The viewpoint, furthermore, does not make sufficient allowance for connecting verse 3 with the activities of heathen ecstatics as portrayed in verse 2 of chapter 12.

A sixth attempt at explaining "Jesus is accursed" envisions a court scene where pressure comes upon Christians to pronounce Jesus accursed so as to secure their freedom from imprisonment and persecution (Barrett, 1968, 279–80). Later on, after being released, and when recounting their experiences to fellow Christians, these same Christians would explain this as a means used by the Spirit to procure their freedom. While it is undoubtedly true that Christians faced such pressure (Barrett, 1968, 280), it is probable that this view presupposed circumstances of a time later in the Christian era. In addition, this manner of approaching the problem posits a heathen legal surrounding, but the context of 1 Corinthians 11–14 has its setting in Christian worship (Schmithals, 1971, 124n).

A seventh approach is similar to the sixth, with the exception that the hypothetical trial takes place in the Jewish synagogue rather than in the heathen court. It is clear from Acts 18:6 that adverse opinion from a Jewish synagogue audience had placed pressure upon Christians in Corinth to renounce Jesus. The Jewish background of *anathema* gives additional credence to this idea (Barrett, 1968, 280). Yet, one of the difficulties with seeing a trial setting remains: the context of the passage is that of a Christian meeting, not one of trial proceedings.

An eighth theory about the identity of the speaker in question suggests "Jesus is anathema" is merely a hypothetical possibility supplying an opposite extreme to the second statement of 12:3, "Jesus is Lord" (Barrett, 1968, 280; Bruce, 1971, 21, 118; Fee, 1987, 581). Those who hold this view doubt that the statement "Jesus is accursed" had ever been heard in the Christian assembly. It is merely a rhetorical device, an extreme example, to teach "that no false or unworthy witness to Jesus can ever be attributed to the Spirit of God" (Bruce, 1971, 118). On the opposite side of the issue, the effectiveness of an argument based on the purely hypothetical and artificial is questionable (Barrett, 1968, 280). In fact, the reality of "Jesus is Lord" as a criterion for testing demands the assumption that "Jesus is accursed" was also a real occurrence (Godet, 1886, 185).

A ninth way of explaining the circumstances of 12:3 relates it to the cries of Christian ecstatics who were resisting the trance or ecstasy they felt coming upon themselves (Barrett, 1968, 280). Support for this explanation comes from parallel experiences of heathen ecstatics who, in fighting off a "spell," would sometimes utter things contrary to their own wills and judgments as it began (Barrett, 1968, 280). A Christian ecstatic who had previous experiences of ecstasy before being converted (12:2) might find himself taken by such a spell, even after conversion. The test in question supplies a means for him and the church to tell the difference between the two kinds of ecstasies, the non-Christian and the Christian. It is questionable, however, whether the Corinthians would have had this kind of difficulty telling the difference between the sources of inspiration. Clearly, inspiration by the Spirit (whether ecstatic or not) could be withstood successfully without any utterance being made (1 Cor. 14:28, 32). From this fact alone it would have been obvious that an oncoming irresistible trance was from a source other than God.

The tenth viewpoint, and the one presented on pages 20–22 combines several elements from the above theories. View one notes the necessity of the speaker's being a professing Christian, as opposed to the idea of view two that makes him an unbeliever. There seems little doubt that the statement did come in the Christian assembly, contrary to the suppositions of views six, seven, and eight. Contextually, a state of inspiration (or ecstasy) is necessitated because of the close tie-in with the heathen condition of 12:2. That state alone is not sufficient to prove the Spirit's part, though it did not exclude it. The anathema and the relationship with Deuteronomy 21:23 (cf. view four) denote some element of Jewish influences behind the statement. And the fact of incipient heresy (cf. view five) plays a vital part in explaining why such a derogatory remark about the person of Christ would have been tolerated in the Corinthian church. In addition to the citations already made under the discussion of view five, evidence for an element of Judaistic heresy in Corinth relate to those who claimed Peter as their leader (1 Cor. 1:12), the Hebrew claims of false apostles (2 Cor. 11:22), and a comparable condition among the Galatian churches at about the same time. Paul's extensive treatment of Christ's resurrection in 1 Corinthians 15 supports the presence of doctrinal aberrations of other kinds as already in existence in Corinth. These, too, were doctrinal tendencies that eventually flowered into the system of second-century Gnosticism. The existence of such a low view of the historical Jesus a few years later in Asia Minor (1 John 2.22; 4:1–3) adds further plausibility to the belief that "Jesus is accursed" in some degree relates to prevailing Corinthian doctrinal beliefs. All these factors together seem to explain the surprising character of the negative test of 1 Corinthians 12:3.

Chapter 2 (Page number following note number tells where the note appears)

1. (p. 25) Some have given *diaireseis* ("varieties"), occurring in 12:4, 5, and 6, the more general meaning of "distribution." With that meaning it does not point to differences that distinguish gifts from one another. The neutral meaning does not commit itself as to whether they are similar or dissimilar. Support for the noncommittal meaning comes from the sense

of the cognate *diairoun* ("distributing") in 12:11, in which verse only the meaning "distributing" will satisfy the idea of the statement. Comparison with the noun's usage in the Septuagint (LXX) and in nonbiblical Greek increases the likelihood of this more general meaning (Godet, 1886, 189). Since the three occurrences in verses 4, 5, and 6 are the only three in the New Testament, usage outside the New Testament becomes substantial evidence for the translation "distributing" here (Robertson and Plummer, 1914, 262–63).

The more specific meaning of "varieties" or "differences" for *diairesis*, of course, has in view the variations that exist between the gifts. That meaning accords best with the emphasis of 12:4–11, especially the list of nine distinct gifts in verses 8–10 (Fee, 1987, 586). As a more definitive meaning, it also best accounts for the adversative *de* occurring in the expressions "but the same Spirit" (v. 4) and "but the same God" (v. 6). No contrast exists between the former and latter parts of verses 4 and 6 unless *diairesis* has the meaning of "differences" (or "varieties" or "diversities"). Since the etymology of the noun allows for such a meaning and the context requires it, this latter alternative is preferable.

2. (p. 27) Analysis of the genitive *tou pneumatos* ("of the Spirit") of 12:7 determines whether the verse speaks of the Holy Spirit as being demonstrated, or of Him as the one who puts on the demonstration. The sense dictated by the objective genitive is, "To each one it is given to exhibit the Spirit." Gifted individuals show forth the Holy Spirit through their charismatic acts, with God the Father the implied divine agent supplying the manifestation (Fee, 1987, 589 n. 30; Kistemaker, 1993, 420). Support for seeing this construction as an objective genitive is gleaned from another usage of *phanerōsis* ("manifestation") with the genitive in 2 Corinthians 4:2, where "the manifestation of truth" cannot be "an exhibition put on by the truth," but must have the sense of "exhibiting the truth" (Meyer, 1879, 1:360–61; Carson, 1987, 54 n. 52). The cognate verb *phaneroō* also carries an active connotation such as is invariably accompanied by a recipient of the action (2 Cor. 2:14; 4:10; Col. 4:4) (Parry, 1916, 179). Yet, these usages of both the noun *phanerōsis* and the verb *phaneroō*, though related, are not exactly the same as the present passage; that is, the notions of truth (2 Cor. 4:2) and the Spirit (1 Cor. 12:7) are different in that one is an abstract quality and the other is a Person (Godet, 1886, 193).

The sense dictated by the subjective genitive of *tou pneumatos* can be paraphrased as follows: "To each one the Spirit-produced exhibition is given." In this sense, it is the Holy Spirit who puts on the display (Hodge, 1959, 243). In a way, this is a self-revelation because He is the one in evidence in the operation of various gifts. This is not difficult, however, since this paragraph looks upon Him as separate from gifts. Support for the subjective genitive derives from the emphasis that pervades verses 4–11, an emphasis upon the gifts' common source, rather than on the variety of the gifts themselves. The paragraph contains no emphasis upon the sameness of output, as would be the case with the objective genitive. In fact, verses 8–10 exemplify the contrary, that is, variety of output. Verse 11 especially specifies that the Spirit is the agent in dispensing the gifts, which is His character as seen in verse 7 when a subjective genitive is the conclusion (cf. also 12:4). This strong contextual flavor for understanding *tou pneumatos* to refer to Him as producer of the gifts takes precedence over good but weaker evidence in favor of the objective genitive.

3. (p. 28) The alternation of *allō* ("another") and *heterō* ("another") in the gift list of 12:8–10 has been subjected to a number of explanations: Some believe that no distinction exists between the two pronouns. They explain that Paul alternates from one to the other only for the sake of rhetorical effect, the repetition of *allos* with each of the last eight members in the series being too monotonous to bear. Basis for this opinion comes from the contextual emphasis on illustrating the variety of gifts but not categorizing that variety. The viewpoint also stems from a companion idea that Paul used the two pronouns in 2 Corinthians 11:4 without a distinction between them (Robertson, 1934, 747), though this conclusion may also be debated (Schmithals,

1971, 133). Good ground exists, however, for understanding an intended distinction between the two words, as it is the normal hermeneutical approach to New Testament synonyms in general to presuppose that an author had some shade of meaning to convey whenever he varied his vocabulary in such a close context. Furthermore, the way Galatians 1:6-7 uses *allos* and *heteros*, leaves little room for doubt that this same author envisioned a dramatic difference between the two words (Robertson, 1934, 747; but see Turner, 1963, 197).

Most scholars understand a distinction between the two synonyms and proceed with attempts to identify the three categories of gifts marked off by the twofold occurrence of *heterō* (Trench, 1958, 361; Fee, 1987, 584–85 n. 9; 591). One concept of the divisions is that the first deals with the mind and understanding, the second with the will and the ability to exercise faith, and the third with the feelings or emotions (Godet, 1886, 194–200). The first two gifts, wisdom and knowledge, occupy that early position because the Corinthians were prone to value the ecstatic gifts more than those gifts that left man in control of his reason (Godet, 1886, 194). The second category communicated force more than meaning and related to the will more than the mind (Godet, 1886, 196). Since the only part of the human personality left untouched by the first two categories is the emotional aspect, the third category pertains to the feelings, with the understanding and will excluded (Godet, 1886, 199). Yet, this threefold division of gifts according to human psychological makeup is somewhat artificial. It leaves no room for other gifts later in the chapter (e.g., "administrations," 12:28) to be fitted under one of the three headings. Nor does the category of emotions seem completely suitable for the gifts of tongues and interpretation. It is a wiser course to understand each of these personality factors—intellect, sensibility, and will—to involve the operation of each of the gifts to a greater or lesser degree (Hodge, 1959, 244).

Another approach that recognizes distinct categories professes an inability to define exactly what that distinction is (Hodge, 1959, 244). This approach notices the unsatisfactory explanations that have sought to define the classifications, stresses that gifts are more like a landscape than a humanly designed building, and concludes it to be an unwise course to force them into man-made groups. Yet, to admit the presence of categories discernible by the human mind and not allow for man's ability to label these categories is unacceptable. If the gifts are definable and common factors within each group exist, the danger of imposing artificial labels is lessened.

It is clear that the first pair of gifts is intellectually oriented. The supernatural character of all the gifts implies that these two pertained to special powers of the mind, without excluding other aspects of the personality (Meyer, 1881, 361). One might, for convenience, term these revelational gifts, for they were special functions of the mind through which God made revelations to men. The next five gifts find their commonality in connection with *pistis* ("faith"). Since faith is an act of the will, this aspect of personality is in the forefront, but without precluding the other two. The fact that these gifts entail demonstrable force, whether in deed or word, serves notice of their evidential character. Yet, the mind remained fully aware of the activity all the while the gift operated. The third category that included tongues with its sequel, interpretation, also conveyed the impression of force, so that the will was prominent in this area also. The difference between this and the second category lay in the degree to which they involved the mind. Tongues provided a much lower degree of comprehension. The mind was more in abeyance, but without being completely excluded.

A major difficulty with this manner of classifying the gifts (Hodge, 1959, 244) is not insuperable. The difficulty is that prophecy rightly belongs with those gifts that are intellectually oriented. Yet, the dual nature of prophecy, whereby it is evidential on the one hand and revelational on the other, allows it to be placed in either section. A comparison with Acts 27:25 and Romans 12:6 establishes its definite correlation with faith. One other possible objection points to the discerning of spirits and the interpretation of tongues and asks how they fit into their respective categories. These gifts stand where they are within the classification, not because of the nature of the gifts themselves, but because of the nature of each one's companion gift.

    4. (p. 28) In the context of Paul's writings, an adequate definition of "the word of wisdom" must include the following features.

1. The gift must focus upon the person and work of Christ. The apostle makes this clear as he treats the subject of wisdom in earlier portions of 1 Corinthians (1:23–24, 30).

2. Direct communication between God and a recipient must occur. He revealed divine truths previously hidden—sometimes referred to as "mysteries"—to men at particular junctures through chosen human instruments. Such divine revelations were particularly necessary for understanding God's will and purpose during the years immediately following Pentecost because God was doing something new, something undisclosed before that time. *Sophia* ("wisdom") often depicts such special acts of communication by God (Rom. 11:25–33; 1 Cor. 2:6–7; Eph. 3:1–10).

3. A distinction exists between God's direct communication that resulted in the written Word and His ministry in illuminating the meaning of what has already been written. Though illumination by the Holy Spirit is a valid biblical teaching (John 16:12–15; 1 Cor. 2:14–3:2; 1 John 2:27), it is not a "wisdom-giving" ministry in the same sense as described under number two above. *Sophia* never appears in direct connection with the Spirit's ministry of teaching the meaning of previously imparted revelation.

4. What God does for all members of Christ's body is distinct from what He does only for certain members. Only a limited number have received each spiritual gift (1 Cor. 12:14, 29–30), including "the word of wisdom." In contrast, all members of Christ's body possess a practical wisdom that equips them to meet the everyday situations of life (Eph. 1:8; Col. 1:9; James 1:5; 3:13, 17). "The word of wisdom" as a separate and limited bestowment, therefore, is different from the more general wisdom available to every Christian.

The above factors facilitate an evaluation of the various viewpoints that have been propounded regarding the nature of "the word of wisdom."

   a. A number of authorities have centered the meaning of this gift in an ability to cope with the practical and sometimes perplexing demands of everyday life. Some believe this ability pertains personally to the holder of the gift (Farrar, n.d., 403; Grossman, 1971, 55; Laurin, 1941, 194; Gould, 1887, 105; Beet, 1883, 215; Grosheide, 1953, 285; Kistemaker, 1993, 421), while others relate it to a practical "know how" in imparting judicious advice to others (Thieme, n.d., n.p.; Kuyper, 1900, 188; Bittlinger, 1968, 28). Obviously, this explanation does justice to the practical nature of wisdom, but it fails to catch the genius of "the word of wisdom," which incorporates direct inspiration and impartation of previously unrevealed truth (see feature 2 above). It also fails to account for the biblical teaching that practical wisdom of the type described is available to all Christians, not just to a select few (see feature 4 above).

   b. Others have viewed "the word of wisdom" as a special ability to understand the written Word of God. Through special insights gained by various means, an individual may penetrate the depths of biblical revelation with unusual perception (Sanders, 1940, 119; Morgan, 1946, 152) and be effective in communicating his findings to others (Parry, 1916, 180; Ironside, 1943, 382). The merit is in recognizing that true *sophia* is bound up in God's inspired revelation, but there is also confusion over the process by which the revelation originally came, and over the process by which the completed product was to be illuminated (see feature 3 above). There is also some confusion here between "the word of wisdom" and the gift of teaching, the latter being the ability to communicate what has been previously revealed (cf. 1 Cor. 12:28). The limited distribution of "the word of wisdom" (see feature 4 above) also contrasts with the universal availability (among Christians) of the Spirit's illuminating ministry.

c. A final grouping of definitions sees "the word of wisdom" to be the avenue adopted by the Holy Spirit in imparting revelations concerning the person and work of Christ (Carter, 1968, 23; Coke, 1812, 2:251; Gill, 1775, 111, 761; DeHaan, 1956, 141; Bruce, 1971, 38; Robertson and Plummer, 1914, 265; Berquist, 1960, 93; Craig, 1953, 152; Morris, 1958, 170; Hodge, 1959, 245; Cook, 1973, 37–49). This is the only explanation of the gift that conforms satisfactorily with the criteria set forth: a principal focus upon the person and work of Christ; a direct communication between God and a recipient (features 1 and 2 above); and distinctions between God's direct communication and His ministry in illuminating what has been written, and between what He does for all members of Christ's body and what He does for only a limited number (features 3 and 4 above). This, therefore, is the definition adopted.

5. (p. 35) Explanations for the nature of the tongues gift are in two categories.

Some explain that the gift of tongues consists of an ability to produce ecstatic utterances that are inarticulate; that is, they do not fall into the classification of any language spoken on earth (Fee, 1987, 598; Kistemaker, 1993, 426). The sounds do not consist of words and are not organized into grammatical relationships. They are, therefore, incoherent and have no natural meaning to anyone, regardless of linguistic background. Usually included under this heading is the angelic language, which proponents of this view generally reckon to be inarticulate according to human standards (cf. "the tongues of angels," 1 Cor. 13:1). Evidences for inarticulate type of speech have come in a wide variety of forms. Discounting the miraculous aspect of the gift, Meyer has noticed the psychological impossibility of a person's speaking a language he has not learned by natural processes (Meyer, 1879, 1:366). In a similar vein, Behm views Christianity as being like any other religion and notes that the practice of speaking ecstatically is a common occurrence in the history of all religions. The phenomenon should be no different in conjunction with Christianity (Behm in *TDNT*, 1964, 1:722–24). Meyer also proposes that if the gift had consisted of foreign languages, Paul would have discussed the same in light of the presence or nonpresence of those who understood these languages (Meyer, 1879, 1:367). Godet adds to the case for inarticulateness by noticing the widespread knowledge of Greek and Latin in New Testament times. No special linguistic ability was necessary in spreading the gospel, he says (Godet, 1886, 2:201). He asks further, What use would a gift with foreign languages have been in the city of Corinth (Godet, 1886, 2:201)? The contribution of Edwards to this side of the issue is twofold. He notices that use of the gift in Corinthians is never evangelistic as it was in Acts (Edwards, 1885, 319). And he also postulates that a change in the nature of speaking in tongues from spoken languages to inarticulate utterances gradually came about over a twenty-five year period between the occurrences of Acts 2 and the writing of 1 Corinthians. It is his theory that the ecstasy associated with foreign languages (Acts 2) loomed larger and larger until it replaced the languages themselves as the focal point of the gift (1 Corinthians 14) (Edwards, 1885, 322–23). The remaining evidences presented in support of the inarticulate position grow out of passages in 1 Corinthians 12–14, which themselves are subject to debate. The exposition and explanatory notes of the following pages will comment on most of these passages (cf. 1 Cor. 13:1; 14:2, 4, 6, 9, 10–11, 14–15, 18–19, 23, 26, 28).

The other viewpoint concerning the nature of glossolalia in the New Testament is that the gift enabled a person to speak languages he had never acquired by natural means. In uttering a foreign tongue, the speaker did what was an impossibility from a psychological and natural standpoint. Whether or not the tongue was foreign to the listeners depended upon their backgrounds. A number of reasons offer support for this conclusion. One is that this is the most likely sense to be attached to *glōssa*, i.e., that it refers to "language" (Behm in *TDNT*, 1964, 1:725–26; Gundry, 1966, 299–300; Edgar, 1996, 134–46). No clear counterpart for its referring to something inarticulate appears elsewhere in the New Testament, though at times in heathendom it referred to archaic or mysterious expressions. Neither is there precedent for making it a technical word referring to angelic language. The normal conclusion must be that it refers to meaningful human speech. No doubt, the gift in Acts 2 consisted of using a language foreign to the language(s) of the speaker in his normal psychological condition (cf. Acts 2:4; Hering, 1962, 127–28). Acts 2 included peoples of Latin, Arabic, Coptic, Cretan, and other linguistic backgrounds. Since the same terminology for the tongues gift occurs in 1 Corinthians 12–14 as in Acts, one must assume a continuity of meaning. The two sources must be consistent unless somewhere a clear-cut change happened and is somewhere documented, which is not the case (Hodge, 1959, 249; Mare, 1976, 263). The association of Luke with Paul makes this continuity even more likely (Gundry, 1966, 300).

Another matter to take into account is the tradition of the church with regard to this phenomenon. From the third century, when tradition first becomes clear, until very recent times, the church has been practically unanimous in understanding this gift as a special ability with foreign languages (Edwards, 1885, 319; Godet, 1886, 2:200–201).

In addition to continuity in the use of *glōssa*, one must also weigh a continuity in the infant church's historical development. To change the nature of one of her basic tools for demonstrating God's presence and activity between Pentecost (Acts 2, A.D. 30) and Paul's writing of 1 Corinthians (1 Cor. 12–14, A.D. 55) injects an unnecessary break in her development that does not lend itself to satisfactory explanation (Hodge, 1959, 248). Besides this, Luke wrote Acts *after* Paul wrote 1 Corinthians. That, too, argues for continuity in the nature of the gift. Other considerations favoring tongues as articulate utterances grow out of specific verses in 1 Corinthians 12–14. Many of these will be subjects of discussion in later parts of this exposition and these explanatory notes, since each of the passages is debatable in itself (cf. 1 Cor. 13:1; 14:2, 4, 7–11, 14–17, 19, 21–22).

In anticipation of the discussions to follow as well as in evaluation of the evidence set forth, the conclusion must be that the second alternative, that is, tongues as a supernatural ability with foreign languages, is the preferable understanding of *genē glōssōn* ("kinds of tongues") in 1 Corinthians 12:10.

6. (p. 37) The nature of "interpretation of tongues" hinges, of course, upon one's understanding of the gift of tongues. Therefore, one could expect to find exegetical evidence pertaining to *hermēneia* ("interpretation") that supports the conclusion reached in regard to tongues (cf. explanatory note 5) if the previous conclusion is valid. Investigation of the gift of interpretation does serve to verify the nature of tongues as previously defined. Strong evidence supports assigning the usual meaning of "interpret" in the sense of translating a foreign language into a language understandable to the listeners. This is the predominant use of the cognate verb in the New Testament (John 1:38, 42; 9:7; Heb. 7:2) and of the compound verb as well (Acts 9:36). No legitimate reason arises for making the gift an ability in assigning intelligible content to a series of sounds that in themselves have no intelligible meaning to anyone anywhere. The concept of translating a language is also what dominates in the LXX's usage of *hermēneuō* (Gundry, 1966, 300). The possibility that the word here means "explanation" or "exposition" is quite remote.

Chapter 3 (Page number following note number tells where the note appears)

1. (p. 41) Much discussion has surrounded the nature of the church's involvement in Christ's person. Five interpretations of that involvement follow.
   1. The church as a body is identical with its leading member, the head, which is Christ. Support for this approach comes mainly from noticing that Christ as the head is a Pauline concept (Eph. 4:15–16, 25; 5:23, 30; Col. 1:18) (Meyer, 1879, 1:373). Yet, Christ's appearance as the head is observed nowhere else in 1 Corinthians, especially chapter 12. In fact, 1 Corinthians 12:21b identifies the head as being other than Christ.
   2. Another viewpoint represents the church as being involved in Christ's person because of believers' being united and identified with Him individually (Morris, 1958, 174; Barrett, 1968, 287–88). The "in Christ" teaching of identification signifies that each individual becomes one with Christ the moment he is born again (1 Cor. 1:30) (Morris, 1958, 174). Such an understanding agrees well with the emphasis upon unity in 1 Corinthians 12 (cf. v. 12) (Morris, 1958, 174). As much as this understanding has to commend it, a distinct difference between a relationship with Christ individually and the church's collective joining to Him is necessary to do justice to the present discussion. This chapter speaks of the church as a collective body, not of the individuals who compose that body. This, then, is not an appropriate place to apply the "in Christ" teaching of the Christian's identity with Christ.
   3. Another way of approaching the issue is to posit that the identity here grows out of a conception of the church as a living organism deriving her life (Parry, 1916, 183) or nature (Robertson and Plummer, 1914, 271) from the glorified Christ. One or the other of these two grounds accounts for the unity that exists. Both of these alternatives are doubtless valid observations regarding the church, but the question is whether the teaching in this context is specific enough to justify them as explanations of the issue at hand. Since examination of the current chapter fails to reveal any attention to either life from Christ or the nature of Christ, both must be ruled unsatisfactory.
   4. A fourth way of explaining the statement is to view "Christ" as a figure of speech called metonymy. In other words, "Christ" is a shortened way of saying "body of Christ," a view that looks to 12:27—"you are the body of Christ"—for support (Fee, 1987, 603; Kistemaker, 1993, 429). The difficulty with this view is that it "generalizes" the text and does not take its specific wording seriously. Paul knew how to write "body of Christ," but he did not do so here. Besides that, the view introduces a new figure of speech into the text without a contextual warrant for doing so. Chapter 12 already uses the figure of a human body. To understand "Christ" to mean "body of Christ" would compound figures of speech to the point of needless confusion.
   5. A final suggestion for explaining the church's involvement in the person of Christ sees Him as the "ego" of the body. The decisions of the body are made by Him. Its feelings and sensitivities as well as its intellectual functions are His. In this sense, He is the true personality of the body (Meyer, 1879, 1:373; Edwards, 1885, 324–25). The concept of the Spirit (of Christ) as the life principle of the body has already found its way into the discussion (cf. v. 7). The functioning of various members (i.e., gifted individuals) is none other than an activity of Christ carried out by the Holy Spirit. It is furthermore recalled that Paul's earliest encounter with Jesus Christ impressed him with the truth that anyone who did anything to Christ's body did it to Christ Himself (Acts 9:5). The only difference in 1 Corinthians 12 is that Paul

links the body's identity with Christ mainly to the flow of activity resulting from various spiritual gifts. To be sure, this explanation limits the all-inclusiveness of the way Christ permeates the body. At the same time, however, no reason for thinking that Paul intended an all-inclusive sense comes to light. He has an immediate objective in the chapter, that of correlating unity in the body with a variety of spiritual gifts, and this device furnishes him a convenient opportunity for doing so. The functioning of gifts, therefore, is none other than a manifestation of Him who is the true personality of this spiritual organism.

2. (p. 42) A minority voice has arisen on behalf of limiting the scope of *pantes* ("all") in 12:13, whether it be the former occurrence (Baker, 1967, 19) or the latter (Ervin, 1968, 45–50). In limiting the former *pantes*, one claims that all the Corinthian Christians of Paul's day had experienced Spirit baptism, but that was not true of all Christians everywhere. The view uses Acts 2, 8, and 19 as cases where people had been converted, justified, and regenerated, and yet were not baptized in the Spirit (Baker, 1967, 19). Associated with this viewpoint also is the unnatural meaning assigned to *eis* ("into") in verse 13, "with a view to" or "in relation to." Baptism of some in the body of Christ is in this argument said to be "for the purpose of" enriching and benefiting the fellowship and life of the total body. In addition to the unnatural meaning given to *eis*, various other difficulties beset this approach to *pantes*. It avoids the obvious universal thrust of 1 Corinthians 12, which encompasses Christians everywhere, and excludes even Paul himself, who was not a native Corinthian. *Pantes* must have in its scope all the apostles (cf. 1 Cor. 12:28), none of whom belonged to the city of Corinth. This view also has against it the questionable practice of interpreting 1 Corinthians 12:13 on the basis of passages from Acts whose assumed interpretation is at best questionable. To limit the scope of *pantes* would be self defeating in that it would distinguish two groups within the body of Christ, one Spirit-baptized and the other not. This completely subverts Paul's avowed purpose of proving unity of the body.

Turning to Ervin's view, one finds a limitation placed on the latter *pantes* in verse 13. Ervin allows the all-inclusive nature of the former *pantes*, but limits the other instance to those individuals who have received power for charismatic witnessing (Ervin, 1968, 16, 51). He sees Paul using "made to drink one Spirit" in the sense that Luke uses "baptized in the Spirit" in Acts. This is doubtful because of the extreme likelihood that these two close missionary associates would use terminology in the same way. Ervin's explanation, furthermore, has the unfortunate consequence of fragmenting the body of Christ, just as does Baker's. Following out his theory to its logical conclusion, one would have to posit that the latter *pantes* (v. 13) stipulates a different group—only a limited number of members—as compared to the former *pantes*, which includes all members of the body. This is not only unfortunate from the standpoint of fragmentation and the creation of disunity but illegitimate from an exegetical point of view (cf. Fee, 1987, 604–5). It is the much saner posture to see both instances of *pantes* in 1 Corinthians 12:13 as inclusive of all Christians (Carson, 1987, 44–45). All are in the body and have their gifts by virtue of this same Spirit baptism. None is excluded. That is not a subsequent or separate act experienced by only a limited number. Neither is being made to drink one Spirit separate from this initial experience of being brought into the body. Unity of the body demands unanimity in the singular experience that is here described.

3. (p. 42) The issue of whether *ebaptisthēmen* ("were ... baptized") in 1 Corinthians 12:13 refers to the ordinance of water baptism, to a purely spiritual transaction, or to both has received wide discussion. The idea that it looks solely at water baptism is not probable because of the Holy Spirit's association with the baptism, as expressly declared in the verse.

1. A dual reference to water baptism and a receiving of the Holy Spirit in conjunction with it has been the view of many. They seek support for this double reference in

the parallel passage of Romans 6:3–5, as well as in Galatians 3:27–28 (e.g., Barrett, 1968, 288). Existence of the same disagreement in these other contexts as in the current verse weakens that argument from comparison. Morris seeks to add credibility to this view by alluding to the parallel meaning of baptism in 1 Corinthians 1:13–17 (Morris, 1958, 174). Just how parallel 12:13 is with 1:13–17, however, is open to question. In chapter 1 of the epistle, discussion revolves around baptism administered by a human agent; this is not the case in chapter 12. A further proof of the combination meaning of the verb in 12:13 points to the overwhelming usage of *baptizø* among early Christians to speak of water baptism (Meyer, 1879, 1:373–74.; Oepke in *TDNT*, 1964, 1:539; Carson, 1987, 43). The fact that the connotation of the word so strongly included water leaves no doubt in the readers' minds that it signified actual baptism here. Again, however, it is questionable whether such a strong water connotation always applied (Fee, 1987, 604). In fact, this is the very issue the present discussion seeks to resolve. Furthermore, a convincing argument that the term's usage does not automatically involve water comes in connection with Mark 10:38–39 and 1 Corinthians 10:2. In other passages such as Luke 12:50 and Acts 1:5, to have *baptizø* signify "baptize in water" would be to introduce a contradiction in sense, whereas the same meaning in John 1:26 and 31 would create tautology (Dunn, 1970, 129).

2. Those holding the other position assert that 1 Corinthians 12:13 has no reference to the ordinance and that it stipulates the spiritual transaction by which the Holy Spirit at the time of conversion places a person into the body of Christ (Kistemaker, 1993, 430). They base their conclusion on the context's emphasis on the body's unity, and notice that to introduce the ordinance of baptism into a discussion with these Corinthians would have an opposite effect. Administration of the ordinance among them had been the occasion of strong disunity (1 Cor. 1:12–17). These also notice a closely parallel usage of *baptizø* ("were baptized") in 1 Corinthians 10:2 that connotes a purely spiritual identification, the absence of water being especially notable. Hodge has well pointed out, in addition, that a dual reference to the ordinance of baptism and to baptism by the Spirit is contrary to historical precedent (Hodge, 1959, 153–54). Earliest teaching on the subject, rather than making the two synonymous, pits them against each other in an emphatic contrast (e.g., Acts 1:5). That Spirit baptism and water baptism are separable from one another is also evident in that the former took place prior to the latter in the experience of Cornelius's household (Acts 10:44–45; 11:15–16) (Parratt, 1971, 235). Paul's extreme care in distinguishing between outward rite and inward spiritual activity would hardly allow him to merge these two into one word (cf. Rom. 2:28–29) (Dunn, 1970, 129–30).

The formidable evidence is on the side of position 2, necessitating exclusion of the ordinance of baptism from the meaning of this verse.

4. (p. 43) Some find a difference between Spirit baptism in 1 Corinthians 12:13a and the Spirit baptism referred to in Acts (Williams, 1953, 3:47; Riggs, 1949, 59; du Plessis, 1961, 70). They make this differentiation because of a difference in the agent performing the baptism. They recognize that every Christian has experienced the Spirit baptism of 1 Corinthians 12:13, where the Holy Spirit is the agent. But they limit the baptism of Acts, where the Spirit is the element instead of the agent, to only those Christians who have experienced the filling of the Spirit and spoken in tongues.

Stott has ably pointed out in response to this position, however, that the Greek construction is precisely the same in the other Spirit baptism passages as it is in 1 Corinthians 12:13, and that no adequate reason exists for referring the Corinthians passage to a separate Spirit baptism (Stott, 1964, 23). Another argument against distinguishing between Corinthians and the rest of the Spirit baptism contexts is to note the Son's integral part as the source of this baptism in Corinthians, the same role He has elsewhere (1 Cor. 12:5). This agrees closely with His agency in baptizing throughout Acts. No room remains for distinguishing two Spirit baptisms because of difference in agent or anything else. All instances speak of the same baptism, one that is not reserved for just a portion of the body of Christ, but one that is common to every Christian, making him a part of that body (cf. Carson, 1987, 46–47).

    5. (p. 43) The *en* ("by") early in 1 Corinthians 12:13 has been subject to a variety of understandings.

      1. One group of interpreters has taken it to be in the locative case. This approach means that *pneumati* ("Spirit") names the sphere in which the baptism of the Spirit takes place. This position emphasizes the normality of understanding the locative case following the preposition *en* and the necessity of a clear contextual indication in the cases where an instrumental meaning is intended (Robertson, 1934, 590). Another argument notes that earlier New Testament teaching regarding this baptismal act makes Christ rather than the Holy Spirit the agent of baptism. The latter would have been the case were *en* to be understood instrumentally (see view 3) (cf. Matt. 3:11; Mark 1:8; Luke 3:16; John 1:33) (Stott, 1964, 16). The view also points out that a parallelism with *en tō Iordanē* ("in the Jordan") in Matthew 3:6 and Mark 1:5 gives credence to the locative sense of the word (Oepke in *TDNT*, 1964, 11 539). Dunn adds to this that *en* with *baptizō* never designates a baptizer. Rather, it is always the element in which the baptized one is immersed (Dunn, 1970, 127–28; cf. Fee, 1987, 605–6). Matthew 3:11 and parallels are sometimes cited in favor of this position as examples showing that *en* should be understood locatively (Morris, 1958, 174). Another comparison that lends credence to taking *en* with a locative interpretation places 1 Corinthians 10:2 alongside the present verse because another instance of *baptizō* with the prepositions *eis* and *en* is found there. The clear function of *en* in 1 Corinthians 10:2, "in the cloud and in the sea," is locative, and this identifies the Pauline habit in such a construction as this, it is claimed. That *en* is necessarily understood locatively in these verses, however, is disputed, and so the evidence that argues thus is largely neutralized.

      2. A second way of understanding *en* is to assign it an instrumental function introducing the means whereby the baptism was carried out. In such a case, *pneumati* names the element employed in the baptismal act. Mark 1:8, Luke 3:16, and Acts 1:5 and 11:16 confirm this fact. In these verses, *hydati* ("with water") without a preposition can hardly represent any other than the instrumental case, for the purpose of designating the means, or element, of the baptism. Spirit baptism being antithetical to *hydati* in these cases, is therefore presumably instrumental also, as opposed to locative (Hodge, 1959, 254). Another reason given for an instrumental-of-means sense is the image of the Spirit's being "poured out" as water. This marks Him as being typified in the other kind of baptism, the one carried out with water as the element. It is further reasoned that since the Spirit is the "means by which" rather than the "agent by whom" in the other six passages dealing with Spirit baptism, He must be viewed in the same light here (cf. Matt. 3:11; Mark 1:8; Luke 3:16; John 1:33; Acts 1:5; 11:16). Supporters of view 2 also note the relevance of *pyri* ("fire") in Matthew 3:11 and Luke 3:1. As *pneumati hagiō* ("Holy Spirit") is in parallel relationship with the *pyri* and as *pyri* must express means rather than agency, they conclude that the preposition points to means rather than agency in 1 Corinthians 12:13 also. The principal deficiencies of this position appear in the form of supports in favor of viewpoint 1, which says *en* governs the locative rather than the instrumental case.

      3. A third viewpoint also takes *en* as governing the instrumental case, but as introducing the agent who carries out the baptism rather than the means by which it was

performed. Support here is forthcoming from the immediate context of 1 Corinthians 12. Specifically, in 12:9, where *en tō autō pneumati* ("by the same Spirit") is found twice, it is difficult to dispute that those two uses of the preposition denote agency rather than means, the Holy Spirit being depicted as the agent who distributes the gifts there alluded to (Kistemaker, 1993, 428). First Corinthians 12:8 and 11, where it is "through [*dia*] the Spirit" that gifts are bestowed, provide confirmation of the present context's emphasis on agency of the Spirit. There "distributing to each one . . . just as He wills" describes the Spirit's active part in allotting the gifts. Coupled with this is the fact that 1 Corinthians 12:4–6 pictures all three Persons of the Trinity as sources of the gifts. It is no surprise, therefore, to find the Holy Spirit as the agent of baptism, a baptism which in 1 Corinthians 12:13 relates primarily to the placement of Christians in the body of Christ according to gifts bestowed. It is no problem that Christ is the one pictured elsewhere as the baptizer (i.e., in a remote sense), whereas the Spirit is the agent of baptism in the present passage (i.e., in a more immediate sense). Neither is it any great problem that an agent of baptism is sometimes unnamed (Acts 1:5; 11:16), or that the element of baptism is always stated elsewhere (cf. Stott, 1964, 16–17). The speech and writing habits of other New Testament figures are not determinative of Paul's practice in conjunction with this doctrine. In fact, contextual considerations in the other six passages taken from the gospels and Acts are somewhat different from 1 Corinthians 12. Furthermore, an element of baptism need not always be mentioned. For example, Paul refers to baptism in Romans 6:3, where no element is present.

The issue involved in this difficult passage is not easily resolved. Each position has much favorable evidence on its side. Yet, in overall evaluation, it seems the preference should be go to the immediate context of 1 Corinthians 12. In that case, view 3 is most accurate: the Holy Spirit is the personal agent for implementing baptism in verse 13.

6. (p. 45) Another issue in 1 Corinthians 12:13 focuses on the word *epotisthēmen* ("were made to drink"). To what does this verb refer?

1. One position is that the verb refers metaphorically to a Christian's receiving the Spirit at the time he receives water baptism. Whether it be a figure for the watering of plants or the taking of water into the human system internally, the position holds that the water of baptism is an apt outward representation of the Spirit's coming to individual Christians (Edwards, 1885, 326; Parry, 1916, 184). Either of the representations follows naturally from a picture of the Spirit's being "poured out" upon Christians (John 7:37–39; Acts 2:17; Rom. 5:5) (Meyer, 1879, 1:374). Some also suggest that water baptism should be included here based upon the conclusion that it is present also in the earlier part of the verse (e.g., Parry, 1916, 184). Objections to this point of view direct themselves only against seeing a reference to the rite of baptism. It is an uncommon thing to have the last half of the verse say the same thing as the first half (Godet, 1886, 2:211), even if one allows that water baptism is in view in verse 13a. A further objection notes that water baptism is a very inexact representation of an inner reception of the Spirit such as is depicted in verse 13b (Godet, 1886, 2:211). Again, it remains to be proven that water baptism is even a part of verse 13a, much less verse 13b.

2. Another widely held approach to this part of verse 13 is to refer it to the ordinance of the Lord's Supper. Again, this grows largely out of seeing an ordinance in verse 13a. When baptism is envisioned there, the other ordinance of the church, the Lord's Supper, is its natural sequel. Further substantiation for this claims the presence of this same communion ordinance in the broader context of this part of 1 Corinthians (cf. 11:17–31). The symbolism thus involved has baptism representing the Spirit in

the form of an external element, whereas the elements of communion present Him as being received inwardly. This view includes an understanding of *epotisthēmen* as a gnomic aorist, referring to the repeated, periodic commemorations at the Lord's Table (Edwards, 1885, 326). Opposition to view 2 comes again in the form of noting it is yet to be proven that verse 13a refers to any ordinance. It also sees the Lord's Supper as being foreign to the context of chapter 12, though the proximity of the chapter 11 account is undeniable (Hodge, 1959, 255). It is also an unnatural expedient to read a gnomic aorist into the present setting. Furthermore, the idea of drinking the Holy Spirit is alien to symbolism at the Lord's Table in that the cup typifies Christ's blood (1 Cor. 11:25) and not the person of the Holy Spirit (Godet, 1886, 2:210).

3. An approach that has merit sees the "being made to drink one Spirit" as a reference to bestowing spiritual gifts on Christians, thereby enabling them to function as one body. Certainly much can be said for this emphasis in the present context, for in verse 14 immediately following, diversity of the body's gifts becomes the subject of discussion (Godet, 1886, 2:211). It is also argued in support that the communication of spiritual gifts is a natural sequel to the ordinance of baptism (Acts 8:17; 10:45–46; 19:6; 2 Tim. 1:6) (Godet, 1886, 2:211). Perhaps the principal difficulty with this approach is the necessity of beginning a new paragraph in the middle of verse 13. It would have Paul talking about unity through verse 13a, but then switching very abruptly and imperceptibly to a new subject of discussion, diversity of gifts, in the middle of his sentence. It is also important to note that the figure of drinking is not effective as a portrayal of active service such as the gifts involve. It speaks more of personal possession or internal inclusion. As argued against viewpoints 1 and 2, it remains to be proven that the ordinance of baptism is a part of verse 13a.

4. A final understanding of *epotisthēmen* in 1 Corinthians 12:13 excludes any reference to an ordinance and refers the verb to the Holy Spirit's indwelling within each member of the body of Christ. At conversion, each Christian has received the Spirit as indweller. Though He is the same Spirit who imparts spiritual gifts, His action referred to by this particular verb is not a direct reference to His bestowal of gifts (cf. Rom. 8:9, 15). Such an inward reception of the Spirit is frequent in Pauline thought (e.g., 1 Cor. 2:12), and drinking Him is an apt representation of thus partaking of Him. Water to be drunk is a well-known figure for the Holy Spirit (John 4:13–14; 7:37–39; Acts 2:17; Rom. 5:5). Contextually, this view is strong in that conceiving of all members as partaking of the same Spirit enhances the major idea of verse 13, that of unity. This view also accords well with and provides a natural explanation for the aorist tense of *epotisthēmen*. Reception of the Spirit occurred at a particular time in the past for each individual Christian, just as did his baptism by the Spirit (v. 13a). It was at that point that the Spirit's dwelling within him began (Hodge, 1959, 255). One apparent inadequacy of viewpoint 4 is the *gar* that introduces verse 14 (Godet, 1886, 2:210). To have verse 13b continue the thrust of unity denies *gar* its usual explanatory emphasis in making a transition from verse 13b to verse 14. If one understands, however, that the *gar* of verse 14 is reaching back to explain verse 11 rather than verses 12–13, the difficulty is circumvented.

The conclusion must be one of a purely spiritual understanding attached to *epotisthēmen*. It refers to the spiritual transaction whereby the Holy Spirit comes to make His abode in the individual Christian at the time of conversion and is therefore in agreement with the conclusion regarding *ebaptisthēmen* in verse 13a. It was in this former case also a spiritual transaction, that of baptism by the Holy Spirit, which is a ministry occurring simultaneously with the initiation of His indwelling ministry.

A more specific question regarding *epotisthēmen* is pertinent. Does it refer to the figure of giving a person something to drink or to the figure of irrigating parched land for agricultural purposes? The latter alternative is Paul's usage of the term in 1 Corinthians 3:6–8, and in this light could be conceived of as carrying on the Old Testament images of the Spirit's being poured out upon the land and the people (Isa. 32:15; 44:3; Ezek. 39:29; Joel 2:26) to make them as a well-watered garden (Jer. 31:12) (Dunn, 1970, 131). This, however, is too repetitious of the emphasis that has already occurred in the *ebaptisthēmen*. It is more convincing to see Paul using the verb in the sense of giving someone something to drink, as he does in 1 Corinthians 3:2. Where persons are involved, this is natural, since this is a vivid picture of their receiving the Spirit inwardly, that is, just as they receive a drink of water. Inward reception forms a natural counterpart to external engulfment such as is found in the baptism of the Spirit.

7. (p. 47) A delicate issue in 12:15 involves the method chosen in rendering the preposition *para* ("for . . . reason"). A more usual meaning of the word is "in spite of." With this meaning, results are twofold. (1) The sentence becomes interrogative: "If the foot says, 'Because I am not the hand, I am not of the body,' is it not in spite of this . . . is it not of the body?" (2) The antecedent of *touto* ("this") is specifically the foot's inferiority to the hand: "Is it not in spite of this inferiority to the hand . . . is it [the foot] not still part of the body?" This understanding of *para* has in its favor the fact that it represents a more normal sense of the preposition, whose common meaning is "alongside of"' or "in spite of" (Godet, 1886, 213). It also is a bit more natural in the present context to have *touto* refer to actual inferiority rather than a supposition or complaint of inferiority. The context does grant that there are differences in importance between different members of the body (Godet, 1886, 213).

A twofold implication also comes from assigning *para* the meaning "because of." (1) The sentence in this case is declarative: "It is not because of this not of the body." (2) The antecedent of *touto*, rather than being actual inferiority, is the complaining nature of the member in the protasis. It is a disgruntled member that voices, "Because I am not the hand, I am not of the body" (cf. Fee, 1987, 610). The sense of the apodosis becomes, "It is not because it gives vent to its discontent not of the body." The position of *para touto* immediately following *ou* ("not") and preceding *ouk* ("not") favors this meaning in that "because of" is the only adequate meaning for *para* with the negation of *ou* applied specifically to the prepositional phrase (Hering, 1962, 130). It is not unique in Paul to find a double negative with one destroying the force of the other (cf. 2 Thess. 3:9) (Robertson and Plummer, 1914, 273). Though "because of" for *para* is not paralleled in the New Testament, it is an accepted sense in Attic Greek (Robertson, 1934, 616). Perhaps the most forceful evidence in support of the second viewpoint is its avoidance of the elliptical construction that the earlier viewpoint necessitates. The smoother syntax is preferred because no factor sufficiently significant to explain an elliptical construction is present, as the meaning "in spite of" would require.

It is better to conclude that *para* means "because of" in verse 15 (as well as in v. 16). It is true that actual inferiority, not just a complaint of it, is present in the context, but it is not so large an emphasis until verses 22–23. Thus, the statement of verse 15 (and v. 16) is that of a disgruntled member.

8. (p. 51) Identification of the members designated by *asthenestera* ("weaker") has been along at least four lines.

1. The term encompasses such members as are vulnerable to outside objects, including the eyes and ears (Meyer, 1879, 377; Parry, 1916, 185). The inability of such members to protect themselves and their consequent "weakness" is indisputable. Yet, this mode of identification violates the sense of verse 21, where the eye is a primary member rather than a secondary or weaker one. This contextual factor is effective enough to discount the probability of such a meaning.
2. Some have said the weaker members are the hand and feet because these occupy a

secondary position in verse 21. This explanation falls short, however, in that the hands and feet are not inherently weak members. In addition, the *alla* ("On the contrary") that introduces verse 22 signals the introduction of members different from those discussed in verse 21.

3. Another approach says that Paul by "weaker" refers to members more susceptible to disease, regardless of what part of the body they are (Alford, 1899, 2:582; Edwards, 1885, 328–29). This view rests heavily on the participle *dokounta* ("which seem," v. 22), and emphasizes that weakness is only apparent. Yet, it is strange that Paul always has particular members in view throughout the rest of his discussion. Such a generalization at this point would be out of harmony with the context.

4. A final view says that *asthenestera* refers to sensitive organs in the body that are protected by virtue of their position. Examples are the lungs and the stomach. This explanation reasons that the *alla* that begins verse 22 necessitates a reference to members even more secondary than the hands and feet. These organs have no protection in themselves, yet they are vital in sustaining life (Hering, 1962, 131; Godet, 1886, 215; Fee, 1987, 613). The main objection to this viewpoint—that is, that throughout the rest of the passage comparison is limited to the body's exterior members—is not serious enough to rule out the view.

9. (p. 53) The meaning of verse 24b depends to a large extent on the relative time significance associated with the aorist participle *dous* ("giving"), that is, whether it stipulates time subsequent to or simultaneous with the sentence's main verb, *synekerasen* ("composed").

1. If it is seen as expressing subsequent time, the bestowal of more abundant honor on the one who lacks is identified with mutual concern currently operative between individual parts of the body. In other words, this is the instinctive sense of self-respect, propriety, and decency naturally imparted in a body, through which comes an automatic equalization of dignity among the members. This concept of mutual concern is certainly present in the immediate context (v. 25b). In fact, the idea of mixing members in the body implies that some members are weaker and some are stronger (Godet, 1886, 217). This is a natural compensation by which members correct the inequality among themselves through a sort of mutual dependency (Parry, 1916, 185; Fee, 1987, 614). A large deficiency in this viewpoint lies in the way it understands the aorist participle *dous*. Subsequent action cannot be the implication of such a participle (Robertson, 1934, 1113; Hering, 1962, 131–32). It should also be noted that this view supplies an inadequate sense for the strong adversative conjunction *alla* in verse 24.

2. Another approach is to say that *dous* expresses simultaneous time, resulting in the following meaning: at the time of creation God's sense of values differed from man's. Man's opinion that some members seem to be weaker (12:22), less honorable, and less comely (12:23) is wrong. The true appraisal is that all members are of equal strength, honor, and beauty. This is the attitude that prevailed in God's mingling of different members in the body. To its credit, this viewpoint assigns a proper grammatical implication to *dous*, that of simultaneous time, and it also gives an adequate thrust to *alla*, allowing it to contrast human evaluation (vv. 22–24a) with divine estimation (v. 24b). A chief deficiency of this viewpoint, however, is that the inferiority portrayed in *hysteroumenō* ("lacked") is actual, not just a human opinion of inferiority. It would seem rather that God recognized the inferiority and did something about it.

3. A third viewpoint sees *dous* corresponding with the creative act, as in view 2, but explains the contrast of *alla* (v. 24) on a different ground. From this perspective, the conjunction is seen as a transition from type to antitype, from the human body to

the body of Christ, which the human body represents in figure. What the human body takes care of by instinct (vv. 21–24a), God has provided for in the spiritual body in conjunction with its creation. In other words, what the human body does intuitively, God has done by direct action for the body of Christ. This approach has the advantages of taking the middle voice of *hysteroumeno̧* (v. 24) in a subjective sense, "to feel need," and of providing for the compassion spoken of in *merimnōsin* ("should have . . . care," v. 25), since compassion is a quality completely foreign to the human body member. It also explains how *timēn* in verse 24 can have its necessary meaning of "honor" rather than the same meaning that it has in verse 23, that of "clothing" or "a covering in token of honor." As Barrett notes regarding verse 24b, "Paul has left the metaphor and is speaking directly of the church. . . . Paul now moves on to a positive point for which there can be no real physical analogy" (Barrett, 1968, 291). This third view provides the most adequate explanation for all the phenomena involved. It tells the reader that an equality already exists regarding the body of Christ and that mutual concern is an outworking of that equality.

10. (p. 56) The exact meaning of the anarthrous (no preceding article) *sōma* ("body") in 12:27 is difficult to define. Various attempts have tried to explain the article's absence.

1. The anarthrous *sōma* is not to be pressed but understood as a specific identification: the church in Corinth is referred to as the complete body of Christ. "You are the body of Christ" is the sense. This meaning sees the *Christou*, a proper name, as rendering the *sōma* definite without the need of an article, and notices that had Paul wanted to indicate their being "part of the body," he would have utilized *ek sōmatos*. The foregoing explanation falls short, however, by failing to explain how Paul himself could have been a member of this body if that were the case (cf. 12:13). It also creates difficulty in understanding why Paul omitted the article in this case when he has used it with *sōma* almost without exception earlier in the chapter (cf. 12:12 [twice], 14, 15 [twice], 16 [twice], 17, 18, 19, 22, 23, 24, 25).

2. The anarthrous construction's purpose is to place emphasis on *Christou*. This approach allows the *Christou* to modify *melē* ("members") as well as *sōma*: "You are Christ's body and members in particular" (Parry, 1916, 185; Fee, 1987, 617 n. 5). This view has the virtue of emphasizing a common relationship to Christ throughout the body on a collective basis (*sōma*), as well as on an individual basis (*melē*). In effect, it circumvents the anarthrous noun issue altogether. Yet, whether this issue can legitimately be circumvented is questionable. The appearance or nonappearance of the Greek article is of sufficient gravity to render this procedure very unwise. That explanation also negates the obviously intended antithesis between *sōma* and *melē* by giving grammatical emphasis to *Christou* rather than *sōma*, a step that is not warranted by the Greek word order.

3. Another way of explaining the anarthrous *sōma* is to understand it in the same sense as the English indefinite article: "You are a body of Christ," the idea being that the Corinthian church was one among many bodies of Christ (Godet, 1886, 219–20). This approach considers no one local assembly to be deserving of the designation "the body of Christ," though each shares in the dignity of the whole, resulting in the right to be called "a body." This view has in its favor the fact that the term *ekklēsia* ("church") is used in a similar dual sense to refer to all believers in a universal sense (cf. Eph. 1:22–23) as well as to a local group of believers (cf. 1 Cor. 1:2). In the face of this reasoning, one can see negatively the difficulty of figurative language that merges a number of bodies to make up one body. This is a difficulty that does not exist with the word "church." It is also difficult that the Corinthians in themselves could not have been a complete body, for they lacked some of the gifts indispensable to the

existence of such a spiritual body (e.g., apostleship, 1 Cor. 12:28). Furthermore, this view misses the point of the anarthrous Greek noun, that is, that it can be equally definite whether it has the article or not.

4. A view that does notice the purpose of an anarthrous noun properly focuses great attention on the body's quality: "You as individuals are of such a character as to be the body of Christ." In this case, "body of Christ" is a quality that characterizes each individual Christian, but not a local congregation collectively. In effect it applies Paul's lessons earlier in the chapter more personally and individually. A weakness appears, however, in that the individual emphasis of *sōma* proposed by this evaluation all but eliminates the antithesis between *sōma* and *melē*. In order for the antithesis to be maintained, verse 27a must be collective and verse 27b individual, a distinction not provided by this understanding.

5. It is also possible to explain the anarthrous *sōma* by viewing the Corinthian church as a miniature representation or exemplification of the universal church: "You as a body of Christ represent the whole body" (Carson, 1987, 49–50; Kistemaker, 1993, 440). In this sense, each individual church represents the ideal or whole body of Christ, a feature also observable when the figure of a temple is used to describe the church (cf. 1 Cor. 3:16) (Meyer, 1879, 380). It is not that each church is a separate body, but that each church as a local group possesses the quality of the whole and should therefore function in an appropriate manner.

View 5 best satisfies the grammatical and contextual criteria pertaining to *sōma*. Hence *sōma Christou* should be understood as teaching that each local church is a visible portrayal of the quality that characterizes the church at large, which is composed of all Christians of all generations throughout the present age.

11. (p. 65) One of the seven questions in 12:29–30 deserves special attention. The *mē pantes dynameis* ("All are not workers of miracles, are they?") is elliptical, and at least two suggestions have been offered on how to resolve the ellipsis: One could either draw upon a verb from the following clause or pattern the question's syntax after the preceding clause.

The first alternative places no punctuation stop after *dynameis* at the end of verse 29. That allows the *echousin* ("have") to govern both *dynameis* and *charismata* as direct objects. *Dynameis* thereby becomes the accusative case, resulting in the sense, "Have all [the power of working] miracles, all gifts of healings?" This interpretation is strong in that it puts "miracles" with another gift of the same category ("healings") (cf. 12:9) and separates "miracles" (which is abstract and refers only to an ability) from the preceding gifts (which are concrete and refer to the men possessing ability). *Dynameis* has more affinity with the gifts that follow than with the gifts that come earlier in verse 29. A disadvantage lies in the position of *echousin*, which presumably would have been prior to *dynameis* if the sense were that suggested by view 1. It is also needless to repeat the *mē pantes* in the second part of the statement when one verb governs two direct objects.

A second alternative places a question mark after *dynameis*, making the noun a predicate nominative. In this case, *dynameis* becomes concrete rather than abstract, referring to gifted persons rather than abilities: "All are not [workers of] miracles, are they?" This explanation notices the unnaturalness of the compound question necessitated by view 1. The absence of a *kai* ("and") militates against view 1, as does the absence of any other compound question in the list, much less one of such an unusual character. This second view also observes how natural it is to continue with a predicate nominative sense after the first three questions of verse 29. Taking *dynamis* to refer by metonymy to a person, Christ Himself, is parallel to 1 Corinthians 1:24, to the credit of this second viewpoint. Furthermore, it is not feasible to group this question with the last three since each of them contains a verb, whereas this one does not.

Both methods of punctuation have their strengths, but in choosing between them the factors favoring view 1 are more persuasive. That choice finds further confirmation by noticing that the *dynamis* referring to Christ in 1:24 is in a somewhat different sense than that needed to support reference to a spiritually gifted person in 12:29.

12. (p. 66) Much discussion has centered on the nature of the verb *zēloute* ("earnestly desire") in 12:31. In what sense is this zeal spoken of? Is it one that the Corinthians already had, or one that they were to initiate? If it was a zeal they were to initiate, were they to desire zealously on an individual basis, or is this advice to the assembly as a whole?

1. *Zēloute* as an indicative carries the meaning that they were already zealous along certain lines and usually includes a note of irony or sarcasm in Paul's statement. In essence, he is deriding the readers because of their flare for the more spectacular or sensational gifts (Bittlinger, 1968, 73–74). To support this viewpoint, 14:36 may be compared, for it also resorts to stinging sarcasm. However, the unnaturalness of sarcasm in the 12:31 context argues against the indicative. It is much saner to take *ta meizona* ("the greater") as a reference to the sequential ranking of 12:28, that is, the greater gifts are those near the beginning of the list. These, of course, are not nearly so appealing to the eye and other senses as those toward the end of the list, such as "various kinds of tongues." *Meizona* thus must be given the meaning required by its own paragraph (contra Fee, 1987, 623–25). Another deficiency in taking *zēloute* as indicative is seen in a comparison with the same form in 14:1 (Fee, 1987, 624). In this later verse, the writer resumes his discussion of spiritual gifts after a brief interlude devoted to love (12:31b–13:13). The necessity of taking 14:1 as imperative greatly enhances the likelihood of an imperative sense in 12:31 also.

2. Assuming an imperative mood with the command addressed toward individual compliance, one can see it as a directive to seek gifts at the top of the list in verse 28, beginning with apostleship. For a person to seek such a gift is not contradictory to the sovereign activity whereby the gifts are bestowed by God (12:11, 18). A divine decision does not exclude the individual responsibility of seeking such gifts as a service to the body of Christ (Hodge, 1959, 264). Even though the best gifts are not available to everyone, the believer is to strive continually for them in case they are available to him (Robertson and Plummer, 1914, 282). Such a zeal accords with the prayer directive of 14:13, in which a person's responsibility to pray in quest of the gift of interpretation is specified.

On the other side of the issue, certain factors appear that make the individual application of *zēloute* less likely. As will be noted later in connection with 14:13, it is not a clear-cut decision that this verse advocates prayer for the gift of interpretation. It is, furthermore, highly unlikely that Corinthian Christians would be instructed as individuals to seek the position of an apostle, in that the eyewitness requirements for an apostle had not been met by any of them, and opportunity no longer existed to meet them (cf. 1 Cor. 15:8–9). In fact, the writer has just indicated this by the series of seven questions in 12:29–30; that is, the best gifts are not available to every Christian. It is one thing to seek the Spirit's sovereignly bestowed saving benefits (cf. Hodge, 1959, 164). It is another, however, to seek spiritual gifts that are also sovereignly bestowed because no gift is universally applicable, unlike the benefits of salvation.

Yet, assuming for the moment that when Paul uses "the greater gifts" he means the greater gifts other than apostleship, one encounters an interesting dilemma in chapter 14. Every single Christian was expected to ask for and receive the gift of prophecy (14: 1). They all were to use the gift on each occasion of their gathering together ("all prophesy," 14:24), and their meetings gave opportunity for every one of them to prophesy and render benefit to the rest of the assembled group over a period of time (14:31). Yet, such a course is clearly contrary to 1 Cor. 12:29, where "all are not prophets, are they?" is written. Such an eventuality was impossible. It is necessary that the sense of 14: 1, "that you may prophesy," called for giving those among them who were prophets the principal opportunities to speak. The "all's" of 14:24 and 31 must also be taken in a sense restricted by the context: "all among you who have the gift of prophecy."

3. To give *zēloute* a collective application to the whole assembly results in a different sense. Rather than each one desiring the greater gifts for himself, he is to desire them for the whole congregation (Kistemaker, 1993, 445–46). Such a desire was gratified by persons being added to the local assembly, either by conversion or by coming to Corinth from another locality. An advantage of this view is its harmony with the upcoming emphasis upon love (12:31b–13:13). Desiring what is beneficial to others is far superior to desiring a gift for oneself. It is also more in accord with 12:15–17, which urges unsung members of Christ's body not to despair but to be content with their current position in the body. No possibility is available to these that they might be "promoted" to a more auspicious or effective office. This view also harmonizes more easily with the clear specifications of 1 Corinthians 12:11 and 18; that is, gifts are not distributed on the basis of human want, but are granted by divine plan.

The collective force of *zēloute* has clear preference over views 1 and 2. This is a command to seek the good of the whole body of believers, not an individual gift.

Chapter 4 (Page number following note number tells where the note appears)

1. (p. 68) At least two diverse opinions define the exact meaning of *kath' hyperbolēn hodon* ("a . . . more excellent way") in 12:31. The issue has to do with the exact relationship of love—the subject of the section to follow—to spiritual gifts, which have been the subject of discussion up to this point.

The first viewpoint takes *kath' hyperbolēn* in an absolute sense and *hodon* in the sense of "manner," a meaning very similar to that of *tropon*. In this explanation, love has an excellence all its own, standing independently: "a most excellent way." The writer does not compare it with something else. As an independent entity, it is the only suitable means for gaining an accurate appraisal of spiritual gifts. By means of love, he urges the readers to seek, obtain, and exercise "the greater gifts." The chief merit of this viewpoint lies in its compatibility with the context. Verse 31a has been speaking of a quest for spiritual gifts, and verse 31b continues that same emphasis. It is not a contrasting way presented in this latter part of the verse. If that were the case, an *alla* would have been found instead of *kai*, or a *homōs* rather than the *eti*. Verse 31b presents love as a way *par excellence* for obtaining spiritual gifts. The sense of the verse is, "Seek the greater gifts, and moreover I show you a most excellent way to do it" (Hodge, 1959, 264; Edwards, 1885, 337; Meyer, 1879, 385). Argument against this viewpoint derives partly from the way it presents love as only a means to an end rather than as an end in itself. Far from being pictured as just a way to obtain greater gifts, love quite clearly in chapter 13 is something desirable because of its own value, as a way that is far better than the gifts with which it is put side by side (Robertson and Plummer, 1914, 283; Morris, 1968, 180). Another disadvantage of this absolute understanding of *kath' hyperbolēn* lies in its assignment of an unnatural meaning to *hodon*. The noun elsewhere does not name the means of accomplishing something else, but depicts a virtue in itself. Its use in such expressions as "the way of peace," "the way of life," and "the way of salvation" clearly shows this (Parry, 1916, 190). Had the author wanted to depict the idea necessitated by view 1, he most probably would have used *tropon* instead of *hodon*.

A second way of understanding *kath' hyperbolēn hodon* is to take the *kath' hyperbolēn* in a relative sense: "a more excellent way." *Hodon* then designates a way independent of, but not contradictory to, the way of spiritual gifts. This separate path has love at its core. It is clearly distinguishable from another path that centers on spiritual gifts. The *kai* of 12:31b, according to this understanding, advances the reader from the pursuit of spiritual gifts to a new pursuit, a higher aspiration, which is a walk in love (Fee, 1987, 625). This approach to *kath' hyperbolēn* is closer to the root idea of the noun *hyperbolēn*, which is more comparative than superlative. In its favor, this view also has the unmistakable support of chapter 13, where love and gifts are put side by side. Verses 1–3 highlight the complete dependence of gifts on love, and 13:8–13 shows the superiority of love to gifts because of love's permanence. Comparison is certainly present in chapter 13. The fact that love is distinct from and therefore more to be desired than gifts is confirmed also in 14:1, which urges the pursuit of both, but the quest for love is to be more intense. Clearly, love is worthy of being sought for its own sake, and not just because it leads to a more intelligent sifting of gifts. A claim against that viewpoint is that it makes the *zēloute* of 12:31a a concession rather than a command. The zeal for gifts becomes only a second best if the comparative force of *kath' hyperbolēn* is accepted (Hodge, 1959, 264; Meyer, 1879, 385). View 2 also places love and spiritual gifts in contrast to each other, which is out of accord with their common origin in the Holy Spirit and with their coexistence as expressed in 14:1.

Yet, it seems this is the comparison that Paul is trying to make, judging from 14:1 and 39. He presents two distinct entities quite clearly, not on an "either . . . or" basis, but on a "both . . . and" basis. One does not exclude the other, but the way of love is most definitely to be preferred above the way of gifts. In other words, comparison, not contrast, is made between love and spiritual gifts. Since the Holy Spirit generates both, they cannot stand opposed to each other.

2. (p. 78) Though the main thrust of 13:8–13 is clearly the temporal superiority of love, the specific manner in which Paul puts his point across has been subject to debate.

1a. There is, first of all, the interpretation that necessitates the equating of *to teleion* ("the perfect") of 13:10 with the completion of the New Testament canon. This view sees the termination of knowledge, prophecy, and tongues at a time when the twenty-seven New Testament books were completed (Unger, 1971, 98–100). The completion of the canon entailed putting away these three gifts (13:10) and introduced a condition of the church illustrated by Paul's personal experience in 13:11. His state of manhood aptly illustrates the coming of age of the church following the last book's completion. The same holds true for the illustration of verse 12, the "now" half of the verse 12 comparisons spelling out obscured vision prior to this point and the "then" half looking forward from Paul's vantage point to the period after New Testament revelation reached its culmination. Projecting this framework into verse 13, the advocate of view 1a compares the continuance of faith, hope, and love throughout the present age with the limited extent of these temporary gifts. Love is superior to the others because it alone continues beyond the present age.

1b. A variation of that viewpoint allows the continuation of knowledge and prophecy throughout the present age by not restricting them to revelational functions, but limits tongues to the period before the canon's completion. In this case, verse 12 illustrates conditions prior and subsequent to Christ's parousia. The contrast of verse 13 is, then, between the gifts that prevail up to the parousia, on one side, and on the other, faith, hope, and love that not only extend throughout the present age but also remain after the parousia. In this case, the ultimate supremacy of love (13:13b) is not a temporal one, but one that is qualitative.

2. A second approach to verses 8–13 sees *to teleion* referring to the perfect condition following the second advent, that is, the parousia. The view defines the three gifts (vv. 8–9) more generally, with the cessation of all three taking place at that future time. Verses 11 and 12 illustrate the difference between the two states prior and subsequent to Christ's coming in a twofold manner: by the comparison of verse 11 and by the explanation of verse 12. Faith, hope, and love differ from the aforementioned gifts by their continuance after the second advent (v. 13). As in view 1b, love's supremacy to the triad of virtues is not temporal but qualitative. F. F. Bruce, Frederic Godet, Charles Hodge, H. A. W. Meyer, Archibald Robertson, Alfred Plummer, Gordon D. Fee, D. A. Carson, and Simon J. Kistemaker, among others, suggest such an analysis or its equivalent. MacArthur proposes a variation of view 2 with his suggestion that *to teleion* refers to the eternal state after the millennium rather than the period immediately after the parousia (MacArthur, 1984, 364–65).

3. A third approach to verses 8–13 sees *to teleion* as referring to "the mature body," rather than "the complete canon" (view 1) or "the perfect state" (view 2). The gifts of verses 8–9 experienced a gradual cessation with increasing maturity of the body of Christ. Various criteria measure a growing maturity, one of them being completion of the whole New Testament. Paul illustrates progressive growth of the church through the critical period of her history by his own personal development from childhood to adulthood (13:11). Ultimate or absolute maturity is another matter, as is illustrated in verse 12, when growth reaches its culmination at the return of Christ. The contrast of verse 13a is, then, that gifts of the earlier part of the paragraph were possibly to extend only through a portion of the church's existence, whereas faith, hope, and love would characterize her entire earthly history. Beyond that, only one of the three virtues will survive the parousia, and this is love itself. For this reason, it is the greatest (13:13b).

A chart showing in summary form how each view answers crucial questions in 13:8–13 is found on page 238.

Factors favorable to view 1*a* include the following.

1. By definition the gifts of prophecy and knowledge pertain to receiving direct revelation, part of which eventually found its way into the New Testament documents (cf. 12:8, 28) (Unger, 1971, 99), a feature provided for under this view. This view also makes adequate allowance for the confirmatory character of tongues (cf. 14:22). Its use as an outward proof of divine revelation revealed through prophecy and knowledge is clear.

2. The partial character of prophecy and knowledge (v. 9) aptly describes the two gifts when comparing them with this interpretation of *to teleion*, that is, the completeness of the New Testament canon.

3. "Complete" is a well-established meaning of *teleios*. Furthermore, of the possible meanings it furnishes the best contrast to *ek merous* ("in part") (vv. 9–10), in that both expressions are quantitative (Unger, 1971, 99; Barrett, 1968, 306).

4. This view also allows for the most natural sense of verse 13, that is, a temporal contrast between the group of three virtues and love alone.

Pronounced weaknesses in this understanding of verses 8–13 include the following.

1. It makes no provision for verse 12 to refer to conditions following the parousia.

2. The context contains no direct reference to the concept of a completed New Testament canon, as this approach presupposes. Indeed, it is doubtful that Paul was assured there would ever be such prior to the return of Jesus Christ.

3. The abrupt shift to the subject of the second advent in verse 13 necessitated by this view is unnatural. The transition from making verse 12 the completed canon to the

Answers to Crucial Questions in 13:8–13

	View 1a	View 1b	View 2	View 3
13:8 When do the 3 gifts cease?	Prophecy and knowledge are revelatory; tongues are confirmatory; all 3 cease with completed canon.	Prophecy and knowledge are nonrevelatory; tongues are confirmatory; only tongues cease with completed canon.	Prophecy and knowledge are nonrevelatory; tongues are nonconfirmatory; all 3 remain to the parousia.	Prophecy and knowledge are revelatory; tongues are confirmatory; all 3 cease with completed canon.
13:10 What is *to teleion*?	The canon	The canon	The parousia	The mature body of Christ
13:11 What does growth to manhood represent?	States before and after completed canon	States before and after completed canon	States before and after the parousia	States before and after the body's relative maturity (as indicated by the canon)
13:12 What are partial and full sight and knowledge?	States before and after completed canon	States before and after the parousia	States before and after the parousia	States before and after the body's absolute maturity (as completed by the parousia)
13:13a What is the comparison between gifts and virtues?	Compares the period prior to canon's completion with the entire age	Compares the entire age with the period following the parousia	Compares the entire age with the period following the parousia	Compares the period prior to the body's maturity (as measured by the completed canon) with the entire age
13:13b How is love superior?	Group of 3 virtues ceases at the parousia, but not love	Qualitatively superior to 3 virtues as a group	Qualitatively superior to 3 virtues as a group	Group of 3 virtues ceases at the parousia, but not love

culmination of the church age in verse 13 is more than the *de* ("but"; first occurrence of v. 13) can bear.

View 1*b* overcomes some of the difficulty of view 1*a*. On the one hand, it allows verse 12 to have its more natural reference to conditions following the parousia. On the other hand, however, view 1b creates additional problems of its own. It is inconsistent to take tongues as a sign gift but not take prophecy and knowledge as revelatory and temporary like tongues. It also has the disadvantage of eliminating the natural temporal contrasts involved in verse 13, thereby making it extremely difficult to delineate an accurate sense of "the greatest of these is love" in verse 13b.

View 2 has a number of arguments in its favor.

1. It gives an adequate explanation to verse 12, that is, a clear reference to conditions instituted after the return of Christ.
2. It allows the aorist tense of *elthē* ("comes," v. 10) to have its natural punctilear meaning, referring it to the precise moment of Christ's return.
3. The meaning "perfect," allowable for *teleion*, is well-suited to describe the existent state after Christ's coming. It will be a flawless condition, ideal in every respect.

Deficiencies in view 2 also exist.

1. In several respects it fails to satisfy verse 11 by interpreting it as having exactly the same meaning as verse 12. The illustration of Paul's gradual development from childhood to manhood can hardly typify the vast transformation associated with the parousia as verse 12 does. See Appendix A at the conclusion of this volume for a detailed explanation of why verse 11 rules out this view.
2. It is questionable whether *teleion* ever carries the philosophical meaning of "perfect" in the New Testament. Furthermore, such qualitative perfection is difficult to construe as a suitable opposite to *ek merou* ("partial," v. 10). See Appendix A for a further development of this point.
3. It fails to allow for the distinctive revelatory character of prophecy and knowledge, as well as the distinctive confirmatory character of tongues (v. 8; cf. 12:8–10, 28).
4. The parousia also excludes the more obvious explanation of the contrasts in verse 13, that is, the explanation allowing a two-stage temporal contrast—first, between the three temporary gifts and the virtues that last through the entire age, and second, between the group of three virtues limited to the present age and love as the only one extending beyond the parousia.

Viewpoint 3 has the following commendable features.

1. Advantages 1 and 4 under view 1*a* apply to view 3 also.
2. This is the only one of the views that allows *teleios* a relative sense. Whenever the adjective appears in connection with *nēpios* ("child," cf. vv. 10–11), it always has the connotation of gradual increase, not an abrupt change (cf. 1 Cor. 2:6 and 3:1; 14:20; Eph. 4:13–14; Heb. 5:13–14). The adjective is well suited to Paul's predicament of not knowing whether or not a New Testament canon would reach completion before Christ's return. It allows either the canon's completion or the return of Christ to come first.
3. A wide variety of exegetical and historical links between Ephesians 4:1–16 and the present passage provides ample ground for understanding the body figure of the church to be in force in verse 10. A sample historical link between the two books and cities lies in the fact that Paul wrote 1 Corinthians from Ephesus and probably instructed the Ephesian church about body truth in conjunction with writing his letter to the Corinthians. His later epistle bearing the name of Ephesus would predictably reflect strains of the same emphasis. Another example of the kinship, this one exegetical, is the emphasis in both broader contexts, Ephesians 4:1–16 and 1 Corinthians 12–14,

upon the subject of edification. Such striking resemblances between the two passages are extensive, indicating the presence of the same train of thought in both passages. See Appendix A at the rear of this volume for further links between the two passages.

4. The figure of a human body representing the church is heavily emphasized in this part of 1 Corinthians (cf. 12:12–27).

5. This is the only view that permits a gradual development and growth in agreement with the illustration of verse 11. For further development of this point, see Appendix A.

6. The view also provides for the ultimate state after the parousia, according to the illustration of verse 12. Maturity is of two kinds: one that is constantly changing and increasing, and the other that is final and absolute. The latter type is in view in verse 12 alongside the illustration of verse 11 that pictures gradual growth.

7. View 3 provides for the contrasts of verse 13. The first is between the church's infancy and adolescence on the one hand and the entire history of the church on the other (the three gifts spanning the former period and the three virtues the latter). The second contrast is between the three virtues that occupy the entirety of the present age, and love, which alone will continue beyond the return of Christ (McRae, 1976, 94).

Possible disadvantages of this view surface.

1. The church as the body of Christ is not in a near enough context to be understood in verse 10.

2. This view assigns a double sense to *teleion*, a hermeneutical weakness.

3. "Mature" is a qualitative term that does not constitute a suitable antithesis to *ek merous* and its quantitative connotation (v. 10).

See Appendix A at the conclusion of this volume for further discussion of objections to this view and their responses.

Since evaluation of these viewpoints involves such a large number of factors, only some of which have been listed above, reaching a decision is a complex matter. In light of the total perspective, it is the author's conclusion that viewpoint 3, which makes *to teleion* a reference to the mature body of Christ, has the most to be said in its favor with the least amount of objection. In looking to the future and speaking of the coming of "the mature," Paul saw its arrival in stages. If the church of Paul's time matured substantially enough to have its own completed body of revelation before Christ's return (which it did), maturity would reach a significant point at which gifts of revelation and confirmation would no longer be necessary. Beyond that, the growth of the body has continued and will continue until the time of the parousia, at which moment maturity will be complete, with the body of Christ collectively mature and conformed to His image. (For additional discussion of the issues of 13:8–13, see Thomas, 1974, 81–89, and Appendix A at the rear of this volume.)

Chapter 5 (Page number following note number tells where the note appears)

1. (p. 87) Two pertinent questions and their answers regarding the *glōssē* ("in a tongue") of 14:2 provide clarification: (1) What is the significance of the singular number in comparison with the plurals found elsewhere in the chapter? (2) Is the noun used instrumentally or locatively (i.e., "with a tongue" or "in a tongue")?

Some scholars answer the first question by saying the singular refers to one foreign language, whereas the plurals are references to more than one. Another explanation is that the singular refers mainly to the single physical member and the plural to "the various motions of the tongue" (Thayer, 1889, 118). In fact, that explanation assumes various categories of movement by the tongue. Yet, to theorize such categories and think of a single organ of the body seems far removed from anything propounded in the present setting. Another idea has been that the singular distinguishes the use of ecstatic language on one occasion from the plural, which views the gift in general (Godet, 1886, 2:265). That distinction breaks down, however, in its failure to explain the difference between singular and plural numbers in verses 4–5. Why should *ho lalōn* ("one who speaks") used with the singular *glōssē̦* in verse 4 refer to a particular occasion, whereas in verse 5 the same participle with *glōssais* refers to the gift in general? Such a distinction is arbitrary. It is more advantageous to see the difference between singular and plural as being one language on the one hand and multiple languages on the other. That explanation is most cogent in light of the "strange tongues" of 14:21, which are foreign languages. It also clarifies the expression *genē glōssōn* ("kinds of tongues") of 12:10 in light of the *genē phōnōn* ("kinds of languages") of 14:10, the latter being a clear reference to multiple foreign languages.

In response to the second issue raised with *glōssē̦,* an instrumental meaning appears to be the correct solution, because the locative case without the preposition *en* is relatively infrequent in comparison with the instrumental case used absolutely. Furthermore, the *tō̦ noi* of 14:19 that furnishes a usage parallel to *glōssē̦* in 14:2 is definitely instrumental. Paul indicates the locative, on the other hand, through such a construction as the phrase *en glōssē̦* ("in a tongue") in verse 19. Hence, throughout the chapter the meaning is more likely "with a tongue," or "with tongues" in cases of the plural.

2. (p. 87) Some have elected to apply a universal sense to *oudeis* ("no one"). The pronoun thus understood, in the sense of "no one living" or "no person anywhere," obviously implies a nature of tongues precluding understanding by any human being on earth (Carson, 1987, 101–2). The argument is that this detail distinguishes tongues in Corinthians from tongues in Acts 2, where all men understood what was said (Morris, 1958, 191). Such an outlook reasons that a foreign language most certainly would have been understood in such a cosmopolitan setting as Corinth, with people from so many different parts of the world present (Godet, 1886, 2:266; Meyer, 1881, 2:4). From the other side comes the answer that all these linguistic groups were not necessarily represented in the Christian assembly of the city. The setting of Acts 2 was such that listeners would understand a wide variety of languages, but the hearers in Corinth may very well have been local citizens such as often compose a local assembly. The scope of such inclusive pronouns as "all" and exclusive pronouns as "no one" must always be subject to limitations imposed by historical and literary contexts, the limitations of the present discussion being the extent of the Christian assembly in that city (Hodge, 1959, 279). The conclusion that *oudeis* requires qualification is obvious from another side of 1 Corinthians 14: an exception to the "no one understands" condition is found whenever an interpreter was present and active (14:5) (Edwards, 1885, 357). If one exception existed, so could others. All in all, therefore, it is wiser to understand a qualified *oudeis* in the sense of "no one present in the Christian meeting" or "no one of the particular linguistic background represented by the tongues speaker."

3. (p. 87) Two dilemmas relate to the *pneumati* ("in his spirit") of 14:2. (1) What is the case and use of the noun and (2) does it refer to some aspect of the Holy Spirit or of the human spirit?

The noun as an instrumental of agency, or means, is the best answer to the first question. The decisive consideration is a parallel situation in verses 14–15. There the use of *pneumati* (twice in v. 15) is comparable to the use of the word in verse 2, and is recognizable as instrumental of agency when the nearby nominative of the same word performs the action of prayer (v. 14, *to pneuma*). Since the parallelism between verse 2 and verses 13–15 is fairly well established, good reason exists for taking the *pneumati* of verse 2 as the same instrumental case.

The second and larger issue connected with *pneumati* in verse 2 pertains to who or what the noun stands for: man's human spirit or the Holy Spirit and some aspect of His activity. If the noun represents the human spirit, it pictures a condition of ecstasy in which human understanding is in suspension. A nonrational part of man's psychological makeup serves as a counterpart to the mind so that a person becomes "destitute of distinct self-consciousness and clear understanding" (Thayer, 1889, 520; cf. Meyer, 1881, 2:5). This is a condition in which a higher organ of the inner life contemplates the divine, but cannot work out such matters on a plane of human understanding to communicate them to others (Meyer, 1881, 2:5). Though a somewhat comparable use of *pneuma* occurs in Romans 8:16, the principal support for this interpretation rests on a debated understanding of verses 14–16 of this chapter. Furthermore, Romans 8:16 is not analogous to the present usage in that human intelligence is not excluded there as it must be here for this verse to apply to the human spirit. Referral of *pneumati* more specifically to the Holy Spirit requires a reference to His activity in manifesting spiritual gifts. That is the meaning of *pneumatōn* in 14:12 and very closely approximates the meaning of *pneumatika* ("spiritual gifts") in 14:1. Such an interpretation accords well with the Pauline habit of using *pneuma* to refer to the third Person of the Trinity (Hodge, 1959, 279). It is also in agreement with an established scriptural manner of describing the Spirit's guidance by means of a dative (instrumental) case, particularly in conjunction with speaking (Hodge, 1959, 279). The noun's usage for the Holy Spirit is so extensive in 1 Corinthians 12–14 that it can be questioned whether it is used of the human spirit at all. Hence, it is better to see in *pneumati* indication of a Spirit-inspired manifestation by assigning *pneuma* the same meaning as is found in 14:12.

4. (p. 88) Whether to take *paraklēsin* ("exhortation") and *paramythian* ("consolation") as further definitions of *oikodomēn* ("edification") in 14:3 or to take the three words as parallel and independent of each other is significant to an overall understanding of the passage. To take them independently is feasible since the last two can in no sense exhaust the first by way of definition. Distinctions between the words are also observable, the first relating to faith, the second to love, and the third to hope (Godet, 1886, 2:267). Nevertheless, the predominant emphasis throughout the paragraph (14:1–5), as well as the rest of the chapter, is upon edification. It is also persuasive to understand exhortation and comfort as supportive of edification, even though admittedly edification is more broadly based than just these two areas (Edwards, 1885, 358). These factors plus the absence of exhortation and comfort as objectives distinct from edification point to the necessity of making the first *kai* in the verse ascensive ("even") and taking *paraklēsin* and *paramythian* as further delineations of *oikodomēn*.

5. (p. 89) Whether or not self-edification of 1 Corinthians 14:4 is a wholesome goal is hotly contested. In favor of taking it as desirable is the positive sense given to *oikodomeō* ("edifies") and its cognates throughout the rest of the chapter. The express personal desire of Paul in 14:5 apparently accords with the wholesome sense (Carson, 1987, 102 n. 89; Kistemaker, 1993, 480), though verse 5a may also be a hyperbolic concession. It would certainly seem that any gift from the Spirit must be beneficial, but balancing off this consideration is a recollection that even gifts from the Spirit are profitless without love (13:1–3). In addition, Jude 20, "building yourselves up on your most holy faith," seemingly advocates self-edification as a healthy practice. In the Corinthian context, however, where a selfish spirit among Christians prevailed, edifying oneself was tantamount to becoming puffed up (13:4–5), and becoming puffed up proved to be the opposite of edifying others (1 Cor. 8:1) (Michel in *TDNT*, 1967, 6:141). Paul's selective use of *zēteō* in contexts of love and edification is also significant. In addition to love's abstinence from seeking the things of itself (13:5), Paul expressly prohibits a Christian from misusing his Christian liberty by seeking his own profit or edification (1 Cor. 10:23–24). That follows the example set down very clearly by Paul himself (1 Cor. 10:33). Instead, the Christian's energies are to be harnessed for edification of the total assembly (14:12). Paul's expression of desire that all speak with tongues in 14:5 must be taken in light

of 12:28–30, which indicates clearly that all did not have the gift of tongues or any other gift, for that matter. In light of the epistle's total emphasis, 14:4a does not measure up to wholesome Christian guidelines (cf. Edgar, 1996, 169–74).

6. (p. 92) Interpreters have proposed joining the *ean* ("if") and *ean mē* ("unless") clauses of 14:6 in two different ways:

Some have taken them in a coordinate relationship, in which case the *ean* clause pertains to the gift of tongues and the *ean mē* clause to the gift of prophecy. From that perspective, Paul taught that he could not under any condition edify the Corinthians with tongues. Benefit could come to the church only by the use of prophecy. This is a feasible explanation in that verses 1–5 have just compared the two gifts, and "revelation" and "prophecy" are known to relate to the prophetic gift (Hodge, 1959, 282; Morris, 1958, 192; cf. 14:29–31). The *nyn de* ("but now") that introduces verse 6 heightens the tie-in with verses 1–5: the sixth verse gives support to the main thought of verse 5, that the prophet is greater than the tongues speaker (Hofmann, cited by Meyer, 1881, 2:6). A weak aspect of the view is that it requires understanding an anacoluthon; that is, the writer begins the sentence talking about one gift and ends it in an entirely different vein.

Others have taken the *ean mē* clause as subordinate to the *ean* clause, in which case the *ean* clause speaks of tongues and the *ean mē* clause, tongues' companion gift of interpretation. According to that perspective, the verse encourages the use of interpretation along with tongues, a line of thought that is an outgrowth of the exception clause of verse 5. Such an epexegesis by the *ean mē* clause follows naturally as a refinement to and a necessary qualification of the earlier *ean* clause (Edwards, 1885, 359). The generalization is that tongues produced no profit (v. 6a). But an exception to the generalization came when interpretation accompanied tongues (v. 6b), for in the latter case, tongues became the practical equivalent of prophecy (Johnson, 1962, 1253–54). The second explanation of the two conditional clauses is more convincing, as Paul seems to drop his discussion of prophecy for the moment and to concentrate on tongues and interpretation in the verses immediately following.

7. (p. 93) A decision on whether to see a reference to the physical organ of speech or one to the gift of tongues in the *tēs glōssēs* ("the tongue") of 14:9 is problematic. The former alternative conceives of the physical member as giving out something unintelligible. It enters the discussion at this point to illustrate the same lesson illustrated in verses 7–8 and 10–11 (Meyer, 1881, 2:9; Fee, 1987, 664). In the latter case, the *dia* ("by") introduces the gift of tongues as an avenue for communication. The absence of listeners with the same linguistic background as the foreign language utilized in the tongues message is the condition outlined. This explanation has in its favor the probability that verse 9 is not an illustration like verses 7–8, but rather an application of the illustrations already given (cf. *houtōs kai hymeis* ["so also you"] vv. 9, 12; Edwards, 1885, 362; Godet, 1886, 2:273). Also supporting this view is the usage of *glōssēs* throughout the present context. It is always a spiritual gift. That evidence is strong enough to conclude that the noun in verse 9 refers to the gift of tongues.

8. (p. 93) Various explanations have suggested Paul's reason in choosing *phōnōn* rather than *glōssōn* to depict foreign languages. One widespread explanation posits that *glōssai* in the present context has been reserved for the spiritual gift consisting of inarticulate utterances. He therefore had to use another word for foreign languages in verse 10 (Parry, 1916, 202; Fee, 1987, 664–65). The other prominent explanation understands both words as referring to foreign languages, in which case the illustration of verses 10–11 is much more to the point (Hodge, 1959, 284–85). In this latter instance, the only difference in significance is that *phōnē* refers to a language learned by natural processes, whereas *glōssa* is one spoken by special pneumatic endowment. Further support for the latter viewpoint lies in the parallelism between the *genē glōssōn* of 12:10 and the *genē phōnōn* of 14:10. The kinship of the two expressions argues convincingly for a similarity in meaning between the two nouns in question.

9. (p. 95) The relationship of the *dio* ("therefore") of 14:13 to the previous context requires a clear definition. Otherwise, unnecessary additional obscurity surrounds the already difficult paragraph of verses 13–19. On the one hand, it is possible to find the particle's basis in the entirety of verses 1–12: "Seeing then how useless it is to speak with a language that no one present understands, let the one speaking with a tongue pray that someone will interpret what he says" (cf. Hodge. 1959, 286). It is true that verses 13–19 present a positive alternative to the criticism against uninterpreted tongues in verses 1–12, but the connection thus indicated is much less direct than having *dio* draw its inference only from verse 12, which is a summary application of verses 6–11. The latter possibility yields the sense, "Seeing then that edification of the church is to be the prime consideration in your zeal for spiritual gifts, let the one speaking with a tongue pray that someone will interpret what he says." This gives a more clear-cut basis for the exhortations to follow and avoids the need to construe verses 13–19 as another summary application of verses 1–12. Verse 12 is itself that application, and a repeated application is not called for. Verses 13–19, then, build on verse 12. Specifically, they define how the edification advocated could become reality in the Corinthian surroundings (cf. *oikodomeitai*, "is . . . edified," 14:17).

10. (p. 96) A number of considerations evidence that the prayer of this verse is a tongues prayer rather than one in a native language. One is the use of the same verb *proseuchomai* ("I pray") in verse 14 in the specific sense of a tongues prayer, along with a connection of the two verses by the explanatory conjunction *gar* (if the textual variant is accepted as genuine; Godet, 1886, 2:279; Hering, 1962, 149–50; Meyer, 1881, 2:13). Had Paul wished to refer to a petition completely intelligible to the one praying, he would have used *aiteō* or *deomai* in verse 13 (Godet, 1886, 2:277–78). Further, tongues are the vehicle in prayer throughout verses 14–17, and the *glōssē* ("in a tongue") qualifying *ho lalōn* ("one who speaks") in verse 13 easily carries over to *proseuchesthō* ("let one . . . pray") of the same verse.

Those who see verse 13 as an intelligible prayer argue that a speaker praying with a tongue could not choose the purpose of his prayer. In other words, making this a tongues prayer is not convincing because it cannot provide a suitable meaning for the *hina* ("that") clause following *proseuchesthō* (Robertson and Plummer, 1914, 311). They also observe that intelligible prayer fits nicely with the meaning of verse 12: praying intelligibly for interpretation to contribute as much as possible to the church's edification (Fee, 1987, 668–69). This view seeks to relieve the necessity of having *proseuchomai* refer to the same kind of prayer in consecutive verses (vv. 13–14) by noting a change from second person plural (v. 13) to first person singular (v. 14). Response to the advocates of the intelligible prayer interpretation consists of noting the dubious wisdom of referring *hina* after *proseuchomai* to the content of prayer in Paul's writings. The supposed parallels to substantiate this practice (Phil. 1:9; Col. 1:9; 2 Thess. 1:11; Cremer, 1895, 720) are open to question because of their inexact correspondence to 14:13. Intelligible prayer in this situation is unlikely also in that it contradicts a principle already set down that any gift (including interpretation) comes not in answer to human quest, but solely according to the dictates of God's sovereign will (cf. 12:11). This interpretation also fails to fit the context, for one could not justifiably speak with a tongue unless an interpretation was assured. The fact that it had been prayed for was not a sufficient guarantee to risk the tongues message's going uninterpreted.

It is best, then, to refer the *proseuchesthō* of verse 13 to prayer with a tongue, though not necessarily ecstatic prayer. Prayer with a foreign language is a suitable option. The view recognizes that the tongues prayer is not an end in itself. The goal is rather the interpretation resulting therefrom. The interpretation is what benefits the church (14:12). In effect, tongues convert into prophecy or teaching through the interpretation that follows (Barrett, 1968, 319). This means that the only suitable justification for a tongues prayer uttered in a Christian assembly was the interpretation to be drawn from it. Paul follows up the exhortation of verse

13 by considering in verses 14–15 and 18–19 how the principle had worked out in his own ministry.

11. (p. 96) Two ways of understanding *hina diermēneuē* ("that he may interpret") have been forthcoming:

If the prayer of verse 13 is taken as a tongues utterance, the clause in question presents an interpreted message as the purpose of that utterance. The speaker's settled aim in that case was to use a tongues prayer only as a means to an end, the end being the substance of intelligible revelation and prophecy that would result from it (cf. 14:6). This understanding coincides with the rest of the chapter, as it makes interpretation the only legitimate justification for using tongues with a predominantly Christian audience (cf. 14:5, 28). Whether it is the tongues speaker or someone else who interprets is not specified. From verse 5 it would appear to be the tongues speaker, but from verse 27, that is not the likely conclusion. Verse 28 shows also that it was uncommon for a Corinthian tongues speaker to possess the gift of interpretation. Since verses 27–28 are more specific in laying down a criterion for public worship, it is better to understand the subject of *diermēneuē* as "someone" (Hering, 1962, 149–50). The important point is not who does the interpreting, but the interpreted message that results.

The *hina* clause discloses the contents of an intelligible prayer if the prayer of verse 13 is so understood (cf. n. 10, 243). In this case, it is a conscious prayer for the ability to interpret. Whereas some evidence may support such a use of *hina* (cf. Col. 4:3; 2 Thess. 3:1), it is more likely that the gift of interpretation would be best described by the noun *hermēneia* than by *hina diermēneuē* (cf. 12:10; 14:26) if it were the object of a request.

Understanding the *hina* clause to connote purpose and to designate the ultimate goal of a tongues prayer is the sounder alternative if one wishes to avoid contradicting the principle of 14:27–28, as well as the divine prerogative of bestowing gifts apart from human merit or desire (cf. 12:11).

12. (p. 97) Identification of the *pneuma* ("spirit") in 14:14 is closely akin to the same issue in 14:2. The use of "my" rules out making this the Holy Spirit, though that is a common Pauline usage of the noun (Olshausen, 1851, 4:365). Also, a direct correlation between the present verse and Romans 8:26 is unproven, even though the Romans passage is also connected with prayer (Barrett, 1968, 320).

Another alternative refers *pneuma* to a fundamental element of the human personality, the human spirit, or some aspect thereof. The present context dictates that it be a nonrational part of man's psychological makeup. The forte of this interpretation is the noun's antithetical relationship to *nous* ("mind") in verses 14–15. The reasoning is that since *nous* is the intellectual part, the corresponding *pneuma* must be some nonintellectual faculty such as the "feelings" (Barnes, 1879, 5:265). Prayer with "my spirit" is, then, some kind of prayerful communion with God, devoid of conscious thought and couched in language that is not comprehensible to the speaker. Several obstacles to this "psychological" understanding exist. One great obstacle is the usage of *pneuma* elsewhere. No New Testament writer, especially Paul, approximates this sense (Barrett, 1968, 320; Hodge, 1959, 287). Though it is true that "in spirit" refers to the human spirit in Romans 1:9, it is not there distinguished from "my mind," nor is it dissociated from conscious thought as it must be in 1 Corinthians. Prophetic trances (Acts 10:10; Rev. 1:10) do not afford suitable parallels to the psychological explanation, for with the prophets, conscious thoughts were couched in intelligible words.

A third alternative, understanding *pneuma* as a spiritual gift, has much to commend it. The view sees the gift as the spiritual agent for producing inspired speech, the gift being from the Holy Spirit, of course. In this case, the gift bestowed was that of tongues (Barrett, 1968, 320; Schweizer in *TDNT*, 1968, 6:423; Carson, 1987, 104; cf. Fee, 1987, 670). Three indispensable contextual elements fit this interpretation. (1) The Holy Spirit is operative in the prayer involved; (2) His work is crystallized into a single gift; and (3) the gift is operative through appropriate psychological channels (Barrett, 1968, 320). Probably the most convincing proof of the view's validity, however, is its adoption of a meaning compatible with the *pneumatōn* in 14:12. Verse 14 is, after all, intimately bound to verse 12 by two conjunctions (*dio* and *gar*), and it is therefore natural to assign the same meaning in the latter verse as in the former. From this perspective, the possessive "my" recognizes the apostle's peculiar manifestation of the Spirit, his own spiritual gift. The gift is, as it were, personified as the source of prayer. *To pneuma mou* is therefore Paul's own peculiar gift of tongues that had been granted him by the Holy Spirit. His self-analysis is, in essence, "For if I pray in a tongue, it is my Spirit-given ability to speak a language foreign to my natural senses that is praying" (14:14a).

13. (p. 97) The meaning assigned to "my mind" in verse 14 must take into account one's understanding of the prayer(s) and song(s) in verse 15. Paul therefore conveniently discussed the two issues together. An important issue in verses 14–15 is proper identification of *nous* ("mind"). Some combine the two prayers of verse 15 and conclude that this is one utterance involving both the human spirit and the mind (Hoekema, 1966, 91–92; Hodge, 1959, 281). They abruptly disconnect verse 15 from verse 14, picturing a contrast between rational prayer in one and irrational prayer in the other (Barrett, 1968, 320). The prayer of verse 15, then, combines intellect and emotion into one prayerful activity (Robertson, 1931, 4:183). But that step is unjustified. Nothing marks strong contrast between verses 14 and 15. Instead, the implication is that of continuity (cf. *oun*, v. 15). No ground exists for dropping tongues prayer from the discussion in verse 15. On the contrary, very good ground exists for retaining it (cf. vv. 16–19, where tongues utterances are clearly in view).

Another meaning assigned to verse 15 is to understand prayer with the spirit as tongues prayer and prayer with the mind as prayer dictated by normal human intelligence (Grosheide, 1953, 326). That meaning has the advantage of embracing the same meaning of *pneuma* as is found in verse 14 (Meyer, 1881, 2:15). It also allows for its ordinary sense, referring to human intelligence (Parry, 1916, 203). It is consistent in carrying on the same meaning of *pneumati* in verse 16. One serious objection to the explanation arises, however: it does not allow for an intimate connection between the two prayers of verse 15. The contextual impression is that the two prayers come together, and the latter in some important sense derives its meaning in relation to the former.

A further possibility for understanding the prayer(s) of verse 15 is to explain prayer with the spirit as a tongues prayer and prayer with the mind as a prayer of interpretation (Meyer, 1881, 2:15; Godet, 1886, 2:280; Kling in Lange, 1868, 6: Lenski, 1963, 7:592–93; Carson, 1987, 104). The view also retains the advantage of understanding *pneuma* consistently throughout the paragraph. It also recognizes in "my mind" a facility for formulating matters intelligently to communicate them to others, an appropriate description of interpretation and an appropriate emphasis in the overall thrust of verses 13–19. Another convincing element is the referral of *tǭ noi* ("with the mind") to a spiritual gift as analogous to its companion *tǭ pneumati* ("with the spirit") in verse 15. The same is true regarding "my mind" and "my spirit" in verse 14. If one designates a spiritual gift, it is natural for the other to do the same. Probably the greatest weakness of the explanation, on the other hand, is its failure to find this meaning for *nous* elsewhere.

All factors considered, the extremely heavy contextual argument for letting *ho nous mou* ("my mind") (v. 14) and *tǭ noi* refer to the gift of interpretation is most persuasive. The unusual nature of the present paragraph is sufficient to explain the appropriation of an unusual meaning for *nous* to emphasize the importance of having interpretation wherever someone used tongues.

14. (p. 97) The precise meaning of "my mind is unfruitful" (14:14) is important to the progress of thought. A decision on its meaning centers on the meaning of *akarpos* ("unfruit-

ful"]—whether the adjective is passive in sense, meaning the speaker himself receives no benefit, or active in sense, meaning his *nous* provides no benefit to others.

The passive sense means the apostle, in the case supposed, received no profit himself because his mind could not grasp the meaning of what his lips said. The validity of the understanding hinges largely on whether potential benefit to the tongues speaker himself is a recommended course in verses 4 and 18 (Parry, 1916, 202, 203). If it is, nothing improper attaches to the situation of verse 14.

Yet, the present paragraph's emphasis is on the obligation of the charismatically endowed person to communicate with others (vv. 12, 13, 16, 17), which he fails to do in the case supposed in verse 14. The active sense of *akarpos* is therefore to be preferred. Failure of the speaker's understanding to produce fruit in others is blameworthy. His responsibility is to communicate comprehensibly with his listeners in Christian worship. Fortifying this active meaning of *akarpos* is the adjective's uniform usage elsewhere (Matt. 13:22; Eph. 5:11; Titus 3:14; 2 Peter 1:8) (Hodge, 1959, 288). In light of the meaning already assigned to *ho nous mou* (v. 14; cf. 97, 246 n. 13), the verse is referring to the hypothetical situation where Paul might have used his tongues gift for prayer without interpretation. Such a combination rendered his interpretative gift ineffective in the lives of others because of disuse. As he goes on to say, that is a practice he never followed.

The view that assigns *akarpos* a meaning of "produces nothing, contributes nothing to the process" (Barrett, 1968, 319–20) is not convincing, because *akarpos* does not mean "inactive." It is a word for results and does not apply to the process through which someone obtains the results. The present discussion does not center on the activity or nonactivity of the tongues speaker's mind, but rather on potential benefit derived by listeners.

15. (p. 98) The issue of whether a tongues speaker comprehended to some degree the nature and/or meaning of his own utterance is in question. One method of approaching the matter is the unqualified position that he understood nothing of his own utterance, this being the reason for his inability to communicate the meaning to others apart from the gift of interpretation. Such an explanation goes hand in hand with relegating *tō noi* ("with the mind") to purely human intellectual comprehension. As already seen, however, *nous* ("mind") can and probably should be understood not in reference to the speaker himself, but to his ability to make himself understood by others.

The larger issue of the nature and degree of ecstasy in tongues speaking also comes up here. Were the tongues speaker's senses in a state of complete suspension or not? If he in no way understood his own utterance, the answer is probably yes.

Another way of approaching the matter, however, is to allow that the tongues speaker did to some extent understand his own utterance, but because his grasp was so limited, he was unable to communicate it to others (Hodge 1959, 281, 287, 291, 292). This approach makes much of the distinction between prayer and singing in verse 15 and of the distinction between blessing and thanksgiving in verse 16. How could a tongues speaker be conscious of the nature of his utterance, for example, whether prayer or singing, without some understanding of what kind of utterance it was (Hodge, 1959, 287, 291)? In fact, thanksgiving could not be true thanks for him apart from at least a general knowledge of what he had said (Hodge, 1959, 291). If the tongues speaker had no inkling of what he was talking about, in no way could the gift have benefited him. Yet, verses 4 and 18 indicate benefit did accrue to him (Hodge, 1959, 281, 292).

The latter position is more convincing. For a tongues speaker to have received edification (14:4), his could not have been a purely emotional experience. It is questionable whether edification ever comes through channels that exclude the intellect (contrary to Edwards, 1885, 358). If the listeners needed to understand to be edified, so did the speaker (Hodge, 1959, 291). That he did, even though his understanding was not precise enough for him to convey it to others (Godet, 1886, 2:268).

16. (p. 98) Translation of *tou idiōtou* ("of the ungifted") in 14:16 is a complex issue. Some presume this person to be a Christian, perhaps even a Christian leader, but one who is excluded from proceedings in the assembly when tongues dominate because of his lack of a gift adequate to understand a tongues message (Edwards, 1885, 376; Meyer, 1881, 2:22). The chief advantages in seeing the person as a Christian come from the context of verse 16 and from verses 23–24. In the former passage, the paragraph obviously has Christians in view (cf. "amen" of v. 16). In the latter section, the person is different from an unbeliever (cf. *apistoi*, "unbelievers"). From another perspective, however, the *idiōtai* of 14:23 are different from the Christian community when pictured as visitors. Also, verses 24–25 show them to be in need of conversion, not edification, which again rules against identifying them as Christians.

Another suggestion has been that the *tou idiōtou* of 14:16 points to a non-Christian, but one who has become interested enough to attend Christian meetings regularly (Parry, 1916, 203, 207). He is "uninitiated" due to his non-Christian status, but at the same time he is different from out-and-out unbelievers (*apistoi*, 14:23) because of his frequent presence at Christian meetings. This allows that the person so named is still in need of a conversion experience (14:24–25) and corresponds to the Jewish practice whereby a section of the synagogue was regularly reserved for non-Jewish "worshipers." The difficulty with the approach is in understanding how that kind of person could add his "amen" to a Christian declaration (v. 16). Furthermore, if he had been a regular attender and had seen the tongues-dominated Corinthian assembly previously, it is unlikely that he would declare, "You are mad" (v. 23) (Barrett, 1968, 324). A conclusion that distinguishes such "half-Christians" as lying somewhere between *apistoi* and *pistoi* needs better support than is available in the present chapter (Schlier in *TDNT*, 1965, 3:217). Another suggestion is that the *idiōtēs* in verse 16 as well as in verses 23–24 is a non-Christian who, of course, does not possess either tongues or interpretation, and is essentially no different from the one designated *apistos* in 14:23 (Hodge, 1959, 297–98). Paul expresses the person's need of a conversion experience (14:24–25). His stronger status at the Christian meeting (14:23–25) adds further weight to this opinion. The big difficulty here is understanding how an unbeliever could add an "amen" to a Christian utterance (14:16). In fact, the whole context of 14:12–19 has a believing assembly in view, making an unbeliever in verse 16 out of place.

The only possible solution to identifying the *tou idiōtou* in 14:16 in a way that will satisfy the use of the same word in 14:23–24 is to see him as one ignorant of the language being used, regardless of whether he be Christian or non-Christian. In this case, the word simply means "ungifted" insofar as tongues, interpretation, and prophecy are concerned (Barrett, 1968, 324–25; Kistemaker, 1993, 493). Contextual differences between 14:16 and 14:23–25 are sufficient to warrant such a broad definition (Cremer, 1895, 838). This means that a person could at the same time be both *idiōtēs* and *apistos*, with the former title viewing him in relation to the language used, an objective designation, and the latter viewing him in relation to Christianity more broadly, a subjective designation. The conjunction *ē* in verses 23–24 connects the two terms, but with this view does not make them mutually exclusive. The usage is legitimate for the correlative (cf. 14:37; Arndt and Gingrich, 1957, 342). Thus, the *tou idiōtou* of 14:16 can be seen as a Christian's adding "amen" to something he understands, whereas the same noun in verses 23–25 represents an unbeliever who is, of course, likewise ungifted and in need of conversion. Though some could accuse proponents of this view of assigning the word two different meanings, one in verse 16 and another in verses 23–25, and of taking the conjunction *ē* in an unnatural sense, these are obstacles far smaller than those encountered by other explanations of the term. This conclusion regarding *idiōtou* carries with it a consequent necessity of taking *ton topon* ("the place") in 14:16, not in the sense of an assigned physical location within the Christian meeting room, but with a metaphorical meaning. Such persons, whether believers or unbelievers, occupy a distinct category according to their liability in understanding the proceedings. They fill the role of an *idiōtēs* due to the nature of the utterances they hear, in other words (Godet, 1886, 2:282–83). Though *topos* in comparable expressions more often has a concrete meaning rather than an abstract (Meyer, 1881, 2:15), sufficient precedent exists for understanding it here in a metaphorical way, especially since geographical locality is not a concern of the present discussion (Cremer, 1895, 838).

17. (p. 99) The adverb *mallon* ("more than") in 14:18 shows the greater degree to which Paul possessed and exercised the gift of tongues. Some have contended on this basis that the gift consisted of inarticulate sounds rather than foreign languages. It refers to a mode of speaking (inarticulate), not to what is uttered (foreign languages), they say (Godet, 1886, 2:285). Paul could have made such a claim about foreign languages apart from his tongues gift, probably being well-enough educated to speak Aramaic, Latin, and Syriac in addition to his native Greek. If tongues consisted of foreign languages, why would he defend his proposition regarding tongues by using himself as an example (Robertson and Plummer, 1914, 314)? Yet, it is not a sufficient argument against foreign languages to reason on the basis of what Paul could have written: "more foreign languages than you all." The superior degree of his gift can apply equally as well to foreign languages as it does to inarticulate utterances. The qualitative distinction between himself and his readers could just as well have quantitative implications (Barrett, 1968, 321). In fact, the quantitative idea is more probably involved, no matter what the nature of the gift. He spoke with tongues more frequently than all his readers. Foreign languages satisfy that criterion just as easily as inarticulate utterances do.

18. (p. 99) Some have preferred to understand verse 18 as though a *hoti* stood between the two verbs, in which case the verse would read, "I give thanks to God for the fact that I speak with tongues more than all of you" (Godet, 1886, 2:284–85). Grammatically, this accords with the practice of classical Greek and other nonbiblical sources in allowing *hoti* to be omitted in indirect discourse (Edwards, 1885, 370; Blass and Debrunner, 1961, 247). Paul himself followed this stylistic habit (1 Cor. 4:16; Phil. 4:3; cf. Luke 14:18; Acts 21:39). Yet, one can argue dissimilarity between this and other New Testament instances because elsewhere the introductory verb is one of exhortation or petition, with the latter verb always being imperative in mood, neither of which is true in verse 18. A serious objection to this manner of connecting the two parts of verse 18 bases itself on what the view does to the continuity of discussion. Verses 18–19 hereby become an island to themselves, without a suitable tie-in with either what precedes or what follows. In fact, one could eliminate the first three words, *eucharistō tō Theō* ("I thank God"), without substantially affecting the sense of the two verses.

It is possible, however, to find a very natural tie-in with verses 12–17 by letting *eucharistō* ("I thank," v. 18) carry on the continuity of *eucharistiai* (v. 16) and *eucharisteis* (v. 17). Since verses 16–17 are evidently tongues utterances, so must be the thanksgiving of verse 18 (Edwards, 1885, 370). If that connection is correct, verse 18 is elliptical: "I give thanks to God [i.e., in the form of a tongues utterance]—more than all of you I speak [i.e., in other kinds of speech, not just thanksgiving] with tongues." The latter part of the statement broadens the former. Rather than limiting tongues speech to just thanksgiving, Paul substitutes a more general statement covering all forms of tongues utterances. Though admittedly this meaning of verse 18 would follow more naturally with a conjunction such is an ascensive *kai* ("even") connecting the two parts, and with the pronoun *egō* ("I") in the first part of the verse to contrast more clearly with the *sy* ("you") of verse 17, the view still presents a more comprehensible interpretation in a setting following verses 13–17. For Paul to compare himself with his readers in this way is not out of character for him (contrary to Meyer, 1881, 2:17) because he does not refer to his private prayers. Nor does he limit the statement solely to prayers when he says, "I speak with tongues." He instead refers to his public ministry with various linguistic groups encountered in connection with missionary travels. Such an extensive use of tongues was open to verification by anyone who chose to investigate his ministry in various places.

19. (p. 100) When Paul refers to his preferred practice "in the church" (14:19), he raises an issue concerning the implied antithesis of the expression. Many have assumed that the opposite of "in the church" is "in private" (e.g., Godet, 1886, 2:311), since the opposite of *en tais ekklēsiais* ("in the churches") later in the chapter (14:34) is *en oikō* ("at home") (14:35). That seems at first to be a valid conclusion. A closer look at 14:35, however, reveals that *en oikō* does not entail a private situation (contra Fee, 1987, 674–75, and Carson, 1987, 105), but includes both husband and wife. Advocates of this interpretation also attempt to support the "in private" connotation from verses 2, 4, and 28, which, however, lend themselves equally well or better to explanations other than the private use of tongues. One of Paul's prime emphases throughout chapters 12–14 is the necessity that a spiritual gift render benefit to persons other than the one using it (12:7, 25; 13:5–6; 14:12, 19, 26). It is highly unlikely in this light that the apostle would set himself up as an example on the basis of his private use of a spiritual gift. Such selfishness is the very thing that needed purging from among the Corinthians. Private use of a God-given ability is certainly nothing to imitate.

The other possible antithesis of "in the church" is a public gathering peopled predominantly by unbelievers. Use of tongues in that surrounding accords well with the gift's primary purpose, serving as a sign for unbelievers (14:22). That is exactly the use of the gift as described elsewhere (Acts 2:1–13; 10:44–46). The fact that the following paragraph (vv. 20–25) speaks of tongues' justifiable use among unbelievers suggests "outside church," that is, among non-Christians, as a suitable opposite to "in church" (v. 19). The apostle valued the gift highly enough to use it extensively, but not in church gatherings (Hering, 1962, 151). As apostle to the Gentiles, his deeper endowment with the gift was necessary as an authenticating symbol while he worked with different dialects and languages of the Greco-Roman world (Unger, 1971, 111). Hence, the valid purpose of tongues was a public one, not a private one.

20. (p. 100) When Paul uses *tō noi mou* ("with my mind") in 14:19, several lessons emerge.

The expression serves as a link with the paragraph begun at verse 13, confirming that verses 18–19 belong to what has gone before, not what follows. The words "with my mind" (v. 19) are an echo of the *ho nous mou* ("my mind") in verse 14.

That *tō noi* pertains to the speaker's ability to communicate with others is also confirmed (cf. 246, note 14). The *kai* ("also") of verse 19, moreover, shows that a tongues speaker grasped the nature and/or meaning of his own utterance to some degree (cf. 247, note 15). The conjunction connotes, "Not only myself, as would be the case with the gift of tongues, but others also" (Godet, 1886, 2:286). *Ho nous* is the faculty by which the speaker conveys his intuitions and thoughts to the assembly. Having made his tongues utterance, he already had personal grasp of these intuitions and thoughts in a broad sense, but communication of them to others was contingent on the functioning of "my mind."

In line with the continuity of thought, *tō noi mou* must be the gift of interpretation. It is not the functioning of prophecy or teaching, though the former is prominent in the broad context of chapter 14. He has not mentioned the gift of prophecy, though frequent in the large context, since verse 5. Prophecy in verse 19 is out of keeping with the *tō noi* in verse 15, since it is not prophecy's nature to produce prayer and thanksgiving. The prophetic gift is prominent once again at verse 24, but it is best to see in verse 19 another reference to the gift of interpretation that, though dependent upon tongues, is the practical equivalent of prophecy (cf. Acts 19:6; 1 Cor. 14:6).

21. (p. 103) The kind of analogy found between Isaiah 28:11–12 and 14:21 has been defined in two ways:

(1) The connection between the two is loose and allegorical. The foreign languages of the Assyrians in Isaiah present a broad outline of the inarticulate nature of the tongues gift. To assume foreign languages in 1 Corinthians 14 is needless just because foreign languages are in Isaiah 28 since the Rabbinic method of interpretation frequently used resulted in a mean-

ing different from the grammatical, historical meaning of the source passage (Behm in *TDNT*, 1964, 1:727; Edwards, 1885, 374). It is sufficient to find a suitable common ground between type and antitype in "the extraordinary phenomenon of strange divine speaking" (Meyer, 1881, 2:18). Here the similarity ends, that is, in the fact that listeners found the utterances unintelligible in each case.

(2) The analogy between the two passages is close enough to demand that the nature of utterance in each case be the same; that is, both are foreign languages. In the Isaiah instance the foreign languages had been learned by normal processes, but in 1 Corinthians 14 the utterance was miraculous. That is certainly the most natural way to understand verse 21 (Evans, 1900, 3:348). If in Isaiah a message was to be heard, and *eisakousontai* ("they will . . . listen," 1 Cor. 14:21) indicates it was, Paul's use of the quotation is totally inappropriate if the message to be heard was not the one in the tongues utterance. A message to be heard can come only in the form of human language. Obviously, the Isaiah passage is more appropriate to the Corinthian circumstances if a foreign language is the meaning in the Corinthians message too. A comparison of the gift of tongues with foreign languages has been so recently in view (14:10–11) that proper interpretation demands it be in view here in verse 21 as well.

22. (p. 103) Paul's specific reason for quoting Isaiah 28:11–12 and his continuity of thought in verses 21–23 are discernible only after extensive consideration.

One explanation is that Paul made an effort to show God's use of foreign tongues among the people as a mark of divine displeasure. The languages are a symbol of God's decision to curse and punish the people. The emphasis of the quotation is upon *eisakousontai mou* ("they will [not] listen to me"); that is, the people are beyond help because of their refusal to listen and obey. The adoption of that emphasis of verse 21 leads to a conclusion in verse 22 that derives from the historical hardness of Israel, and foreign tongues among God's people become a sign of divine displeasure and consequent approaching judgment on the people who use them. The unbelieving of verse 22 are not those who have merely failed to believe, but those who have hardened their hearts to the point of removing all possibility of future salvation. To such obdurate, obstinate rejecters of the truth tongues become a sign (*sēmeion*, v. 22) of inevitable divine punishment. The carry over of this interpretation requires a general conclusion (v. 23) that speaking in languages not understood by the listeners is useless and even undesirable (Godet, 1886, 2:289–91; Edwards, 1885, 372–74; Evans, 1900, 3:349–51; Hodge, 1959, 294–96; Robertson and Plummer, 1914, 317–21; Barrett, 1968, 323–27; Fee, 1987, 681–82; Carson, 1987, 113–15; Kistemaker, 1993, 500–501).

The above explanation depends heavily on the historical context of Isaiah 28, where the Assyrians' coming and the use of their language in addressing Israel were indicative that God had turned His back on this people because of their rebellion. The childish vanity of the Corinthians was likewise judged, the sign of God's displeasure being the gift of tongues (Edwards, 1885, 372). The use of tongues in their assembly was indicative of unbelief of a character found in ancient Israel (Godet, 1886, 2:291). To both people, tongues were a sign that God's retribution was at hand (Edwards, 1885, 373). Attempts to justify that interpretation, however, have failed to give due consideration to a lack of correspondence in details. In the Assyrian situation, tongues users were God's punitive agents against His own people, but such is not the case in the Corinthian situation. The Corinthians themselves are the speakers, not the objects of the tongues speech, as was Israel of old. The gift's use in Acts certainly does not emphasize tongues as a sign of rejection, but rather as an aid to faith. Even in 1 Corinthians, no hint of the gift's being a sign of divine punishment is present. A further difficulty with this explanation is the way it forces upon *apistos* ("unbelievers," v. 22) a sense beyond what it can rightly bear. *Apistos* in 14:23–25 certainly cannot connote one insensible to further gospel opportunities. Moreover, the meaning fostered by view 1 for *sēmeion* ("a sign") is unparalleled in New Testament usage. The unlikelihood of this explanation is even greater because of the way it eliminates any genuine beneficial use of tongues, with verse 22 pointing out it can bring no benefit to unbelievers, and verse 23 ruling it out for use among believers. Spiritual gifts as otherwise known do not have that character.

Another explanation suggests the reason for a citation of Isaiah 28 is to show tongues as a sign of unbelief on the part of those addressed by them. Rather than being a sign of retribution (cf. view 1), they are a sign of rejection; that is, unbelievers are thereby rendered recognizable! This view entails no connotation of divine judgment (Meyer, 1881, 2:20). The theory removes an objectionable aspect of viewpoint 1 in that it does not see tongues as a penal sign. In fact, nothing results from the gift's usage. It is simply symbolic of unbelief (Meyer, 1881, 2:20). The same meaning carries over into verse 22: people thus addressed are identified as unbelievers (Godet, 1886, 2:292). This is a much more satisfactory identification of the *apistois* of verse 22 as contrasted with the *tois pisteuousin* ("those who believe"; cf. 1 Cor. 6:6; 7:12–15; 10:27) (Meyer, 1881, 2:20). Since tongues are useful only in identification of unbelievers, they have no use in the Christian assembly (v. 23).

The view does not go nearly far enough, however. If the historical condition of Isaiah 28 is to be stressed, one should note that Israel's condition was far more serious than simple failure to believe. The nation was actively rebellious and had reached a point of callousness. In fact, the citation of 1 Corinthians 14:21 says nothing about foreign tongues as a means of recognizing unbelievers. Also, attention to the meaning of *sēmeion* (v. 22) is inadequate here. The term has far deeper implications than just a means of recognition. *Tois apistois* following *sēmeion* would probably have been a genitive case rather than a dative if that were the meaning. "A sign pointing to unbelievers" is unnatural for this construction (Hodge, 1959, 294–95). Insofar as verse 23 is concerned, the explanation seemingly would have produced an opposite conclusion. If tongues were an indicator of unbelief, why should not their use have been appropriate in any gathering where unbelievers were present, for example, in the case supposed?

Some have suggested that the primary lesson to be drawn from the Isaiah citation is that tongues are ineffectual in convincing those not already convinced (Parry, 1916, 206; Barrett, 1968, 321). The expression that caught Paul's eye was "men of strange tongues," and he derives this rather than the historical setting of Isaiah from the quotation. The point of contact between the two instances is tongues' failure to arouse a response in unbelievers. The tongues method will not render unbelievers obedient (v. 22), nor will it profit for use among Christians who are already convinced (v. 23) (Hodge, 1959, 294). Tongues will do no good in the former case, that is, the case of disobedience as among the Hebrews (v. 21). In the latter case, prophets are far more productive (vv. 24–25) (Hodge, 1959, 296). From that perspective, "unbelievers" (v. 22) are not the callous ones (view 1) but simply those who have not exercised faith (view 2). The "sign" of verse 22 is a means of their recognition. The meaning of verses 23–25, then, takes for granted that Christians are already convinced. Why waste tongues on them? The thrust of the view is that tongues are effective only with those who use them, and not with any others. The glaring weakness of this view is the obvious fact that tongues did get a response from unbelievers in Acts 2. This view also denies the basic nature of a spiritual gift. If it has no function in reaching beyond the speaker himself to build up the body of Christ, the apostle is actually arguing against himself in this very chapter. Verse 22 does not dwell on the failure of tongues, but on their success in accomplishing a positive goal. "A sign to unbelievers" (v. 22), because of the overtones of *sēmeion*, must mean spiritual benefit for unbelievers. Plain language and the larger context demand that tongues have some objective in lives other than the speaker's.

A more satisfactory explanation of Paul's use of Isaiah 28:11–12 stems from observing the unusual changes he makes in the last clause. From the *ouk* of Isaiah 28:12 (LXX) comes an *oud'* ("not even") in Paul's citation, followed by the addition of *houtōs* ("thus, so"). "Not even thus" expresses utter amazement at so remarkable a sign as a divine spokesman in a foreign tongue. Here is one of extraordinary character. His facility in strange languages validates him as God's official representative. That is a special means adopted to attract people, a sign of verification or authentication, a proof of divine presence and activity. Yet, "not even thus" would the people of Israel respond.

Though this interpretation varies from the historical meaning of the Old Testament source, it is not infrequent for Paul to adapt an Old Testament quotation for his own purposes. Here he dwells on the provocative nature of the sign rather than the judicial enactment against Israel. This approach accords well with the meaning and emphatic position of *sēmeion* in verse 22. It also agrees with the overall positive purpose of any spiritual gift, as suggested throughout 1 Corinthians 12–14 (cf. *pros ton sympheron* ["for the common good"], 1 Cor. 12:7). The body of Christ grows as unbelievers respond positively in faith to this remarkable sign. Every unbeliever is a potential addition to the body, as verses 24–25 indicate. Furthermore, view 4 affords a satisfactory meaning for *sēmeion*, a miracle with an ethical purpose, or "finger-post of God" (Trench, 1953, 343). Paul's usage of *sēmeion* is especially instructive. It stands for a miraculous authenticating pointer (Rom. 15:19; 1 Cor. 1:22; 2 Cor. 12:12; 2 Thess. 2:9), and is an authenticating sign elsewhere (Rom. 4:11; 2 Thess. 3:17). Usage throughout the New Testament substantiates this (cf. Acts 2:22; 14:3). The view also allows *apistos* to be taken in a consistent sense throughout verses 22–24. Verses 23–25 point out the inappropriateness of tongues in an assembly composed primarily of believers. The gift had a perfectly valid purpose in a group where unbelievers predominated (v. 22), but prophecy is much more useful among Christians (note the specific way of identifying the gathering as a Christian assembly in verses 23–25). This view provides the only adequate way of reconciling verse 22 with verses 23–25. The nature of the listening audience relates to the way the two sections connect. Rather than being objects of the sign value of tongues, as listeners would be in a non-Christian audience (v. 22), outsiders visiting a Christian assembly became "yardsticks for estimating the value of ministries" (E. Schweizer, *Church Order in the New Testament,* cited by Barrett, 1968, 325). They bear witness to the folly of tongues' being used in the presence of Christians only and are in agreement with the verdict of verse 22 that tongues are not the appropriate gift for believers to use among themselves.

In the three instances of tongues in Acts (chapters 2, 10, and 19), unbelievers, that is, people who prior to the occasion had not converted to faith in Jesus Christ, were involved. Hence, tongues in those three cases do have their evidential value in connection with *apistoi,* though at times the evangelists were tongues spokesmen (Acts 2), and at times the ones evangelized did the speaking (Acts 10 and 19) (Burdick, 1969, 29–31). In the first case, the tongues messages preceded actual conversion and prepared the way for it. In the last two instances, tongues followed conversion and served to confirm what had happened. In any event, however, tongues were instrumental in each of the evangelistic endeavors. The Acts 2 kind of situation is what Paul has primarily in mind as he draws his inference from Isaiah 28:11–12. Yet, when unbelievers were in a minority among believers, prophecy was a more effective tool evangelistically (vv. 24–25).

23. (p. 105) Whether or not the idea of *eis sēmeion* ["for a sign"] in 14:22a is applicable to 14:22b has been a matter of debate.

A number of versions have continued the force in the latter part of the verse, with such renderings as the NASB's: "Prophecy is for a sign, not to unbelievers, but to those who believe." Support for that rendering emphasizes the parallelism of clauses in verse 22 (cf. Hodge, 1959, 294; Parry, 1916, 206). The same dative expressions appear in the latter half, and verse 22b has no verb, necessitating a carryover of *eisin* ("are") from the former part of the verse. For the antithesis to be meaningful, it is argued, the meaning of *eis sēmeion* must also carry over (Meyer, 1881, 2:21). Closer perusal reveals, however, that *sēmeion* cannot have the same meaning in two parts of such an antithesis. Whether it be a sign of judgment, a sign whereby unbelievers are recognized, or an evidential sign for unbelievers, the meaning is contrary to what is known about the gift of prophecy. If the prophetic gift has benefit chiefly for its sign value in verse 22, the Scripture never alludes to such elsewhere.

The other alternative is that repetition of *eis sēmeion* is unnecessary. Correctly understood, the latter part of the verse says, "Prophecy is not for unbelievers, but for those who believe" (Olshaussen, 1851, 228; Robertson and Plummer, 1914, 317). Explaining verse 22b in this manner avoids the elliptical construction of view 1 and leaves the grammar and meaning of the sentence in perfect order. A dual antithesis between believers and unbelievers, one in the former part of the verse and one in the latter, overshadows the supposed parallelism between tongues and prophecy. In fact, the very reason for contrasting objects of the two gifts is that one is a sign and the other is not (Olshausen, 1851, 228). That explanation of verse 22b is still more impressive in that the sign value introduced in the 14:21 quotation has nothing to do with prophecy. It deals only with "men of other tongues and other lips." The necessity of taking *tois pisteuousin* ("to those who believe") and *tois apistois* ("to unbelievers") with different case significations in the two parts of the verse (Hodge, 1959, 294) is not serious enough to overthrow this viewpoint. In the latter part of verse 22, an insertion of an implied "is" fills out the meaning of the nominal clause satisfactorily: "Prophecy [is] not for unbelievers."

24. (p. 110) The question of whether the *de* in 14:28b is adversative (NEB) or explanatory (RSV, NASB) is significant. In the former case, it would contrast public tongues with private tongues, whereas in the latter it would introduce an explanation of how the tongues speaker is to keep silent in church. With the adversative meaning, verse 28b introduces a setting other than a public assembly, a situation where tongues speaking is in private: "Let him keep silent in church, but let him speak to himself and to God [privately]" (cf. Fee, 1987, 692–93; Mare, 1976, 276; Kistemaker, 1993, 507). Favorable to this understanding is the use of *laleō* ("let him speak") throughout the chapter to refer to audible speech rather than inaudible (Meyer, 1881, 2:27). The chapter also uses *de* often as an adversative (14:4, 5, 22). Yet, this would involve suppressing the moving of the Spirit until another occasion, something the tongues speaker could not arbitrarily do since he would not be sure when another such moving might come (Godet, 1886, 2:302). That Paul would advocate private tongues as a substitute for use in public is unlikely in that throughout chapters 12–14 the proper function of gifts is to benefit other members (cf. vv. 26, 31).

The other explanation of verse 28b is that *laleitō* refers to inaudible utterances: "Let him keep silent in church, [and let him do this by means of] speaking to himself and to God only." The way *en ekklēsia* ("in the church") continues its force from verse 28a shows the greater plausibility of such a meaning. Wherever the silence takes place is the same place where the speaking to oneself and to God is to transpire. Verse 28b is a proverbial way of depicting meditation, in other words (Edwards, 1885, 379), similar to the English idea of "talking to oneself." *De* frequently introduces explanatory additions (cf. 1 Cor. 14:2, 15 [twice], 24 [second occurrence], 40).

Since the context of 11:2–14:40 has public surroundings in view and makes no clear reference to private activities, *de* in an explanatory sense is the preferable interpretation.

25. (p. 111) If the *hoi alloi* ("the others") in 14:29 referred to all others present at the meeting, no suitable antecedent for the pronoun is available in the immediate context. All Christians did have a test of discernment to apply (1 Cor. 12:3; cf. 1 Thess. 5:20–21) (Barrett, 1968, 328), but the kind of testing exercised on the immediate occasion of a prophetic utterance was more specific, necessitating a special gift. Fee considers that everyone in the congregation was a potential prophet and therefore capable of discerning the validity of the utterances (Fee, 1987, 694), but this view is in clear violation of 12:28–30, which makes clear that all did not have the gift of prophecy or any other gift, for that matter. Carson says "the

others" refers to the church as a whole (Carson, 1987, 120; cf. Kistemaker, 1993, 508–10), but overlooks what the natural antecedent is in this context and rejects without any grounds the connection of this evaluation with the gift of discernment in 12:10. Grudem does essentially the same (Grudem, 1988, 72–73). But both have the insurmountable grammatical problem of overlooking the natural antecedent of *alloi*.

Identifying "the others" as the other prophets present at the meeting has much greater plausibility. Such is the natural antecedent of *hoi alloi*. It is very appropriate that those with the gift for discerning prophecy should themselves be prophets. Discernment was a special endowment (cf. 1 Cor. 12:10) and hence could not belong to the whole congregation (Meyer, 1881, 2:27–28). Verification for this antecedent of *hoi alloi* comes in the *allō* immediately following in verse 30. For revelation to have been given to another (*allō*, v. 30) required that he be a prophet also. That continues and confirms the same antecedent for *hoi alloi* in verse 29.

26. (p. 112) Whether the first speaker was to go on until he had concluded his remarks or stop immediately to allow a prophet with more recent revelation to speak has been debated. In favor of allowing the initial speaker to continue until finished is the preference in this context for orderly procedures free from interruptions (14:33a, 40) (Hodge, 1959, 302). That he be allowed to complete his discourse also seems feasible from the explanation following in verse 31. Each one was to await his own turn, according to verse 31. The passage says nothing to support the idea of an earlier speaker's quitting to open the way for another (Hodge, 1959, 302). The sense, then, is to let the first be silent *before* the other begins. The other way of understanding *sigatō* ("let . . . keep silent") in 14:30 is as an instruction to an earlier speaker to cease at the moment he receives indication another prophet has received new revelation. The procedure gave precedence to an undelayed prophetic revelation and kept any one speaker from dominating the whole service (Robertson and Plummer, 1914, 322). That latter explanation is more convincing because the command of the imperative *sigatō* pertains to the earlier speaker, and, therefore, he is the one who must obey it, not the speaker following him. That characteristic emerges again in the imperatives of the same verb in verses 28 and 34.

27. (p. 113) Possible meanings for the *pneumata* in 14:32 are threefold.

The noun can refer to the spirits of persons possessing prophetic gifts. With that meaning, the reference includes the inward impulses and revelations granted these persons via their human spirits. Each prophet is capable of controlling his own impulses. Such an emphasis is in line with the need for mutual submission among the prophets as just discussed in verses 31–32. If this were Paul's meaning, however, it is difficult to see why he would not have expressed mutual submission in a much more direct way: "prophets must be in subjection to one another" (Robertson and Plummer, 1914, 323; Godet, 1886, 2:306). It is quite unnatural, furthermore, to say that a man's own spirit is subject to himself (Edwards, 1885, 380). That is a truth obvious in itself. Moreover, if the verse were inculcating mutual submission, it would read "ought to be subject" rather than "are subject."

These are angelic spirits (Ellis, 1974, 134). Similar passages that reflect a plurality of such good spirits are 1 John 4:1–3 and Revelation 22:6, the view holds. Paul elsewhere associates angels with activities of pneumatics in 1 Corinthians 11:4–10; 13:1; and Galatians 1:8, among others (Ellis, 1974, 138). Contrary to the somewhat persuasive evidence offered by this view, however, an explicit statement about the part of good angels in the functioning of spiritual gifts is lacking. Furthermore, to posit the presence and activity of angels in this capacity goes against the obvious directness of the Holy Spirit's personal part in assigning and acting in the outworking of the gifts (1 Cor. 12:4, 8, 9, 11, 13).

Pneumata identifies its meaning with that of the *pneumatōn* ("spiritual gifts") in 14:12 (Barrett, 1968, 329; Godet, 1886, 2:307; Kistemaker, 1993, 510). This essentially is the Spirit manifestations or spiritual gifts of the prophets. The statement requires something separate from the individual personality, and both this chapter and elsewhere justify this sense for *pneuma* (cf. 1 Cor. 12:10; Rev. 22:6). God is the source of prophetic revelation, and He imparts such revelation through the spiritual gift of prophecy. The gift in turn is subject to control by the prophet possessing it, meaning he can choose to speak or not to speak, whichever is appropriate to the occasion.

28. (p. 114) How to connect *hōs en pasais tais ekklēsiais tōn hagiōn* ("as in all the churches of the saints") with its context is problematic.

To connect the words with what precedes by placing a comma after *eirēnēs* ("of peace") and a period after *hagiōn* ("saints") makes the clause a conclusion to the paragraph 14:26–33. Finding a suitable thought with which to connect it in the preceding verses is not easy, however. To read it with the words of verse 33a, that is, reverent submission to order is everywhere a characteristic of the churches, relegates God's peaceful and orderly character merely to church situations. Had Paul wished to dwell upon or demonstrate the universality of God's character as a God of peace, as this connection presupposes, he would not have sought evidence in the way God is seen in the behavior of all the churches (Godet, 1886, 2:308–9). That is poor proof, as evidenced not only by the Corinthian situation but elsewhere as well (e.g., Gal. 5:15; Phil. 4:2). Furthermore, this assumed reasoning by Paul is incomprehensible. What value is there in seeking to prove an undeniable quality of God by appealing to the authority or experience of the church (Hodge, 1959, 304)? Verse 33a is universally true of God, not just in the churches and not as proven by the churches. Even though a similar clause concludes a paragraph in 11:16, that is insufficient warrant for climaxing so weighty a paragraph as this with such a self-evident truth.

To make the words a comparative analogy with verse 32 results in the sense, "It is universally true in all the churches that prophets have the ability to control their gifts." Against this mode of connection, however, is the necessity it entails of making verse 33a with its weighty character, a mere parenthetical insertion. If the *hōs* clause is made a comparative analogy with verse 31b, the sense becomes, "church-wide instruction and encouragement are practiced in all the churches." Yet verse 31b is even more remote than verse 32, and there is very little likelihood that verses 32–33a are parenthetical.

Since none of the possible connections with the previous context yields a satisfactory meaning, the *hōs* clause must go with what follows in verse 34, necessitating a period after *eirēnēs* and a comma after *hagiōn*. The sense becomes, "Let the women keep silent in the assemblies, as is the universal practice in all the churches" (Hodge, 1959, 304; Meyer, 1881, 2:30–31; Carson, 1987, 122). A similar phrase in 11:16 has dealt with women's deportment, and an additional word regarding a universal custom of women occurs there. Custom elsewhere is further highlighted at the conclusion of this same paragraph (v. 36) (Godet, 1886, 2:309). Objection that this connection renders *en tais ekkiēsiais* in verse 34 superfluous (Barrett, 1968, 330) is weak because of different usages of *ekkiēsiais* in the two places. In verse 33, the noun depicts local groups of believers, whereas in verse 34 it refers to actual worship sessions (Godet, 1886, 2:309–10). It is true that Paul rarely begins a new paragraph with a dependent (comparative) clause. More commonly he places a vocative such as *hai gynaikes* ("the women") (v. 34) first (cf. Eph. 5:22, 25; 6:1, 5; Col. 3:18–22) (Robertson and Plummer, 1914, 324). Yet, sufficient factors are present here to justify differentiating this passage from his practice elsewhere. All in all, view 2 is most free from unanswerable objections such as beset all three alternatives of view 1.

29. (p. 115) Additional discussion of the five possible interpretations of *hai gynaikes en tais ekkiēsiais sigaōsan* ("Let the women keep silent in the churches") confirms the preference for the fifth alternative. Fee's proposal that verses 34–35 were not authentic parts of the original text (Fee, 1987, 699–705) is beyond question ill-advised because of the overwhelming manuscript evidence that places the verses in the text at this point (Carson, 1987, 124). That

support is so strong that Fee has to base his whole case on internal evidence alternative 5 below shows to be quite insufficient.

1. To limit the restriction to only certain occasions when women were not allowed to speak in the assembly implies that female participation became a problem only at Corinth and only at certain times. Because of local abuse, Paul had to impose on the Corinthian women this especially stringent limitation, it is argued. The assumption is that the guideline did not apply except in cases of abuse. First Corinthians 11:5–6 indicates that women did participate vocally even at Corinth, with even Paul's approval to do so. Their possession of vocal spiritual gifts (Acts 2:17; 21:9) also argues for their participation. Where else could they use them if not in a local assembly? Occasions of sudden revelation to a prophetess supposedly were justification for her to speak in exception to her normal practice of silence (Godet, 1886, 2:116–17). This feminine privilege might have extended more widely, the view claims, had things not degenerated so radically in Corinthian worship (Barrett, 1968, 332–33). Because conditions were as they were, careful distinction had to be maintained between a preaching woman and one who was merely a member of the congregation (Hering, 1962, 154). As persuasive as this logic may be, it is insufficient to overrule the universal applicability stated so specifically in 14:33b and 14:36. Female participation had become an issue elsewhere (e.g., at Ephesus, 1 Tim. 2:8–15), and what Paul was requiring of the Corinthians was no different from what he required of other churches. Because of the excesses of Corinthian abuse, he conceded a manner of dress appropriate if the women insisted on speaking in defiance of his warning (Parry, 1916, 210–11). He would have preferred their public speaking ministry to be limited to groups composed only of women and/or children, however (cf. Titus 2:3–5). The fact that his first choice was their complete abstinence from any kind of speech is evident from his restriction even upon their asking questions in public (14:35).

2. To limit the restriction of verse 34 to utterances by way of tongues or prophecy has a persuasive ring in light of chapter 14's exclusive attention to these two gifts (Metz, 1968, 454). It comes to the point that *laleō* ("to speak") in this setting (cf. *lalein*, v. 34) almost assumes a technical idea of "speaking by inspiration." Only the authority implied by these two gifts is in violation of the female status of submission (cf. *hypotassesthēsan*, "let them subject themselves," 14:34b). The impressiveness of this interpretation fades, however, in comparison with verse 35. It is not just to a certain type of inspired utterance that the restriction applies. Women were denied even the privilege of asking questions in public meeting and had to control their curiosities until they were at home with their husbands.

3. A third understanding of 14:34 comes by giving special attention to concepts of authority and submission found in 1 Corinthians 11:10 and 14:34–35 (Hommes, 1969, 5–22). According to this understanding, the limitation of 14:34 is applicable to any type of speaking whereby a woman might assume an authoritative role in the local assembly. Paul prescribes two remedies for female speech of this character. (a) She may refrain from speaking entirely (14:34); or (b) she may proceed to speak by wearing a covering to symbolize her submission while speaking. A similar emphasis addressed to another church is found in 1 Timothy 2:11–12. The obstacle to adopting this interpretation is careful attention to what chapters 11 and 14 do and do not say. What they do not describe are two ways of stopping women from becoming authoritarian figures in the local assembly. What they do deal with is a woman's proper apparel if she speaks in the local assembly (chapter 11), and the universal principle in all the churches of not allowing vocal participation by women (chapter 14).

4. The fourth alternative has Paul restricting women from giving spoken criticisms of

prophecies uttered in a church service (Grudem, 1988, 220–25; Kistemaker, 1993, 512). They were allowed to form opinions in their own minds, but were not allowed to voice them in the assembled congregation. The effort to support this view tries to derive a contextual argument that says, "Let the others [that is, the rest of the congregation] weigh what is said [by the prophets . . . but] the women should keep silence in the churches" (Grudem, 1988, 220–21). The major problem with this view is the contextual improbability that Paul would still be talking about evaluating prophecy five verses after he has concluded that subject. Verses 30–33 intervene between that discussion and his beginning to talk about the roles of women, the subject of the intervening verses having to do with orderliness in worship and not confusion. Another problem with the view is its understanding of "the others" in v. 29 to speak of the whole congregation rather than just the prophets, as the context of that verse requires (see discussion of that point at v. 29).

5. The fifth alternative is that Paul was laying down a blanket principle to govern all situations. Any other regulations apparently to the contrary must be adjusted in light of that principle. First Corinthians 11:5–6 does not grant women the right to prophesy and pray in the assembly, but says that if a woman insists on speaking in spite of the rule of 14:34–35, she should clothe herself in a certain manner. The earlier context of Corinthians deals with dress, not with the propriety of women's speaking in church. As difficult as this position is to apply, it is the one that accords best with the plain sense of 14:34. It also aligns well with Paul's viewpoint as known from his other writings (1 Tim. 2:11–15). Certainly, if Paul denies women the right to ask questions (14:35), he also denies them the right to speak on a more formal basis (Godet, 1886, 2:312; Mare, 1976, 276–77). Paul sometimes withdraws his apparent permission to engage in a certain practice later in the same writing after he has laid more groundwork (cf. 1 Cor. 6:4, 7; 8:10; 10:21–22), as seems to be the case in this instance (Godet, 1886, 2:116). The reasons supporting this regulation are unrelated to a local Corinthians problem, but go far deeper, growing out of teaching from the law of Moses (14:34b) and the general convention of antiquity (14:35b) (Hodge, 1959, 305).

With the addition of the universal emphasis of 14:33b and 14:36, it is inescapable that Paul intended 14:34 as an absolute rule. Yet, if the Corinthians were not ready to accept the ideal, he provided them with a less desirable substitute in 11:5–6.

Chapter 6 (Page number following note number tells where the note appears)

1. (p. 119) A more general sense for *pneumatikos* ("spiritual") in 14:37 is conceivable. With such a connotation, a spiritual person possessing any one or more of the spiritual gifts alluded to in chapters 12–14 is in view. That meaning results from giving the conjunction *ē* (v. 37) the sense of "or in general." Hence, a *pneumatikos* may even have been a *prophētēs* (v. 37). This explanation clearly matches most closely with the meaning of *pneumatikos* in its other, nearby uses (cf. 1 Cor. 12:1; 14:1). Nowhere else is it limited to just one gift (Parry, 1916, 211). The same may be said regarding the meaning of *pneuma*, the cognate noun, in 14:12 (cf. 1 Thess. 5:19) (Schweizer in *TDNT*, 1968, 6:423).

The necessity of seeing *pneumatikos* always in a general sense is questionable, however. Earlier discussion has shown the probability of limiting *pneuma* to just one gift, the gift of tongues (14:2, 14, 15) or the gift of prophecy (14:32). If the present context justifies a similar limitation for *pneumatikos*, such a meaning in verse 37 is quite viable. In order to correlate the substantive *pneumatikos* with *prophētēs* in 14:37, it is best to limit it to one spiritual gift, the one that along with prophecy has been so prominent throughout chapter 14. That provides a more natural function for $\bar{e}$ (cf. $\bar{e}$, with its exclusive sense in 14:36), that is, to separate the expressions it connects. It is safe to conclude that the Corinthians, in light of their pagan background and in light of Paul's present evaluation of their condition, were predisposed to view the gift of tongues as the spiritual gift *par excellence.* Here, therefore, Paul ironically concedes their evaluation of the gift (Behm in *TDNT,* 1964, 1:724). He poses *pneumatikos* as the epitome of *pneumatika* (cf. 14:1). Such a tone of biting sarcasm is a fitting continuation of the sharpness of verse 36. Tongues have been the only prominent gift aside from prophecy, a prominence appearing again two verses later (14:39).

Furthermore, a comparison of the hypothesis of 14:37 with the principle that every Christian is a gifted part of Christ's body (cf. 12:7, 11) reflects that Paul had no reason to speak hypothetically unless he was giving *pneumatikos* a restricted meaning. The term's general meaning, including all gifts, leaves no room for doubt about any Christian's being a "spiritual person." Every Christian is a spiritual person by virtue of his endowment with at least one spiritual gift (cf. *hekastō* ["to each one"], 12:7, and *idia hekastō* ["to each one individually"], 12:11). So then, *pneumatikos* is Paul's way of referring ironically to the tongues speaker. This is his sarcastic concession to those who considered this the highest of all gifts.

2. (p. 120) The choice between *agnoeitai* (Nestle-Aland text) and *agnoeitō* (*Textus Receptus*) in 14:38 substantially affects the verse's meaning. With the indicative *agnoeitai* ("he is not recognized"), a person so characterized is not known by God and hence is to be ignored by the church. Such ostracism is appropriate treatment in return for his failure to recognize God's authoritative representative (cf. v. 37). To read the imperative *agnoeitō* carries with it the threat of perdition. Refusal of apostolic authority renders hopeless the condition of such a rejecter. He is so puffed up that he has become unreachable. The imperative reading is supported by two early manuscripts (*Chester Beatty* and *Vaticanus*), but geographically, support for such a reading is not widespread until the fifth century and later. The reading's origin is easy to explain as conforming to other imperatives in the immediate context (14:37, 39, 40), but it is extremely problematic in that it amounts to pronouncing anathema on persons who disputed Paul's apostolic authority. Such quick transitions—from sarcasm in verses 36–37 to a strong denunciation in verse 38, and then to more gentle commands in verses 39–40—are too harsh to be probable.

On the other hand, the indicative reading has respectable early and widespread support (*Sinaiticus, Alexandrinus, Old Latin, Palestinian Syriac,* and *Coptic*) (Metzger, 1971, 566). The reading is also plausible on internal grounds: for the writer to alternate between active and passive verbs is unusual, but not unprecedented (cf. 1 Cor. 8:2–3). A direct meaning is also obtained through the indicative, one that is at first difficult to discern but after reflection adequately satisfies contextual considerations. Paul does not venture to say that a person who is not recognized is not among God's elect. In this context, the statement means that he is not recognized as a prophet or spiritual person for purposes of participation in public meetings. If he does not know with certainty the authoritative nature of Paul's writings (14:37), he forfeits his right to have a speaking part in the church's services.

Appendix A (See pages 123–32)

1. Robert L. Thomas, "Tongues ... Will Cease," *JETS* 17/2 (spring 1974): 85–89; cf. idem, *Understanding Spiritual Gifts* (Chicago: Moody Press, 1978), 106–13, 199–204.

2. E.g., see note 31.

3. Wayne A. Grudem ("The New Testament Gift of Prophecy: A Response to My Friends" [paper presented to the Forty-fourth Annual Meeting of the Evangelical Theological

Society in San Francisco, November 21, 1992], 18) has called 1 Corinthians 13:10 an "im-movable stumbling block" for the view that the gift of prophecy has ceased.

4. F. David Farnell, "When Will the Gift of Prophecy Cease?" *Bibliotheca Sacra* 150 (April-June 1993): 191–93. In his defense of view (5), Farnell agrees with the position advo-cated in the present discussion.

5. Grudem ("Response," 15) continually injects the qualitative notion as the meaning of *ek merous* (13:10): "This . . . [is a statement] about the imperfect nature of our activity of prophesying" ("Response," 17) and "He states quite clearly that these imperfect gifts will last until the time of Christ's return" ("Response," 18). On the contrary, *ek merous* speaks of the gifts' partial nature, not their imperfection in quality. Grudem is in conflict with himself at this point. In 1982, he wrote that the phrase refers to quantitative rather than qualitative imperfection (Wayne A. Grudem, *The Gift of Prophecy in 1 Corinthians* [Washington, D.C.: University Press of America, 1982], 148–49 n. 59). Now in speaking of the same phrase as referring to "the imperfect *nature*" [italics added] ("Response," 17; cf. also 17 n. 24), he unfor-tunately appears to have switched to a qualitative sense for the same phrase.

6. *Webster's Ninth New Collegiate Dictionary*, 872.

7. Gerhard Delling, "*telos, teleō, k.t.l.*," *Theological Dictionary of the New Testament*, 8:77.

8. Ibid., 8:69–72.

9. R. Schippers, "*telos*," *New International Dictionary of New Testament Theology*, 2:62.

10. In Colossians 4:12 *teleioi* is "a term evidently chosen to counteract the Gnostic aspi-ration to 'perfection' by their regimen and cult" (Ralph Martin, "Colossians and Philemon," in *New Century Bible* [Grand Rapids, 1973], 134).

11. Grudem erroneously uses Matthew 5:48 and Romans 12:2 to illustrate the meaning of "perfect" for *teleios* ("Response," 14–15). "Complete" is a better English word for those two passages because the concept behind *teleios* is the Hebrew *tāmîm* or *šālôm*, "wholeness," not the philosophical connotation of perfection in a qualitative or ultimate sense as the word "perfect" implies (Delling, "*telos*," 8:74, 76–77).

12. Delling, "*telos*," 8:75.

13. Delling, "*telos*," 8:76. Oepke notes the concept behind childhood in ancient times: "Antiquity primarily sees in the child the element of immaturity or childishness" (Albrecht Oepke, "*pais, paidion, k.t.l.*," *Theological Dictionary of the New Testament [TDNT]*, 5:642). The opposite of this state is maturity. *Nēpios* was used for small children between the ages of 1 and 10 (Georg Bertram, "*teleios anēr, nēpiazō*," *TDNT*, 4:912). The goal of human develop-ment was *teleios anēr*. As the adult sets aside the nature of a child, so the Christian with the coming of *to teleion* sets aside the *gnōsis* essential during the stage of the *nēpios* (ibid., 919). *Anēr* indicates an adult man as distinct from a boy (Albrecht Oepke, "*anēr, andrizomai*," *TDNT*, 1:361, 363).

14. Robert L. Reymond, *What about Continuing Revelations and Miracles in the Pres-byterian Church Today* (Phillipsburg, N.J.: Presbyterian and Reformed, 1977), 31–36, and Walter J. Chantry, *Signs of the Apostles, Observations on Pentecostalism Old and New* (Edinburgh: Banner of Truth, 1976), 50–54, capture the overlapping meaning of *teleios* but weaken their position by a refusal to apply 13:12 to the situation following the parousia. John R. McRay, "*To Teleion* in I Corinthians 13:10," *Restoration Quarterly* 14 (1971): 172–74, also notes the twin meanings of the term, but concludes that 1 Corinthians 12–14 must be ex-plained on the basis of the entire argument of Ephesians, particularly the Jewish-Gentile issue prominent in that book (174–83). Reymond and Chantry refer verse 12 to the comple-tion of the New Testament canon, but McRay refers it to the final stages of Paul's work among the Gentiles (183). Both positions differ from that defended in the present study.

ENDNOTES

15. Archibald Robertson and Alfred Plummer, *A Critical and Exegetical Commentary on the First Epistle of Paul to the Corinthians*, 2d ed. (Edinburgh: T. & T. Clark, 1914), 297–98; Thomas Charles Edwards, *A Commentary on the First Epistle to the Corinthians* (London: Hodder and Stoughton, 1885), 349.

16. "In Eph 4:13 . . . the *teleios anēr* is the adult . . . in contrast to the *nēpios* of v. 14" (Gerhard Delling, "*plērēs, pleroō*," *Theological Dictionary of the New Testament*, 6:302).

17. Du Plessis notes that *teleios* in Ephesians 4:13 is characterized in three ways: (1) Growth is involved. A body-building process or a dynamic development transpires throughout the period of the church's existence. (2) The dynamic is corporate in nature. Though composed of many members, the body of Christ grows as a unit. (3) Since the image of *teleios* is in the character of an exhortation, it is maturity progressively realized in the present state of the church's existence (Paul Johannes Du Plessis, *TELEIOS, The Idea of Perfection in the N. T.* [Kampen: J. H. Kok, 1956], 188–93).

18. Robertson and Plummer, *1 Corinthians*, 297.

19. A. T. Robertson, *A Grammar of the Greek New Testament in the Light of Historical Research* (Nashville: Broadman, 1934), 900, 971.

20. Thomas, "Tongues . . . Will Cease," 85. In fact, in verse 12 he refers to himself personally (i.e., in the singular) as currently having only partial knowledge (*ginōskō*).

21. Farnell, "When . . . Cease?" 193.

22. Cf. Robertson, *Grammar*, 896.

23. Robertson and Plummer, *1 Corinthians*, 298; cf. Frederic L. Godet, *Commentary on St. Paul's First Epistle to the Corinthians*, 2 vols., Rev. A. Cusin, trans. (1957; reprint., Grand Rapids: Zondervan, 1986), 2:252.

24. Robertson and Plummer, *1 Corinthians*, 297.

25. The relevant quotations of Wayne Grudem and Gordon Fee from which these objections derive include the following:

1. "This view fails to recognize that vs. 11, which speaks of Paul in the first person and in the past, is merely an illustration, and our understanding of what it illustrates must conform to vs. 12, which speaks of believers generally ("we") and in the future ("shall know"). And only vs. 12 has *tote* which links it clearly to the *hotan* in vs. 10. Vs. 11 illustrates not the maturity of the church (an idea which is nowhere discussed in this context) but the fact that something complete or perfect replaces something incomplete or imperfect" (Grudem, *1 Corinthians*, 215 n. 60). "Whereas Christ's return is mentioned clearly in 1 Corinthians 13:12, no verse in this section mentions anything about the completion of Scripture . . . or the 'maturity' of the church (whatever that means—is the church really mature even today?). All of these suggestions [including the one about 'maturity'] bring in new elements not found in the context to replace one element—Christ's return—which clearly is right there in the context already" (Wayne A. Grudem, *The Gift of Prophecy in the New Testament and Today* [Westchester, Ill.: Crossway, 1988], 238–39).

2. "The precise reference of the word [*teleios*] must be determined by the individual context, and there, as we have seen, the context indicates that 'when the perfect comes' refers to the time of Christ's return" (Grudem, *New Testament*, 236).

3. "Such views [i.e., those that see 'when the perfect comes' as some time before Christ returns] all seem to break down at 1 Corinthians 13:12, where Paul implies that believers will see God 'face to face' 'when the perfect is come'" (Grudem, *New Testament*, 238).

4. "This view has nothing to commend it except the analogy of v. 11, which is a misguided emphasis at best" (Gordon D. Fee, *The First Epistle to the Corinthians* [Grand Rapids: Eerdmans, 1987], 645 n. 23).

5. "Even though Paul says 'we know in part,' the emphasis is not on the immaturity of the Corinthians, but on the relative nature of the gifts" (Fee, *1 Corinthians*, 645 n. 24).

26. Grudem, *1 Corinthians*, 215 n. 60; Fee, *1 Corinthians*, 644–45 nn. 23, 25.

27. Fee, *1 Corinthians*, 645.

28. Grudem, *1 Corinthians*, 215 n. 60; cf. also idem, "Response," 15.

29. Grudem, *New Testament*, 238–39; Fee, *1 Corinthians*, 645; cf. also Grudem, "Response," 14.

30. First Corinthians 12:12: "For just as the body is *one* and has *many members*, and *all the members* of the body though they are *many* are *one* body, so also is Christ." First Corinthians 12:27: "Now you are [such a thing as the] *body* [an anarthrous collective term] of Christ and *members individually*." Ephesians 4:13–14: "until *we all* attain to the unity of the faith and of the full knowledge of the Son of God, to a mature *man*, to the measure of the stature of the fulness of Christ, that *we* may be no longer children, tossed about and carried around by every wind of doctrine through the trickery of men in craftiness to the deceit of error...." [italics added]

31. Fee, *1 Corinthians*, 644–55, whose criticism of the mature-body view is off-target when he says that the contrast between immaturity and maturity "will not do since the contrast has to do with the *gifts*' being 'partial,' not with the believers themselves."

32. Grudem, *New Testament*, 238–39.

33. Contra Grudem, *New Testament*, 238.

34. Grudem, *New Testament*, 236, 238.

35. Ibid.; Fee, *1 Corinthians*, 645 nn. 23, 25.

36. E.g., "the ambiguity of the first analogy [childhood and adulthood]," Fee, *1 Corinthians*, 644.

37. Cf. Appendix C, "The Spiritual Gift of Prophecy in Rev 22:18."

38. C. K. Barrett, *A Commentary on the First Epistle to the Corinthians*, Harper New Testament Commentary (New York: Harper & Row, 1968), 306.

39. Grudem's proposed single contrast—"when Christ returns, prophesy will cease" ("Response," 18)—is too simplistic to account for all the exegetical data of the passage.

Appendix B (See pages 133–42)

1. Westchester, Ill.: Crossway, 1988.

2. Michael G. Maudlin, "Seers in the Heartland," *Christianity Today* (January 14, 1991): 20.

3. Ibid.

4. The essential contents of the Ph.D. dissertation with some additions were published as *The Gift of Prophecy in 1 Corinthians* (Washington, D. C.: University Press of America, 1982). The present review focuses primarily on the 1988 publication.

5. Saucy and Gentry mention other endorsements of Grudem's work (Robert L. Saucy, "Prophecy Today? An Initial Response," *Sundoulos* [spring 1990]: 1, and Kenneth L. Gentry Jr., *The Charismatic Gift of Prophecy*, 2d ed. [Memphis, Tenn.: Footstool, 1989], iii).

6. Grudem, *Gift of Prophecy in the New Testament and Today*, 206.

7. Ibid., 206–8.

8. Ibid., 184–86.

9. Ibid., 162–64.

10. Ibid., 137–38.

11. Ibid., 156–58.

12. Ibid., 149–53.

13. Ibid., 229.

14. Apparently Grudem defines prophecy as "an unreliable human speech act in response to a revelation from the Holy Spirit" (ibid., 95). In the absence of an explicit definition, one must piece together Grudem's concept of the gift. By contrast, the gift of prophecy properly perceived is "speech directly inspired by the Spirit of God and therefore fully authoritative" (Saucy, "Prophecy Today? An Initial Response," 5).

15. Grudem refers to his approach as "my *somewhat new* definition of the nature of Christian prophecy" (*Gift of Prophecy in 1 Corinthians*, xv, emphasis added).

16. Grudem, *Gift of Prophecy in the New Testament and Today*, 108–9, 112, 241–42. For an overview of prophecy's termination after the apostolic era, see Appendix C, 143–53.

17. Grudem, *Gift of Prophecy in the New Testament and Today*, 108.

18. Ibid., 32.

19. Ibid., 67–68, 199–200, 209.

20. Ibid., 145.

21. Ibid., 154; cf. 168.

22. Ibid., 156–57, 168.

23. Ibid., 144–45.

24. Ibid., 169.

25. Ibid., 153–54, 168.

26. Ibid., 145.

27. Ibid., 80–81, 250.

28. Ibid., 144–45, 167.

29. Ibid., 116–17.

30. Ibid., 81–82, 100. The thought of the human tendency to fail to communicate an accurate picture of what has been received from God is strongly reminiscent of the crisis theology of Karl Barth and Emil Brunner that so captivated much of professing Christendom during the middle decades of the twentieth century. The system held to the belief that once the crisis point of God's communication to an individual had passed, any attempt by the individual to share it with others degenerated into a distorted recollection composed of something like "merely human words" (ibid., 80, 82, 86–87, 90, 95, 99, 112–13, 165). Yet, Grudem with his insistence on biblical inerrancy and the sufficiency of Scripture would certainly be unwilling to associate himself with the neo-orthodoxy of Barth and Brunner.

At stake here is the ability of an omnipotent God to transmit to mankind an accurate account of what He reveals. After all, what good is a revelation if it is distorted in transmission and has to be sifted by human judgment before it is useful? Borrowing from the terminology of Grudem's book, someone could suggest that the book's whole scheme of prophecy, if it originated with a revelation from God, has become terribly twisted in the process of being reported to others.

Unfortunately, D. A. Carson (*Showing the Spirit* [Grand Rapids: Baker, 1987], 93–100, 160–65) and C. Samuel Storms ("A Third Wave View," in *Are Miraculous Gifts for Today? Four Views*, ed. Wayne A. Grudem [Grand Rapids: Zondervan, 1996], 207–12) concur with Grudem in his "neo-orthodox" view of divine revelation through the gift of prophecy.

31. Ibid., 63. In his earlier work, Grudem said there were two distinct gifts (*Gift of Prophecy in 1 Corinthians*, 3–5, 110–13), but he attributes that to his need to conform to scholarly terminology and has modified his terminology in his later work by postulating one gift of two distinct types—authoritative and nonauthoritative.

32. Grudem, *Gift of Prophecy in the New Testament and Today*, 63–64, 160. Though Grudem generally views apostolic prophecy as authoritative, he apparently sees Paul's use of it in 1 Corinthians 13:8–13 as nonauthoritative (ibid., 121–23, 230). Since Paul included himself with his use of the first person plural in this discussion about prophecy's nonauthoritative

nature, he made himself a nonauthoritative prophet, says Grudem. That contradicts the author's representation of apostolic prophecy elsewhere.

33. Ibid., 275–76.

34. Ibid., 251–52, 331 n. 143.

35. Ibid., 234–35.

36. Grudem has a brief word about *teleios* (*Gift of Prophecy in 1 Corinthians*, 213, with n. 58), but he does not explore the limitations imposed on the word by New Testament usage. For a fuller discussion of this point, see *Theological Dictionary of the New Testament*, s.v. "*teleios*," by Gerhard Delling, 8:69–77; Robert L. Thomas, "Tongues . . . Will Cease," *Journal of the Evangelical Theological Society* 17 (spring 1974): 83–85; and the earlier exposition (78–83) and Appendix A (123–32) of this work.

37. Grudem grants passing notice to the "maturity" view (*Gift of Prophecy in the New Testament and Today*, 236), but does not treat it in detail (ibid., 238). In his earlier work, he refers to that view but dismisses it with the comment that the maturity of the church appears nowhere in the context (*Gift of Prophecy in 1 Corinthians*, 215 n. 60). In fact, he does not state the view correctly. The view builds on the figurative concept of the maturing of *the body* of Christ (Thomas, "Tongues . . . Will Cease," 85–89), not the maturing of *the church* literally, as he states it. The body of Christ is most assuredly in the context (1 Cor. 12:12–27) as is a reference to the maturity of individual members of that body (14:20). Paul's major challenge in 1 Corinthians 12–14 was for the Corinthians to build up or edify that body (12:7; 14:3–5, 12, 26). In the companion passage of Ephesians 4:1–16, written a short time later by Paul to the city where he lived while writing 1 Corinthians, the edification of this body through spiritual gifts is tantamount to contributing to its corporate maturity (Eph. 4:13, 16; cf. the earlier exposition in this work, 79, 126–27).

38. Grudem, *Gift of Prophecy in the New Testament and Today*, 171–82. *Sēmeion* in the New Testament most frequently is in association with "miracles, signs, and wonders" that served as credentials for divine spokesmen (Donald W. Burdick, *Tongues: To Speak or Not to Speak* [Chicago: Moody Press, 1969], 26–31). Grudem considers only *abused* tongues as a sign, and that to signify God's disfavor. However, the text does not say abused tongues are a sign. It says tongues are a sign. This reviewer has written elsewhere on 1 Corinthians 14:20–25 as follows: "After a discussion of the impropriety of uninterpreted tongues, clarification of the proper surroundings and purpose of this gift is next in order. A mature Christian outlook recognized tongues to be designed for unbelievers rather than believers. Conversely, prophecy had its function among believers, not unbelievers. Even an unbelieving visitor in Christian worship, with no experience in tongues, could verify this fact. He could certify the propriety of prophecy, not tongues, for a believing audience. Tongues provided a sign such as was needed where non-Christians listened, but such an evidential mark was superfluous among Christians" (earlier exposition of this work, 15; see 101–7 for a more detailed explanation of 1 Cor. 14:20–25).

39. Grudem is usually careful to use an expression such as "less authoritative" to describe prophecy (e.g., *Gift of Prophecy in the New Testament and Today*, 86, 108, 110). In effect, this means nonauthoritative, however. It requires no obedience by the recipients (e.g., ibid.), the prophecy has no authority. At one point, he validates this equation (in the expression "non-divinely authoritative nature of prophecy," ibid., 250).

40. Ibid., 46–47.

41. Ibid., 55–56.

42. Ibid., 49–57.

43. Ibid., 49–51. For a refutation of Grudem's interpretation of Ephesians 2:20 from a grammatical perspective, see F. David Farnell's excellent discussion in "Fallible New Testament Prophecy/Prophets?" *The Master's Seminary Journal* 2 (fall 1991): 162–69, and Thomas R. Edgar,

Satisfied by the Promise of the Spirit (Grand Rapids: Kregel, 1996), 76–79. In his research on this subject, Grudem had the advantage of expert guidance by a widely recognized grammatical authority, C. F. D. Moule (referred to in *Gift of Prophecy in 1 Corinthians*, xvi), but apparently he chose to disregard Moule's counsel on this grammatical point (cf. C. F. D. Moule, *An Idiom Book of New Testament Greek* [Cambridge: Cambridge University Press, 1960], 110).

44.   Charles Hodge, *A Commentary on the Epistle to the Ephesians* (1856; reprint, Grand Rapids: Baker, 1980), 149; F. F. Bruce, *The Epistles to the Colossians, to Philemon, and to the Ephesians* (Grand Rapids: Eerdmans, 1984), 315 n. 29. Grudem's later rebuttal of the evidence in Ephesians 4:11 acknowledges that prophets are separate from apostles, but he says these prophets were different from the ones in 2:20 (*Gift of Prophecy in the New Testament and Today*, 59). That conclusion is arbitrary and exegetically invalid, for nothing in the intervening verses reflects a shift in meaning to a second group of prophets (see also Gentry, *Charismatic Gift of Prophecy*, 30–31).

45.   John R. W. Stott, *God's New Society: The Message of Ephesians* (Downers Grove, Ill.: InterVarsity, 1979), 107; Richard B. Gaffin Jr., "A Cessationist View," in *Are Miraculous Gifts for Today? Four Views*, ed. Wayne A. Grudem (Grand Rapids: Zondervan, 1996), 43–44; Robert L. Saucy, "Open But Cautious," in *Are Miraculous Gifts for Today? Four Views*, ed. Wayne A. Grudem (Grand Rapids: Zondervan, 1996), 111–12.

46.   Grudem, *Gift of Prophecy in the New Testament and Today*, 51–54.

47.   Ibid., 286.

48.   Ibid., 287.

49.   Also see Gentry, *Charismatic Gift of Prophecy*, 33. Grudem comes close to admitting the authority of Luke's writings, but attributes it to Luke's close association with Paul (*Gift of Prophecy in the New Testament and Today*, 329 n. 130). His suggestion, however, dodges the central point that nonapostle Luke, not Paul, was the human instrument responsible for the authoritative revelatory content of Luke and Acts. (See Appendix D of this work, "Correlation of Revelatory Spiritual Gifts and New Testament Canonicity," for more discussion of the gift of prophecy as a means for transmitting inspired words of Scripture.)

50.   Grudem, *Gift of Prophecy in the New Testament and Today*, 62–63.

51.   The prophetic nature of the last book of the Bible is a formidable obstacle to Grudem's effort to prove the existence of nonauthoritative prophecy. If prophecy is nonauthoritative, as Grudem suggests, how can the Book of Revelation, which claims to be prophecy, have authority? He attempts to overcome the obstacle by claiming that the book's authority rests on *apostolic* prophecy (ibid., 43–45). Yet, the author of Revelation never alludes to apostolic authority. From beginning to end, the binding doctrinal and ethical standards John presented rest on the book's self-claim of being a prophecy (e.g., Rev. 1:3; 22:18–19). That is the basis of its authoritative principles. This book has divine authority not because it was written by an apostle but explicitly because it is prophecy.

52.   Ibid., 96–100.

53.   Ibid. 100–102.

54.   Gentry, *Charismatic Gift of Prophecy*, 43.

55.   See also Robert L. Thomas, *Exegetical Digest of 1 Corinthians 12–14* (Sun Valley, Calif.: by the author, 1988), which deals more directly with the Greek text.

56.   Contra Grudem, *Gift of Prophecy in the New Testament and Today*, 70–71.

57.   Contra ibid., 72–73.

58.   Contra ibid., 73–79.

59.   Contra ibid., 78.

60.   Saucy states an appropriate corrective to Grudem regarding the gift of discernment: "The discrimination deals not with the level of prophetic authority, but with the separation of prophecy from that which is not prophecy" ("Prophecy Today? An Initial Response," 3).

61. Contra Grudem, *Gift of Prophecy in the New Testament and Today,* 74, 76–80, 121. Grudem cites a situation in which teaching or preaching could be interspersed with prophecy (ibid., 143, 257). If the former was authoritative, as he asserts it is, and the latter is nonauthoritative, this raises the puzzling challenge of how to recognize which parts of a message require obedience and which do not.

62. Contra ibid., 81–83. In Appendix C of Grudem's 1988 work, "subjective impressions" are apparently a substitute for "divine revelations" the author speaks about elsewhere (ibid., 301, 330 n. 141). This points out a basic error of the work, that of using the words "divine revelation" to refer to what the New Testament calls the leading of the Spirit in a Christian's life (Rom. 8:14). At another point, Grudem seems willing for the sake of compromise to use "illumination" instead of "revelation," though he insists that New Testament usage supports the revelatory terminology (ibid., 249; cf. 133, 170).

63. Contra ibid., 167.

64. Contra ibid., 68–69, 209–10.

65. Contra ibid., 325 n. 99.

66. Contra ibid., 228–33.

67. For lists of elements or characteristics of New Testament prophecy with accompanying documentation see Appendix C, 143–44, and Robert L. Thomas, *Revelation 1–7: An Exegetical Commentary* (Chicago: Moody Press, 1992), 25–29.

68. Saucy shows the defect of Grudem's attempt to distinguish between Old Testament and New Testament prophets and to equate Old Testament prophets with New Testament apostles ("Prophecy Today? An Initial Response," 2–3).

69. See Appendix C of this volume. Grudem concedes the applicability of Revelation 22:18–19 to the closing of the New Testament canon (*Gift of Prophecy in the New Testament and Today,* 290–91), but he does not mention the obvious correlation of the gift of prophecy with the inspiration of the books of that canon. Revelation 22:18–19 speaks of the termination of prophecy and all inspired utterances and writings given through it for the body of Christ.

70. Grudem's cessationist stance regarding the gift of apostleship and his noncessationist stance regarding other revelatory gifts with their confirming signs reflects his middle-of-the-road approach to spiritual gifts. As noted above, that is one of the conflicting elements in his view.

71. Ibid., 14.

72. Ibid., 249 [emphasis added]. Also see his remarks on pages 14–15. Grudem wrote, "But even though I do not agree fully with either group, I hope that in my somewhat new definition of the nature of Christian prophecy both pro-charismatics and anti-charismatics may be able to find a 'middle ground' with a considerable potential for reconciling their current differences" (*Gift of Prophecy in 1 Corinthians,* xv).

Appendix C (See pages 143–53)

1. Some examples of these definitions are of interest. M. E. Boring's definition: "A prophet is an immediately inspired spokesman for the (or a) deity of a particular community, who receives revelations which he is impelled to deliver to the community" ("'What Are We Looking for?' Toward a Definition of the Term 'Christian Prophet,'" SBLASP [Missoula, Mont.: Scholar's, 1973], 2. 43–44). He more specifically limits his definition to a Christian prophet by saying that he is "a Christian who functions within the Church as an immediately inspired spokesman for the exalted Jesus, who receives intelligible revelations which he is impelled to deliver to the Christian community" (p. 44). Regarding the Christian prophet,

D. Aune says, "The Christian who functions in the prophetic role (whether regularly, occasionally or temporarily) believes that he receives divine revelations in propositional form which he customarily delivers in oral or written form to Christian individuals and or groups" (cited by Boring, 58). J. Lindblom says prophets "are inspired personalities who have the power to receive divine revelations. They act as speakers and preachers who announce what they have to say" (*Prophecy in Ancient Israel* [Philadelphia: Fortress, 1973], 6). D. Hill defines a Christian prophet in this way: "A Christian prophet is a Christian who functions within the Church, occasionally or regularly, as a divinely called and divinely inspired speaker who receives intelligible and authoritative revelations or messages which he is impelled to deliver publicly, in oral or written form, to Christian individuals and or the Christian community" (*New Testament Prophecy* [Atlanta: John Knox, 1979], 8–9). G. Friedrich says that "primitive Christian prophecy is the inspired speech of charismatic preachers through whom God's plan of salvation for the world and the community and His will for the life of individual Christians are made known" (*"Prophētēs," TDNT*, 6:828).

2. Almost every source cites this feature as a prominent part of prophecy. Lindblom writes, "Common to all representatives of the prophetic type here depicted is the consciousness of having access to information of the world above and experiences originating in the divine world, from which ordinary men are excluded" (*Prophecy*, 32–33). Prophets in early Christian communities regarded themselves as spokesmen for an ultimate authority (D. E. Aune, *Prophecy in Early Christianity and the Ancient Mediterranean World* [Grand Rapids: Eerdmans, 1983], 204). Possession of a direct revelation from God was one thing that distinguished true prophecy from false prophecy (W. A. Grudem, *The Gift of Prophecy in I Corinthians* [Washington, D.C.: University Press of America, 1982], 142). Evidence for this characteristic of prophecy is readily available in the Apocalypse where prophets are a group whose special task is to mediate divine revelation to the churches (Rev. 22:6, 9; cf. 1:1; Aune, *Prophecy*, 206).

3. This is in line with the "forth-teller" etymology of the word *Prophētēs* (Krämer, *"Prophētēs," TDNT*, 6:783–784). That part of the two-part structure of present/future is easily illustrated in the sayings of Jesus (Aune, *Prophecy*, 188). The prophet gives God's call to repentance, which torments some (e.g., Rev. 11:3, 10), but which convicts others to turn to God (e.g., 1 Cor. 14:24–25; Friedrich, *"Prophētēs,"* 829). He is essentially a proclaimer of God's Word (ibid.). His *paraklēsis* results in the *oikodomē* of the Christian community (Hill, *Prophecy*, 141). In particular, the Apocalypse is a series of messages to bring consolation and exhortations (C. Brown, "Prophet," *New International Dictionary of New Testament Theology*, 2:88).

4. The prophet instructed the church regarding the meaning of Scripture and through revelations of the future (D. Hill, "Prophecy and Prophets in the Revelation of St. John," *NTS* 18 [1971–72]: 406). The prophetic gift should not be confused with that of the teacher, however. The ministry of prophets was more spontaneous, being based upon direct divine revelations. Teachers, on the other hand, preserved and interpreted Christian tradition, including relevant Old Testament passages, the sayings of Jesus, and traditional beliefs of earlier Christian teaching (Aune, *Prophecy*, 202).

5. This was the "foretelling'" part that is suggested by the *pro-* prefix but that was a later development in the evolution of the word's meaning (Krämer, *"Prophētēs,"* 783–84; Friedrich, *"Prophētēs,"* 832–33). This is chiefly the sense of the word in the Apocalypse, but Paul also predicted the future (e.g., Acts 20:22–23; 20:29; 27:22ff.; Rom. 11:25ff.; 1 Cor. 15:51ff.; 1 Thess. 4:13ff.; ibid., 840). Friedrich notes that in Paul exhortation is dominant in prophecy but that in the Apocalypse prediction is the main focus (ibid., 828–29; cf. Aune, *Prophecy*, 5). That, he says, puts John more in the category of Old Testament prophecy than in company with early Christian prophets. Aune disagrees with this appraisal (ibid., 6). The predictive element is one

of several features that C. Brown uses to relate Luke's understanding of the gift to Old Testament prophets too ("Prophet," 87). Hill observes that prediction is clearly not the main function of prophets in Acts (*Prophecy*, 108). The degree of prediction as compared to exhortation is probably not sufficient ground to remove any New Testament writer's idea of the gift from the realm of New Testament prophecy, however. Though he could predict the future, the New Testament prophet should not be confused with the *mantis*. This latter figure belonged strictly to a secular setting and discharged nothing of the hortatory function of a prophet.

6. Since they were spokesmen for God, they claimed no personal part in the communication they gave (Aune, *Prophecy*, 204), so it is inevitable that they possessed authority (Hill, *Prophecy*, 87). The limited nature of this authority is obvious. Utterances of New Testament prophets were in many cases challengeable in ways that those of an Old Testament prophet would never have been (cf. 1 Cor. 14:30; ibid., 135). This limitation may be missed if one takes the prophecies of Paul (1 Cor. 7:10; 14:37–38) and John (Rev. 22:18–19) as typical. Paul's absolute authority is clear throughout his writing (Hill, *Prophecy*, 114), and in the Apocalypse, John seemingly places himself into the category of the Old Testament prophets through such things as his inaugural vision (1:9–20), his use of symbolic acts (10:10), and his use of oracular formulas (chapters 2–3; Rendtorff, "*Prophētēs*," TDNT, 6:812; Friedrich, "*Prophētēs*," 849; Hill, *Prophecy*, 87–88). It must be recalled that Paul and John were also apostles, a fact that enabled them to write with a higher degree of authority. This was not possible for the nonapostolic New Testament prophet (ibid., 132).

7. In 1 Corinthians 14:29, Paul speaks of the need for some to evaluate whenever a prophet was speaking in the local assembly of that city. Though there is some disagreement about the identity of the discerners in the verse, the most probable answer is that "the others" referred to are the other prophets in the congregation (Friedrich, "*Prophētēs*," 855; Hill, *Prophecy*, 133; Aune, *Prophecy*, 196).

8. Friedrich, "*Prophētēs*," 842; E. E. Ellis, "The Role of the Christian Prophet in Acts," *Apostolic History and the Gospel*, W. W. Gasque and R. P. Martin, eds. (Grand Rapids: Eerdmans, 1970), 55. Such ability was widely regarded as a prophetic phenomenon by Jesus' contemporaries (cf. Mark 2:5, 8 par.; 9:33ff.; 10:21 par.; 12:15 par.; Luke 6:8; 9:47; 11:17; 19:5; Matt. 12:25 par.; John 2:24–25; 4:17ff.; Hill, *Prophecy*, 60). This ability was a distinctive part of the effectiveness of the gift for Paul (1 Cor. 14:24–25; Friedrich, "*Prophētēs*," 842).

9. Here is another trait it has in common with Old Testament prophecy. Agabus signified Paul's coming imprisonment this way (Acts 21:10–11). John swallows a small book (Rev. 10:8–11) and measures the temple with a reed (11:1; Friedrich, "*Prophētēs*," 849).

10. Hill, *Prophecy*, 90.

11. There had to be some kind of public communication of the revelation received. Without it the *apokalypsis* could not be characterized as prophecy (Grudem, *Gift*, 143–44). In spite of the importance attached to written prophecies such as the Apocalypse, most early Christian prophets appear to have delivered their messages orally (Hill, *Prophecy*, 93).

12. For the most part, the New Testament prophet did not follow stereotyped oracular formulas. A noteworthy exception here is the use of the *tade legei to pneuma to hagion* formula by Agabus and John (Hill, *Prophecy*, 107). Aside from this type of rare indicator, Christian prophecy had to be recognized on other grounds (Aune, *Prophecy*, 317).

13. Hill holds that the Christian prophet was always controlled by the Spirit (*Prophecy*, 90). This is doubtful, since the Corinthian prophets appear to have been anything but Spirit-filled. Yet, they were users or potential users of the gift.

14. Some might take issue with this, based on the list of Ephesians 4, but the parallels of Ephesians 4 with 1 Corinthians 12–14 and Romans 12:4 make more likely a grouping of the Ephesians list with ministries rather than offices (Hill, *Prophecy*, 138–39).

15. This point is debated (T. Callan, "Prophecy and Ecstasy in Greco-Roman Religion

and in I Corinthians," *NovT* 27 [1985]: 139), and how the term "ecstasy" is defined is not agreed upon. Nevertheless there was something different about the prophet's condition as he was receiving divine revelation (Friedrich, *"Prophētēs,"* 829).

16. The method of using the Old Testament was one that resembled the practice of the Qumran community in its *pesharim* (Aune, *Prophecy,* 252). The practice consisted of finding hidden or symbolic meanings that could be revealed only through an interpreter possessing divine insight (Hill, *Prophecy,* 91; Aune, *Prophecy,* 133). Paul illustrates this in his handling of Isaiah 59:20–21 and 27:9 in Romans 11:25–26 (Aune, *Prophecy,* 252). Aune feels this practice could have been followed by one with the gift of teaching also (ibid., 345–46), but that is doubtful.

17. Hill, *Prophecy,* 137. First Corinthians 13:8–13 makes this point, though the extent of the limited time is debated.

18. Friedrich, *"Prophētēs,"* 849.

19. Ibid.

20. Ibid. Another difference between Old Testament and New Testament prophecy lies in the absence of oracular formulas from the latter. None of those with the gift of prophecy attempted to pattern their prophecies after the Old Testament prophetic models (Aune, *Prophecy,* 130). Closely related to this is the failure of any collections of oracles to be preserved from the first century of Christian history. This is in "marked contrast to ancient Israelite prophecy and Greco-Roman oracular tradition" (ibid., 247).

21. Ibid., 230.

22. G. Mallone writes, "If the source of the preacher's sermon is the Word of God, then it can be said that he is fulfilling a prophetic function when he preaches" (*Those Controversial Gifts* [Downers Grove, Ill.: InterVarsity Press, 1983], 38).

23. E. Best, "Prophets and Preachers," *SJT* 12 (1959): 145.

24. Among the characteristics of prophecy that are missing from preaching is the direct revelation that is necessary for a speech to be prophetic. As Friedrich notes, "All prophecy rests on revelation, 1 C. 14:30. The prophet does not declare what he has taken from tradition or what he has thought up himself. He declares what has been revealed to him" (*"Prophētēs,"* 853). When it is noted that preaching includes teaching, Friedrich's further comment is relevant: "Whereas teachers expound Scripture, cherish the tradition about Jesus and explain the fundamentals of the catechism, the prophets, not bound by Scripture or tradition, speak to the congregation on the basis of revelations" (ibid., 854).

25. In contrast to the *mantis* who may have been in a state of rage, out of his senses, the prophet speaks while in control of himself (Peisker, "Prophet," *New International Dictionary of New Testament Theology,* 2:76). In some circles, the experience of a state of inspiration tended to pass on into a state of ecstasy that might even be accompanied by a foaming at the mouth (Lindblom, *Prophecy,* 6; Krämer, *"Prophētēs,"* 790). Yet, all ecstasy was not of this type (Friedrich, *"Prophētēs,"* 851).

26. Friedrich, *"Prophētēs,"* 851.

27. He received his revelation either through a possession trance according to which the Spirit took control of him or through a vision trance through which his soul left, as it were, his body to receive the revelation (Aune, *Prophecy,* 86). After the trance, he delivered his prophetic message. The frequent use of "I saw" indicates that prophecies were "secondary narrations of experiences which had occurred earlier" (ibid., 150).

28. Grudem, *Gift,* 110–13; idem, "Prophecy—Yes, But Teaching—No: Paul's Consistent Advocacy of Women's Participation Without Governing Authority," *JETS* 30/1 (1987): 11–13; D. A. Carson, *Showing the Spirit* (Grand Rapids: Baker, 1987), 94–100, 160–65.

29. Grudem, *Gift,* 73–74; idem, "Prophecy—Yes," 12–15.

30. Such places use "clusters" of technical terms that speak of direct divine communication

to the prophetic instrument. The same clusters appear in both passages (e.g., *prophēteuō* and *prophētēs* —1 Cor. 12:28–29; 13:9; 14:1–6, 24, 29, 31–32, 37, 39 = Eph. 2:20; 3:5: *oikodomē* and *oikodomeō*— 1 Cor. 14:3–5, 12, 17, 26 = Eph. 2:20–21; *mystēria*—1 Cor. 13:2; 14.2 = Eph. 3:3–4, 9; *apokalypsis* and *apokalyptō*—1 Cor. 14:6, 26, 30 = Eph. 3:3, 5; *kryptō* and its cognates—1 Cor. 14:25 = Eph. 3:9; *apostolos*—1 Cor. 12:28–29 = Eph. 2:20; 3:5; *sophia*—1 Cor. 12.8 = Eph. 3:10). The two passages provide no basis for saying that the gift is different in the two places.

31. J. Jeremias, *New Testament Theology: The Proclamation of Jesus* (New York: Scribner's, 1971), 2. Jeremias bases this conclusion on Christ's seven letters to the seven churches in Asia Minor (Rev. 2–3 and other of His sayings that have been handed down in the first person (e.g., 1:17–20; 16:15; 22:12ff.).

32. Hill, *Prophecy*, 165.

33. Aune, *Prophecy*, 108. According to this pattern, a work to which the term "apoca-lyptic" is applied has an author who is a seer and who records visions he has experienced with their meaning that is usually supplied in a conversation between the seer and an angel. The revelatory visions tell of an imminent intervention of God in human history to end the present evil world system and replace it with one that is perfect. Such is accomplished by punishing the wicked and rewarding the righteous (ibid., 108, 376 n. 39).

34. Peisker, "Prophet," 80; Hill, "Prophecy and Prophets," 403; idem, *Prophecy*, 72. Along with its lack of pseudonymity is its lack of a claim to antiquity through an appropriation of the name of an ancient worthy such as Elijah, Enoch, Ezra, or Baruch. Another distinction between Revelation and apocalyptic lies in their distinctive views of history. Prophecy such as is in the Apocalypse is firmly rooted in salvation history, while apocalyptic gives very little attention to the acts of God on which salvation was based (G. von Rad, *Theology of the Old Testament* [San Francisco: Harper & Row, 1965], 2:303–8).

35. Friedrich, *"Prophētēs,"* 853.

36. Some of these include the use of the *tade legei* formula (Revelation 2–3), the position-ing of the vision of prophetic calling (1:9ff.; cf. Isa. 6:1ff.; Ezek. 1:1ff.), the swallowing of a small book (Rev. 10:8–11; cf. Ezek. 2:8–3:3), the measurement of the temple (Rev. 11:1; Friedrich, *"Prophētēs,"* 849; Aune, *Prophecy*, 206), John's authority and prophetic role in rela-tion to other prophets, and the proportion of predictive prophecy in comparison with horta-tory prophecy (Aune, *Prophecy*, 206–7).

37. Aune, *Prophecy*, 207–8.

38. E. Käsemann gives these words as an example of the "sentences of holy law" that originated in prophetic utterances ("Sentences of Holy Law in the New Testament," in *New Testament Questions for Today* [Philadelphia: Fortress, 1969], 76). Aune observes that the tendency of apocalyptists in early Christian prophecy to view themselves as witnesses is evidence that the statements fit the pattern of oath formulae used so widely in prophetic practice (Aune, *Prophecy*, 115). He also labels these words as an "integrity formula" such as was used in prophetic writings to preserve the accuracy of the revelatory text (ibid., 115–16).

39. H. B. Swete, *The Apocalypse of John* (Grand Rapids: Eerdmans, n.d.), 311; G. B. Caird, *The Revelation of St. John the Divine* (New York: Harper & Row, 1966), 287–88.

40. Caird, *Revelation*, 287.

41. I. T. Beckwith, *The Apocalypse of John* (New York: Macmillan, 1919), 778–79; G. E. Ladd, *A Commentary on the Revelation of John* (Grand Rapids: Eerdmans, 1972), 295; R. H. Mounce, *The Book of Revelation*, NICNT (Grand Rapids: Eerdmans, 1977), 395.

42. Swete, *Apocalypse*, 311.

43. H. Alford, *The Greek Testament* (New York: Longmans, Green, 1903), 4:749; Swete, *Apocalypse*, 311–12; Beckwith, *Apocalypse*, 779.

44. Hill, "Prophecy and Prophets," 415, 417–18.

45. Aune, *Prophecy*, 206.

46. R. E. Brown, *The Epistles of John,* AB (Garden City: Doubleday, 1982), 503.

47. A similar test of spiritual gifts appears in 1 Corinthians 12:3 (cf. also the gift of discernment through which other prophets could test an utterance of a fellow prophet [1 Cor. 12:10; 14:29]; R. Brown, *Epistles,* 503–4).

48. Hill, *Prophecy,* 191; Aune, *Prophecy,* 14.

49. The missionaries about whom John warns in 2 John were most likely claiming prophetic authority for their false teaching. The unusual injunction to inhospitality in 2 John 10–11 is explainable on this basis (R. Brown, *Epistles,* 690–91; Aune, *Prophesy,* 224–25). Another challenge to John's authority came in Diotrophes' refusal to receive missionaries who were propagating the truth (3 John 9–10). Diotrophes had assumed primacy and refused to recognize John's leadership (R. Brown, *Epistles,* 744–45).

50. Hill, *Prophecy,* 191.

51. Friedrich, *"Prophētēs,"* 860. In these two noncanonical works, similar to 1 John, misbehavior was the key to distinguishing false prophets from true prophets, though their misbehavior was of a different type than what is described in 1 John (Aune, *Prophecy,* 209, 211, 227).

52. Aune, *Prophecy,* 218.

53. Ibid.

54. Ibid.

55. Ibid., 218–19. Aune speculates about why the Apocalypse never mentions bishops, presbyters, and deacons, who surely existed in these Asian churches (ibid., 205–6). He concludes that John intentionally ignored them to bring his message to the communities at large and not just to their leaders. His egalitarian concept of all Christians sees apostles, prophets, and the rest of the saints as sharing the same fundamental obligations and responsibilities as Christians in general (cf. 11:16; 16:6; 18:24). They all must remain faithful to the testimony of Jesus and the word of God (cf. 1:2, 9; 6:9; 12:17; 19.10; 20:4).

56. Space limitations prohibit a detailed discussion of the warning against taking away words of the book of this prophecy, but they probably addressed the listeners to ensure that the totality of the Apocalypse was read in their assemblies without any omissions. Someone claiming prophetic authority could have through an alleged prophetic revelation deleted something that John had written. The fear that leaders might omit something that should be read recalls Paul's strong adjuration in 1 Thessalonians 5:27. For additional discussion of Revelation 22:19 in this connection, see Robert L. Thomas, *Revelation 8–22* (Chicago: Moody Press, 1995), 516–19.

57. A significant issue in verses 18–19 pertains to whose words the verses contain, those of Jesus or those of John. A detailed resolution of that question is beyond the scope of this paper (for further discussion of this issue, see Thomas, *Revelation 8–22,* 513–14), but will be injected as a brief consideration below.

58. Hill, "Prophecy and Prophets," 405. The futurist sees chapters 2–3 as encompassing the entire period of the church, however long that may be, and chapters 4–19 as the period of future tribulation, and then the millennium and eternal state following. The continuous-historical school finds in chapters 2–20 the entire scope of church history until the second advent of Jesus Christ, and then the eternal state. The preterist who allows for a reference to the second coming of Christ in the book is no exception. He sees the book as carrying through to the end also. The only exception to this rule is the idealist, who does not take the details of the book as having prophetic significance.

59. J. P. M. Sweet, *Revelation* (Philadelphia: Westminster, 1979), 319.

60. Ladd, *Commentary,* 295. Some might question the exhortations to patience (13:10; 14:12) or to faithfulness unto death (2:10; 3:10). There will always be those who say, "Let him make speed, and hasten his work, that we may see it" (Isa. 5:19; 2 Pet. 3:4). Prophecies in conflict with this are the perverting additions that John feared someone might make (W. Lee, "The Revelation of St. John," *The Holy Bible,* F. C. Cook, ed. (London: John Murray, 1881), 4.843).

61. G. R. Beasley-Murray, *Revelation*, NCB (Grand Rapids: Eerdmans, 1978), 346–47.

62. Käsemann, "Sentences," 76.

63. Hill, "Prophecy and Prophets," 403; Beasley-Murray, *Revelation*, 347.

64. H. Y. Gamble, *The New Testament Canon: Its Making and Meaning* (Philadelphia: Fortress, 1985), 94.

65. W. C. van Unnik, "A Formula Describing Prophecy," *NTS* 9 (1962–63): 190.

66. Aune, *Prophecy*, 209.

67. Ibid.

68. Ibid., 210, 303.

69. Friedrich, *"Prophētēs,"* 859–60; Hill, *Prophecy*, 187.

70. Aune, *Prophecy*, 209.

71. S. M. Burgess, *The Spirit and the Church: Antiquity* (Peabody, Mass.: Hendrickson, 1984), 52; cf. Hippolytus, "Treatise on Christ and Antichrist," *ANF*, 5:204–19, esp. 205, 211.

72. Friedrich, *"Prophētēs,"* 859–61; Hill, *Prophecy*, 187; Aune, *Prophecy*, 189, 209. Another study has sought to trace prophecy on into the third century (R. A. N. Kydd, *Charismatic Gifts in the Early Church* [Peabody, Mass.: Hendrickson, 1984], 4, 87), but it lacks any substantial evidence.

73. Aune, *Prophecy*, 189.

74. Friedrich, *"Prophētēs,"* 860; Hill, *Prophecy*, 191; Aune, *Prophecy*, 14. It is Aune's opinion that "throughout the entire second century prophecy was primarily tied to dissenting voices and movements within various phases of Christianity" (ibid., 338; cf. Hill, *Prophecy*, 191).

75. Friedrich, *"Prophētēs,"* 860–61; C. Brown, "Prophet," 89.

76. Montanism had more in common with movements of Second Temple Judaism than it did with the kind of prophetic activity that characterized Christianity during the first half of the second century (Aune, *Prophecy*, 189).

77. Friedrich, *"Prophētēs,"* 860; E. Käsemann, "An Apologia for Primitive Christian Eschatology," in *Essays on New Testament Themes* (Philadelphia: Fortress, 1964), 188.

78. The explanation for why this was true for apostles is relatively easy: Apostleship, by definition, was a temporary gift with its responsibility taking the apostle to different parts of the first-century world. A person so gifted was called upon to evangelize and lay the foundation for new Christian communities. The explanation for the failure to integrate the prophet into local church structure is not so easy, however, since in many cases early Christian prophets were permanent residents in their communities (Aune, *Prophecy*, 203).

79. Ibid., 204–5. Two additional sociological reasons of lesser significance may be added to the above list: (1) The increasing Hellenization of the church and the accompanying emphasis on the rationality of the faith (ibid., 14). Such a trend was evident as second-century leaders sought to defend the Christian faith in a society thoroughly entrenched in its Greek philosophical background. It is doubtful, however, that this influence was more than secondary. (2) A neglect of the distinction between two types of New Testament prophecy, one having a divine authority of actual words and another having only an authority of general content (Grudem, *Gift*, 111–12). Grudem tentatively suggests that prophets who had only the latter type of revelation mistakenly took it for the former, leading eventually to the downfall of the prophetic gift altogether. If the consensus that there was only one New Testament gift of prophecy is accurate, however, this could hardly have been a factor.

80. Hill, *Prophecy*, 191; Aune, *Prophecy*, 7.

81. If the prophetic revelations did not coincide perfectly with apostolic truth already received, the prophet himself became suspect and may have even been accused of being a false prophet. For Ignatius, only inspired utterances that agreed with the values he was already teaching to his congregations were considered genuine (Aune, *Prophecy*, 293). There seemed to be a growing inability on the part of prophets to transmit apostolic truth accu-

rately, so the task had to be committed to others who were more reliable (Hill, *Prophecy*, 191; Aune, *Prophecy*, 14).

82. Peisker, "Prophet," 84.

83. In opposition to the foundational nature of prophecy, it has been suggested that Ephesians 2:20 refers only to prophets who were apostles and not to "church prophets" (Grudem, "Prophecy—Yes," 12–13). This explanation is grammatically possible but not probable in light of equal access to revelatory data that must be granted to church prophets as was granted to prophets who were apostles. The vocabulary of 1 Corinthians 12–14, which pertains to church prophecy, is the same as that in Ephesians 2–3 where apostolic prophecy is usually identified. The same vocabulary is found in the Apocalypse where the writer makes no claim to apostolic authority (*prophēteuō* and cognates [Rev. 1:3; 10:11; 19:10; 22:6–7, 9–10, 18–19]; *mystēria* [1:20; 10:7; 17:5, 7]; *apokalypsis* [1:1]; *kryptō*, [2:17]; *apostolos* [2:2; 18:20; 21:14]; *sophia* [13:18; 17:9]). He claims only the authority of a prophet commissioned by Jesus Christ. Hence it is better to identify the prophets of Ephesians 2:20 as a group wider than the apostles and not identical with them (see Appendix B of this volume for further discussion). The prophetic gift belonged to the period of foundation, and the edifice built upon the foundation was relegated to individuals with other types of gifts (Aune, *Prophecy*, 7).

84. The *Didache* blends together apostles and prophets and emphasizes the need to distinguish between true and false prophets or apostles (D. G. Dunbar, "The Biblical Canon," in *Hermeneutics, Authority and Canon* [Grand Rapids: Zondervan, 1995], 327). Ignatius bears the same testimony. He wrote that Christian prophets should be heard because they had "lived according to Jesus Christ" and were "inspired by his grace" (*Magn.* 8.2). He said further that Christians should love not only the gospel and the apostles but also the prophets because they had announced the advent of Christ and became his disciples (*Phld.* 5.2; Dunbar, "Canon," 325). If the end of the first century marked the end of the apostolic gift, it is probable that it marked the end of the other also. The Muratorian Canon also associates these gifts with each other as it declares the termination of apostleship and prophecy: In speaking of the *Shepherd of Hermas*, it says, "It cannot be read publicly to the people in church either among the prophets, whose number is complete, nor among the apostles" (Gamble, *Canon*, 95).

85. H. A. Guy, *New Testament Prophecy* (London: Epworth, 1947), 25; Peisker, "Prophet," 80; Hill, *Prophecy*, 21–22, 31, 33, 49.

86. Aune, *Prophecy*, 103, 106, 189; Meyer, "*Prophētēs*," *TDNT*, 6:813–15, 817–19.

87. Aune, *Prophecy*, 109.

88. C. Wordsworth, *The New Testament of Our Lord and Saviour Jesus Christ in the Original Greek* (London: Rivingtons, 1870), 277 [emphasis in the original].

89. The proposal of R. H. Charles (*A Critical and Exegetical Commentary on The Revelation of St. John*, ICC [Edinburgh: T. and T. Clark, 1920], 2:222–23) and others (J. Moffatt, "The Revelation of St. John the Divine," *Expositor's Greek Testament*, 5:492–93; Beckwith, *Apocalypse*, 779) that these words are a later interpolation is without foundation among the manuscripts that preserve the text of Revelation.

90. Additional reasons for choosing Jesus as the speaker appear in Swete, *Apocalypse*, 311; Lee, "Revelation," 482–83; Mounce, *Revelation*, 396; Thomas, *Revelation*, 8–22, 513–14.

Appendix D (See pages 154–72)

1. R. Laird Harris, "Preface," in *Inspiration and Canonicity of the Scriptures* (Greenville, S.C.: A Press, 1995), 3.

2. Ibid., 285.

3. Ibid., 234–47.

4. Ibid., 247.
5. Ibid., 241.
6. Ibid., 245.
7. See discussion of these issues earlier in this volume, 34–35, 111, 254–55 n. 25.
8. N. B. Stonehouse, "The Authority of the New Testament," in *The Infallible Word*, N. B. Stonehouse and Paul Woolley, eds., 3d rev. printing (Phillipsburg, N. J.: Presbyterian and Reformed, 1980), 115–16.
9. Charles Hodge is among those who define "the word of wisdom" as the avenue adopted by the Holy Spirit in imparting revelations concerning the person and work of Christ (*An Exposition of the First Epistle to the Corinthians*, 6th ed. [London: Banner of Truth, 1959], 245).
10. Ibid., 245–46.
11. For evidence that apostles and prophets in Eph. 2:20 were two gifts rather than one, see Appendix B of this volume; F. David Farnell, "Does the New Testament Teach Two Prophetic Gifts?" *BSac* 150 (January-March 1993): 62–88.
12. W. Mundle, *"apokalyptō," NIDNT* 3:314.
13. Of course, the Apocalypse is full of information about how God communicated revelation to John on the island of Patmos, but that apocalyptic revelatory activity was somewhat exceptional.
14. *Vaticanus* and *Beza* are among an impressive list of sources that support *martyrion* instead of *mystērion* in 1 Corinthians 2:1. The latter receives strong support from p[46], Sinaiticus, Alexandrinus, and other witnesses.
15. F. W. Grosheide says "the deep things of God" are God Himself in His infinitude, including particularly His plan of salvation in Christ as referred to in Romans 11:33 (*Commentary on the First Epistle to the Corinthians, NICNT* [Grand Rapids: Eerdmans, 1953], 68). C. Brown refers the term to God's "secret wisdom" (*"theos," NIDNT*, 2:75). J. Blunck says it is "the paradox of unveiling and veiling which is Christian," in other words, revelation (*"bathos," NIDNT*, 2:198).
16. *Systematic Theology* (London: Thomas Nelson, 1880), 1:162.
17. Cf. 29–30 earlier in this volume.
18. See Appendix, 137–38, for a defense of the inerrancy of this prophecy.
19. Harris, *Inspiration and Canonicity*, 245.
20. Ibid., 324.
21. F. F. Bruce, *The Canon of Scripture* (Downers Grove, Ill.: InterVarsity, 1988), 264–65.
22. *Prophēteia* occurs seven times (1:3; 11:6; 19:10; 22:7, 10, 18–19), *prophētis* once (2:20), *prophēteuō* twice (10:11; 11:3), and *prophētēs* eight times (10:7; 11:10, 18; 16:6; 18:20, 24; 22:6, 9).
23. Rolf Rentdorff, *"prophētēs k.t.l.," TDNT*, 6:812; G. Friedrich, *"prophētēs k.t.l.," TDNT*, 6:849; David Hill, *New Testament Prophecy* (Atlanta: John Knox, 1979), 87–88.
24. D. E. Aune, *Prophecy in Early Christianity and the Ancient Mediterranean World* (Grand Rapids: Eerdmans, 1983), 196.
25. Robert L. Thomas, *Revelation 8–22, An Exegetical Commentary* (Chicago: Moody Press, 1995), 112.
26. Aune, *Prophecy in Early Christianity*, 197; Robert H. Mounce, *The Book of Revelation, NICNT* (Grand Rapids: Eerdmans, 1977), 232.
27. Cf. Appendix C of this volume, 147–48.
28. G. R. Beasley-Murray, *The Book of Revelation*, NCB (Grand Rapids: Eerdmans, 1978), 268.
29. See Appendix C, 146–53; Thomas, *Revelation 8–22*, 513–19.
30. Hippolytus, "Treatise on Christ and Antichrist," *ANF*, 5:204–19, esp. 205, 211; cf. Stanley M. Burgess, *The Spirit and the Church: Antiquity* (Peabody, Mass.: Hendrickson,

1984), 52; Ronald E. Heine, "The Role of the Gospel of John in the Montanist Controversy," *The Second Century* 6 (1987–88): 12.

31. Chrysostom, *Homilies in First Corinthians*, Homilies 29, 36; cf. F. David Farnell, "When Will the Gift of Prophecy Cease?" *BSac* 150 (April-June 1993): 195–96 n. 79.

32. E.g., David G. Dunbar, "The Biblical Canon," *Hermeneutics, Authority, and Canon*, ed. D. A. Carson and John D. Woodbridge (Grand Rapids: Baker, 1995), 356; cf. Lee M. McDonald, *The Formation of the Christian Biblical Canon*, rev. and expanded ed. (Peabody, Mass.: Hendrickson, 1995), 142–43.

33. Harris, *Inspiration and Canonicity*, 235–45.

34. Ibid., 293–94.

35. Ibid., 191; Benjamin B. Warfield, *The Inspiration and Authority of the Bible* (Philadelphia: Presbyterian and Reformed, 1970), 163–65, 415–16.

36. Harry Y. Gamble, *The New Testament Canon, Its Making and Meaning* (Philadelphia: Fortress, 1985), 72.

37. Clement of Alexandria quotes from an epistle of Clement of Rome as though it were Scripture (Clement, *Stromata*, iv.17, in *ANF* 2:428–29).

38. Bruce M. Metzger calls attention to the use of *theopneustos* by early Christians to refer to such writings as Basil's commentary on the first six days of creation, a synodical epistle from the Council of Ephesus, and an epitaph on the grave of Bishop Abercius (*The Canon of the New Testament, Its Origin, Development, and Significance* [New York: Oxford, Clarendon, 1988], 256). He also notes that Augustine said Jerome wrote under the dictation of the Holy Spirit (ibid., 255) and that Clement of Alexandria quoted "inspired" passages from the epistles of Clement of Rome and of Barnabas, the *Shepherd of Hermas*, and the Apocalypse of Peter, as well as ascribing to Jesus sayings not found in the four canonical gospels (ibid., 134).

39. See Edward J. Young, "The Authority of the Old Testament," in *The Infallible Word*, ed. N. B. Stonehouse and Paul Woolley, 3d rev. printing (Phillipsburg, N. J.: Presbyterian and Reformed, 1980), 55–91.

40. Harris, *Inspiration and Canonicity*, 248–59.

41. Bruce, *Canon of Scripture*, 257–58.

42. Ibid., 265–66.

43. Stonehouse, "Authority of the New Testament," 114, 119.

44. Harris, *Inspiration and Canonicity*, 255, 281–82.

45. Ibid., 273–74.

46. Ibid., 283.

47. Ibid., 295.

48. J. B. Lightfoot, "Lost Epistles to the Philippians?" *St. Paul's Epistle to the Philippians*, 6th ed. (1913 reprint; Grand Rapids: Zondervan, 1953), 138; cf. Metzger, *Canon of the New Testament*, 272 n. 12, 284 n. 34.

49. This essay assumes the traditional authorship of all the New Testament books. In the case of the Epistle to the Hebrews, along with many individuals in the early church, it assumes an unknown authorship.

50. Harris, *Inspiration and Canonicity*, 285.

51. Gamble, *New Testament Canon*, 68; cf. Steven Voorwinde, "The Formation of the New Testament Canon," *Vox Reformata* 60 (1995): 25.

52. In dealing with the Muratorian Canon, this discussion accepts the late second-century date of composition (cf. C. E. Hill, "The Debate over the Muratorian Fragment and the Development of the Canon," *WTJ* 57/2 [Fall 1995]: 437–52; William Horbury, "The Wisdom of Solomon in the Muratorian Fragment," *JTS* NS 45 [1994]: 158–59).

53. Gamble, *New Testament Canon*, 46.

54. Bruce, *Canon of Scripture,* 164.

55. Ibid., 166; Metzger, *Canon of the New Testament,* 307 n. 8.

56. See Heine, "Gospel of John in the Montanist Controversy," 13; contra Gary Steven Shogren, "Christian Prophecy and Canon in the Second Century: A Response to B. B. Warfield" (paper read at the 47th Annual Meeting of the Evangelical Theological Society, Philadelphia, November 18, 1995), 19.

57. The only possible allusion to the Old Testament is indirect, when the compiler refers to "Wisdom also, written by Solomon's friends in his honour." *The Wisdom of Solomon* is a book of the Old Testament Apocrypha, making its mention in this list surprising. Metzger calls this "a puzzle that has never been satisfactorily solved" (Metzger, *Canon of the New Testament,* 198). As a reason for its inclusion here, Bruce suggests its writing came closer to New Testament times than to the period of the Old Testament (Bruce, *Canon of Scripture,* 165). William Horbury has suggested the compiler did not intend to include Wisdom among the canonical books, but his discussion of it toward the close of his list indicates it was among disputed books from *both* testaments ("The Wisdom of Solomon in the Muratorian Fragment," 152–56).

58. L. W. Hurtado, "Muratorian Fragment," *ISBE,* ed. Geoffrey W. Bromiley, 3:433.

59. Cf. Dunbar, "The Biblical Canon," 327.

60. Cf. ibid., 325.

61. *Dialogue with Trypho,* chap. 119, in *ANF,* 1:259; cf. Brooke Foss Westcott, *A General Survey of the History of the Canon of the New Testament,* 6th ed. (Cambridge and London: Macmillan, 1889), 173. That Tertullian included the author of the Apocalypse among the prophets is evident from his words in *Dial.* chap. 100.81: "Moreover also among us a man named John one of the Apostles of Christ, prophesied in a revelation made to him that those who have believed on our Christ shall spend a thousand years in Jerusalem" (Westcott, *General Survey,* 121).

62. Westcott, *General Survey,* 168.

63. Harris, *Inspiration and Canon,* 268.

64. Cyprian *Exhortation for Martyrdom* 11; Victorinus *On the Apocalypse* 1.7, on Rev. 1:20; Jerome *Epistle* 53:9.

65. L. Gaussen, *Theopneustia, The Plenary Inspiration of the Holy Scriptures,* rev. ed., trans. David Scott (1949; reprint, Chicago: Moody Press, n.d.), 83–85.

66. Bruce, *Canon of Scripture,* 259–63.

67. Ibid., 260.

68. Ibid., 171–72.

69. Ibid., 151–52.

70. Gamble, *New Testament Canon,* 69–70.

71. Bruce, *Canon of Scripture,* 260.

72. Ibid., 261.

73. Gamble, *New Testament Canon,* 70.

74. Bruce, *Canon of Scripture,* 261.

75. See discussion above under "Test of Propheticity"; cf. Bruce, *Canon of Scripture,* 262.

76. Gamble, *New Testament Canon,* 70–71.

77. Metzger, *Canon of the New Testament,* 237, 253.

78. See Gamble, *New Testament Canon,* 70.

79. Ibid., 71; Bruce, *Canon of Scripture,* 263.

80. Gamble, *New Testament Canon,* 71.

SELECT BIBLIOGRAPHY OF
WORKS CITED

(Works cited in the Appendixes do not necessarily appear in the following listing.)

Alford, Henry. *The Greek Testament.* 4 vols. London: Longmans, Green, 1899.

Arndt, William F. A. *Greek-English Lexicon of the New Testament and Other Early Christian Literature.* Translated and adapted by William F. Arndt and F. Wilbur Gingrich. Chicago: University of Chicago Press, 1957.

Baker, John. *Baptized in One Spirit.* Plainfield, N.J.: Logos, 1967.

Barnes, Albert. *Notes, Explanatory and Practical, on the First Epistle of Paul to the Corinthians.* New York: Harper, 1879.

Barrett, C. K. *A Commentary on the First Epistle to the Corinthians.* Harper's New Testament Commentaries. New York: Harper & Row, 1968.

Beet, Joseph Agar. *A Commentary on St. Paul's Epistles to the Corinthians.* 2d ed. London: Hodder and Stoughton, 1883.

Behm, Johannes. *"Glōssa."* In *Theological Dictionary of the New Testament,* edited by Gerhard Kittel, translated by Geoffrey W. Bromiley, 1:719–27. Grand Rapids: Eerdmans, 1964.

Berquist, Millard J. *Studies in First Corinthians.* Nashville: Convention, 1960.

Bittlinger, Arnold. *Gifts and Graces, A Commentary on 1 Corinthians 12–14.* Translated by Herbert Klassen and supervised by Michael Harper. Grand Rapids: Eerdmans, 1968.

Blass, Friedrich W., and Albert Debrunner. *A Greek Grammar of the New Testament and Other Early Christian Literature.* Translated and revised by Robert W. Funk. Chicago: University of Chicago Press, 1961.

Bruce, F. F., ed. *"1 and 2 Corinthians."* In *New Century Bible,* edited by Ronald E. Clements (Old Testament) and Matthew Black (New Testament). London: Oliphants, 1971.

Burdick, Donald W. *Tongues: To Speak or Not to Speak.* Chicago: Moody Press, 1969.

Carson, D. A. *Showing the Spirit: A Theological Exposition of 1 Corinthians, 12–14.* Grand Rapids: Baker, 1987.

Carter, Howard. *Spiritual Gifts and Their Operation.* Springfield, Mo.: Gospel Publishers, 1968.

Coke, Thomas. "The First Epistle of St. Paul the Apostle to the Corinthians." In *A Commentary on the New Testament,* 2:166–292. New York: Published by Daniel Hitt for the Methodist Connexion in the United States, 1812.

Cook, Leroy. "The Spiritual Gift of the Word of Wisdom." Master's thesis, Talbot Theological Seminary, 1973.

Craig, Clarence T., and John Short. *The First Epistle to the Corinthians.* Vol. 10 of *The Interpreter's Bible.* Edited by George A. Buttrick. New York: Abingdon, 1953.

Cremer, Hermann. *Biblico-Theological Lexicon of New Testament Greek.* Edinburgh: T. & T. Clark, 1895.

DeHaan, M. R. *Studies in 1 Corinthians.* Grand Rapids: Zondervan, 1956.

Du Plessis, David J. *The Spirit Bade Me Go.* Dallas, Tex.: (n.p.), 1961.

Dunn, James D. G. *Baptism in the Holy Spirit.* Naperville, Ill.: Allenson, 1970.

Edgar, Thomas R. *Satisfied by the Promise of the Spirit.* Grand Rapids: Kregel, 1996.

Edwards, Thomas Charles. *A Commentary on the First Epistle to the Corinthians.* London: Hodder and Stoughton, 1885.

Ellis, E. Earle. "Spiritual Gifts in the Pauline Community." *New Testament Studies* 20 (1974): 128–44.

Ervin, Howard M. *These Are Not Drunken as Ye Suppose.* Plainfield, N. J.: Logos, 1968.

Evans, Canon. "1 Corinthians." In *The Holy Bible, with an Explanatory and Critical Commentary,* edited by F. C. Cook. London: John Murray, 1900, 3:239–376.

Farrar, F. W., et al. "1 Corinthians." In *The Pulpit Commentary,* edited by H. D. M. Spence and Joseph S. Exell. Vol. 44. Rev. ed. New York: Funk & Wagnalls, n.d.

Fee, Gordon D. "The First Epistle to the Corinthians." In *New International Commentary on the New Testament,* edited by F. F. Bruce. Grand Rapids: Eerdmans, 1987.

Gaffin, Richard B., Jr. "A Cessationist View." In *Are Miraculous Gifts for Today? Four Views,* edited by Wayne A. Grudem. Grand Rapids: Zondervan, 1996.

Gill, John. "The First Epistle of Paul the Apostle to the Corinthians." In *An Exposition of the New Testament, Both Doctrinal and Practical.* Rev.

ed. London: Printed for George Keith, in Gracechurch Street, 1775, 3:628–837.

Godet, Frederic L. *Commentary on St. Paul's First Epistle to the Corinthians.* Vol. 2. Translated by Rev. A. Cusin. 1886. Reprint, Grand Rapids: Zondervan, 1957.

Gould, E. P. *A Commentary on the Epistles to the Corinthians.* Vol. 5 of *An American Commentary on the New Testament,* edited by Alvah Hovey. Chicago: Amer. Bapt. Pub. Soc., 1887.

Grosheide, F. W. "Commentary on the First Epistle to the Corinthians." In *The New International Commentary on the New Testament.* Vol. 7. Grand Rapids: Eerdmans, 1953.

Grossman, Siegfried. *The Gifts of the Spirit.* Translated by Susan Wiesmann. Wheaton, Ill.: Key, 1971.

Grudem, Wayne A. *The Gift of Prophecy in 1 Corinthians.* Washington, D.C.: University Press of America, 1982.

_____. *The Gift of Prophecy in the New Testament and Today.* Westchester, Ill.: Crossway, 1988.

Gundry, Robert. "'Ecstatic Utterance' (NEB)?" *Journal of Theological Studies* 17 (1966): 299–307.

Hering, Jean. *The First Epistle of Saint Paul to the Corinthians.* London: Epworth, 1962.

Hodge, Charles. *An Exposition of the First Epistle to the Corinthians.* 6th ed. London: Banner of Truth Trust, 1959.

Hoekema, Anthony A. *What about Tongue-Speaking?* Grand Rapids: Eerdmans, 1966.

Hommes, N. J. "Let Women Be Silent in Church." *Calvin Theological Journal* 4 (1969): 5–22.

Ironside, H. A. *Addresses on the First Epistle to the Corinthians.* New York: Loizeaux, 1938.

Johnson, S. Lewis. "The First Epistle to the Corinthians." In *The Wycliffe Bible Commentary,* edited by Charles F. Pfeiffer and Everett F. Harrison, 1227–60. Chicago: Moody Press, 1962.

Kistemaker, Simon J. *Exposition of the First Epistle to the Corinthians.* Grand Rapids: Baker, 1993.

Kling, Christian F. *The First Epistle of Paul to the Corinthians.* Vol. 6 of *Lange's New Testament Commentary,* translated by Daniel W. Poor. New York: Scribner, Armstrong, 1868.

Kuyper, Abraham. *The Work of the Holy Spirit.* Translated by Henri de Vries. London: Funk & Wagnalls, 1900.

Laurin, Roy L. *Life Matures! Devotional Exposition of the Book of First Corinthians.* Los Angeles: Stationers, 1941.

Lenski, R. C. H. *The Interpretation of St. Paul's First and Second Epistles to the Corinthians.* Minneapolis: Augsburg, 1963.

Mare, W. Harold. "1 Corinthians." In *The Expositor's Bible Commentary,* edited by Frank E. Gaebelein. Grand Rapids: Zondervan, 1976.

John MacArthur, Jr. "1 Corinthians." In *The MacArthur New Testament Commentary.* Chicago: Moody Press, 1984.

McRae, William J. *The Dynamics of Spiritual Gifts.* Grand Rapids: Zondervan, 1976.

Metz, Donald S. "1 Corinthians." In *Beacon Bible Commentary,* 8:293–486. Kansas City: Beacon Hill, 1968. .

Metzger, Bruce M. *A Textual Commentary on the Greek New Testament.* London: United Bible Soc., 1971.

Meyer, Heinrich August Wilhelm. *Critical and Exegetical Handbook to the Epistles to the Corinthians.* Revised and edited by William P. Dickson, translated by D. Douglas Bannerman. Vol. 1. Edinburgh: T. & T. Clark, 1879.

_____. Vol. 2, 1881.

Michel, Otto. *"Oikos, oikia, k. t. l."* In *Theological Dictionary of the New Testament,* edited by Gerhard Kittel, translated by Geoffrey W. Bromiley, 5:119–59. Grand Rapids: Eerdmans, 1967.

Morgan, G. Campbell. *The Corinthian Letters of Paul: An Exposition of 1 and 2 Corinthians.* New York: Revell, 1946.

Morris, Leon. *The First Epistle of Paul to the Corinthians.* Tyndale New Testament Commentaries. Grand Rapids: Eerdmans, 1958.

Oepke, Albrecht. *"Baptō, baptizō, k. t. l."* In *Theological Dictionary of the New Testament,* edited by Gerhard Kittel, translated by Geoffrey W. Bromiley, 1:529–46. Grand Rapids: Eerdmans, 1964.

Olshausen, Hermann. *Biblical Commentary on St. Paul's First and Second Epistles to the Corinthians.* Vol. 20 of *Clark's Foreign Theological Library.* Edinburgh: T. & T. Clark, 1851.

Parratt, J. K. "Holy Spirit and Baptism." *Expository Times* 82 (1971): 231–35, 266–71.

Parry, R. St. John. "The First Epistle of Paul the Apostle to the Corinthians." In *Cambridge Greek Testament for Schools and Colleges.* Cambridge: Cambridge University Press, 1916.

Riggs, Ralph M. *The Spirit Himself.* Springfield, Mo.: Gospel Pub., 1949.

Robertson, Archibald, and Alfred Plummer. *A Critical and Exegetical Commentary on the First Epistle of St. Paul to the Corinthians.* 2d ed. Edinburgh: T. & T. Clark, 1914.

Robertson, Archibald T. *Word Pictures in the New Testament.* 6 vols. Nashville: Broadman, 1931.

_____. *A Grammar of the Greek New Testament in the Light of Historical Research.* Nashville: Broadman, 1934.

Sanders, J. Oswald. *The Holy Spirit and His Gifts.* Grand Rapids: Zondervan, 1940.

Saucy, Robert L. "An Open But Cautious View." In *Are Miraculous Gifts for Today? Four Views,* edited by Wayne A. Grudem. Grand Rapids: Zondervan, 1996.

Schlier, Heinrich. *"Idiōtēs."* In *Theological Dictionary of the New Testament,* edited by Gerhard Kittel, translated by Geoffrey W. Bromiley, 3:215–17. Grand Rapids: Eerdmans, 1965.

Schmithals, Walter. *Gnosticism in Corinth: An Investigation of the Letters to the Corinthians.* Translated by John E. Steely. Nashville: Abingdon, 1971.

Schweizer, Eduard. *"Pneuma, pneumatikos, k. t. l."* In *Theological Dictionary of the New Testament,* edited by Gerhard Kittel, translated by Geoffrey W. Bromiley, 6:332–455. Grand Rapids: Eerdmans, 1968.

Storms, C. Samuel. "A Third Wave View." In *Are Miraculous Gifts for Today? Four Views,* edited by Wayne A. Grudem. Grand Rapids: Zondervan, 1996.

Stott, John R. W., *The Baptism and Fullness of the Holy Spirit.* Chicago: InterVarsity Press, 1964.

Thayer, Joseph Henry. *A Greek-English Lexicon of the New Testament.* New York: American Book, 1889.

Thieme, Robert. "Spiritual Gifts." *Nutshell Notes,* Scripture Tape Library Fellowship, compiled by Marge Milliren from tapes by Robert Thieme, n.p., n.d.

Thomas, Robert L. *Revelation 1–7: An Exegetical Commentary.* Chicago: Moody Press, 1992.

_____. *Revelation 8–22: An Exegetical Commentary.* Chicago: Moody Press, 1995.

_____. "Tongues . . . Will Cease." *Journal of the Evangelical Theological Society* 17 (1974): 81–89.

Trench, Richard C. *Synonyms of the New Testament.* Grand Rapids: Eerdmans, 1958.

Turner, Nigel. *Syntax: A Grammar of New Testament Greek,* edited by James H. Moulton and Nigel Turner. Vol. 3. Edinburgh: T. & T. Clark, 1963.

Unger, Merrill F. *New Testament Teaching on Tongues.* Grand Rapids: Kregel, 1971.

Williams, Ernest S. *Systematic Theology.* 3 vols. Springfield, Mo.: Gospel Pub., 1953.

SCRIPTURE INDEX

SUBJECT INDEX

(Page–number listings are not exhaustive for frequently occurring subjects such as prophecy and tongues.)

AUTHOR AND ANCIENT SOURCE INDEX

(Superscript number following a number indicates number of occurences on that page or within that note.)

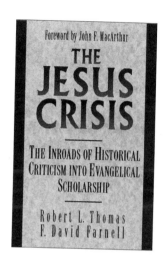

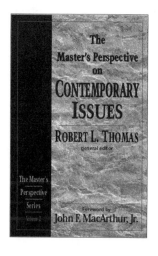 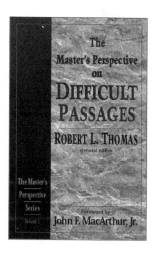